Government, Business, and the American Economy

Government, Business, and the American Economy

Second Edition

Robert Langran
and
Martin Schnitzer

ROWMAN & LITTLEFIELD PUBLISHERS, INC.
Lanham • Boulder • New York • Toronto • Oxford

ROWMAN & LITTLEFIELD PUBLISHERS, INC.

Published in the United States of America
by Rowman & Littlefield Publishers, Inc.
A wholly owned subsidiary of The Rowman & Littlefield Publishing Group, Inc.
4501 Forbes Boulevard, Suite 200, Lanham, Maryland 20706
www.rowmanlittlefield.com

PO Box 317
Oxford
OX2 9RU, UK

British Library Cataloguing in Publication Information Available

Library of Congress Cataloging-in-Publication Data

Langran, Robert.
Government, business, and the American economy / Robert Langran and Martin
Schnitzer.—2nd ed.
p. cm.
Includes index.
ISBN-13: 978-0-7425-5323-1 (cloth : alk. paper)
ISBN-10: 0-7425-5323-X (cloth : alk. paper)
ISBN-13: 978-0-7425-5324-8 (pbk. : alk. paper)
ISBN-10: 0-7425-5324-8 (pbk. : alk. paper)
1. Industrial policy—United States.   2. Trade regulation—United States.
I. Schnitzer, Martin.   II. Title.

HD3616.U47L354   2007
338.973—dc22   2006003892

Printed in the United States of America

♾ ™ The paper used in this publication meets the minimum requirements of American
National Standard for Information Sciences—Permanence of Paper for Printed Library
Materials, ANSI/NISO Z39.48-1992.

Contents

PART I
THE ROLE OF GOVERNMENT

PART V
GOVERNMENT AND FOREIGN TRADE

Tables and Figures

TABLES

FIGURES

Preface

The purpose of *Government, Business, and the American Economy* is to integrate economics, business, and U.S. politics into a unified whole. Most Americans cite the economy as their major concern. When times are good, as they have been in recent years, Americans are satisfied, and this bodes well for politicians on election day; when times are bad, Americans are not satisfied, and this means trouble for politicians. Business is the centerpiece of the American economy, and private enterprise employs the great majority of American workers. Moreover, American business firms operate all over the world. Government is important to the economy and business in several ways: It regulates the functions of business, such as foreign trade, consumer product safety, labor relations, and competition. It also purchases many kinds of goods and services, and is a major employer of workers. Finally, it affects the American cconomy through taxation and expenditures.

This book also covers some of the major developments of the past century and extends them into the twenty-first century. Probably the most important development is the creation of the European Union, which represents the economic and political integration of most of the countries of Europe. A common currency unit called the euro has also been created. In the Western hemisphere, two major trading blocs have been created: Canada, Mexico, and the United States signed a free trade agreement called NAFTA, which is designed to promote the flow of trade among these countries. In South America, a customs union called the South American Community of Nations includes all countries except for French Guyana. Economic integration is also occurring in other parts of the world.

A cross-disciplined approach gives the book a flexibility that will broaden its appeal. It is adaptable to many courses. It can be used in courses taken by public administration and pre-law majors. It also can be used in government and business courses that are normally taught in business schools and in introductory courses in colleges where economics and political science may be integrated. The book's strength is that it is topical and it covers a wide range of events that are relevant to the twenty-first century.

The book utilizes cases that are related to topical events. An example involves sexual harassment at Mitsubishi, a Japanese conglomerate with plants in the United States. Other cases involve product liability lawsuits, with the pharmaceutical serving as the most visible example. Another very important case involves the federal government's antitrust lawsuit against Microsoft. At the end of each chapter, there are "Questions for Discussion," which can be used to stimulate class participation or as examination questions. A list of "Recommended Readings" is also presented at the end of each chapter.

ACKNOWLEDGEMENTS

Many people have contributed to the preparation of this book: We are deeply indebted to other authors who have informed us, and, where appropriate, we have cited their works. We thank Jennifer Knerr, formerly of Rowman and Littlefield, for her faith in our doing the book, and to Renee Legatt of Rowman and Littlefield for helping it come to fruition. Martin Schnitzer thanks his daughter Marcy who served as lead researcher for this book. He also thanks his wife, Joan, and his research assistant, Daniela Fernandez, for their invaluable assistance in putting together his part of the book. He also thanks Larry Thompson of Refugees International, who has traveled extensively in Africa and East Asia; and Dr. Harrison Fox, former aide to Senator John Danforth, who provided the information on special interest groups. Robert Langran thanks his wife, Eleanor, for her patience and support during the writing of this book, and the people at Rowman and Littlefield for their encouragement throughout this endeavor.

I

THE ROLE OF GOVERNMENT

1

The State in a Changing World

The role of the state has changed throughout history. From earliest times people have grouped together into larger associations, starting with clans and extending to the modern state of today. States have come in various forms depending on a mix of factors including culture, natural endowments, and geographical location. Athens developed as a state because its location provided it opportunities for trade.[1] Its economic underpinning was based on slave ownership. Rome developed on a much larger scale. Its success was based on its coercive power, as represented by its legions, over all individuals and organizations within its territories. Its wealth was based on the spoils of war, and its legal system gave it authority in key areas such as commerce.[2] The city-state of Venice developed as a maritime power because of its location on the Adriatic Sea. It was ruled by an oligarchy that provided goods and services to the people in return for their support.[3]

By the end of the fifteenth century, the balance of economic and political power had begun to shift away from Venice, Genoa, and other city-states to the maritime countries of Spain and Portugal. Spain had become a nation-state with a consolidated territory and population. Authority was centralized and encompassed separate judicial, legislative, and executive functions. State intervention played a vital role in the development of Spanish colonies and markets in North America and South America. Mercantilism involved a major state role in the promotion of trade. The proponents of mercantilism were concerned with national wealth because they perceived national power as resting on an economic foundation. They believed that government ought to undertake actively to guide the activities of its citizens along those lines that were conducive to national well-being.[4]

Notions of the role of the state began to change in the eighteenth and nineteenth centuries, largely as a result of the Industrial Revolution. It consisted

mainly of the application of machinery to manufacturing, mining, transportation, and agriculture. The factory system replaced the traditional method of
small-scale production in the home, and a new class of industrial capitalists
was created. It was they who shaped the course of economic development by
reinvesting their earnings in new enterprises. It was the individual, not the
state, who created wealth, and it was generally recognized that the market was
the best instrument for allocating resources.[5] The state was best held to certain
core functions—providing public goods such as defense, educating its citizens,
and enforcing contracts—deemed essential for the market to flourish. Redistribution of income came mainly through private charity and other actions.

    The twentieth century changed the role of the state in several ways. World
War I ended the monarchies in Germany, the Austro-Hungarian empire, and
Russia.[6] The Russian Revolution of 1917 led to the rise of a new political and
economic system by which private property ownership was abolished, the
state was put in control of resource allocation through central planning, and
the Communist Party ruled. The Depression of the 1930s caused economic
and social devastation in the Western world. The role of government in the
United States, Canada, and Western Europe expanded. This role took several
forms. The first was the use of fiscal and monetary policies to stimulate economic activity in order to create jobs.[7] The second was the provision of welfare benefits to provide assistance for those who were unemployed and for
those who were too old to work.

    But the role of government increased significantly during the period after
the end of World War II up to the present. The war destroyed most of Europe,
and government expenditures supported by Marshall Plan aid from the
United States were necessary to rebuild it. Fear of a return to the mass unemployment of the Depression led governments to adopt a policy to promote
full employment through the use of Keynesian economic policies designed to
promote consumption through government expenditures. The welfare state
expanded through the transfer of income from the public sector to the private
sector. The role of the state, as measured by expenditures, doubled between
1960 and 1996. Sweden, the consummate example of the welfare state,
increased its expenditures relative to Gross National Product (GNP) by 800
percent from 1937 to 1996.

THE ROLE OF GOVERNMENT
IN THE AMERICAN ECONOMY

For the purpose of organization, government intervention and participation in
the American economy can be divided into four areas that provide the subject
matter of the remainder of this chapter. First, there is the area of public
finance, in which government is a purchaser of goods and services as well as

a tax collector. Government economic stabilization policies can be considered a part of this area. Second, government regulation and control prescribe specific conditions under which private economic activity can and cannot take place. It may interpose itself in employer-employee relations by prescribing rules of employment. It may also influence business operations both directly and indirectly through antitrust and other laws. Third, government is the single largest employer in the U.S. economy, and as such competes directly with private industry for labor. Fourth, government is a major provider of credit.

PUBLIC FINANCE

Public finance involves the spending and taxing activities of government. Government spending for goods and services divert resources from the private to the public sector of the economy. Taxes give the government control over an economy's resources and also affect the distribution of income among groups of people. The public sector of an economy differs from the private sector because the state has the sovereign power to compel individuals to make financial contributions and to accept certain services. Another difference is the nonmaterial and general welfare character of most government activities. Unlike private business, government is not always expected to yield financial returns. Moreover, if financial returns are expected from a given government activity, the returns need not be immediate and may be adjusted to a cost basis rather than a profit basis.

Federal Government Budget

The importance of the federal government's budget to the American economy cannot be minimized. It exerts an influence on the economy in terms of the level of revenues and taxes, of whether or not it is balanced, and of the specific expenditures it authorizes. It is the focal point for the presentation and implementation of the government's economic policy. It is often used as a means of publicizing government policies toward particular sectors, groups of people, or industries, either in an attempt to improve the chances of success for the proposed measures or at times, as a substitute for any specific measure. Finally, through the implementation of fiscal policy, the budget can be used to raise or lower the level of national income.

Resources

The budget of the federal government is financed from two income sources—taxes and borrowing. As table 1.1 and figure 1.1 indicate, the two

**Table 1.1   Federal Government Revenue by Source for the Year 2004
(Billions of Dollars)**

Source	Amount
Individual income taxes	849.9
Corporate income taxes	169.1
Payroll taxes	810.9
Excise taxes	70.9
Estate and gift taxes	23.4
Customs duties	20.7
Miscellaneous receipts	38.5
Adjustment for uncertainty*	
Total revenues	**1,922.0**

*These amounts reflect an additional adjustment to receipts beyond what the economic and tax models forecast and have been made in the interest of cautious and prudent forecasting.

Source: Budget of the United States Government: Browse Fiscal Year 2004, Office of Management and Budget. http://www.gpoaccess.gov/usbudget/fy04/index.html

most important tax sources of federal government revenues are the personal income tax and payroll taxes, which accounted for 86 percent of total revenue for the fiscal year 2004. The corporate income tax, which was once the most important source of federal government revenue, is of little importance today,

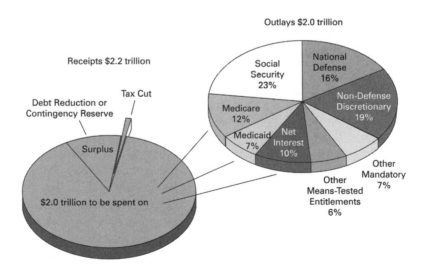

"Means-tested entitlements are those for which eligibility is based on income. The Medicaid program is also a means-tested entitlement."

Figure 1.1.   The Federal Government Dollar—Where It Comes from and Where It Goes
Source: A Citizen's Guide to the Federal Budget, Executive Office of the President, fiscal year 2002. www.whitehouse.gov/omb/budget

accounting for 8.8 percent of total revenue. Excise taxes are a minor source of government revenue, accounting for 3.6 percent in 2004. Excise taxes are consumption-based taxes and are levied on the sale of a particular commodity. Excises are levied on the consumption of gasoline, alcohol, tobacco,[8] and other products. They can be employed as "user charges" to collect part or all of the cost of services enjoyed by specific taxpayers.

Payroll taxes were introduced into the federal revenue system by the Social Security Act of 1935 and have increased in importance to the point that they are now second to the personal income tax as a source of revenue. Payroll taxes are earmarked through trust funds to finance Social Security programs of which there are two types. The first type is a federal system of old age, survivors, disability, and health insurance (OASDHI), which is financed by payroll taxes collected from employers and employees in equal amounts. The second type is a federal and state system of unemployment compensation, which is financed mainly by a payroll tax on employers. Payroll taxes constitute a significant part of the tax payments made by lower income groups.

The difference between federal government revenues and expenditures is made up by borrowing, which is the responsibility of the U.S. Treasury. It can borrow by issuing three types of debt obligations, ranging from the sale of short-term Treasury bills to long-term Treasury bonds. Borrowing is an easy way out for politicians and the public. Politicians can spend more money, and the public can "have their cake and eat it too," in that they can postpone payment until a later date. But living beyond one's means can create problems for governments as well as individuals. It has increased interest payments, which is a fixed cost in the federal budget. Borrowing also has affected the foreign trade deficit, and has made the United States the world's leading debtor nation.

Expenditures

Federal government expenditures for the fiscal year 2005 are an estimated $2.7 trillion, which is around 20 percent of the U.S. Gross Domestic Product (GDP).[9] Federal spending has risen 33 percent since 2001. Expenditures can be divided into two major categories—discretionary and mandatory. Discretionary expenditures cover a wide variety of government functions and activities. About half of all discretionary expenditures goes for national defense. Annual spending on domestic security and the military in 2005 was $205 billion higher than in 2001. The remaining expenditures are for housing, agriculture, education, environmental protection, law enforcement, space exploration, research and development, international aid, and government operations, and have climbed 31 percent from 2001–2005. Conversely, mandatory expenditures consist mainly of large entitlement programs, such as Social Security, Medicare and Medicaid, and of interest payments on the federal debt. For most mandatory spending programs, the federal government is obligated to spending levels that depend on factors that are beyond its direct control.

Table 1.2 and figure 1.1 present a breakdown of estimated federal government expenditures for the fiscal year 2004. Discretionary expenditures made up approximately one-third of the total net interest on the public debt, which is a fixed cost that has to be met, and accounted for $819 billion. Mandatory entitlement expenditures, which have risen rapidly over the last twenty-five years, can be expected to continue to increase. Beginning about the year 2010, the first wave of the baby-boom generation will reach retirement age, bringing unprecedented pressure on federal financing for Social Security, Medicare, and Medicaid programs. At about the same time, the number of people working and paying taxes to support these and other programs will rise more slowly. It is for these reasons that Congress and the President are currently considering measures to reform Social Security.

State and Local Governments

The political structure of the United States is that of federalism, with sovereignty legally and constitutionally divided between the federal and state governments. Despite the increasing importance that the federal government has assumed since the start of World War II, any consideration of public finance would be incomplete without the inclusion of state and local government financial systems. One major item of federal government spending is national defense, a function that clearly belongs under its control. Related items such

Table 1.2   Federal Government Expenditures for the Year 2004[1] (Billions of Dollars)

Source	Amount
Discretionary	
Defense	390
Non-defense	429
Total discretionary	**819**
Mandatory	
Social Security	493
Medicare	255
Medicaid and SCHIP	185
Other	301
Total mandatory	1,234
Net interest	176
Total mandatory	**2,229**

[1]Estimate
Source: Executive Office of the President, Office of Manpower and Budget, *Budget of the United States Government, Fiscal Year 2004* (Washington, D.C.: OMB, 2004), p. 312.

as foreign aid, aid to veterans, and interest on the national debt are also clearly the responsibility of the federal government. Social Security, which dates back to the Depression of the 1930s, is another responsibility of the federal government in order to assure uniformity in taxes, benefits, and standards.

The essential division of responsibility in a federal political system is that drawn between the powers of the federal government and those of the state governments. Within each state there is also a second division of responsibility between the powers of the state and those of local government units—counties, cities, school districts, and so forth. This division of responsibility is more administrative and legislative than constitutional. All local units of government are creations of the states, which hold the residual power to destroy them. The division of financial authority between the states and their subordinate local government units varies from state to state, and the administrative devices for coordinating their expenditure and tax systems are diverse. Broadly speaking, the more divisible and concentrated the benefits are from the service provided, the more advantageous it is to have the service provided by the local unit of government.

State and Local Government Revenues

For state governments, the sales tax is the single most important revenue source. Normally, the tax is imposed as a percentage of the retail selling price of goods and services. Income taxation is a second source of revenue for state governments. However, states tend to be limited in their usage of income taxation by the fact that the national economy is an integrated market. The freedom of migration for both humans and other resources across state boundaries tends to insure that state government will set relatively low tax rates on income. Local governments may also impose income taxes. Transfers from the federal government to state and local governments, which take the form of grants-in-aid, are a third important source of revenue. Property taxes are the primary revenue source for local governments. Property is not subject to federal government taxation, and state governments have generally left this revenue source to the localities.

State and Local Government Expenditures

State and local government expenditures for 2000 amounted to $1.75 trillion.[10] Education is the single most important component of expenditures, accounting for one-third of the total. One of the most striking of the post World War II phenomena was the rapid increase in population, which continues to grow. Education expenditures increased almost six-fold during the period following World War II to the present. Moreover, as the United States has shifted from mass production industries to knowledge-based industries, demand for an educated labor force has increased. More students are finishing

high school and more are going to college. New physical facilities are constantly in the process of construction. Expenditures on highways, hospitals,
and other public facilities have also shown a marked increase in recent years.
Affluence and the aging of the population are contributing factors.

A COMPARISON OF GOVERNMENT
EXPENDITURES BY COUNTRIES

Government expenditures represent a transfer of resources from the private
sector of an economy to the public sector, and they also represent the contribution of the government sector to the total Gross Domestic Product (GDP)[11]
As figure 1.2 shows, total government spending amounted to 28 percent of
U.S. GDP in 2002, while private spending contributed 72 percent. The federal
government spent about 18 percent of GDP, and state and local governments
contributed 9 percent.

However, in comparison with other countries, total government expenditures expressed as a percentage of GDP is much smaller in the United States
than in other major industrial countries with the exception of Japan. This can
be attributed to the fact that income transfer payments in these countries are
much higher than they are in the United States. They would include family
allowances, free medical care, paid maternity leave, old-age pensions, unem-

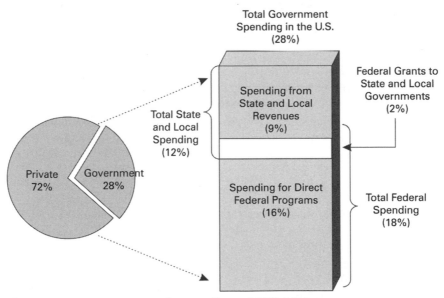

Figure 1.2.   Government Spending as a Share of GDP, 2002
Source: A Citizen's Guide to the Federal Budget, Executive Office of the President, fiscal
year 2002. www.whitehouse.gov/omb/budget

ployment compensation, free college education, and accident benefits. However, there is also a reverse side to these expenditures; somebody has to pay for them. Thus, the level of taxation in these countries is going to be much higher than it is in the United States. In such countries as France and Sweden, it is going to be over half of their GDP.

ECONOMIC STABILIZATION POLICIES

It is generally accepted that the economic and political objectives of U.S. society are a high level of employment, price stability, economic growth, and a balance-of-payments equilibrium. Each goal does not necessarily lend itself to precise definition, and the attainment of one may not help achieve the others. Considerable government intervention is necessary. This intervention takes the form of macroeconomic stabilization of fiscal and monetary policies that are implemented by the federal government's use of taxation, payments, and transfer payments, and by the Federal Reserve's control over the money supply and interest rates.

Fiscal Policy

The term fiscal policy refers to the tax and expenditure policies of the federal government.[12] Its objective is either to increase or decrease the level of aggregate demand through changes in the level of government expenditures and taxation. For example, an expansionary fiscal policy is supposed to stimulate economic growth and employment through an increase in government spending, a decrease in taxation, or both. Conversely, fiscal policy can be used to contract the level of aggregate demand. Taxes can be raised, expenditures can be reduced, or a combination of these approaches can be used. The federal budget, because of its sheer size, exercises a considerable influence on the American economy.

Monetary Policy

Monetary policy is used by the Federal Reserve to control the level of national output and the price level through variations in the money supply.[13] An increase in the money supply will lower interest rates and stimulate private and public spending; a decrease in the money supply will raise interest rates and reduce public and private spending. The Federal Reserve cannot fix the amount of credit and its cost independently. If it wants to restrain the rate of growth in the money supply, it must allow interest rates to rise as high as possible. If it wants to keep interest rates low, it has to accept the consequences of an increase in the money supply. Monetary policy is independent from fiscal policy in that control over it is not in the hands of the federal government.

GOVERNMENT REGULATION

The legal basis for federal government regulation of certain economic activities is based on the Constitution of the United States. Its single most important provision is found in Article 1, Section 8—the Commerce Clause that states that Congress shall have the power to regulate commerce among the states and with foreign nations. Eventually, federal regulation of commerce became restricted to interstate commerce, as opposed to intrastate commerce that came under state jurisdiction. In addition, Article 1, Section 8 gave Congress the power to levy and collect taxes; to pay debts and provide for the general welfare of the people; and to coin money and regulate its value. Regulations to promote the general welfare of the people are usually of a negative character. For example, the producers of food may not ship their products in interstate commerce unless they meet certain purity standards prescribed by law.

Rationale for Government Regulation

There are several reasons for government regulation. One is competition, which is considered one of the basic institutions of a capitalist free market economy. It is based on the notion that it contributes to social welfare. It is a regulator of economic activity, and is thought to maximize productivity, prevent excessive concentration of economic power, and protect consumer interests. But both business and government have intervened in different ways to circumvent competition, which is a hard taskmaster, for there are losers as well as winners. Business firms have formed various combinations, such as cartels and trusts, to eliminate competition. They have also engaged in collusive practices, such as price fixing and tying agreements to eliminate competition. Government subsidies and restraint on foreign competition also protect businesses, farmers, and other groups against competition.

Economic Regulation

Antitrust laws provide an example of economic regulation. They are based on two premises. The first is the English common law as it evolved through court decisions over a period of time. In general, these decisions held that restraints on trade or commerce are not in the public interest. In interpreting the common law, courts in England and the United States ruled that contracts or agreements to restrain or attempt to restrain trade were illegal. A second example of economic regulation involves control over certain industries that directly affect the public interest. An example would be regulation of a natural monopoly, which refers to a market in which a single seller is required for efficient production. Public utilities can be natural monopolies, but the services they provide are regulated; otherwise, they would charge monopoly prices.

Social Regulation

Other defects in the market system are the inability of consumers to express negative wants in the marketplace through the price mechanism, and externalities such as pollution which are an external cost of production. Many people would be happier if they could prevent the production and sale of cigarettes or the emission of noxious fumes from a chemical plant. But there is no way in which the market price mechanism can take these preferences into account, except through government control over the output and use of goods deemed deleterious to the public interest. Pollution is an example of an externality because producers can impose a cost on consumers without having to pay compensation. Consumer spending cannot mandate a clean environment, but government regulation can. Thus, a series of laws were passed by the federal government that require the cleaning up of various forms of pollution.

State and Local Government Regulation

State and local governments have often enacted legislation in advance of the federal government. For example, a number of Midwestern state governments enacted a series of laws designed to regulate railroad abuses in the period immediately following the Civil War. In 1871 Illinois created a railroad commission authorizing it to fix maximum rates for intrastate freight and passenger service. Federal regulation of the railroads did not occur until 1887. State and local governments were the first to pass laws to protect consumers. Sanitary regulations, inspection of weights and measures and the like were established local government functions at the beginning of the nation's history. State laws to protect consumers against the adulteration of food and drugs was first passed in Virginia in 1848 and Ohio in 1853. The federal government passed the Pure Food and Drug Act in 1906.

GOVERNMENT AS AN EMPLOYER

One measure of the public sector's size and importance to the American economy is the number of people employed by various government units. In 2002, 2.7 million people—including military personnel—were employed by the federal government, while state and local governments employed 18.3 million people.[14] The total number of government employees—federal, state, and local—amounted to 21 million, which was approximately 14 percent of a total American labor force of 146.5 million workers. Of this total, 12 million, or approximately 55 percent, worked for local governments and 4.7 million, or approximately 22 percent, worked for state governments.[15] State and local government employment are expected to increase in the future since the demand for social services will increase, particularly as the population continues to grow older.

Two sets of administrative hierarchies, one public and the other private, have grown at different times for different reasons to carry out different functions. The public hierarchy developed much later than the private hierarchy. In 1929 the federal government's labor force in Washington was a great deal smaller than that of U.S. Steel or General Motors; today, it is much larger than both companies combined. Numerous federal agencies have been created, and a new administrative culture has developed. The work, attitudes, and perspectives of the private sector administrator and the government administrator have become and will remain almost as distinct and separate as those of the scientist and humanist. The attitudes of these two hierarchies define relations between the private and public sectors of the American economy.

GOVERNMENT AS A LENDER AND INSURER

The federal government is the nation's single largest source of credit and underwriting of risk. It has a number of programs that offer financial assistance to its citizens. These programs give assistance to students, business firms, farmers, homebuyers, banks, and exporters. Some of them are an important source of credit for various sectors of the American economy. For example, the housing industry relies on the various federal mortgage credit programs. The Direct Student Loan Program provides several types of loans for students, which carry interest rates lower than the going market rate. Rural electrification and telecommunications loans are for the construction and operation of generating plants, electric transmission, and distribution lines or systems. Exporters can obtain financial assistance from the Export-Import Bank (Eximbank).

Direct Loans

Direct loans have several characteristics. First, they are designed to promote socially useful activities rather than to remove imperfections in the credit market. Second, they contain a subsidy element in that interest rates charged are lower than prevailing market rates. Third, they are financed directly out of federal budget revenues. Fourth, foreign loans are the largest single component of direct loans. In quantity, the most important types of foreign loans are development loans and loans made by the Export-Import Bank (Exim-bank). Both loans create a foreign demand for U.S. goods and services.

Loan Guarantees

From the standpoint of the amount of money involved, insured loans are by far the most important segment of federal government credit. The government may either insure or guarantee loans made by private lenders. The difference between loan insurance and loan guarantees is that a fee is generally charged for insurance. The best example of loan insurance is the Federal Housing Administration (FHA) mortgage program, which is designed to encourage lenders to make credit available to expand home ownership. It predominantly serves borrowers that the conventional credit market does not adequately serve: first-time homebuyers, minorities, lower-income families and residents of under-served areas. The Federal Family Education Loan program is an example of a loan guarantee program.

Government-Sponsored Financial Institutions

A third way in which the federal government allocates credit, although indirectly, is through privately owned government sponsored financial enterprises. These enterprises have been created by the government to perform special credit functions. Three of them, the Federal National Mortgage Association (Fannie Mae), the Federal Home Loan Mortgage Bank (Freddie Mac), and the Federal Home Loan Banks, serve the housing market. The Farm Credit System finances agriculture, and the Student Loan Market Association (Sallie Mae) makes a secondary market in federally guaranteed student loans. Each issues securities and uses the proceeds to finance its lending activities, and their earnings are exempt from state and local income taxes. They can borrow at interest rates significantly lower than even the best-rate private borrowers, and can make loans at interest below prevailing market rates.

GOVERNMENT AND THE WORLD ECONOMY

The world has changed more rapidly since 1990 than at any time since the end of World War II in 1945. Probably the seminal event of this century has been the collapse of communism in 1989. The Soviet Union is now a thing of the past, and its former republics have become independent countries that are proceeding unevenly toward democracy and free market capitalism. Poland, the Czech Republic, Hungary, and other Eastern and Central European countries that were once a part of the Soviet bloc are, for the most part, well on their way to becoming democratic market economies. Most state-owned enterprises are now privately owned. Throughout most of the world, from Germany to Argentina, a trend toward privatization of state-owned enterprises has occurred.

A new type of economic and social revolution is also underway. The factor that is transforming the world environment and the relationship of the United States within it is technological change, which is moving more rapidly than at any time in history. Advances in computers and telecommunications have shrunk distances, eroded national boundaries, and enlarged the domain of the global economy. This is the most significant force that will shape the first half of this century. Money is immediately transferable; on a given day, some $1 trillion will cross country borders throughout the world. Many services have become internationally tradable and easier to ship from one country to another than goods are. The power of international market forces to allocate resources certainly will have an impact on the role of government in the future.

So, does this mean the end of national governments? It is argued by some that the Internet will make avoiding taxes so easy and riskless that sovereignty will shift to individuals, leaving governments to die of fiscal starvation. Another argument is that the volume of world money is so large that its movements in and out of a currency have an enormous impact on world financial markets. It has total mobility, serves no economic function and finances nothing, and is easily panicked by a rumor or unexpected event.[16] Currency instability is created by forces over which governments have little or no control. A third argument is that large corporations have become transnational. In a transnational company, there is only one economic unit, the world, and national boundaries have largely become irrelevant. This means that there will have to be the development of supranational organizations to make and enforce rules in a global economy.

Nevertheless, governments will continue to play an important role in their respective countries. In many countries, entitlements have become accepted as a right by their citizens. In fact, not only are entitlement expenditures the single largest component of the U.S. federal budget, they are also the single largest component of the budgets of other industrialized nations. Spending on public consumption, such as education, health, and pensions, has risen substantially. The most important cause of the increase in government expenditures has been the development of the modern welfare state and the growth in income transfers and subsidies.

SUMMARY

A considerable amount of government intervention is an indispensable requisite for the establishment of even the freest type of economy. The very atmosphere for the conduct of economic activity is created by the ability of government to establish and maintain private property, freedom of enterprise, money and credit, and a system of civil laws for adjusting the private disputes of individuals. Government regulation exists for several reasons. It is used to intervene between sellers and buyers in order to protect either or both from certain harmful practices that may arise. For example, it is unlawful to market certain drugs unless they have been approved by the Food and Drug Administration. Antitrust policies are designed to deal with industry conduct, such as price fixing, that discriminates against consumers. A third area of regulation involves the misuse of public resources, such as air and water, which causes pollution.

QUESTIONS FOR DISCUSSION

1. What is the role of government in a market economy such as the United States?
2. What is the difference between discretionary and mandatory government expenditures?
3. It is said that technology will reduce the importance of national governments in the world economy. Do you agree?
4. What are the differences between direct loans and loan guarantees?
5. Discuss the differences between economic and social regulation.
6. What are entitlements? Why are they the fastest growing component of the federal budget?

RECOMMENDED REFERENCES

A Citizen's Guide to the Federal Budget, Executive Office of the President, fiscal year 2002. www.whitehouse.gov/omb/budget

Economic Report of the President, fiscal year 2006, U.S. Government Printing Office. www.gpoaccess.gov/eop/2006/2006_erp.pdf

Federal Budget of the United States, fiscal year 2006, U.S. Government Printing Office. www.gpoaccess.gov/usbudget/fy06/browse.html

Statistical Abstract of the United States, 2006, 125th Edition U.S. Census Bureau. www.census.gov/statab/www/

NOTES

1. The naval victory of Athens over Persia at Salamis in 480 B.C. made Athens the leading sea power of the Eastern Mediterranean for some 100 years; hence its dominance in trade.

2. The Roman legal system became the foundation for civil, or code, law which is used in Europe, Latin America, Japan, and the state of Louisiana.

3. Venetian traders traveled as far as China. Venice developed a banking system and used letters of credit in foreign trade.

4. Mercantilist policies have been used to promote foreign trade in Japan and other East Asian countries.

5. Laissez-faire was developed by Adam Smith as a rule of practical economic conduct. According to Smith, the individual, if permitted to pursue his or her own self-interest, will promote the well-being of all.

6. Even without the war, the monarchical system of government was on its way out.

7. This can be called *Keynesian economics*.

8. In the case of taxes on tobacco, revenues are used to treat tobacco users who become ill from smoking.

9. This is much lower than it is in such countries as Sweden, where government expenditures are more than 50 percent of GDP.

10. U.S. Department of Commerce, Bureau of the Census, *Statistical Abstract of the United States 2004–2005* (Washington, D.C.: U.S. Government Printing Office, 2004), 277–78.

11. Gross Domestic Product (GDP) measures the value of all goods and services that are produced each year in a country.

12. Fiscal policy is associated with what is called Keynesian economics, which is a school of economic thought based on the work of John Maynard Keynes, particularly *The General Theory of Employment, Interest, and Money*. Keynesian economics holds that government purchases of goods and services and tax collections are key instruments of government economic policy.

13. The money supply is the total quantity of money existing in an economy at a particular time.

14. U.S. Department of Commerce, Bureau of the Census, *Statistical Abstract of the United States 2004–2005* (Washington, D.C.: U.S. Government Printing Office, 2004), 298.

15. *Statistical Abstracts*, pp. 298, 371.

16. A very good example was the collapse of East Asian stock markets in October and November 1997.

2

Government Regulation

The United States of today has changed considerably from the United States of the past. A laissez-faire economy existed through much of its history, predicated on the belief that government that governed the least, governed the best. Business owners ran their businesses pretty much as they pleased without government intervention. Consumers had little protection, with caveat emptor ("let the buyer beware") being the rule of the land. In terms of employment, the concept of employment at will prevailed. The employer owned property, set wages, and dictated working conditions. Workers could take it or leave it. If they did not like their jobs, they could quit; if they did not go to work, they were fired; and if they joined a union, they were also fired. But all this changed drastically during the twentieth century. Government heavily regulates business. Local regulations tell a company where it may do business. State regulations cover the selling of securities, loan rates, and highway weight limits. Federal regulations are all encompassing. Antitrust laws are designed to promote competition and to prevent various unfair business practices such as price-fixing. Consumers are protected by a variety of laws covering the sale of food and drugs, lending, warranties, and product safety. Federal and state regulations address pollution and the safety of employees in the workplace. There is also extensive federal and state regulation of labor, ranging from minimum wages to collective bargaining. In addition, there are federal and state laws designed to provide equal employment opportunity for persons who were historically foreclosed from the workplace.

THE POLITICAL SYSTEM OF THE UNITED STATES

The United States possesses what can be called a "marble cake" government. With the exception of Germany, the United States is unique in that it has a federal form of government that is divided into three parts—federal, state, and local. However, of the three levels, the federal government is clearly dominant in terms of its impact on business, consumers, taxpayers, and other groups. The Constitution of the United States provides for a distribution of power among the legislative, executive, and judicial branches of government. This provision was made to prevent an undue concentration of power within the federal government. An additional restriction on the exercise of political power was subsequently developed in the practice of judicial review. Soon after the federal courts began to function, they faced the question of whether or not certain acts of Congress were in harmony with the Constitution.[1]

LEGISLATIVE BRANCH

Congress is the most important legislative body in the land. It passes the laws that affect all of us. Sources of ideas for legislation are unlimited, and proposed drafts of bills can originate from many diverse sources, but only Congress can pass a bill. The United States today is composed of many special interest groups, each with its own constituency. The goals of these interest groups are often directly opposite—for example, pro-life versus abortion on demand. There is a trend toward a divided society and a multiplicity of special interest groups, and money is not likely to be lacking for any group with a good-sized bloc of voters. Congress is where the action begins, and the exercise of political power requires communication.

COMMITTEES

The committee system is the crux of the legislative process and is the basis for most legislative action. Ninety percent of all federal and state legislation is passed in the form reported by a particular committee. Some committees are of particular importance. At the federal level, the House Ways and Means Committee has the power to tax; all revenue-raising bills emanate from this committee. No one thing has more impact upon any individual or group than the power to tax. The House and Senate Appropriations Committees are also of prime importance for they determine how the money will be spent. The House Rules Committee is important because it has control over the order in which bills will be introduced in the House. The Senate Finance Committee and the Senate and House Judiciary Committees are also important.

Subcommittees

In addition to the committees, there are various subcommittees. The framework and parameters of most bills are settled in committees and subcommittees. Many subcommittees and their chairpersons and senior members have assumed considerable influence over the generally smaller slice of legislation they command. These subcommittees also have staff members, and chairpersons and higher-ranking members also employ staff experts in the subject matter covered by these units. Staff members may play a major role in shaping legislation because their expertise is often greater than that of the typical legislator who has to be concerned with a myriad of other issues, constituent matters, and other problems. Thus, the power of Congress is dispersed, with legislative influence over policy decisions scattered over a large number of members who serve on many subcommittees.

EXECUTIVE BRANCH

The executive branch is the second branch of government. At the federal level of government, the executive branch consists of the president of the United States, his cabinet, and the bureaucracy. The framers of the Constitution created a presidency of limited powers. They wanted a presidential office that would stay clear of parties and factions, enforce the laws passed by Congress, deal with foreign governments, and help the states put down disorders. However, American presidents have been extending the limits of executive power, aided and abetted by Congress and the courts. In times of national emergency, Congress has increased the rule-making discretion of the executive branch. The growth in the role of the federal government has also enlarged the responsibility of the president. The presidency has increased in power, and White House aides are able to claim that it is the only place in government where it is possible to set national priorities.

The president of the United States has several responsibilities. First, the president is responsible for priority setting and policy formulation. Particularly since the New Deal, presidents have been expected to assume more responsibility in directing economic policy—fighting inflation and promoting economic growth. Second, the president is responsible for handling national emergencies. The military role of the president has increased in importance, as witnessed by U.S. involvement in the Persian Gulf region. Finally, the president is supposed to be the strongest mobilizer of public influence in the American system of power. This is facilitated by ready access to all communications media, which provides immediate contact with the people.

Departments and Agencies

However, the executive branch is by no means limited to the president. There is a host of departments and agencies that come under the jurisdiction of the executive branch. There is the Executive Office of the President, which consists of the Office of Management and Budget, the Council on Environmental Quality, the National Security Council, and other staff units. These units are supposed to coordinate administration policies before the Congress, help the president plan and set priorities, and monitor and evaluate progress toward achieving national objectives. Then there are the various departments of government, the heads of which are appointed by the president and form his cabinet. Then comes the government bureaucracy, which is the administrative arm of the government. Bureaucracy cannot be dismissed as simply part of the executive branch of government. Its power has increased and it has become an important force in the government system.

Bureaucracy

For practical purposes, the federal bureaucracy and Congress have the greatest impact upon the American public. Congress makes the laws and the bureaucracies of the many federal agencies enforce them. Only a small part of the bureaucracy works in Washington. The vast majority is employed in regional, field, and local offices scattered throughout the country. When one speaks of "big government," one is speaking about the bureaucracy. It provides an inviting target for politicians and the general public, because many have been hassled from time to time in dealing with such agencies as the Internal Revenue Service, which has been very much in the news, or the dozens of national regulatory agencies that have been created over the last thirty years.

JUDICIAL BRANCH

Courts, taken together, make up one of the three branches of government; therefore, as is also true of the legislative and executive branches, they are generally provided for in the federal and state constitutions. For example, Article III of the U.S. Constitution vests the judicial power of the United States "in one Supreme Court and in such inferior courts as the Congress may from time to time ordain and establish." The judicial branch of government has the power that allows the courts to make the ultimate decision as to where and how the other two branches of government may properly exercise their powers. There are two types of courts based on jurisdiction—federal court and state courts. Federal jurisdiction is derived from Article III of the Constitution. It would include all regulations of federal administrative agencies. For example, if a person is denied a job because of race, that would raise a federal question. State courts have the power to hear all matters with respect to state laws.

Federal Courts

The Supreme Court sits at the apex of the American judicial system. It is the only court created by the Constitution. It has nine judges, called justices, who are nominated by the president and confirmed by the Senate, and they serve for life. It has affected every stage in the transformation of government's role in the economic life of the United States, from its modest functions in 1789 to its all-pervasive role in the economy of today. However, its power is negative, one of veto rather than origination. Thus future economic and social policies are diverted into permitted channels confined within the orbit of judicial approval. For example, in recent years the Supreme Court has expanded the legal concept of class action to facilitate a much broader use of litigation as a form of interest-group social policy. It has also struck at various forms of discrimination.

In addition to the Supreme Court, the federal judicial system includes other types of courts. Congress has created federal district courts in each state. Each state has at least one; some states have many. The courts contained in each district constitute the general trial courts of the federal system. The district courts are grouped into circuits. There are thirteen circuits. Each circuit has a court of appeals in which appeals from the trial courts are heard. They do not retry the case; rather, they review the record to determine whether the trial court made errors of law. The decisions of these circuit courts of appeal are often final. In a few cases, further appeal may be made to the Supreme Court. Finally, there are specialized courts. An example would be the U.S. Claims Court.

In order for a lawsuit to be filed in a federal district court, it must come within the classes of cases to which the Constitution extends the federal judicial power: cases between citizens of different states and cases involving questions under federal laws or under the U.S. Constitution. Decisions of the district court are appealable, as a matter of right, to the appropriate U.S. court of appeals, and in a few cases directly to the Supreme Court of the United States. Most of the cases that reach the Supreme Court from the courts of appeals come by way of certiorari. In such cases, the party who lost the case is not given the right to appeal to the Supreme Court, but must persuade the Court that it should exercise its discretion and take the case for review because of some special importance it has.

State Courts

State courts include inferior trial courts, which include municipal courts, juvenile courts, domestic relations courts, and traffic courts. Then there are courts of general jurisdiction, meaning they have the power to hear all matters with respect to state law. In some jurisdictions, two courts may exist at this level: one to resolve all questions of law, and the other to resolve all matters of equity. Each state also has at least one court of appeals. It is usually, but not always, called the supreme court. Sometimes intermediate courts of appeals also exist, as in the federal system. These courts review the trial court record to determine whether or not there are any errors of law.

THE ADMINISTRATIVE AGENCIES

Almost every type of business activity falls within at least the indirect influence of a number of administrative agencies. It is important to study these agencies and their functions, though some general points should be made. Administrative agencies, regardless of responsibility, acquire their authority to act from the legislative branch of government. Because they do most of the day-to-day work of government, they make many significant policy decisions. Administrative agencies can be divided into two categories: independent regulatory commissions and agencies that are part of the executive branch of government.[2] In many areas of domestic policy formulation, independent agencies exercise more control, although different economic and political needs have produced administrative agencies exercising vast legislative and adjudicative powers that cannot be classified as independent regulatory agencies. Many executive agencies perform regulatory functions as part of their broader responsibility.

Most regulatory agencies that function within the executive department possess both quasi-legislative and quasi-judicial powers, just as the independent regulatory commissions do. The power to make rules and regulations has been delegated to these agencies by legislative fiat. The only important difference between an agency rule and a law enacted by a legislative body is that the rule may be only slightly more susceptible to attack because it was not made by elected officials. Administrative agencies can also implement policy or legislation through a process of initiating and settling specific cases. They also engage in administrative adjudication, which includes procedures used in deciding cases. For many types of cases, the procedures are carefully outlined: hearings are frequently prescribed, records are required, and so on. Furthermore, if the agencies overstep the boundaries of their authority, redress can always be secured in the courts.

Administrative agencies, as agents of Congress, reflect group demands for positive action. They are not supposed to be arbiters like the courts; rather, they should be activists who initiate policy in accordance with their mandate. For example, when the Federal Trade Commission (FTC) ferrets out deceptive business practices, either through its own investigation or through information gained from outside sources, it initiates action in the name of the FTC against the party involved. It then adjudicates the very case it initiates. If the case reaches a formal hearing and goes to a hearing examiner for an initial decision, it is not, at that point, subject to commission control. But after the examiner renders a decision, the Commission may reverse it. The result is that the FTC can control the decisions rendered in almost all the cases it initiates.

Sanctions

Government intervention carries with it the threat and the actual application of sanctions to achieve desired economic and social outcomes. Sanctions may often be positive, taking the form of subsidies and tax incentives to promote a desired activity such as the construction of low-rent housing. When the target is an undesirable economic or social activity, negative sanctions are often used to enforce compliance with the law. They can designate noncompliance either as a criminal offense requiring the imposition of fines, imprisonment, or both, or as a civil offense involving the loss of the right or privilege to engage in economic transactions through the loss of licenses, permits, and franchises. For example, the Clean Air Act of 1970 subjects willful polluters to fines and jail sentences. Plants can be shut down and permits to operate canceled if pollution continues. In applying negative sanctions, the intent is to use the coercive power of the state to enforce compliance. This is done by announcing to society or its components that various actions are not to be carried out and to ensure that fewer of them are. There is no choice other than to comply with a mandatory standard if the regulatory agency has sufficient enforcement tools. In addition, the regulatory agencies are expected to amass facts, to apply the law to these facts, and to impose the appropriate sanctions when noncompliance is found. Thus, the intent and process of regulation is more like adjudication than other types of political action. It can be said that violators of economic and social regulation differ from violators of criminal law only in the degree of responsibility for societal harm that is attributed to them by regulators and the community as a whole.

Major Regulatory Agencies

Some regulatory agencies are economic in their objectives, while other regulatory agencies have social goals, such as a clean environment. There are also some regulatory agencies that may have both economic and social goals. Economic regulation pertains to a specific industry. The Interstate Commerce Commission (ICC) was created in 1887 and was phased out in 1996. During its existence, it had control over rates and services that railroads, trucks, and buses could charge and provide in interstate commerce. Social regulation reflects concern for public welfare across all industries. Its aim is a better quality of life for all through the provision of a clean environment, better working conditions, and safe consumer products. For example, the Food and Drug Administration (FDA) protects consumers against the consumption of unsafe food, drugs, cosmetics, and other potentially hazardous products.

The Federal Trade Commission (FTC)

The Federal Trade Commission (FTC) is an example of a federal government agency that is engaged in both economic and social regulation. It was created by the Federal Trade Commission Act of 1914 to enforce compliance with the provisions of the Clayton Act that was also passed in 1914. Subsequent antitrust laws—such as the Robinson-Patman Act of 1936 and the Hart-Scott-Rodino Act of 1976—are also enforced by the FTC. The goals of these laws are economic. They are designed to promote competition. The Federal Trade Commission Act specifically prohibits unfair methods of competition, including price discrimination, and gives the FTC enforcement powers to seek civil and criminal remedies against violators of the act. The FTC, along with the antitrust division of the Justice Department, has jurisdiction over mergers.

However, the FTC is also involved in social regulation. It protects the public by preventing the dissemination of false or misleading food and drug advertising. It also has jurisdiction over various labeling laws, such as the Wool Products Labeling Act, that are designed to protect consumers from the misrepresentation of the product. Then there are various credit laws, such as the Truth-in-Lending Act of 1968, which require that borrowers be made aware of basic information about the terms and cost of credit. Finally, the Consumer Product Warranty Act of 1975 provides minimum disclosure standards for written consumer product warranties and defines federal content standards for these warranties.

The Securities and Exchange Commission (SEC)

The Securities and Exchange Commission (SEC) was created by the Securities Exchange Act of 1934 to prevent the widespread and flagrant abuses in the securities markets during the 1920s. The SEC consists of five members appointed by the president with the consent of the Senate, with each holding office for a period of five years. The act condemned a number of manipulative practices and gave the SEC the authority to check their use. Manipulation of stock prices in any manner is outlawed. Under the act, corporate directors, officers, and insiders are not permitted to sell their company's stock short, and they must make public any intent to exercise stock options. Willful violations of an unfair practice are punishable by fines or imprisonment, or both. The act also requires all securities listed on national exchanges be registered with the SEC by the issuer, and that financial reports be in a form prescribed by the SEC. Significant regulatory changes occurred in the wake of several corporate scandals in the early 2000s, leading to the passage of the Sarbanes-Oxley Act of 2002. These changes are among the most significant in the history of the SEC.[3]

The Food and Drug Administration (FDA)

The Food and Drug Administration (FDA) is one of the most important social regulatory agencies in Washington. It monitors most laws involving food and drugs, and some laws dealing with disclosure. An example would be the Flammable Fabrics Act of 1953, which requires the labeling of highly flammable clothing. Also coming under FDA's jurisdiction are laws pertaining to the consumption of tobacco products. Cautionary notices have to be put on cigarette and small cigar packages as well as on containers of smokeless tobacco. An example is the Smokeless Tobacco Act of 1986 that requires producers, packagers, and importers of smokeless tobacco to label their products with such warnings as: "This product may cause mouth cancer," or, "This product may cause tooth disease and gum loss." The FDA also requires the testing of drugs before they can be sold to the public.

The Environmental Protection Agency (EPA)

In July 1970, President Richard Nixon submitted to Congress a reorganizational plan to create an independent environmental protection agency. The organization was approved and the EPA was created in the executive branch of government. Functions that formerly belonged to the Department of the Interior relating to studies on the effects of insecticides and pesticides were transferred to this agency. Also transferred were functions belonging to the Department of Health, Education, and Welfare, including the creation of tolerance norms for pesticide chemicals under the Food, Drugs, and Cosmetics Act of 1938. The EPA was given supervision over air pollution standards as set forth in the Clean Air Act of 1970 and its subsequent amendments. The EPA was also given control over water pollution control programs, particularly those set forth later in the Water Pollution Control Act of 1972, including the setting of water quality standards. The jurisdiction of the EPA was also later extended to the Noise Control Act of 1972, and it became responsible for setting noise emission standards for products identified as major sources of noise. Subsequent environmental laws are also under the jurisdiction of the EPA.

The Occupational Safety and Health Administration (OSHA)

OSHA was created as an agency of the Department of Labor to administer the Occupational Safety and Health Act of 1970. The purpose of the act is to assure safe and healthful working conditions. It requires employers to comply with safety and health standards promulgated by OSHA. In addition, every employer is required to furnish for his or her employees work free from recognizable hazards that cause or are likely to cause death or serious injury. Recognized hazards are defined as those that can be detected by the common human senses, unaided by testing devices, and that are generally known in the industry as hazardous. Further, a firm can be penalized under the general duty clause if the unsafe conditions have been cited by an inspector and the employer has refused to correct it in the specified time. However, ergonomic standards are voluntary. In 2002, 5,524 workers died in work-related accidents.

The Federal Communications Commission (FCC)

The Federal Communications Commission is an example of an economic regulatory agency in that it is concerned with the way business is done in a specific industry—telecommunications. It was created by the Communications Act of 1934. Prior to the passage of the act, Congress had given the Interstate Commerce Commission (ICC) jurisdiction over the operations in interstate commerce of telephone, telegraph, and radio companies. The FCC has control over maximum and minimum rates (except broadcasting charges), controls entry of new companies, and controls services companies can offer. It was eventually given control over the television industry; for example, the right to operate a local television station. The Telecommunications Act of 1996 impacted the authority of the FCC, particularly with a long-distance entry approval procedure involving the regional Bell operating companies (RBOCs).

The Consumer Product Safety Commission (CPSC)

The Consumer Product Safety Commission was created in 1972 by the Consumer Product Safety Act, and functions as an independent regulatory commission. It has jurisdiction over most consumer products and has the power to inspect facilities where consumer products are made, stored, or transported. It can also require all manufacturers, private labelers, and distributors to establish and maintain books and records and to make available additional information if deemed necessary. It can require the use of specific labels that set forth the results of product testing. The greatest impact this requirement has is in the production process, in which the design of numerous products must conform to federal standards. Since safety standards are often formulated at various government and independent testing stations, a company may find that a finished product may no longer meet federal standards, and modification is necessary.

The Equal Employment Opportunity Commission (EEOC)

The EEOC was created by the Civil Rights Act of 1964 as an independent commission, and its enforcement authority was greatly increased by the Equal Employment Opportunity Act of 1972. It has the power to investigate and act on a charge of a pattern or practice of discrimination, whether filed by or on behalf of the person or group claiming to be aggrieved. It has the right to initiate civil suits against employers, labor unions, and any other group accused of practicing employment discrimination. Moreover, private individuals and groups have the right to sue under Title VII of the Civil Rights Act of 1964. The EEOC can also investigate company records to see whether a pattern of discrimination exists and can subpoena company records if necessary. Any organization subject to the Civil Rights Act of 1964 and subsequent executive orders must keep records that can determine whether unlawful practices have been committed.

State and Local Government Regulatory Agencies

It is important to realize that state and local governments have their counterparts of the federal regulatory agencies. For example, federal laws pertaining to employment practices are not the only laws that affect business and other organizations; state and local government laws also exist. The degree of state and local government laws varies—some provide agencies to enforce laws, whereas others have voluntary enforcement. State and local governments also have environmental laws. The first consumer protection laws were passed by state and local governments long before consumer protection laws were introduced by the federal government. Regulations governing occupational safety and health and the sale of food and drug products are also among state and local laws.

INTERNATIONAL REGULATION

The globalization of national economies began with the communications revolution and continues unabated. Problems that were once the province of a particular country have become global. One problem is pollution of the environment that transcends national borders. Examples are pollution of the ocean and global warming. A second problem pertains to trade among nations. To prevent the use of deterrents to trade, such as protective tariffs and import quotas, most of the leading trading nations are signatories to the General Agreement on Tariffs and Trade (GATT) and its successor, the World Trade Organization (WTO). In 1994, Canada, Mexico, and the United States signed the North American Free Trade Agreement (NAFTA), creating a free-trade zone. Finally, in 1997, member nations of the Organization for Economic Cooperation and Development (OECD) agreed to create new laws to make bribery of a foreign public official illegal.

Extraterritorial Jurisdiction

A question of jurisdiction is that of the power of a nation to regulate activities occurring beyond its borders. As markets become more global, the problems of regulating various types of unfair business conduct become more complex. In the United States, courts and regulators have struggled with the issue of the reach of their power. Some cases are relatively simple, involving conduct of foreign-owned businesses within the United States. In those instances, the jurisdictional principle of presence affords a basis for American courts or regulatory agencies to act. A more difficult question of authority arises when the alleged illegal conduct occurs in a foreign country but has an effect on the commerce of the United States. However, through legal precedence, U.S. laws, particularly in the areas of antitrust, employment, and corrupt practices, have been extended to actions of U.S. companies outside the United States.

Antitrust Laws

Although a number of countries have antitrust laws, they are not as far-reaching as those of the United States. As a consequence, actions taken by American corporations operating in a foreign country may be legal under its laws, but illegal in the United States. The American view that a freely competitive economic system is the most efficient, most desirable form of society, is not necessarily the view held by other major industrial countries. To compete more successfully in international commerce, the western European countries and Japan have permitted the use of such anticompetitive devices as cartels and other forms of business combinations that would be illegal in the United States.[4] One result is that the extent of industry and banking concentration is greater in those countries than in the United States.[5]

The application of American antitrust laws has been applied extraterritorially to American firms engaged in international commerce, thus subjecting their worldwide activities to national control. The first major international application of U.S. antitrust law came in the landmark American Tobacco case of 1911.[6] The American Tobacco Company and the Imperial Tobacco Company of Great Britain had agreed to divide world markets, with Imperial agreeing not to sell its tobacco products in the United States, except through American Tobacco. The two companies then formed a third corporation, the British-American Tobacco Company, which took over the foreign businesses of both companies. The U.S. Supreme Court ruled that this allocation of markets illegally restrained trade under the provisions of the Sherman Act.

Employment Laws

The U.S. government, particularly the Equal Employment Opportunity Commission (EEOC), has made an effort to apply U.S. employment laws to American firms operating overseas. These laws are the Civil Rights Act of 1964, particularly Title VII, the Age Discrimination in Employment Act (ADEA) of 1967, the Americans with Disabilities Act (ADA) of 1990, and the Civil Rights Act of 1991. The last act made clear that Americans employed abroad by U.S.-owned or U.S.-controlled firms can avail themselves of the protection of the Title VII, the ADEA, and the ADA unless compliance with these laws will constitute a violation of the laws of the country in which the American firm operates. American employment laws also apply to American workers employed by foreign firms operating in the United States, unless there is a need for these firms to employ their own citizens.

Bribery is an accepted way of life in many countries, a way to get things done. The moral implications of bribery are irrelevant in these countries, if indeed moral considerations are taken into account. Foreign firms, then, are often faced with a dilemma—do they play by the rules of the game, give a bribe and get what they want done, or do they stand on principle and refuse to play by the rules of the game. In an effort to address this problem, Congress passed the Foreign Corrupt Practices Act in 1977, which is an amendment to the Securities Exchange Act of 1934. The act prohibits the giving of money or anything else "of value" to foreign officials with the intent to corrupt. Enforcement comes under the jurisdiction of the Securities and Exchange Commission.

THE IMPACT OF REGULATION ON SOCIETY

There is more to regulation than the creation of a number of new government agencies. The laws creating these agencies also defined ambitious health, safety, and equity goals and in some cases established strict deadlines for attaining them nationally. Frequently, the laws have restricted agency discretion to moderate regulatory standards in view of economic or other considerations. They empower citizens' complainants and advocacy groups to sue business firms for damages and government officials for failure to promulgate strict rules of enforcement. Business firms are required to undertake extensive reporting of their compliance efforts. Local governments and school districts that fail to meet federally prescribed regulatory requirements have been threatened with debarment from federal grants-in-aid and contracts.

Costs of Regulation

There are two types of regulatory costs—direct and indirect. Direct costs are of two types—paperwork and compliance. Paperwork costs involve the keeping of records and the filling out of required forms.[7] Compliance costs involve the installment of machinery and equipment. A university has to comply with the provisions of the Americans with Disabilities Act of 1990 by providing ramps, elevators, special parking facilities, and other devices necessary for use by individuals with disabilities. The Clean Air Act of 1970 required the purchase of equipment, such as the catalytic converter and scrubbers, by companies to reduce the emission of pollutants into the atmosphere. Regulation also requires the creation of government regulatory agencies that employ people who are a part of the government payroll.

The indirect costs of regulation usually show up in higher prices for goods and services. For example, an automobile costs more because of government regulation. Federal safety standards promulgated in the 1960s and early 1970s involved accident avoidance, crash protection, and postcrash survivability. Accident avoidance standards were set for braking systems, tires, windshields, lamps, and transmission controls. Occupant protection standards included requirements for safety belts, head restraints, and highly penetration-resistant safety glass. Exterior penetration standards included the absorption capacity of front and rear bumpers. These and other standards add to the price of the average automobile.

Opportunity Costs

Opportunity costs are a type of indirect cost. Since resources are scarce, the decision to use them means that something else must be given up. When resources are used in a certain way, there is a simultaneous choice not to use them another way. The opportunity cost then can be defined as the value of the benefit lost as a result of choosing one alternative over another. It is an important concept because the real cost of any activity is measured by its opportunity cost, not by its outlay cost. Thus, if resources are used to control pollution or build safer automobiles, society gives up all the other goods and services that might have been obtained from the use of these resources. For example, resources devoted to the production of pollution control equipment might have been used to produce houses instead.

Cost-Benefit Analysis

The motive for incorporating cost-benefit analysis into the regulatory decision-making process is to achieve a more efficient allocation of resources. In making an investment decision, for example, it is necessary to compare the costs to be incurred to the expected benefits, namely, revenues. Very likely the investment will be pursued only if the expected costs are less than the expected revenues. If an investment will yield $20 and the cost is $10, the benefit obtained will be $10. Cost-benefit analysis can be applied to opportunity costs. For example, suppose that an individual has $10 that he or she wishes to spend on some benefits. His or her rational response would be to examine a number of possible uses of the money and ask which of them would yield the greatest benefit.

Table 2.1 provides an example of cost-benefit analysis applied to automobile safety regulation. The costs of safety standards are the original cost of meeting them as well as the costs of complying with them after the companies have had sufficient time to redesign the vehicles to accommodate the standards at the lowest cost. The benefits include a reduction in premature deaths, a large portion of which occurs among teenagers and adults. There has been a reduction in the number of highway deaths per 100 million vehicle miles driven. In 1965 the highway deaths were 5.52 per 100 million vehicle miles driven; in 1985 there were 2.21 highway deaths per 100 million vehicle miles driven; and in 2002 there were 1.5 highway deaths per 100 million vehicle miles driven.[8] These reductions can be attributed in part to improved safety standards for automobiles, but also in part to other factors such as drivers education and the 55 mile-per-hour speed limit then in effect.

Regulatory Impact Analysis (RIA)

In 1981 President Reagan issued Executive Order No. 11291, which required that expensive new regulations should be implemented only if their benefits to society outweighed costs. Major regulations with an impact of $100 million or more required a regulatory impact analysis (RIA) from the sponsoring agency before going into effect. RIAs are used in environmental regulation where calculation of costs includes costs to industries for the installation of abatement measures, plant closures, lost jobs, medical costs, and the value of lives lost. In recent years the EPA has valued lives at between

Table 2.1 Estimates of the Benefits and Costs of Automobile Safety Regulation

BENEFITS	
Reductions in premature deaths	23,400
Reductions in all deaths	35,100
Value at $1 million per fatality avoided (billions of dollars)	35.1
Value at $300,000 per fatality avoided (billions of dollars)	10.5
COSTS	
Cost per car (1981 dollars)	671
Annual cost (billions of dollars)	7.0
Annual cost without bumper standards (billions of dollars)	4.9
Benefits less costs—first estimate = 35.1 less 7.0 =	28.1
Benefits less costs—second estimate = 10.5 less 7.0 =	3.5

Source: Robert W. Crandall, Howard K. Gruenspecht, Theodore E. Keeler, and Lester B. Lave, *Regulating the Automobile* (Washington, D.C.: The Brookings Institution, 1986), p. 77.

$400,000 and $7 million each.[9] The benefits of any environmental improvement can be the sum of the monetary values assigned to the effects of that improvement by those persons directly or indirectly affected by the action. Health benefits would be an example. Health can be improved by a reduction in pollution.

DEREGULATION

A number of industries, including airlines, banking, railroads, trucking, natural gas, electricity, and telecommunications have been deregulated in recent years. The regulation was economic in nature, with regulatory agencies, such as the Civil Aeronautics Board (CAB), regulating specific industries. Most of these industries were natural monopolies. This can happen when economies of scale are so extensive in relation to the size of the market that only one firm can operate efficiently within that market. Thus, it is given a monopoly over a specific area. In return for its control over a given service area, a natural monopoly is subject to direct control of rates, services, and other functions by federal and state agencies to ensure the protection of the public interest. In both electricity and telephones the most important natural monopoly was the local distribution network. It was considered wasteful to lay a set of parallel electric cables or telephone lines through cities and towns to enable different sellers to compete for customers. Accordingly, electricity and telephone service used to be provided by companies that managed virtually every aspect of the industry from top to bottom. Telephone services were largely the domain of the American Telephone and Telegraph Company (AT&T) which provided most local networks, long-distance services, and telephone equipment. Electric power companies generated power and transmitted it over high voltage lines to their local distribution networks, which in turn delivered it to homes, offices, and factories. Both industries were subject to both federal and state regulation.

   Deregulation has occurred for several reasons. The first is that technological change has eroded the natural monopoly characteristics of regulated industries. The telephone industry has seen the development of wireless technologies, along with the reductions in the cost of fiber-optic transmission lines. Second, it is felt that deregulation produces economic benefits when it leads to competition. If markets are competitive and function smoothly, they will lead to prices at which the amount sellers want to supply equals the amount sellers will demand. The benefits that accrue are a reduction in the cost of services and technological and operating innovation. Third, markets have information-processing skills and the preservation of individual incentives superior to those of the government when it comes to running an economy. Table 2.2 lists the various deregulatory initiatives that have occurred since 1978 when the airline industry was deregulated.

REDEFINING THE ROLE OF GOVERNMENT IN THE U.S. MARKET ECONOMY

Attitudes toward the role of government in the U.S. market economy are in the process of change. For most of the twentieth century, government has expanded its role as regulator of economic activity in industries ranging from banking to public utilities. The traditional relationship was between government mandated regulation and reliance on market forces. But developments in the latter part of the 20th century forced a reappraisal of the proper role of government in the United States and throughout the world. The collapse of the centrally planned economies of the Soviet Union and Eastern and Central Europe demonstrated that state ownership and control of resources led to inefficiency, waste, and corruption. In Germany and other Western European countries, it has been demonstrated that excessive regulation has inhibited individual initiative and created high unemployment rates.[10]

A major problem confronting the United States and, for that matter, Canada, Western Europe, Japan, and the rich countries of the world is what to do about social security. In the United States, social security was introduced at a time when the average recipient, who was a male, lived only three years

Table 2.2 Major Deregulatory Initiatives, 1978–1996

Year	Initiative	Purpose
1978	Airline Deregulation Act	Deregulate interstate air transportation
1978	Natural Gas Policy Act	Deregulate interstate natural gas prices
1980	Motor Carrier Reform Act	Reduce federal control over entry and pricing of interstate trucking
1980	Depository Institutions Deregulation & Monetary Control Act	Reduce limitations on interest payable on bank depository accounts
1980	Staggers Railroad Act	Give railroads flexibility in setting rates
1982	Bus Regulatory Reform Act	Deregulate interstate bus transportation
1984	Cable Communications Policy Act	Deregulate 90 percent of cable TV rates by the end of 1986
1984	Breakup of AT&T	Promote more competition in the telephone industry
1996	Telecommunications Act	Deregulate the telecommunications industry
1996	Federal Energy Regulatory Commission, Orders No. 888 & 889	Set rules for opening up interstate transmission networks to all generators and resellers of electricity

after the retirement age of sixty-five. But times have changed in the United States, and recipients are living an average of fourteen years after retirement. Thus, one of the most topical issues of the day is how to fix the social security system so that benefits will be available for those who retire in the future. One proposal is to allow citizens to use the money they would invest in the social security system to invest in stocks, bonds, and mutual funds.[11]

It is also argued that the links between government and those citizens who reap the benefits and who bear the costs are very weak. In his book, *The Rise and Decline of Nations*, Mancur Olsen combined economics and politics to explain why nations rose and declined.[12] The main reason was the rise in political importance of special interest groups. As they form, each gains and then fiercely defends some benefit for its members, usually with the help of government. Subsidies and other transfer payments flow to these groups, and a specialized class of lawyers, bureaucrats, and lobbyists who know how to work the system are created. Redistributive struggles displace productive ones when it comes to allocating resources. As a special interest group increases in numbers, its political clout increases, and it becomes more difficult to initiate reforms.[13]

The Proper Role of Markets and Government

The United States has a modified market economy where there is a primary reliance on the market mechanism to allocate resources, but also a considerable amount of government intervention in the form of regulation. The relationship between the market and government has been that one should be a substitute for the other and vice-versa. Those who advocate complete reliance on the market mechanism claim that it is much more efficient than government when it comes to resource allocation. Those who support an active role for government compare market failures with an idealized vision of a government possessing unlimited information and purely beneficial objectives. It can also be argued, based on the deregulation of telecommunications and electric power, that the relationship between the market and the government should be one of complementariness rather than substitution.[14]

The Proper Role of the Market

The price mechanism is the linchpin of a market system. Its function is to provide a coordinating mechanism for millions of decentralized production and distribution units. Because market prices measure the marginal benefits of goods and services, firms that maximize their profits also maximize the difference between benefits and costs. As tastes, technology, and resource availability change, market prices will also change to direct resources to the newly created ends. The interaction between prices and profits are supposed to keep economic mistakes down to a reasonable level. Profit, which depends on the selling price of goods and the cost of making them, indicates to businesses what people are buying.[15] In a market economy, profit is necessary for survival; it is the payment to owners of capital.

Given the institution of private property, which is indispensable for a market economy to function, the attempt of individuals and companies to further their economic self-interest results in competition. Competition is a requisite part of a market system. It is, therefore, not surprising that by statute and common law, the U.S. legal system has been actively concerned with the promotion of competition in the marketplace.[16] Certain benefits to society are thought to be derived from competition. The first benefit is that it expands consumer choice by providing a wide variety of goods and services. A second benefit is that it encourages product innovation. Finally, it promotes efficiency in that efficient firms are profitable and inefficient firms go bankrupt.

The Proper Role of Government

Government is necessary because it sets the formal rules—laws and regulation—that are a basic part of a country's institutional environment. These rules, along with the informal rules of the broader society, are the institutions that mediate human behavior. Without a government legal system to guarantee property rights and to enforce contracts, market exchange would virtually be impossible. Without regulation, firms can hinder competition through such devices as an agreement among themselves to maintain high prices or through the division of markets. The government also provides public goods, such as roads and education, that can have a spillover effect in the market sector. An example would be scientific research.[17] Finally, market efficiency is not the only way to judge an economy. Markets can be consistent with inequalities of opportunities and income resulting from various forms of discrimination.[18]

The Complementary Role of Markets and Government

Markets and government can complement each other. There are certain things that the market does best and there are certain things that government does best. Public policies can make the markets perform better, and market incentives can improve the performance of government. An example of the former is government deregulation of local telephone services and electricity generation to bring about competition and cost reduction to consumers. Conversely, markets can help the government to do its job more efficiently. An example is the use of tradable permit programs, in which the government issues rights to emit some pollutants and then allows firms to allocate those rights across their plants and to buy and sell them among themselves.

SUMMARY

Regulatory growth in the late 1960s and early 1970s created a number of new and important agencies that were social in nature. They included the Consumer Product Safety Commission, the Equal Employment Opportunity Commission, and the Environmental Protection Agency. These agencies were given the right to regulate certain business activities, including employment practices and the production of consumer goods. In the later 1970s and early 1980s, other industries were deregulated, and federal regulatory agencies that were economic in nature were eliminated. The Airline Deregulation Act of 1978 ended regulation of the fares, rates, schedules, and routes of passenger airlines in interstate commerce, eased entry into the airline industry, and phased out the Civil Aeronautics Board. The telecommunications and electric utilities industries were deregulated in the 1990s.

QUESTIONS FOR DISCUSSION

1. Discuss some of the reasons for the rapid expansion of the role of government in the American economy during the twentieth century.
2. What is the legal basis of government regulation of the American economy?
3. Discuss the differences between economic regulation and social regulation. Give examples of each type of regulation.
4. Discuss the division of responsibilities in the political system of the United States.
5. What is the role of profit in a market economy?

RECOMMENDED READING

Buchanan, James M. "Why Does Government Grow?" In *Budgets and Bureaucrats: The Sources of Government Growth*, ed. Thomas Borcherding. (Durham, NC: Duke University Press, 1977).

Executive Office of the President, Office of Manpower and Budget. *A Citizen's Guide to the Federal Budget, Fiscal Year 2002*. (Washington, D.C.: U.S. Government Printing Office, October, 2001). *not produced since 2002.*

Budget of the United States Government, Fiscal Year 2004. (Washington, D.C.: U.S. Government Printing Office, 2003).

Helm, Dieter, ed. *The Economic Borders of the State*. (Oxford, England: Oxford University Press, 1992).

Israel, Arturo. The Changing Role of the State: Institutional Dimension. *PRE Working Paper 495*. (Washington, D.C.: Country Economics Department. The World Bank 1990).

Lawrence, Robert Z., Albert Bress, and Takatoshi Ito. *A Vision for the World Economy.* (Washington, D.C.: The Brookings Institution, 1996).

Rodrik, Dani. Why Do More Open Economies Have Larger Governments? (Cambridge, MA: John F. Kennedy School of Government, Harvard University, 1996).

A Survey of the World Economy: The Future of the State. *The Economist.* (London, England. September 20, 1997): pp. 1–48.

The World Bank, *World Development Report 2005: A Better Investment Climate for Everyone.* (New York: Oxford University Press, 2004).

NOTES

1. *Marbury v. Madison*, 1 Cranch 137, 2 L.ED. 60 (1803).

2. An example of an independent regulatory agency is the Federal Trade Commission; an example of an agency that is a part of the executive branch of government is the Equal Employment Opportunity Commission.

3. For further discussion of the SEC and corporate governance reform, see the Economic Report of the President, 2003.

4. This would represent a direct violation of Section 2 of the Sherman Act of 1890.

5. In Germany three major banks—the Dresdner Bank, the Commerz Bank, and the Deutsche Bank—dominate the credit market of the country.

6. *U.S. v. American Tobacco Co.*, 221 U.S. 10 C, 31 Sup. Ct. 632 (1911).

7. It is estimated that paperwork costs amount to around $30 billion a year to business firms and public institutions.

8. U.S. Department of Commerce, Bureau of the Census, *Statistical Abstract of the United States 2004–2005, 124th ed.* (Washington, D.C.: U.S. Government Printing Office, 2004), p. 697.

9. EPA evaluations of life are based on earnings surveys of dangerous occupations that try to measure the wage premium paid to attract people to risky work.

10. If anything, Russia has performed even worse since the 1990s. Corruption is widespread, income inequality has increased, crime is endemic, many workers do not get paid on time, and living standards for many people have declined.

11. This approach is predicated on the assumption that the stock market will continue to rise in the future. The performance of the stock market in the spring of 2000 shows that stocks can also fall and people can lose money.

12. Mancur Olsen, *The Rise and Fall of Nations* (New Haven, CT: Yale University Press, 1983).

13. The United States provides a number of good examples beginning with the AARP.

14. See Chapter 7, "Government Regulation in a Free-Market Society," in *Economic Report of the President 2004* (Washington, D.C.: U.S. Government Printing Office, 2004), pp. 149–156.

15. The reverse of profit is loss, and in a competitive market economy there are also losers.

16. It involves the Darwinist concept of "survival of the fittest."

17. Numerous recent initiatives, such as the Department of Transportation's programs to provide financing for public highways and private toll rolls, can generate benefits by promoting regional economic development.

18. There are a number of factors that inhibit true equality of opportunity. They would vary from country to country. In England, it would probably be social class and schools attended. It helps in life to have attended Eton or Harrow.

3

Special Interest Groups and the Public Interest

The National Rifle Association (NRA) is one of the better-known special interest groups in the United States. Its purpose is to protect the rights of individuals to own guns as guaranteed by the Constitution of the United States.[1] Its spokesperson for many years was the well-known actor Charlton Heston who, among his acting accomplishments, parted the Red Sea and won a chariot race.[2] In Europe, Japan, and other parts of the world, the right to own guns is circumscribed by law. They must be registered before a permit is issued. But the American psyche is different from the rest of the world. It is individualistic, and the individual is pretty much free to do what he or she pleases, including owning guns. American males, in particular, seem to be attached to owning guns.

School violence involving the use of guns has increased public interest in laws regulating gun ownership, which the NRA has adamantly opposed. However, the massacre of students at Columbine High School in Littleton, Colorado, in April 1999, galvanized public support in favor of laws regulating the use of guns, particularly by minors. In May 1999, as part of a bill aimed at curbing juvenile violence, the U.S. Senate passed measures mandating child safety locks on handguns and requiring background checks to be made on anyone who buys a weapon at a gun show. The House of Representatives began watering down the mandatory background checks. Both Democrats and Republicans participated in emasculating the measure, and gun control did not pass. The NRA was roundly blamed for its defeat.

However, the NRA is just one of a number of special groups that are involved in the making of public policy. As the United States has become a more pluralistic society, special interest groups have increased. One of the better known and most powerful interest groups is the American Association of Retired Persons (AARP), which represents that segment of the population that depends on Social Security for retirement. The National Association of Women (NOW) represents women on such issues as choice and affirmative action. The National Association of Manufacturers (NAM) represents the interest of business. Veterans are a special interest group and so are unions. Special interest groups are active at all levels of government. In Virginia, the Virginia Education Association (VEA) represents the interests of teachers. Special interest groups have learned the tools of political influence. They have become insiders in the high stakes game of public policymaking.

THE HISTORY OF SPECIAL INTEREST GROUPS

There is nothing new about special interest groups. Efforts to influence public policy through appropriate organizations have been a cardinal feature of the American economy since its inception in 1789. The three most important special interest groups over time have been those representing agriculture, business, and labor. In the period from 1789 to the beginning of the Civil War, canal builders and road builders looked to Washington and to state governments for financial help. Railroads and shipping companies also got support from Washington and the states to build railroads and steamboats. Small manufacturers petitioned Washington to raise tariffs on manufactured goods from Europe, arguing that they needed protection from more advanced European industries. Agrarian interests pressed for lower tariffs because they wanted to buy cheaper manufactured goods from Europe.

Agriculture

Agriculture discontent after the Civil War asserted itself through the Grange movement. The discontent began for several reasons. The first was the decline of agricultural prices during the 1870s, and the others were high railroad rates, price gouging by middlemen, difficulty of getting credit, and a growing conflict between agrarian interests and commercial interests. The National Grange was created in 1867 and moved like a prairie fire across the Midwest. During the depression of 1873 it turned to politics, calling for regulation of warehouses and railroads, control of monopolies, creation of a Department of Agriculture, and broader government services for agriculture. In a short time it built up a membership of one million, captured control of several Midwestern state governments, and passed laws regulating railroads and warehouses. But the Grange movement, like many political movements in America, was short-lived.

Populism

With the return of agricultural distress in the late 1880s, another movement called Populism developed. Two separate Farmers' Alliances, one in the Midwest and the other in the South, were created. They supported antimonopoly regulation, railroad regulation, and currency reforms. Their electoral successes stimulated agitation for the creation of a national party, and in 1892 the Populist Party was born. It wanted nationalization of the railroads, inflation based on a silver standard, regulation of banks, and rate regulation. Its peak was reached in 1892 when it polled twenty-two electoral votes and over one million votes. Like all third parties, it was absorbed into one of the major political parties.

Veterans

Veterans have been one of the strongest special interest groups in the United States.[3] After the Civil War, thousands of Union soldiers were disbanded and became the backbone of the Republican Party. Support of veterans came mainly from the states, which provided pensions, land grants, and special poverty relief for disabled veterans. Many more Americans served in World War I than in the Civil War. Veterans formed a political group called the American Legion. It lobbied for veterans' hospitals and pensions for veterans and their dependents. One of the largest and most important special interest groups ever created in the United States was the veterans of World War II, some nineteen million of them. The Veterans' Administration helped them buy homes by providing them with loan guarantees; the federal government passed the GI Bill of Rights that provided them with free education; and various veterans' hospitals around the country provided them with free medical services. They were given preferential treatment when it came to getting jobs.

Labor

Unions have become an important force in American politics. Much of their power developed during the 1930s, although they had been around a full century prior to this decade. Unions were generally split up into two types—those who recruited only skilled workers and those who recruited semiskilled and unskilled workers. The first were called craft unions, and the second were called industrial unions. Craft unions concentrated on "bread and butter" issues. They concentrated on the improvement of their own wages, hours, and working conditions, and showed little interest in wider reform or in politics in general. The first union to become actively involved in the political process was the Industrial Workers of the World (IWW), which supported a program of militant unions and the creation of a socialist economy. Its espousal of radical politics cost it any support it might have received from the craft unions, and it was outlawed during World War I with the passage of the Espionage Act. Labor became a major special interest group during the Depression of the 1930s. The balance of power was strongly in favor of employers, who used every measure possible to keep unions from unionizing their workers. The typical device was the company union. As the Depression deepened, unions as represented by the American Federation of Labor increased their demands for government assistance.

Unions made enormous gains during the 1930s. Collective bargaining over wages, hours, and working conditions was recognized as legitimate and treated as legally enforceable. Gains in membership were made in the steel, tire, automobile, electric manufacturing, and other industries. Social legislation of interest to unions was passed, including retirement benefits, minimum wages, and overtime pay. The unions became one of the most powerful special interest groups as their membership increased. Most of the unions have traditionally supported the Democratic Party, particularly on social issues. They have supported protection against foreign imports when the issue is losing jobs. They were opposed to the North American Free Trade Agreement (NAFTA), because they visualized many American jobs being exported to Mexico if the agreement were passed.

However, union membership in the United States has been on a steady decline since its peak membership in 1983.[4] Membership is now down to 12.5 percent of all U.S. wage and salary workers. The declining strength of unions overall, plus their contentious role in U.S. election politics, resulted in an epic splitting off in 2005 of the Teamsters Union and the Service Employees International Union from the AFL-CIO. The unions believe that the AFL-CIO "neglected the movement's loss of members and influence in favor of politics."[5] The loss of the two unions, with a combined total of almost 15 million members, is catastrophic for the AFL-CIO and raises questions about future directions for trade unionism in the United States.

Consumers

Consumers are a special interest group, although they are not as well organized as other groups. They share a common interest in the most efficient conversion of their income into goods and services. They want accurate information about products they use—their variety, quantity, quality, price, and safety. They want a defense against product misrepresentation and injury. Consumers, who are all of us, are too many to organize into one organization, but they can coalesce around a single issue to demand product safety legislation. The sale of unsafe food and drugs led to consumer protest and the creation of the Food and Drug Administration in 1906. Automobile safety became an issue in the 1960s, leading to laws requiring the installation of seat belts and shatterproof glass. Various groups, such as the Consumers Union and Consumer Research, provide information and ratings of products that are available to consumers.

Business

Business is one of the most important special interest groups in the United States. Its concern with government dates back to the beginning of the country. It is the most visible element in American society. Attitudes toward business have fluctuated from good to bad during the two hundred years of our country's existence. During the latter part of the nineteenth century, such persons as John D. Rockefeller and Andrew Carnegie were referred to as "robber barons" and "malefactors of great wealth." Business had a bad name during the Depression of the 1930s and in the 1980s when corporate takeovers became common. In the 1990s, given the prosperity of the American economy, the image of business has improved as the number of billionaires and millionaires has increased. This all changed in the 2000s, with wave after wave of corporate scandals, which resulted in new legislation and significantly reduced American trust in corporations.

Traditionally, business input into the political process has been done through the organization of industry trade associations and of regional and local business groups. In addition to crystallizing and registering the interests of the particular industry or area, these groups are important media for arousing and focusing general business reactions to broader policy issues. They attempt to speak for the business community as a whole. The two most important business groups are the National Association of Manufacturers (NAM) and the Chamber of Commerce. NAM concentrates on representing manufacturing firms and is opposed to any form of government encroachment on the business decision-making process. The Chamber of Commerce represents a broader constituency. It is effective in presenting business views to legislative and administrative agencies and informing the business community of its stake in public policy issues.

Environmentalists

Pollution of the environment is by no means a recent phenomenon. In one form or another it has existed since antiquity. In the United States, pollution as we know it today is a by-product of industrialization, urbanization, and population growth. In the nineteenth century, industrial cities such as Chicago and Pittsburgh were cited by foreign visitors as being particularly foul.[6] The largest assembly of stockyards in the world added a mephitic odor to Chicago's air, as if a poisonous or foul-smelling gas were being emitted from the earth. Natural drainage was nonexistent, flooding was habitual, and the surface of the Chicago River was so thick with grease that it looked like a liquid rainbow.[7] In New York, refuse including the carcasses of dead animals was thrown into the rivers or the Atlantic Ocean.

There is nothing new about environmentalism. Interest in preserving the environment dates back to John Audubon, who developed bird sanctuaries, and to the administration of Theodore Roosevelt, whose friend was the naturalist John Muir. Roosevelt set aside thousands of acres of forestland and designated them public property. But the one person who had the greatest impact on the environmental movement was Rachel Carson, who wrote the book *Silent Spring* in 1962.[8] She warned of the dangers of pesticides, in particular DDT. The use of DDT in the southern states against fire ants caused widespread damage to living creatures so that it had to be canceled. But pollution involves more than the use of pesticides. Rivers and lakes were polluted by runoffs of waste materials by chemical plants, paper mills, and oil refineries. The air in the cities was polluted by emissions from cars. Protection of the environment became very important to a large segment of the public, and another special interest group developed.

There are a number of environmentalist groups today and they are politically powerful. A number of these groups have more than half a million members and annual budgets in the tens of millions of dollars. They have large staffs who are able to churn out information and policy papers, and information still equates power with Congress and the news media. Some of the environmentalist groups, such as the Audubon Society, have been around for many years, which gives them credence in terms of their staying power.

Senior Citizens

People are living longer in the United States and many have reached that stage in life at which they have the title of senior citizen bestowed on them. It entitles them to many dispensations, including discounts at restaurants and stores, and fawning attention from the politicians.[9] It was not always that way. In 1900 the average American did not reach the age of fifty. There were many things that carried people off—poor dietary habits and a plethora of diseases ranging from typhoid fever and influenza to minor infections. Even when Social Security was created in the 1930s, the average American male lived only three years after he reached the age of sixty-five. But all this has changed dramatically, as healthier diets and the eradication of fatal diseases have increased the longevity of Americans and thereby increased the costs of pensions, medical care, and social services for retirees.

Older people, as represented by the American Association of Retired Persons (AARP), represent the strongest special interest group in the United States. No politician worth his or her salt would dare cross this group, because they vote more consistently than voters in any other special interest group. Their lobbyists are active at all levels of government for larger pensions, lower taxes, increased medical coverage, nursing home regulation, and other benefits of interest to the group. The entitlements for this special interest group comprise the largest expenditure in the federal budget, which will increase as more Americans grow older. The most recent increase occurred in the early 2000s with the passage of the Prescription Drug Benefit legislation, the cost of which has vastly exceeded estimates.

Other Special Interest Groups

There are many other special interest groups in the United States. They represent nonprofit organizations as well as profit organizations. They do not have to be American; they can represent the interests of other countries. China is an example. They can represent a large number of people or a small number of people. Although the number of farmers is declining nationally, in some states they are large enough to have a political impact. In Virginia, Kentucky, and North Carolina tobacco is an important product and tobacco farmers are a group that has an impact on how politicians from their states vote on tobacco legislation. Sugar beet farmers, although limited in number, have until recently been successful in having restrictions placed on the import of cane sugar from other countries, even though it is cheaper than the beet sugar produced in the United States. In 2005, their opposition failed to stop the passage of the Central American Free Trade Agreement (CAFTA) in Congress. Maritime unions have protected the jobs of their members by having requirements imposed on shipping goods on U.S. ships.

PROMOTION OF AN AGENDA

The public sector has grown rapidly because there has been a proliferation of economic and social responsibilities that various interest groups have asked government to perform. As a result, the federal government has extended its involvement in the market system. State and local governments have also become involved. More and more government effort is being directed toward cushioning individual risks and regulating personal and institutional conduct. The cumulative impact of its actions impinge upon all of us but in different ways, so we coalesce into special interest groups. There are a number of ways in which support or opposition to a particular measure that affects us can be expressed, the first of which is through lobbying.

Lobbying

When Bill Clinton was running for president back in 1992, one of the things he promised to do if elected was to rid Washington of "lobbyists wearing Gucci shoes."[10] That promise, once he was elected, was promptly forgotten, probably because of his financial support from various lobbys.[11] As the number of special interest groups has increased, so has the number of lobbyists.

Washington has many of them, most of whom are lawyers who have had government experience in one form or another. Congresspersons who were defeated for reelection are likely to remain in Washington and become lobbyists for interest groups. The same holds true for government officials. Their knowledge of the ways of the political process is a strong selling point.

Although lobbyists are normally associated with the activities of the federal government, this is hardly the usual case. As state and local governments have increased in importance, so have the number of lobbyists. In Virginia the political action is in Richmond, and that is where the lobbyists are. There are 2,083[12] registered lobbyists in Richmond, and few of them wear Gucci shoes. They span a very diverse group of interests, ranging from Philip Morris, the Norfolk and Southern Railroad, and the Newport News Shipyards to volunteer environmental groups, home schoolers, and firefighters. The two major universities in the state—Virginia Tech and Virginia—also have lobbyists to represent them in Richmond before the state legislature.[13] The lobbyists have to be aware of shifting public sentiment and its impact on state education.[14]

Federal Lobbyists

One may wonder what politicians do when they are not reelected to Congress. Do they go back to the districts from which they were elected and socialize with the people who elected them? Not hardly! Did Bob Dole go back to Russell, Kansas, his boyhood home, which he extolled when he was running for president in 1996? Not hardly! Do they emulate former president Jimmy Carter by working for Habitat for Humanity? Not hardly! So what do they do with themselves? They become lobbyists. But one does not have to be a former politician to become a lobbyist. One can be a former member of a congressional staff, or be involved one way or another with government, or have contacts with important people who usually do not live in Russell, Kansas. Vernon Jordan comes to mind.

As of 2005, there were 34,785 lobbyists in Washington.[15] The reported total billings of Washington lobbyists was $2.4 billion for the year 2003.[16] Add the revenues from subsidiary operations that do not require public disclosure, such as strategic advice and public relations services, and total income probably doubles. They are part of the power elite in Washington, and shape the decision-making process. They know what buttons need to be pushed in order to get things done. The backgrounds and clients of some of the most successful lobbyists in Washington are presented in the following paragraphs. Cassidy and Associates is one of the top lobbying firms, having some 187 clients. Gerald Cassidy was a former general counsel to Senator George McGovern's Committee on Hunger. Presumably this motivated him to build his company into Washington's most powerful lobbying firm. He earned a $4.5 million fee for getting the White House to allow an entry visa for Lee Teng-hiu, the president of Taiwan, so he could attend his Cornell University class reunion, as well as promoting Taiwan's entry into the World Trade Organization. To get the entry visa, Cassidy had influential Cornell graduates write their representatives and senators, and the president got his visa. Taiwan continues to pay Cassidy a retainer fee, and Cornell got a $2.5 million gift from its Taiwan alumni.

Vernon Jordan is well known. He played golf with Bill Clinton and supposedly tried to help Monica Lewinsky get a job. He is associated with the law firm of Akin, Gump, Straus, Hauer, and Feld. He is not a registered lobbyist as is required under the Lobbying Disclosure Act of 1995, but he has the contacts and he brings in hundreds of thousands of dollars in retainers to his firm. Beyond that, he sits on more corporate boards of directors than any other attorney in the United States. He is on the board of directors of JC Penney, Union Carbide, Sara Lee, Ryder Systems, and recently and rather appropriately joined the board of directors of Calloway Golf.

Robert Packwood, former senator from Oregon, achieved national notoriety for kissing almost every woman he could lay his hands on, and resigned his Senate seat. Rather than return to Oregon, he became a lobbyist with Sunrise Research Corp. He is an expert on the tax code of the United States. A coalition of lumber mills and small business firms hired him to secure cuts in estate taxes to make it easier for heirs to keep businesses they inherit. He was successful in having the tax code changed. He also represents Northwest Airlines, which wanted to maintain its dominance in the Japanese market, by opposing the open-sky treaty that would let other airline companies in. He has also represented Marriott, GTE, and the American Public Power Association, among others.

But men have no monopoly on becoming top lobbyists. Women are also lobbyists and an example is Deborah Steelman, who once worked for Senator John Danforth and then worked for the Bush administration in developing Social Security and Medicare policies and is now an adviser to presidential candidate George W. Bush of Texas. She is a lobbyist on health-care issues and represents such companies as Aetna, Eli Lilly, Johnson and Johnson, and Pfizer. She lobbied to defeat the Clintons' proposed health-care overhaul. Ann Wexler, a former aid to President Clinton, also has expertise on health care and is adept at building coalitions in support of such clients as Johnson and Johnson to increase Medicare funding for nonprescription drugs. She also represents ComCast Corp., American Airlines, and the Hong Kong Trade Development Council.

Lobbying is justified on the grounds that it gives more people access to the political decision-making process, but that is hardly the case. Special interest groups can afford to hire lobbyists; most people cannot. There is a redistribution of income in favor of groups that can pay to hire the best lobbyists. A state university that has a paid lobbyist is more likely to get funding for a new building than a state university without a lobbyist. Consumers are often the losers. When union and automobile company lobbyists lobbied Congress to use import quotas to reduce the number of Japanese cars that could be sold in the United States, the intent was to protect workers against loss of jobs and the automobile industry against possible bankruptcy. The end result was that consumers had to pay $3,000 more for both American and Japanese cars. The automobile companies made money, their executives got richer, and the jobs that were saved were eventually lost to automation. Nevertheless, the use of lobbyists is growing as more groups realize that this sort of direct appeal to politicians may be a more effective means of achieving federal assistance for their projects.

THE BIPARTISAN CAMPAIGN REFORM ACT OF 2002

In 1997, the first version of campaign finance reform was brought to the Senate. The McCain-Feingold bill, sponsored by Senators John McCain of Arizona and Russell Feingold of Wisconsin, represented a bipartisan attempt to reform campaign financing. The bill sought to limit personal and corporate spending, restrict out-of-state contributions, eliminate soft money contributions to parties after existing limits on contributions to individual candidates had been reached, and ban corporate and labor union contributions to political parties. In addition, the bill would bar contributions by noncitizens. Testimony at Senate investigatory hearings showed that China, Indonesia, and other countries employed a variety of agents and intermediaries to funnel money to the Clinton campaign.

After almost five years, and fierce opposition, the Bipartisan Campaign Reform Act of 2002 was passed. The BCRA increased contribution limits from individuals and placed a cap on the amount received from political action committees (PACs). It also placed restrictions on campaign advertising funded by PACs. Thus, BCRA recognized the influence of PAC contributions on the election system. However, it left a major loophole open in the form of 527 organizations.

Political Action Committees (PACS)

American politics is very expensive. Candidates for office at every level of government, from local government officials to the president of the United States, are forced to spend money to get elected. Costs range from a few thousand dollars in local elections to tens of millions of dollars for U.S. senate and presidential elections. Thus, long before the presidential election of

2000, the candidates were beating the bushes for donations. By July 1999 George W. Bush, the governor of Texas, had already raised more than $30 million, and he eventually got the Republican nomination for president. Vice-President Al Gore raised more money than his opponent Bill Bradley, close to $20 million by July 1999, and he eventually got the Democratic nomination for president. Both men are wealthy and have friends who are wealthy.

An important way in which candidates raise money to run for political office is through financial support from Political Action Committees (PACs). PACs are independently incorporated organizations that can solicit contributions from employees, union members, or shareholders, and then channel the funds to those seeking political office. Companies that have organized PACs are not permitted to donate corporate funds to the PAC or to any political candidate; all donations to company-organized PACs must come from individuals. Labor unions also have PACs, as do trade and health organizations. One of the more important trade organizations is the National Association of Realtors. Table 3.1 presents the funds raised by PACs by committee type. The top categories of donors are Organized Labor and the Finance/Insurance industry.

The Federal Election Commission has established rules to regulate PACs. For example, PACs are not allowed to give more than $5,000 to a single candidate for a single election. These limits were imposed on all PACs to reduce

Table 3.1   Funding from Political Action Committees by Committee Types, 2003–2004

| | 2003–2004 Election Cycle | | | |
Grouping	Democrat	Republican	Other	Total
Organized Labor	$46,322,380	$7,267,477	$106,600	$53,696,457
Finance, Insurance	$15,356,367	$28,398,936	$3,750	$43,759,053
Health Care	$11,156,127	$21,404,033	$17,250	$32,577,410
Transportation	$5,963,938	$13,809,095	$0	$19,773,033
Energy, Natural Resources	$5,243,309	$13,928,334	$3,500	$19,175,143
Business—Retail, Services	$5,067,568	$13,692,816	$0	$18,760,384
Communication, Technology	$6,898,639	$11,178,649	$0	$18,077,288
Real Estate/Construction	$5,261,896	$11,790,525	$10,000	$17,062,421
Agriculture	$5,102,962	$10,856,040	($1,000)	$15,958,002
Law	$6,160,697	$5,247,729	$5,000	$11,413,426
Defense	$2,545,770	$4,727,545	$0	$7,273,315
Manufacturing	$1,414,326	$4,368,873	$0	$5,783,199
Miscellaneous	$613,745	$662,282	$4,500	$1,280,527
Public Employees	$425,675	$219,250	$0	$644,925
Undetermined	$201,142	$361,369	$0	$562,511
City/County	$58,894	$71,519	$0	$130,413
Foreign Countries	$0	$1,000	$0	$1,000

Source: PAC/Party Profile Search. Political Moneyline. http://www.politicalmoneyline.com/cgi-win/x_pac_init .exe?DoFn =

the role of concentrated wealth in determining the result of elections to public office. Candidates and donors get around these limits by using loopholes. One popular method of the past was the payment of "soft money." This loophole refers to funds directly donated to political parties to support party activities such as televised commercials that do not support a specific candidate, get out-the-vote drives, and other activities in conjunction with presidential and congressional races.

527 Organizations

The 2002 BCRA sought to eliminate soft money from campaigns. That bill has led to a rise in "527 organizations," so called because of their IRS tax code designation. These organizations may not specifically contribute to a particular candidate, but instead raise funds to support issues or to "get out the vote." By law, these organizations cannot be controlled by or coordinated with candidate campaigns. Because they do not explicitly support a particular candidate, but instead focus on issues, these groups are not regulated by the Federal Election Commission. Nevertheless, some groups are explicitly partisan, and the funding that they raise for political advertising can have a large influence in elections. During the 2004 Presidential elections, a group calling itself "Swift Boat Veterans for Truth" ran a series of damaging television advertisements questioning the military service of Democratic candidate John Kerry. Table 3.2 lists the top 527 organizations in the 2004 elections.

The 2004 Elections

In 2004, spending on election campaigns reached a record high. The majority of the funds involved came through soft money loopholes, primarily 527 orga-

Table 3.2   527 Committees in the 2004 Presidential Election

527 Committee	Leaning*	Funds raised
Victory Campaign 2004	Democrat	$71,811,666
America Coming Together	Democrat	$54,251,097
SEIU Political Education and Action Local Fund	Democrat	$46,141,905
Progress for America Voter Fund	Republican	$44,929,178
Republican Governor's Association	Republican	$33,848,421
Democratic Governor's Association	Democrat	$24,172,761
AFSCME Special Account	Democrat	$22,227,050
Swift Boat Veterans for Truth	Republican	$17,008,090
Media Fund	Democrat	$15,044,184
College Republican National Committee, Inc.	Republican	$12,780,126

Source: Silent Partners: How Political Non-Profits Work the System. The Center for Public Integrity. http://www.publicintegrity.org/527/default.aspx?cycle = 2004&sub = 1

nizations. Not counting spending by 527 organizations, however, total spending by both candidates reached $343.1 billion, which surpassed the 2000 total of 239.9 million. Some $405 million was raised by 527 organizations, approximately one quarter of which went to pay for political advertising. Democratically oriented 527 groups outperformed Republican ones by a margin of almost 4 to 1. However, Republicans learned their lesson, and 527 groups, unchecked, are likely to prove a major force in future elections. To address this loophole in the 2002 Bipartisan Campaign Finance Reform Act, a bipartisan effort has been launched in Congress. The 527 Fairness Act of 2005, would raise the current limits on individual and PAC contributions, remove limits on party contributions, and eliminate contributions by 527 organizations.

Individual and corporate contributions still play a major role. Tables 3.2 and 3.3 present sources of funding for the political campaigns in 2004. Some gave more money to Republicans, while others gave money to Democrats. None of them gave money out of the goodness of their hearts or because they had a conversion experience on the road to Damascus; all of them wanted something in return. Financial institutions gave money to both Democrats and Republicans in order to sway them from imposing restrictions on the industry. Labor unions and groups such as EMILY's List gave money to the Democrats because they are more likely to be supportive of their causes.[17] Republicans received greater funding in almost every PAC category except organized labor, which was dominated by the Democrats. The recent split of the AFL-CIO is a response to the priority that organized labor has placed on elections; thus the split may have a historic impact on the political influence of unions.

The Changing Face of Campaign Finance

The great majority of Americans give $200 or less to political campaigns, and that is not likely to buy them a cabinet seat or an ambassadorship to the

Table 3.3   Top 10 Contributions to Campaigns in 2004[1]

Contributor	Total Contributions	Democrat	Republican
Goldman Sachs	$6,511,573	62%	38%
National Assn of Realtors	$3,853,027	48%	52%
Microsoft Corp	$3,549,015	62%	37%
Time Warner	$3,411,967	81%	19%
Morgan Stanley	$3,395,496	41%	59%
EMILY's List	$3,295,470	100%	0%
JP Morgan Chase & Co	$3,120,866	53%	48%
Citigroup Inc	$2,899,575	51%	49%
Laborers Union	$2,748,355	87%	14%
Bank of America	$2,710,937	47%	53%

[1]Based on data released by the FEC on Monday, May 16, 2005.
   Source: 2004 Election Overview: Top Overall Donors. Center for Responsive Politics. http://www.opensecrets.org/overview/topcontribs.asp?cycle=2004

Court of St. James.[18] The political process is subverted by the use of money, but there is nothing new about it. Politicians since time immemorial have rewarded their faithful followers based on services performed. What is new are the flagrant violations that are involved in campaign financing. One of the most egregious violations of campaign financing which occurred during the Clinton administration is the selling of a night at the White House. Apparently, spending a night at the White House is a prestige symbol for which some people are willing to pay a lot of money. To sleep in the Lincoln bedroom can cost a contributor $250,000, not including breakfast. To schmooze with a government official of the contributor's choice can cost an additional $50,000, but as a happy businessman said: "If I had known all the contacts I was going to make, I would have given $600,000."

Times have changed from the old days when all a politician had to do to get reelected was to attend fish fries, march in the Fourth of July parade wearing his VFW hat to proclaim he was a veteran, and send congratulatory notes to graduating high school seniors even though most of them had never heard of him. He usually maintained one office in his district; his office staff in Washington plus the office staff at home numbered around five or six people.[19] But times have changed drastically from the old days. As the country has become more complex and the number of special interest groups has multiplied like dandelions, political campaigns have become expensive and costs have skyrocketed for virtually every local, state, and elected official. The high cost of running for political office in the United States has had a deleterious effect on the American political process. Politicians must now engage in continuous fund-raising; there was a time when fund-raising was done just before an election, but this is no longer true.

One factor that has driven up the cost of elections is the need for media exposure, which has become very expensive. In the old days, advertising in the local newspapers was a good way to get exposure or, as Harry Truman did in the 1948 presidential election, "whistle-stopping" throughout the country by railroad. Television has become the most important medium to reach the most people. Ads can cost thousands of dollars. A candidate also has to hire a pollster to tell him or her what issues to stress. Then there are campaign managers and their assistants, so a politician has to employ a retinue of experts to turn out policy papers. Advertising firms are also hired to turn out clever commercials that voters remember when they go to the polls to vote.

Partisanship

Both the 2000 and 2004 elections demonstrated a level of national partisanship rarely seen in Presidential elections. The 2000 election ended in a statistical dead heat between Republican candidate George W. Bush and Democrat Al Gore. Gore won the popular vote with 50,999,897 votes, or 48.38 percent, while Bush received 50,456,002, or 47.87 percent; however, the election was decided in the electoral college. The election came down to a single state, Florida, whose Governor, coincidentally, was the brother of candidate Bush. Voting irregularities were alleged, most particularly that blacks in many counties were systematically prevented from voting. Recounts were held in the state, and the election was hotly contested until the recounts were ultimately ended by the Supreme Court in its 5–4 vote in *Bush v. Gore*. The Court's decision was also viewed as partisan, as the decision was split between conservative and liberal justices, with Justice O'Connor providing the swing vote.

The 2004 election was also close, although not as close as the previous election. Candidate Bush received 50.73 percent of the vote, while candidate Kerry received 48.27 percent. Nevertheless, the elections had the highest voter turnout since 1968, and some joked that more people voted *against* President Bush than had ever voted against a candidate before. The election reflected a bitter divide between "red states" (those which went for Bush) and "blue states" (which went for Kerry). Blue states were viewed as more traditionally liberal, more urban, and with higher electoral college votes. Red states were described as more conservative and more rural. Voting occurred almost strictly along party lines. "Traditional values" played a large role in the 2004 election, with issues such as same sex marriage serving as a catalyst for conservative voter turnout.

The Bush victory has perhaps the most decisive influence on the Supreme Court. The year 2005 saw the death of Chief Justice William Rehnquist and the resignation of Justice Sandra Day O'Connor. Efforts to replace both justices have been contested on a largely partisan basis. Religious conservatives, emboldened by the support of President Bush, have voiced strong support for judicial nominees who will overturn *Roe v. Wade*. Democrats, chastened by their loss, as well as a bitter fight over the use of the filibuster in opposing judicial nominees, are nevertheless concerned about preserving a woman's right to choose. Judicial nominees have not been forthcoming about their positions on the issue. Chief Justice John Roberts, a well-respected conservative judge, was confirmed on September 29, 2005. Roberts's stance on abortion rights creates concerns for pro-choice advocates, and his narrow interpretation of the Commerce Clause is viewed as a warning sign for environmental advocates. O'Connor's replacement has yet to be confirmed.

SUMMARY

Campaign spending has reached record highs in the United States, which purports to be democratic country but in reality is not. Wealth counts because the wealthy can buy influence through campaign donations. Then there are congeries of special interest groups that combine their resources and form PACs to lobby for their chosen objectives. Politicians have come to depend on much of their support from these groups, whose objectives are often mutually exclusive. In the early 2000s, efforts to reduce the influence of PACs have resulted in the rise of unregulated 527 organizations, and intense partisanship has led to deep divisions along issue lines. These issues occur at a time when the Supreme Court is changing composition, thus the deep political divisions are likely to have far-reaching impacts. The influence of special interest groups is a well-grounded part of U.S. politics, and is likely to remain so.

QUESTIONS FOR DISCUSSION

1. Do lobbyists perform a useful service for society? Discuss.
2. What are special interest groups? Why have they increased in recent years?
3. What impact do special interest groups have on the redistribution of income in the American economy?
4. What are PACs? Do they serve a useful purpose?

RECOMMENDED READING

Birnbaum, Jeffrey H. *The Money Men.* (New York: Times Books, 2000).

Corrado, Anthony, et. al. *The New Campaign Finance Sourcebook.* (Washington, DC: Brookings Institution Press, 2005).

Drew, Elizabeth. *The Corruption of American Politics.* (New York: Overlook, 2000).

Johnson, Haynes, and David S. Broder. *The System: The American Way of Politics at the Breaking Point.* (Boston, MA: Little, Brown and Company, 1996).

Lewis, Charles. *The Buying of the President 2004: Who's Really Bankrolling Bush and His Democratic Challengers—and What They Expect in Return.* (New York: Harper Paperbacks, 2004).

Phillips, Kevin. *Arrogant Capital: Washington, Wall Street, and the Frustration of American Politics.* (Boston, MA: Little, Brown and Company, 1994).

NOTES

1. The Second Amendment of the Constitution is as follows: "A well Regulated Militia, being necessary to the security of a free State, the Right of the people to bear Arms, shall not be infringed." At the time of the writing of the Constitution, the idea was to create a citizens' militia to provide for the defense of the new nation. The possibility of incursion by Indians or foreign powers was real. Also, hunting was necessary for most people to put provisions on their tables. There is little relevance to today's world.

2. The movies were *The Ten Commandments* and *Ben Hur*, the latter for which Heston won the Academy Award for best actor.

3. Most of the veterans of World War II are now deceased. There are, of course, veterans of the Viet Nam War, the Gulf War, and the current war in Iraq, but their numbers are smaller.

4. Union Members Summary. *Bureau of Labor Statistics*. January 27, 2005. "The year 1983 was the first year for which comparable union data are available."

5. U.S. Unions split off main movement. *BBC News World Edition*. July 25, 2005. news.bbc.co.uk/2/hi/americas/4713625.stm.

6. Rudyard Kipling, *Actions and Reactions* (New York: Doubleday and Page, 1909).

7. Lewis Mumford, *The City in History* (New York: Harcourt, Brace, and World), p. 461.

8. Rachel Carson, *Silent Spring* (Boston, MA: Houghton-Mifflin, 1962).

9. The author of this chapter had a politician friend who wanted to change Social Security for the elderly. He is no longer in office.

10. There is an element of populism here because most Americans do not know what Gucci shoes are, but the name sounds foreign.

11. The China lobby that was involved in Clinton's election campaign comes to mind.

12. Lobbyist Registration Database, 2005–2006. *Commonwealth of Virginia*. www .commonwealth.virginia.gov/Lobbyist/database.cfm

13. The lobbyist for Virginia Tech has the campus title of Director of Government Relations.

14. A former governor of Virginia once said: "Shrubs are shrubs and we don't need to pay a bunch of farm extension agents to tell people how to grow them." Virginia Tech did not fare well during his administration.

15. Jeffrey H. Birnbaum, "The Road to Riches is Called K Street," *Washington Post*, June 22, 2005. p. A01. Subsequent data on the top lobbyists is available from the Senate Office of Public Records: U.S. Lobby Registration and Reporting Disclosure page: sopr .senate.gov/cgi-win/m_opr_viewer.exe?DoFn = 0.

16. Lobbyists Double Spending in Six Years. *Center for Public Integrity: Investigative Journalism in the Public Interest*, April 7, 2005. www.publicintegrity.org/lobby/default .aspx?act = summary

17. On July 9, 1999, a California jury awarded plaintiffs in an automobile damage suit $107 million in compensatory damages and $4.8 billion in punitive damages. The lawyers for the plaintiffs hailed the award as a victory for consumers, but did not mention the fact that the award was also a victory for them. If the award stands, they will collect probably a third of it. In Alabama a jury awarded plaintiffs, in a suit involving overcharging for the purchase of a television disc, $529 million.

18. To put things in perspective, 99.97 percent of Americans do not give more than $200 in political contributions, which means that .03 percent of the population has the strongest political influence.

19. In the 1960s the congressman from the author's district had a total of seven staff members, two of whom worked in his office in the district, and the rest were in his office in Washington. Today, the congressman from the same district has around forty people on his staff.

II

GOVERNMENT AND ANTITRUST LAWS

4

The Supreme Court and the Sherman Act

On July 2, 1890, the Congress of the United States passed "An Act to Protect Trade and Commerce against Unlawful Restraints and Monopolies," more commonly known as the Sherman Antitrust Act. The Justice Department is charged with enforcing it, and in 1903 created a special antitrust division for that purpose. Section 1 of the law states that "Every contract, combination in the form of trust or otherwise, or conspiracy, in restraint of trade or commerce among the several States, or with foreign nations, is declared to be illegal." These offenses, known as per se violations, include some price-fixing; divisions of customers, markets, and volume of production; boycotts or concerted refusals to sell; and tie-in sales.

Section 2 of the law states that "Every person or persons, who shall monopolize, or attempt to monopolize, or combine or conspire with any other person to monopolize any part of the trade or commerce among the several States, or with foreign nations, shall be deemed guilty of a misdemeanor." Section 4 of the law allows for civil suits to be brought by the Attorney General, with such remedies as dissolution, divestiture, or divorcement, as well as the remedy of an injunction. Section 7 of the law allows for private parties to sue for three times the amount of damages sustained.

Important Provisions of the Sherman Antitrust Act:
Section 1: prohibits price-fixing; divisions of customers, markets, and volume of production; boycotts or concerted refusals to sell; tie-in sales
Section 2: prohibits monopolies or attempts at monopolies
Section 4: allows civil suits for divestiture and injunctions
Section 7: allows private parties to sue for triple damages

Should the government decide to use criminal penalties, violations of Sections 1 and 2 are subject to fines, not to exceed $100,000 for each violation, or by imprisonment, not to exceed three years, or both. The government often brings suits alleging violations of both Sections 1 and 2, and there are sometimes cases in which the government brings a criminal action to which the defendant will plead nolo contendere. If accepted by the Court, this means the defendant, without making a contention of guilt or innocence, agrees to accept whatever penalties the Court imposes. In addition, there are instances in which a private party will bring a suit under another law, such as the Clayton Antitrust Act, and a court in arriving at a decision might rely upon the Sherman Act for guidance.

Sherman Act cases are heard in U.S. District Courts, with appeals, if any, to the U.S. Courts of Appeals. A case of relative importance might well end up in the Supreme Court of the United States. The Court has, indeed, rendered decisions in many Sherman Act cases over the years, and that has resulted in the development of case law in this area that is constantly evolving and changing.

One point worth noting is the lack of antitrust suits involving professional sports leagues. The 1961 Sports Broadcasting Act exempted them from antitrust regulation so that member teams, acting as a group, could sell TV rights to one or more networks. Baseball, in particular, has enjoyed an immunity from antitrust suits, but the 1998 Curt Flood Act ended its exemption in dealing with its players, but kept it in effect for everything else. It was largely a symbolic statute because of the 1975 arbitration ruling for free agency for the players.

SHERMAN ACT CASE LAW DEVELOPMENT

The Early Years

The first time the Court looked at the Sherman Act, it gave such a narrow interpretation of it that the law might have been doomed from the start except for subsequent cases. That case, in 1895, was *United States v. E.C. Knight Co.*[1] The government was attempting to make the American Sugar Refining Company, chartered in New Jersey, divest itself of the stock it had acquired of four Philadelphia refineries who refined 33 percent of the sugar in the United States and who were competitors with American. The acquisition gave American 98 percent control of the sugar refining in the United States, and, once refined, the sugar went into commerce among the several states. However, an 8–1 Court, speaking through Chief Justice Fuller, held that the Sherman Act was inapplicable because it is based on the government's commerce power, and the refineries in question were involved with the manufacture of the product. Commerce succeeds to manufacture and is not part of it, according to Fuller. He did not find any intention to put a restraint upon trade or commerce, and the fact that trade or commerce might be indirectly affected was not enough. Only Justice Harlan dissented.

Fortunately for the government, the Court in 1897 was going to find a Sherman Act violation, although by only a 5–4 vote. The case was *United States v. Trans-Missouri Freight Association*,[2] and the defendant was a grouping of eighteen railroads formed for the purpose of balancing the freight rates between the states. Any rate change was to be made at a monthly meeting. If one of the railroads felt compelled to cut a rate between meetings and that rate was in violation of the agreement, the offending railroad was fined $100 by the group. Justice Peckham held that the Sherman Act applies to all contracts in restraint of trade or commerce, not just those that are unreasonable, and therefore Section 1 was violated. The government does not have to prove the purpose as long as restraint is the necessary effect, as in this case. The dissenters felt that railroads came under the Interstate Commerce Act and not the Sherman Act.

Once the government was able to dissolve the Association, it was able to do it again the next year in a case in which thirty-one railroads operating between Chicago and the Atlantic coast had joined together on rates.[3] However, later that year the Court ruled against the government in two cases involving Live Stock Exchanges,[4] finding only an indirect and incidental effect upon interstate commerce. The government did gain a major victory in the 1899 case of *Addyston Pipe and Steel Co. v. United States*.[5] Once again Peckham authored the opinion, this time unanimous, in dissolving an association of six companies who were practically the only manufacturers of cast iron in the United States. They agreed not to compete with each other in the sale of pipe and they allotted territories. If a sale took place in a territory not assigned to a member, the association decided which one would get the bid, and the others would then submit higher bids to insure the one they selected would get the sale. Peckham said the direct effect of the association was to regulate interstate commerce and therefore there was a Section 1 violation.

Significant government antitrust victories in the Supreme Court are listed below:

Government Antitrust Victories in the Supreme Court, 1895–1939:
1. *United States v. Trans-Missouri Freight Association*, 1897.
2. *United States v. Joint Traffic Association*, 1898.
3. *Addyston Pipe and Steel Company v. United States*, 1899.
4. *Northern Securities Co. v. United States*, 1904.
5. *Swift & Company v. United States*, 1905.
6. *Standard Oil Co. v. United States*, 1911.
7. *United States v. American Tobacco Co.*, 1911.
8. *United States v. Union Pacific Railroad Co.*, 1912.
9. *Eastern States Retail Lumber Dealers' Association v. United States*, 1914.
10. *American Column and Lumber Co. v. United States*, 1921.

11. *United States v. American Linseed Oil Co.*, 1923.
12. *United States v. Trenton Potteries Co.*, 1927.
13. *Sugar Institute v. United States*, 1936.
14. *Interstate Circuit, Inc. v. United States*, 1939.

Into the Twentieth Century

The year 1904 found the Court sharply divided in a case of national importance. It was *Northern Securities Co. v. United States*,[6] and involved a holding
company organized in New Jersey that held the stock of two railroad giant
competitors: the Great Northern and Northern Pacific, along with the stock
of the Chicago, Burlington, and Quincy. President Theodore Roosevelt was
advocating the breakup of the holding company, and Justice Harlan, for a 5–4
Court, agreed with him. Harlan felt that every corporation created by a state
is subject to the supreme law of the land and therefore cannot circumvent the
Sherman Act. The railroads whose stock was held had substantially parallel
lines and Congress, in regulating interstate commerce, cannot be subordinate
to the will of the states. If the Sherman Act cannot cover this, said Harlan,
then the plain intention of Congress would be defeated. Although happy at
the result, Roosevelt was disturbed that Justice Holmes, his first appointment
to the Court two years earlier, had dissented, saying that the holding company
was not in and of itself an interstate commerce company.

Holmes redeemed himself in Roosevelt's eyes one year later, in 1905 in
the case of *Swift & Company v. United States*.[7] The issue was a combination
of the dominant dealers in fresh meat throughout the United States to regulate
prices. Holmes wrote the unanimous decision dissolving the combination, as
he said it embraced and was directed at commerce among the states and
therefore had a direct effect upon it. He found intent, not merely to restrict
competition among the parties, but to aid in an attempt to monopolize commerce. He found a current of commerce, meaning that even though the combining companies were located in the same place, the fact that the meat
originated in other states and would eventually end up in other states made
for interstate commerce and the application of the Sherman Act. The next
year the Court held that a city is a person and can bring a Sherman Act Section 7 triple damage suit.[8]

Although the Sherman Act was directed against business it did not explicitly say that, and thus the Court was able to uphold its use against a labor
union in the 1908 case of *Loewe v. Lawlor*.[9] A combination of labor organizations had tried to compel a manufacturer whose goods were sold almost
entirely in other states (he made hats in Danbury, Ct.) to unionize. The union,
United Hatters of North America, which was part of the American Federation
of Labor, was sued by the manufacturer for triple damages because of the
boycott, and Chief Justice Fuller for a unanimous Court agreed with him and

awarded him $240,000. Fuller held that the Sherman Act includes restraints of trade aimed at compelling third parties and strangers involuntarily not to engage in the course of interstate trade except on conditions that the combination imposes. The persons in the combination do not themselves have to be engaged in interstate trade, and organizations of farmers and laborers were not exempted from the Sherman Act.

The year of 1911 saw the Court render three Sherman Act decisions. In one of them, it ruled that a system of contracts between manufacturers and wholesale and retail merchants to control prices fell under the Sherman Act.[10] Then came two attempts by the government to break up giant corporations: *Standard Oil Co. v. United States*[11] and *United States v. American Tobacco Co.*[12] In the former, John D. Rockefeller had chartered the company in New Jersey and it had control of over thirty-seven subsidiary corporations. When Theodore Roosevelt was president he called Standard Oil a bad trust and had the Justice Department try to dissolve it. Chief Justice White, for a unanimous Court, agreed with the president and, in so doing, formulated the rule of reason. He thought Standard Oil was guilty of violating both Sections 1 and 2 of the Sherman Act, but Section 2 only because the monopoly was unreasonable (i.e., it was achieved by unnecessarily abusive business practices). He found a prima facie presumption of intent and purpose to maintain dominancy over the oil business. The end result was that Standard Oil was divested into thirty-four smaller companies, each dominant in their region and run by the same persons who had run the parent company. Nevertheless it was a big victory for the government, and was followed by a similar victory in the second case.

In that case, American Tobacco and sixty-four other American companies along with two English companies were tied together by their stock and controlled 86 percent of the cigarettes produced in the United States. They also had big monopolies in other aspects of the tobacco industry. White, again unanimously and again using the rule of reason, agreed that Sections 1 and 2 had been violated. As in the previous case, the subsidiaries became new companies, and because American Tobacco was not totally unreasonable, only two other full-line companies were created to give it competition: Liggett and Myers, and P. Lorillard.

The Interim Period

Once the Court formulated the rule of reason, it began to swing back and forth in its Sherman Act decisions. For example, in the following year (1912) it did not find a violation when the holder of a patent for making stencil-duplicating machines would license the machines with a restriction that his unpatented articles, such as the stencil paper, ink, and other supplies, must be the only ones used by the licensee.[13] However, it did find Sections 1 and 2 violated when one railroad bought 46 percent of the stock of a competitor.[14] Similarly, two years later the Court held that Section 1 was violated by a report circulated among a retail lumber dealers' association listing wholesale dealers who sold directly to customers, which tended to prevent members of the association from dealing with those consumers.[15] Yet four years after that it found no violation when the Chicago Board of Trade prohibited its members from purchasing, or offering to purchase, anything other than what the closing bid had been at the time the Board closed in the afternoon until it opened the next morning.[16] It also found no violation later that year when the government charged a company who had, through patents and acquisitions, ownership or control of all concerns engaged in the manufacturing of all kinds of shoe machinery.[17] Again, a year later it upheld the resale price arrangements made by a manufacturer with its dealers.[18]

Significant government antitrust losses in the Supreme Court are listed below:

Government Antitrust Losses in the Supreme Court, 1895–1939:
 1. *United States v. E.C. Knight Co.*, 1895.
 2. *Hopkins v. United States*, 1898.
 3. *Anderson v. United States*, 1898.
 4. *Board of Trade of the City of Chicago v. United States*, 1918.
 5. *United States v. United Shoe Machinery Co.*, 1918.
 6. *United States v. Colgate*, 1919.
 7. *United States v. U.S. Steel Corporation*, 1920.
 8. *Maple Flooring Manufacturers' Association v. United States*, 1925.
 9. *Cement Manufacturers' Protective Association v. United States*, 1925.
10. *United States v. General Electric Co.*, 1926.
11. *United States v. International Harvester Co.*, 1927.
12. *Appalachian Coals, Inc. v. United States*, 1933.

The Conservative 1920s

The Court's increasing reluctance to interfere with big business was never more evident than in the 1920 case of *United States v. U.S. Steel Corporation*.[19] The government was attempting to break it up due to its being a monopoly, but Justice McKenna, for a unanimous Court, refused to do so. While conceding that the company had more power than any one competitor, he said that it was not greater than that possessed by all the competitors, so there was no monopoly. Mere size is not illegal. Even though the corporation actually was a holding company for twelve manufacturers, he felt there was no public interest served by dissolving it or by separating it from some of its subsidiaries. Instead, such action would actually pose a risk of injury to the public interest and would hurt this country in foreign trade.

The next year, in 1921, the Court decided *Duplex Printing Press Co. v. Deering*.[20] It was a mixture of Sherman and Clayton Acts, since, under the latter, peaceful picketing by labor was not supposed to be enjoined by federal courts, and labor was not commerce and thus should not be prevented from doing legitimate activities. In this case, a union was trying to get a manufacturer of printing presses to unionize its factory in Michigan. Since the union of machinists was in New York, they engaged in a boycott of the company's products in New York City and vicinity. The Court, in a 6–3 decision given by Justice Pitney (Holmes, Brandeis, and Clarke dissenting), allowed the injunction against the boycott, saying that the Sherman Act, as amended by the Clayton, permitted it because the boycott was a secondary one, which is illegal, and under Clayton, labor organizations and its members cannot do illegal conspiracies. Therefore, the section forbidding injunctions was not applicable.

The government did win a case later that year when the Court found Section 1 violated by manufacturers of one-third of the hardwood output in the United States. They had instituted a plan by which they exchanged full and minute disclosures of their business to a central office, which then distributed back to them analytical digests of the information, plus suggestions for future production and prices by an expert agent, supplemented by frequent meetings and discussions.[21] Similarly, two years later (1923) the government won again when twelve corporations entered into agreements to suppress competition in trade between the states. Each company had to reveal to all the others the intimate details of its business affairs.[22] However, two years later, in 1925, the government lost companion cases. In the first one, twenty-two corporations controlling 74.2 percent of the total production of maple flooring gathered information and disseminated it, and in the second one several companies gathered and disseminated pertinent information with respect to the sale and distribution of cement.[23] Again the following year, in 1926, the government lost when it tried to prevent a company who owned patents for electric lamps with tungsten filaments from licensing them out but fixing the prices while doing so.[24] One year later the government did manage to win a victory involving an agreement by twenty-three corporations controlling over 82 percent of the business of manufacturing and distributing sanitary pottery in the United States to fix prices.[25]

In that year of 1927, the Court heard another case similar to *Duplex* in that it concerned labor, combined the Sherman and Clayton Acts, and also went against labor. It was *Bedford Cut Stone Co. v. Journeymen Stone Cutters' Association of North America*.[26] At issue was a conspiracy by a union of stonecutters to restrain the interstate commerce of certain building-stone producers by declaring their stone, cut by nonunion workers, "unfair" and forbidding members of the union to work on it in building construction in other states. Justice Sutherland, in a 7–2 opinion (Brandeis and Holmes dissenting), found the union to be in violation of the Sherman Act because it directly and substantially curtailed, or threatened to curtail, the natural flow of interstate commerce of a very large proportion of the building limestone of the entire country. It was a strike against the product in order to coerce or induce the local employers to refrain from purchasing such a product. Due to the illegal activity, an injunction under Clayton was appropriate.

Fittingly for the 1920s, in that same year the Court refused to divide a company, a combination of five separate firms controlling 85 percent of the harvesting machinery business, into separate and distinct corporations in order to restore the competitive conditions that had existed some sixteen years previously. The company had already agreed to limit its sales agencies and dispose of some of its lines to independent manufacturers, and the Court felt that was sufficient for competitive conditions to exist.[27]

Significant private antitrust suits in the Supreme Court are listed below:

Private Antitrust Suits in the Supreme Court, 1895–1939.
Victories for Plaintiffs:
1. *Chattanooga Foundry and Pipe Works v. City of Atlanta*, 1906.
2. *Loewe v. Lawlor*, 1908.
3. *Dr. Miles Medical Co. v. John D. Park & Sons Co.*, 1911.
4. *Duplex Printing Press Co. v. Deering*, 1921.
5. *Bedford Cut Stone Co. v. Journeymen Stone Cutters' Association of North America*, 1927.
6. *Story Parchment Company v. Paterson Parchment Paper Company*, 1931.
Loss by Plaintiff:
Henry v. A. B. Dick Co., 1912.

The Depression and War Years

As would be expected, Sherman Act cases were few in number during the Depression years. In 1931 the Court did allow a company to collect triple damages based on a Section 2 allegation that three companies were monopolizing interstate trade and commerce in vegetable parchment with the resultant price-cutting against the company. What made the case interesting was the holding that the damages can be based on estimated prices.[28] Two years later, in 1933, the Court refused to break up a corporation formed by some 137 producers of bituminous coal to act as their selling agent with authority to set the prices. The group had 73 percent control in the immediate region, but the great bulk of their coal was marketed in another and highly competitive region. The fact that the industry was one in grave distress helped the Court arrive at its decision.[29] However, three years later, in 1936, the Court did break up a trade association formed by fifteen companies that controlled 70–80 percent of the refined sugar in the United States. Its purpose was to do away with unfair merchandising practices, especially the granting of secret concessions and rebates. The association made each member publicly announce in advance its prices, terms, and conditions of sale, and also imposed numerous supporting restrictions. The Court concluded that the end did not justify the illegal means.[30] Three years after that, the Court upheld the use of Section 1 to stop distributors of 75 percent of interstate motion picture films from making agreements with the owners of theaters in certain cities that showed first-run exhibitions of movies. The agreements said that when the distributors licensed other theater owners in the same cities for subsequent runs of the films, the licenses would mandate a minimum price of admission, and the theaters would not show another picture with it. This would maintain the higher prices of the first-run theaters and protect them from competition.[31]

Once the country started to get out of the Depression, the government began to initiate Sherman Act cases with renewed determination. In 1940 the Court held that Section 1 was violated by a company that was making agreements in the Midwestern area to fix prices in interstate commerce. Even though the company contended that there were competitive abuses or evils that it was trying to stop, the Court held that price-fixing is illegal per se.[32] The following year, labor unions finally received a big boost from the Court in the antitrust area. In *United States v. Hutcheson*[33] the government charged a union with violating Section 1, but Justice Frankfurter, in a 6–2 opinion, held that the Clayton Act and the 1932 Norris-LaGuardia Act immunized trade union activities from being a violation of any U.S. law, including the Sherman Act. He did say, however, that this immunization would be lost if labor combined with nonlabor groups to restrain trade. In that same year the Court held that the United States was not a person under the Sherman Act and therefore could not bring a civil action for triple damages.[34] However, the following year it did consider a state a person for damage awards.[35]

Also in 1942, the Court held that Sections 1 and 2 were violated by ten companies who either made or sold building materials. Each was tied to the dominant company by an agreement that expressly recognized the validity of that company's patents during the life of the agreement and that required the distribution of the patented products at fixed prices. Again, the price-fixing made for the illegality.[36] The next year, on the other hand, the Court made states immune from the Sherman Act, since that law makes no mention of states and there is no suggestion of a purpose to restrain state action in its legislative history.[37]

Significant government antitrust victories and losses in the Supreme Court are listed below:

Government Antitrust Victories in the Supreme Court, 1940–Present:
1. *United States v. Socony-Vacuum Oil Company*, 1940.
2. *United States v. Masonite Corporation*, 1942.
3. *American Tobacco Company v. United States*, 1946.
4. *United States v. Yellow Cab Company*, 1947.

  5. *United States v. National Lead Company*, 1947.
  6. *International Salt Company v. United States*, 1947.
  7. *United States v. United States Gypsum Company*, 1948.
  8. *United States v. Griffith*, 1948.
  9. *Schine Chain Theatres v. United States*, 1948.
10. *United States v. Paramount Pictures*, 1948.
11. *Timken Roller Bearing Company v. United States*, 1951.
12. *Northern Pacific Railway Company v. United States*, 1958.
13. *United States v. Parke, Davis and Company*, 1960.
14. *United States v. Loew's Incorporated*, 1962.
15. *United States v. First National Bank and Trust Company of Lexington*, 1964.
16. *United States v. General Motors Corporation*, 1966.
17. *United States v. Arnold, Schwinn & Company*, 1967.
18. *United States v. Container Corporation of America*, 1969.
19. *United States v. Topco Associates, Inc.*, 1972.
20. *Otter Tail Power Company v. United States*, 1973.
21. *National Society of Professional Engineers v. United States*, 1978.
Government Antitrust Losses in the Supreme Court, 1940–Present:
  1. *United States v. Hutcheson*, 1941.
  2. *United States v. Cooper Corporation*, 1941.
  3. *United States v. Columbia Steel Company*, 1948.
  4. *Times-Picayune Publishing Company v. United States*, 1953.

The Postwar Years and the Fifties

In a 1946 case that was a preview of what was going to occur in the 1990s, the Court ruled that three tobacco companies had a monopoly of over two-thirds of the domestic cigarette market and over 80 percent of comparable cigarettes, with the resultant fixing and controlling of prices.[38] The next year, the Court found that there was a combination and conspiracy to restrain and monopolize interstate trade and commerce in the sale of motor vehicles for use as taxicabs to the principal cab companies in certain cities. The companies bought their cabs exclusively from one manufacturer and an appreciable amount of interstate commerce was affected. In addition, two of the defendants in the case would not compete with a third one for contracts with railroads or railroad terminal associations to transport passengers and their luggage, and that involved a stream of interstate commerce.[39]

In 1947 the government continued with its string of victories. It won a case against an international cartel that was retraining trade and commerce in the titanium products industry among the several states and with foreign nations by pooling patents and allocating markets.[40] Another case was won against a firm owning patents on machines utilizing salt that leased them subject to the condition that the salt be purchased from them.[41] The next year the Court found Sections 1 and 2 violated by six corporations that conspired to restrain and monopolize trade in gypsum products through patent licensing. The dominant firm granted the patents and the others accepted. The Sherman Act bans patent exploitations such as this, and the efforts to monopolize the patents were unreasonable.[42]

Also in 1948, the Court in companion cases held Sections 1 and 2 violated. In one case, four affiliated corporations operated motion picture theaters in three states, and used their monopoly power to prevent their competitors from obtaining first- or second-run films. In the other case, a company and five subsidiaries owned or had a financial interest in a large chain of motion picture theaters in six states. In negotiating for films, they combined theaters in towns in which they had a monopoly with those in towns in which they had competition.[43] In yet another case that year, Sections 1 and 2 were again used against eight corporations in the motion picture industry for price-fixing and monopoly.[44] Finally, in that year, the government lost when the Court refused to dissolve a merger in which a major steel company got the assets of the largest steel company on the West Coast. The Court found a normal business purpose, namely the expansion of facilities to meet the needs of new markets of a community. Vertical integration was not illegal per se.[45]

In 1951 the Court upheld both a triple damage suit due to an agreement among competitors in interstate commerce to fix the maximum resale prices of their products,[46] and a Section 1 case against a company that made antifriction bearings but that combined with a British corporation and a French corporation to allocate territories and fix prices. The latter case, even though it involved foreign trade, still fell under our antitrust laws.[47] In 1953 the Court refused to use Sections 1 and 2 against a publishing company that put out a morning and evening newspaper (there was only one other evening paper in the city) and that adopted a unit rate for advertising space (i.e., one who buys advertising space in the morning paper must also buy it in the evening paper). The Court found no intent to put an unreasonable restraint on interstate commerce nor had it had that effect, and there was no intent to monopolize.[48] Similarly, in 1954 the Court refused to allow triple damages or an injunction in the case brought by a suburban theater owner who claimed that a film distributor conspired to restrict first-run pictures to downtown theaters. It held that proof of parallel business behavior does not conclusively establish agreement, nor does such behavior itself violate the law.[49]

The government did win a Section 1 case in 1957 against a railroad for preferential routing agreements made in deeds or leases to several million acres of land in several northwestern states. Under these agreements, all commodities produced or manufactured on the land would have to be shipped over the railroad's lines. The Court said that a tying arrangement per se is unlawful whenever the seller has sufficient economic power and a substantial amount of interstate commerce is affected.[50] One year later the Court upheld a triple damage award because a chain of department stores had violated Sections 1 and 2 by conspiring with ten national manufacturers and their distributors either not to sell to a particular company, or to do so only at discriminatory prices and highly unfavorable terms. The law forbids all contracts and combinations that tend to create a monopoly, even if done one company at a time rather than in large groups.[51]

The First Seventy Years in Retrospect

The Supreme Court gave varying interpretations of the Sherman Act during its first seven decades of cases involving the law. It broke up monopolies and refused to break up others. It found restraints of trade in some combinations but not in others. It developed the rule of reason and the current of commerce. It even applied it to labor, despite Congress's attempt in the Clayton Act to prevent that. It is true that seldom do two cases have identical facts, so the Court can make differentiations between them. Nevertheless, the Court consists of nine persons who bring to it their own political, social, and economic values, and those values also play a role in decision-making. Therefore, there is an explanation to the Court's decisions, and whether one agrees with a decision or not the fact remains that the Court does have the ultimate say as to what the Sherman Act means. In those first seventy years, both supporters and opponents of vigorous Sherman Act enforcement could find a mixed bag of Court opinions.

The 1960s

The last decade for sheer volume of Sherman Act cases before the Court was that of the 1960s. It began with a 1960 case. The government won an injunction due to a Section 1 violation in which a company had combined and conspired to maintain resale prices of its more than six hundred pharmaceutical products in areas that did not allow that practice. The company refused to deal with retailers who failed to observe suggested minimum prices or who advertised discount prices; five other wholesalers were persuaded to do the same. The company also told a number of retailers that if each would adhere, so would one of their principal competitors. Once a retailer agreed to stop the price-cutting, it could resume purchasing the products. The Court held that the law had been broken even though the plan was not based on any contract.[52] The next year, 1961, the Court did not find Sections 1 and 2 violated and thus refused to issue an injunction or award triple damages to a group of trucking companies and their trade association. The truckers brought the case against a group of railroads, a railroad association, and a public relations firm that had conducted a publicity campaign against the truckers. The campaign's goal was to get laws and law enforcement practices hostile to truckers and to create an atmosphere of distaste for truckers among the general public, thus impairing relationships between the truckers and their customers. The Court felt that people have the right to get together to get laws passed or enforced.[53]

In 1962 the government won a Section 1 suit against six major distributors of pre-1948 copyrighted motion picture feature films for television exhibition. These distributors engaged in blockbooking—selling one or more films on condition the station buy a block of less popular or inferior films.[54] Two years later, in 1964, the government again won, this time a Sections 1 and 2 case stopping the consolidation of the largest and fourth largest of the six commercial banks in a county, even though there was no predatory purpose.[55] In 1966 the Court ruled against a conspiracy wherein a company restrained trade by eliminating sales of its new automobiles through discount houses and referral services. The company got promises from every dealer in the area not to deal with any discounters. The result was a substantial restraint upon competition, a goal unlawful per se when sought to be effected by a combination or conspiracy.[56]

One year later, in 1967, the Court found Section 1 violated by a manufacturer and its distributors who established exclusive territories, meaning the distributors could only sell within their territory and could only sell that product, not those of competitors. The manufacturer also sold to franchised retailers who could sell competitors' products as long as its product was given equal prominence and they did not sell to discounters. Anyone breaking the agreement would be terminated. The Court felt that one should be able to dispose of products purchased from a manufacturer without restrictions. Only those who received a product on consignment could have restrictions imposed, as the manufacturer still retains ownership and has not parted with the title.[57] The next year the Court upheld a triple damage suit brought by an independent newspaper carrier who sold the papers at a price higher than that set by the publisher and was terminated. The problem of fixing maximum prices was revisited by the Court in the 1990s.[58]

In 1969, the Court upheld a Section 1 suit against companies who controlled about 90 percent of the shipment of corrugated containers from plants in the southeastern United States. Each of the companies would, upon the request of a competitor, furnish information as to the most recent price charged or quoted to individual customers, with the expectation of reciprocity and the understanding that it represented the price currently being bid. The Court felt the exchange was concerted action to establish a combination or conspiracy, and the price stabilization had an anticompetitive effect in the industry, thus hurting price competition.[59] That same year, the Court upheld an injunction and triple damages against a company and its wholly owned subsidiary due to violations of Sections 1 and 2. In order to obtain credit at advantageous terms, a housing developer would have to purchase at artificially high prices prefabricated houses made by the manufacturer. The Court held it to be an illegal tie-in sale because there was a substantial volume of commerce foreclosed due to the total volume of sales.[60]

Significant private antitrust suits in the Supreme Court are listed below:

Private Antitrust Suits in the Supreme Court, 1940–Present:
Victories for Plaintiffs:
1. *Georgia v. Evans*, 1942.
2. *Kiefer-Stewart Company v. Seagram & Sons, Inc.*, 1951.
3. *Klor's Inc. v. Broadway-Hale Stores, Inc.*, 1959.
4. *Albrecht v. Herald Company*, 1968.
5. *Fortner Enterprises, Inc. v. United States Steel Corporation*, 1969.
6. *Goldfarb v. Virginia State Bar*, 1995.
7. *Cantor v. Detroit Edison Company*, 1976.
8. *Continental TV., Inc. v. GTE Sylvania, Inc.*, 1977.
9. *Catalano, Inc. v. Target Sales, Inc.*, 1980.
10. *Arizona v. Maricopa County Medical Society*, 1982.
11. *Monsanto Company v. Spray-Rite Service Corporation*, 1984.
12. *National Collegiate Athletic Association v. Board of Regents of the University of Oklahoma*, 1984.
13. *Aspen Skiing Company v. Aspen Highlands Skiing Corporation*, 1985.
Losses by Plaintiffs:
1. *Parker v. Brown*, 1943.
2. *Theatre Enterprises, Inc. v. Paramount Film Distributing Corporation*, 1954.
3. *Eastern Railroad Presidents Conference v. Noerr Motor Freight, Inc.*, 1961.
4. *Broadcast Music, Inc. v. Columbia Broadcasting System, Inc.*, 1979.
5. *Jefferson Parish Hospital District No. 2 v. Hyde*, 1984.
6. *Business Electronics Corporation v. Sharp Electronics Corporation*, 1988.
7. *State Oil Company v. Khan*, 1997.

The 1970s and 1980s

In 1972 the Court upheld a Section 1 suit against a cooperative association of twenty-five supermarket chains in thirty-three states. They had a company that was their purchasing agent with more than one thousand items, most of which bore its name. The sales of the members were exceeded only by three national grocery chains. No member was allowed to sell the agent's brand products outside the territory in which it was licensed to sell unless the member whose territory was being invaded agreed. Also, no member could sell any product supplied by the association at wholesale without permission that was subject to conditions. The Court found it a horizontal restraint, a per se violation that minimized competition at both the retail and wholesale levels.[61] One year later the government again won, this time a Section 2 case against a supplier of electric power to many municipalities in the Midwest. When its franchises expired and the towns wanted to establish their own power systems, the supplier refused to sell wholesale power to them. The company also refused to transfer power over its facilities from other sources, litigated in order to delay things, and invoked transmission contract provisions to forestall other companies from supplying power. The Court found that the company used its monopoly power to foreclose competition or gain a competitive advantage, or to destroy a competitor, all in violation of the antitrust laws.[62]

In 1975 the Court found a Section 1 violation by a state bar association for enforcing fees set by a county bar association. The decision found that the practice established a fixed, rigid price floor that affected interstate commerce.[63] One year later the Court held illegal as a tie-in arrangement a practice of the sole supplier of electricity in a part of a state of furnishing its customers, without charge, almost 50 percent of the most frequently used standard size light bulbs.[64] The next year, in 1977, the Court again found a Section 1 violation, when a manufacturer of television sets limited the number of retail franchises granted for any given area and required each franchisee to sell the product only from where it was franchised. The Court felt the company acted unreasonably and that location restriction is per se illegal because it limits the retailer's freedom to dispose of the purchased products and reduced intrabrand competition. The Court did not differentiate between sale and nonsale transactions, such as in consignments: All were illegal if they included location restrictions.[65]

The year 1978 saw the government win a Section 1 case in which the canon of ethics of engineers prohibited members of their national society from submitting competitive bids for engineering services. This was a suppression of competition.[66] One year later the Court refused to find a Section 1 violation by two organizations in the music industry that awarded blanket licenses to copyrighted musical compositions at fees negotiated by them. Blanket licenses are included in the 1976 Copyright Act. They guard against unauthorized copyright use, which would be difficult and expensive protection if left to individual users and copyright owners. Therefore, the blanket licenses were reasonable.[67]

In a 1980 case the Court ruled that Section 1 had been violated by some wholesalers who made an agreement to eliminate the short-term credit formerly granted to retailers, requiring them instead to make payment in cash. It was anticompetitive in that it eliminated discounts, since discounts had been given by the wholesalers when they competed with each other on credit terms.[68] Two years later the Court again found Section 1 violated, this time by a county medical society that established maximum fees that doctors could claim. It was illegal, horizontal price-fixing that did not enhance competition.[69] In 1984 the Court found vertical price-fixing, and held illegal the refusal of a manufacturer to renew an agreement to sell to a wholesale distributor because the latter was selling at discount prices. Other distributors either refused to sell their products to the discounter or sold them too late to be of use (the product was herbicides). The Court said the standard for finding a conspiracy in these cases must be evidence that reasonably tends to prove that the manufacturer and others had a conscious commitment to a common scheme designed to achieve an unlawful objective. That standard was reached in this case.[70] However, in that same year the Court did not find Section 1 violated by a tying arrangement in the form of a contract between a hospital and a firm of four anesthesiologists requiring all anesthesiology services for hospital patients to be performed by that firm. There was no evidence that price, quality, or supply and demand had been adversely affected and no showing that the market as a whole had been affected at all by the contract.[71]

Also in 1984, the Court did find Section 1 violated by the National Collegiate Athletic Association when it made contracts to televise football games but limited both the total of games telecast and the number of times any one college could appear. It further said that no school could act independently. When the major football schools formed their own association and made their own television contract the NCAA threatened sanctions. In its ruling the Court could find no legitimate procompetitive purpose, saying that the NCAA had restricted rather than enhanced the place of intercollegiate athletics in the nation's life by these actions.[72] The following year, in 1985, the Court found Section 2 violated and awarded triple damages to a skiing company when a rival company made changes in the pattern of distributing tickets under a joint marketing program that had been in effect for several years. When the changes became economically detrimental to the smaller company it refused to go along, and the larger company then refused to deal with it. The Court found no valid reasons for that; rather, the only reason was to harm a smaller competitor and there was no efficiency justification for its pattern of conduct.[73] Three years later in 1988, the Court did not find Section 1 violated by a company who terminated another company because the latter sold the former's product at low prices. The Court said a vertical restraint is not illegal unless it includes some arrangement on price or price levels, which did not happen here.[74]

The 1990s and the 2000s

The Court in 1997 rendered a decision that was of major significance. The case was *State Oil Company v. Khan,*[75] and the issue was whether a manufacturer or supplier necessarily violates Section 1 by placing a ceiling on the retail price a dealer can charge for its products. Even though an earlier case had held that all limits on retail markups were a violation, Justice O'Connor, for a unanimous Court, said that the legality of markup limits will now be determined case by case with reasonableness being the standard. In this particular case, the oil company had tried to tell a gasoline dealer that he had to rebate to it any excess over the allowed markup of 3.25 cents a gallon. The Court felt there was insufficient economic justification to prohibit the practice, and that an inability to limit markups could actually harm consumers by leading to monopoly behavior by dealers who serve exclusive territories, as well as causing higher prices. The Court noted, however, that it is still illegal for a manufacturer to impose minimum prices on dealers.

In 2004 an 8–0 decision by Justice Breyer held that a 1982 amendment to the Sherman Act, the Foreign Trade Antitrust Improvement Act, does not apply to transactions that take place overseas and that cause harm unless a company's actions have contributed to the harm. The defendants pled guilty to international price fixing after a United States investigation and paid the biggest criminal fine, $500 million, ever obtained by the Justice Department, in addition to heavy civil penalties imposed by the European Union and several foreign governments. The Act does not cover foreign effects of anticompetitive behavior unless the defendants' domestic behavior can be shown to have contributed to those effects.[76]

MICROSOFT

In 1998, the Justice Department and nineteen other parties (eighteen states plus the District of Columbia) initiated an antitrust suit against Microsoft. This was a long trial, and the case is significant in several respects. First of all, it was the first antitrust suit of major proportions brought by the government in many years. Microsoft is a major company in the computer field with its Explorer browser and Windows, and the fact that the Justice Department decided to take it on, alleging predatory practices in order to hurt its competitors, was a major step forward in antitrust law enforcement. The last major case brought by the government that ended at the Supreme Court level was in 1978. This case did not reach the Supreme Court, but neither did the case against AT&T, which will be discussed in a later chapter.

The Microsoft case is also significant in that the field of communications, which includes the computer area, has been the scene of many megamergers in recent years. Is this case a portent of things to come, or is it an isolated case based solely on a dominant company's particular practices? Yet another significant point in the Microsoft case is its effect on this country's ability to engage competitively in international trade. U.S. companies already think our laws and regulations hurt them in this field.

The trial judge for the Microsoft case felt that Microsoft plotted to control the browser markets and bullied rivals into altering their products, and he did rule that Microsoft is a monopoly. In April 2000, the judge found Microsoft guilty of violating the Sherman Act due to using anticompetitive means to maintain a monopoly for its PC operating system software, attempting to monopolize the Web-browser software market, and tying its Internet Explorer browser to the Windows operating system. The only point in which the judge ruled for Microsoft was his holding that its marketing contracts with other companies did not deprive Netscape of the ability to distribute its Web browser.

In June 2000, the judge issued his remedy, recommended by the Justice Department and seventeen of the other nineteen plaintiffs, and the most important part of it called for splitting Microsoft into two companies. One company would make the Windows operating system, and the other would make the applications that are run by the operating system, and would also include Microsoft's Internet and computer hardware businesses. The two entities would have separate employees, assets, and intellectual properties, and there would be separate stock. The judge also issued a long list of restrictions on Microsoft's conduct that would last three years if the breakup order withstood appeals, and ten years if it did not. Microsoft appealed the breakup plan and asked that the conduct restrictions be stayed while the appeal proceeded, and the judge did stay them. In 2001 a Court of Appeals overturned the remedy and sent the case back to a new judge, alleging improper conduct by the trial judge; namely, secret interviews with members of the media plus offensive statements about Microsoft officials made in public statements outside the courtroom, such as comparing Bill Gates to Napoleon and the company to a drug-dealing street gang. Microsoft, the government, and nine of eighteen states (but not D.C.) now reached a settlement, which was approved in 2002. The other states not settling had a new trial but all lost in 2002 and settlements were made.

The settlement with the government included the following points:

1. Icons: PC makers can display icons on their machines for non-Microsoft browsers, multimedia players and other products, and remove Microsoft icons. PC makers also can automatically launch a non-Microsoft product during boot-up of the PC. The judge eliminated a loophole which prevented that unless Microsoft launched a competing product.

2. Uniform license: Microsoft must offer Windows to all PC makers at the same price and other terms. The company may give discounts based on volume. It also can give special discounts, called "market development allowances" (MDAs) based on "objective, verifiable criteria," such as PCs that boot up faster or have extra memory. This was all to be done by 2007, but in 2004 Microsoft was given until 2009.

3. Disclosure: Microsoft must disclose Windows' code so competing browsers, media players, computer services and other products can work smoothly with the dominant PC operating system.

4. Exclusive contracts: Microsoft cannot strike exclusive deals requiring Internet services to aggressively promote its browser, media player, or other software in return for favors, such as coveted promotion on Windows. The judge modified a provision that would have exempted agreements in which Microsoft licenses intellectual property from the Internet service. Instead, the intellectual property license must be the "principal purpose" of the deal to meet the exemption.

5. Enforcement: Microsoft must form a compliance committee of three outside members of the board of directors. The committee will hire a

compliance officer to ensure Microsoft abides by the settlement. The compliance officer will no longer be a Microsoft employee and has new powers to report violations of the settlement to the government. The judge also gave herself broad powers to monitor compliance.

6. Anti-retaliation: Microsoft cannot retaliate or threaten retaliation against PC makers or software developers who promote non-Microsoft browsers, media players, or other products that can run applications. The judge bolstered the settlement by barring threats as well as actual retaliation.

Microsoft paid only the legal fees ($1.54 billion) but was not required to distribute the browser or the media player separately.

There were other suits against Microsoft by rivals, all accusing it of using its dominant position in the operating system market to give it an illegal advantage in other markets. In 2003 it agreed to pay AOL Time Warner $750 million and will grant it a seven year royalty free license to its Internet browsing software (Explorer) and faster and greater access to its Windows operating system, making it easier for AOL online services to work with Windows software. It also granted AOL a long-term license to its software (Media Player) for delivering music and movie video over the Internet and will work closely with them to develop software to protect AOL's movie and music assets from piracy. In 2004 Microsoft settled with Sun Microsystems for $1.9 billion, including $700 million to resolve antitrust issues, and also settled with Novell for $536 million, although the latter has since filed a second antitrust suit on a different issue. In 2005 it settled with Gateway for $150 million and the two will work together on the marketing and development of Gateway personal computing products. In 2005 it also settled with IBM for $775 million, addressing all discriminatory pricing and overcharge claims. IBM in return agreed to defer consideration of filing claims related to IBM's server hardware and server software business for two years. Also in 2005 Microsoft settled with RealNetworks for $761 million and the two companies agreed to form a partnership in which the former will use Microsoft's software and the latter will distribute RealNetworks' digital media, especially its subscription music service Rhapsody.

As if all these suits in the United States were not enough, Microsoft was also investigated by the European Union, and in 2004 was found guilty of being a monopoly. It appealed, but a European court held that sanctions will take effect even though the appeal is pending. Microsoft must offer a version of its Windows operating system without its software (Media Player) for playing digital music and movies on personal computers. Also, it must divulge some trade secrets to competitors to allow them to produce server software that works with Windows, which operates more than 95 percent of personal computers around the world. Microsoft in 2006 agreed to do it but is appealing the $665.5 million fine, which has been deposited in an escrow account, and a demand that the company make changes in its business practice.

In 2005 the competition commissioner of Europe agreed to exclude open-source developers, who distribute their software free and do not use patents, from learning the details on Windows until the appeal is finished. Microsoft did agree to share the details globally, not just inside Europe, and to break up the protocols into clusters so developers can buy selected details, rather than all or nothing, and one that has no patent or copyrights will be free. The Commission accepted Microsoft's offer to sell a second version of Windows that has Media Player stripped out, which will give RealPlayer (RealNetworks) and Quick Time (Apple) fairer access to Windows users. As part of its 2005 settlement with Microsoft, RealNetworks will no longer be involved in the European case.

Another European Union antitrust investigation with a United States corporation ended more amicably in 2005 when the European Commission formally accepted Coca-Cola Company's promise to ease its grip on the market for soft drinks. Coke has committed itself to end exclusivity agreements, target and growth rebates and to stop using its strongest brands to sell less popular products. Coke will also reserve up to 20 percent of its cooler space for rivals in locations where retailers have only a Coca-Cola cooler from which to sell chilled beverages.

WHAT DOES IT ALL MEAN?

Sometimes it is difficult for people to understand the significance of the Sherman Act and the Supreme Court decisions interpreting it. One reason for that is the recent decline in these cases. Why has the government not been as active in this area as formerly, especially in view of the fact that it has been remarkably successful in winning its suits? Is it because business has, to a large extent, stopped its Sherman Act violations? The answer to the latter depends on the viewpoint of the person being asked, because there is so much subjectivity in the law. For example, as can be seen from the cases, it used to be that only monopolies were subject to the rule of reason, meaning that only bad monopolies violated the law, and what was bad depended upon various players, such as the president, the Justice Department, and the Court. Now even placing ceilings on retail prices, which used to be illegal per se no matter how reasonable the price, can be reasonable. This, coupled with the fact that recent administrations have tended to be more business-friendly, has led to the decrease in cases brought by the government.

Still another reason for the decline of cases has been the perception that the federal courts, including the Supreme Court, are also more business-friendly than before and thus would be more likely to rule against the government. This is due to the influx of judges appointed by more conservative presidents, such judges usually taking the side of business against the government. The reality is that this perception is probably right, but just the perception itself is enough to make the government decide not to bring a suit even if it were inclined to do so.

A further reason for the decline of cases is that there has also been a decline in Sherman Act cases brought by businesses and individuals, although not as noticeable a decline as government cases. That is due in part to the above-mentioned perception that the federal courts are more conservative and therefore less likely to find illegality in business activities. It is also due in part to the tendency of businesses, especially big ones, to cooperate more with each other than to fight each other, with the resultant increase in practices such as mergers. A healthy economy is also conducive to more friendly relations among businesses.

Will this trend continue? On the surface it would appear so, but history tends to be cyclical, and thus one cannot rule out a renewed interest in Sherman Act prosecutions such as the Microsoft suit. However, Republican administrations tend to be more business-friendly than do Democratic administrations.

One other important point is that the Sherman Act is not the government's only antitrust law. There are others that can be used, as we will see in the next chapter.

SUMMARY

The Sherman Act was the government's first major law to try to curb the abuses of big business (except for the railroads, as will be shown in a later chapter, which were regulated three years earlier). As with any important law, its significance depends upon its enforcement by the executive branch, and its interpretation by the judicial branch, especially the Supreme Court. This chapter has attempted to show the Court's interpretation by pointing out the most significant cases brought both by the government and by private persons, including corporations, in a chronological manner so as to see the Court's growth in this area. As was shown, the growth has been steady, albeit uneven at times, but no study of the role of government and business in the American economy can be complete without this inclusion. With the relative dearth of cases in recent years, there is a tendency to downplay the significance of antitrust history. As mentioned previously, that may or may not change, but whether it does or not is insignificant due to the role it has played. It is sometimes hard to find where antitrust history fits, but indeed it does, as this and the next chapter should make abundantly clear.

QUESTIONS FOR DISCUSSION

1. What does a per se violation of the Sherman Act mean?
2. What does the "rule of reason" mean with regard to the Sherman Act?
3. What is the importance of allowing private parties to sue for triple damages?
4. What is meant by the "current of commerce" doctrine?
5. Was the Sherman Act meant to be applied to labor?
6. Was the Supreme Court consistent or inconsistent in its interpretation of the Sherman Act?
7. Why has the government not pursued antitrust suits despite their high winning percentage?
8. Do private antitrust suits stand a better chance of victory in the courts than do government suits?
9. Do you agree that the rule of reason should apply to maximum resale prices?
10. Why has the government renewed its antitrust activity?
11. Are antitrust suits helpful or detrimental to the economy?
12. Is the Sherman Act still an important law?
13. Is the Microsoft settlement a good one for all?

RECOMMENDED READING

Langran, Robert W. *The Supreme Court: A Concise History*. New York: Peter Lang Publishing, Inc., 2004
———. *The United States Supreme Court*. 5th ed. Needham Heights, MA: Pearson Custom
Publishing. 2004. Chapters 4–15.
Schnitzer, Martin. *Contemporary Government and Business Relations*. 4th ed. Boston, MA: Houghton Mifflin Co., 1990. Chapters 6, 7, and 9.

NOTES

1. 156 U.S. 1 (1895).
2. 166 U.S. 290 (1897).
3. *United States v. Joint Traffic Association*, 171 U.S. 505 (1898).
4. *Hopkins v. United States*, 171 U.S. 578 (1898); *Anderson v. United States*, 171 U.S. 604 (1898).
5. 175 U.S. 611 (1899).
6. 193 U.S. 197 (1904).
7. 196 U.S. 375 (1905).
8. *Chattanooga Foundry and Pipe Works v. City of Atlanta*, 203 U.S. 390 (1906).
9. 208 U.S. 274 (1908).

10. *Dr. Miles Medical Company v. John D. Park & Sons Co.*, 220 U.S. 373 (1911).
11. 221 U.S. 1 (1911).
12. 221 U.S. 106 (1911).
13. *Henry v. A.B. Dick Co.*, 224 U.S. 1 (1912).
14. *United States v. Union Pacific Railroad Co.*, 226 U.S. 61 (1912).
15. *Eastern States Retail Lumber Dealers' Association v. United States*, 234 U.S. 600 (1914).
16. *Board of Trade of the City of Chicago v. United States*, 246 U.S. 231 (1918).
17. *United States v. United Shoe Machinery Co.*, 247 U.S. 32 (1918).
18. *United States v. Colgate*, 250 U.S. 300 (1919).
19. 251 U.S. 417 (1920).
20. 254 U.S. 443 (1921).
21. *American Column and Lumber Co. v. United States*, 257 U.S. 377 (1921).
22. *United States v. American Linseed Oil Co.*, 262 U.S. 371 (1923).
23. *Maple Flooring Manufacturers' Association v. United States*, 268 U.S. 563 (1925); *Cement Manufacturers' Protective Association v. United States*, 268 U.S. 588 (1925).
24. *United States v. General Electric Co.*, 272 U.S. 476 (1926).
25. *United States v. Trenton Potteries Co.*, 273 U.S. 392 (1927).
26. 274 U.S. 37 (1927).
27. *United States v. International Harvester Co.*, 274 U.S. 37 (1927).
28. *Story Parchment Co. v. Paterson Parchment Paper Co.*, 282 U.S. 555 (1931).
29. *Appalachian Coals, Inc. v. United States*, 288 U.S. 344 (1933).
30. *Sugar Institute v. United States*, 297 U.S. 553 (1936).
31. *Interstate Circuit, Inc. v. United States*, 306 U.S. 208 (1939).
32. *United States v. Socony-Vacuum Oil Co.*, 310 U.S. 150 (1940).
33. 312 U.S. 219 (1941).
34. *United States v. Cooper Corporation*, 312 U.S. 600 (1941).
35. *Georgia v. Evans*, 316 U.S. 159 (1942).
36. *United States v. Masonite Corporation*, 316 U.S. 265 (1942).
37. *Parker v. Brown*, 317 U.S. 341 (1943).
38. *American Tobacco Co. v. United States*, 328 U.S. 781 (1946).
39. *United States v. Yellow Cab Co.*, 332 U.S. 218 (1947).
40. *United States v. National Lead Co.*, 332 U.S. 319 (1947).
41. *International Salt Co. v. United States*, 332 U.S. 392 (1947).
42. *United States v. United States Gypsum Co.*, 333 U.S. 364 (1948).
43. *United States v. Griffith*, 334 U.S. 100 (1948); *Schine Chain Theatres v. United States*, 334 U.S. 110 (1948).
44. *United States v. Paramount Pictures*, 334 U.S. 131 (1948).
45. *United States v. Columbia Steel Co.*, 334 U.S. 495 (1948).
46. *Kiefer-Stewart Co. v. Seagram & Sons, Inc.*, 340 U.S. 211 (1951).
47. *Timken Roller Bearing Co. v. United States*, 341 U.S. 593 (1951).
48. *Times-Picayune Publishing Co. v. United States*, 345 U.S. 594 (1953).
49. *Theatre Enterprises, Inc. v. Paramount Film Distributing Corporation*, 346 U.S. 537 (1954).
50. *Northern Pacific Railway Co. v. United States*, 356 U.S. 1 (1958).
51. *Klor's Inc. v. Broadway-Hale Stores, Inc.*, 359 U.S. 207 (1959).
52. *United States v. Parke, Davis and Co.*, 362 U.S. 29 (1960).
53. *Eastern Railroad Presidents Conference v. Noerr Motor Freight, Inc.*, 365 U.S. 127 (1961).

54. *United States v. Loew's Inc.*, 371 U.S. 38 (1962).

55. *United States v. First National Bank and Trust Co. of Lexington*, 376 U.S. 665 (1964).

56. *United States v. General Motors Corporation*, 384 U.S. 127 (1966).

57. *United States v. Arnold, Schwinn & Co.*, 388 U.S. 365 (1967).

58. *Albrecht v. Herald Co.*, 390 U.S. 145 (1968).

59. *United States v. Container Corporation of America*, 393 U.S. 333 (1969).

60. *Fortner Enterprises, Inc. v. United States Steel Corporation*, 394 U.S. 495 (1969).

61. *United States v. Topco Associates, Inc.*, 405 U.S. 596 (1972).

62. *Otter Tail Power Co. v. United States*, 410 U.S. 366 (1973).

63. *Goldfarb v. Virginia State Bar*, 421 U.S. 773 (1975).

64. *Cantor v. Detroit Edison Co.*, 428 U.S. 579 (1976).

65. *Continental TV, Inc. v. GTE Sylvania Inc.*, 433 U.S. 36 (1977).

66. *National Society of Professional Engineers v. United States*, 435 U.S. 679 (1978).

67. *Broadcast Music, Inc. v. Columbia Broadcasting System, Inc.*, 441 U.S. 1 (1979).

68. *Catalano, Inc. v. Target Sales, Inc.*, 446 U.S. 643 (1980).

69. *Arizona v. Maricopa County Medical Society*, 457 U.S. 332 (1982).

70. *Monsanto Co. v. Spray-Rite Service Corporation*, 465 U.S. 752 (1984).

71. *Jefferson Parish Hospital District No. 2 v. Hyde*, 466 U.S. 2 (1984).

72. *National Collegiate Athletic Association v. Board of Regents of the University of Oklahoma*, 468 U.S. 85 (1984).

73. *Aspen Skiing Co. v. Aspen Highlands Skiing Corporation*, 472 U.S. 585 (1985).

74. *Business Electronics Corporation v. Sharp Electronics Corporation*, 485 U.S. 717 (1988).

75. 118 S. Ct. 275 (1997).

76. *F. Hoffmann-LaRoche Ltd. v. Empagran S.A.*, 542 U.S. _____ (2004).

5

The Supreme Court and the Federal Trade Commission and Clayton Acts

When Woodrow Wilson became president in 1913, he perceived that the Sherman Act needed augmenting. As a result, Congress in 1914 passed two more laws to try to keep our market system competitive and to curb abuses. The first one, the Federal Trade Commission Act, was passed on September 26. It created an independent regulatory commission, the Federal Trade Commission, composed of five members appointed by the president with Senate approval, with each member holding office for seven years. Section 5 of the act gives the FTC the power to prevent unfair methods of competition and unfair or deceptive acts or practices in or affecting commerce. The second part, concerning unfair or deceptive acts or practices, was actually added in 1938 when Congress amended Section 5 with the Wheeler-Lea Amendment due to a Supreme Court decision, to be examined later, that did not think unfair methods of competition prevention included efforts to protect consumers. The amendment also specifically forbids false or misleading advertisements for food, drugs, cosmetics, and therapeutic devices sold in interstate commerce. However, the Commission cannot award monetary damages to victimized consumers under the amendment, thereby weakening the consumer's incentive to lodge complaints and weakening the seller's incentive to comply. A fraudulent seller, if successfully prosecuted, will not be allowed to continue or repeat the violation, but may keep any of the profits obtained during the period of the violation. The respondent has sixty days to appeal the Commission's cease and desist order to a court of appeals, but once the order is finalized, any subsequent violation subjects the respondent to contempt proceedings and a civil penalty of up to $5,000 for each day of continuing violation or for each separate offense.

The second law, the Clayton Antitrust Act, was passed on October 15,

1914. Probably its most important provision is Section 2, which deals with primary-line price discrimination (i.e., a geographic line where goods are sold at a higher price in one area and a lower price in another, to the injury of a local seller). It may also occur within the same geographic area. One cannot engage in price discrimination in the sale of goods of like grade or quality when the effect is to injure or prevent competition. In 1936, Congress amended the Clayton Act, especially Section 2, when it passed the Robinson-Patman Act, commonly known as the Chain Store Act. It prohibits secondary-line price discrimination, which is the sale of the same goods to different buyers in the same geographic area at different prices when there is no cost difference. One cannot practice price discrimination when the end result is to lessen competition, when it tends to create a monopoly in any line of commerce, or when it injures, destroys, or prevents competition with any person who either grants or knowingly receives the benefits of such discrimination. The law does permit a seller to show that lower prices to some buyers are based on cost differences related to different methods or quantities involved in the sale or delivery of the product. Other actions prohibited are the payment of brokerage fees when no independent broker was involved (some chains had been demanding the regular brokerage fees at a discount when they purchased directly from the manufacturers), and advertising allowances, unless they were made on equal terms to all competing purchasers.

Section 3 of the Clayton Act prohibits tying contracts, which are the lease or sale of a particular product conditional on the lessee's or purchaser's use of associated products sold by the same manufacturer, and exclusive dealing arrangements, in which one firm induces another not to deal with the former's competitors. These have generally been condemned by the courts only when the seller enjoys substantial market power and they result in a lessening of competition.

Section 4 allows a person to sue for triple damages, and the important Section 7 prohibits any corporation engaged in commerce from acquiring the stock of another corporation when the effect may be to reduce competition substantially or to create a monopoly in any line of business and in any section of the country. It applies to both interstate and foreign commerce. In 1950, Congress passed the Celler-Kefauver Act to plug a loophole in Section 7. It is now illegal for one corporation to acquire the stock or assets of another corporation when the end result might be to lessen competition substantially or to tend to create a monopoly. It makes a merger illegal if there was a trend toward concentration in an industry. Small firms that merge to improve their competitive position are generally not challenged, but mergers that would ordinarily be allowed in concentrated industries may well be challenged if a large firm acquires a small competitor.

Section 8 applies to interlocking directorates (but exempts banks), saying that no person shall be a director in two or more corporations if they are competitors and if they have capital, surplus, and undivided profits in excess of one million dollars. The government does not have to prove that competition has been reduced. The fact of the interlock itself makes for illegality.

Section 14 provides that individual directors or officers of a corporation can be fined as much as $5,000, or sentenced to prison for up to one year, or both, and the Federal Trade Commission was given joint responsibility with the Justice Department to enforce the act, the violations of which are considered civil offenses. Section 15 gives the U.S. district courts jurisdiction over these cases, and Section 16 permits any person or firm to sue for and have injunctive relief against potential loss or damage by violations.

Important Provisions of the Federal Trade Commission Act and the Clayton Act:
FTC Act
Section 5: prohibits unfair methods of competition and unfair or deceptive acts or practices
Clayton Act
Section 2: prohibits price discrimination
Section 3: prohibits tying contracts and exclusive dealing arrangements
Section 4: allows a person to sue for triple damages
Section 7: prohibits anticompetitive acquiring of stocks or assets
Section 8: prohibits anticompetitive interlocking directorates
Section 14: provides for fines and jail sentences
Section 15: gives jurisdiction to U.S. district courts
Section 16: provides injunctive relief

Before looking at the major Court cases, there is one other law of note with regard to antitrust law. It is the 1976 Hart-Scott-Rodino Act, and it made a number of procedural changes. The Justice Department now has the authority to issue civil investigative demands to third parties, such as competitors of those companies under investigation, and to compel oral testimony and answers to written questions. It also requires notice to the antitrust division of the Justice Department and to the Federal Trade Commission, thirty days in advance, of mergers involving companies with stock or assets of $100 million or more that plan to merge with companies worth $10 million or more when the transaction involves acquisitions of more than $15 million in stock or assets. This gives them time in which to challenge the merger, because the firms must provide the government with extensive information pertaining to the merger. The government might decide to approve the merger subject to certain conditions. This provision benefits the government because once a merger takes place it is often difficult to stop it since the length of time needed to arrive at decisions allows firms time to consolidate their assets; it also benefits the firms because they will know of the challenge before the merger is finalized rather than after it has been finalized. Finally, the law authorizes state attorneys general to bring triple damage suits on behalf of state citizens injured by violations of the Sherman Act. This has increased the amount of antitrust enforcement by state governments, and the courts will exclude from the amount of monetary relief any amount duplicating an award for the same injury.

An important point to remember about antitrust enforcement is that the majority of cases initiated by the federal government are settled by a consent decree approved by the judge, a violation of which would result in contempt of court. Although saving the time and expense of a trial, its drawback is that if the government had won the suit that would have constituted prima facie evidence of the violation and would be used by a private plaintiff in a triple damage suit. In 2003 a federal judge fined a medical device maker $1 million for violating a 1995 consent order, the largest ever for a FTC antitrust order.

FEDERAL TRADE COMMISSION AND CLAYTON ACT CASE LAW DEVELOPMENT

The Early Years

The Federal Trade Commission tried using its own law in the 1920 case of *FTC v. Gratz*[1] by bringing unfair competition charges against a company for refusing to sell steel ties unless prospective purchasers bought bagging to be used with them. However, Justice McReynolds, for a 7–2 Court, ruled against the FTC, saying it was up to the courts to decide what is unfair competition. Since Gratz sold at fair prices to those willing to take those terms, the public did not suffer injury and therefore the law was not broken.

Two years later, in 1922, the Federal Trade Commission again brought a case to the Court involving its own law, but this time fared better. The Court ruled against a company who refused to sell to those who did not observe the resale price set by it, even though there was no contract to fix the price, and it refused to sell to those who sold to other dealers who failed to sell at the set price. The Court felt it was a suppression of competition after the company had sold the products, which was unfair competition.[2] That same year the Court voided a contract under Section 3 of the Clayton Act. Under it a manufacturer who controlled 40 percent of the industry bound a retailer to sell only the manufacturer's products. However, the retailer stopped selling those products and began selling those of a rival company. The Court held that the law condemns sales of agreements where the effect may be to substantially lessen competition or tend to create a monopoly.[3] Again that year, the Federal Trade Commission won another case enforcing its law, this time against a manufacturer selling products with misleading labels as to what fabric was in the products. The Court found unfair competition even though competitors and eventually retailers knew what the company was doing.[4]

In 1923 the Court ruled against an attempt by the Federal Trade Commission to use its own law as well as Section 3 of the Clayton Act. The case was *FTC v. Curtis Publishing Co.*,[5] and it involved a contract made between the publisher and a distributor to consign publications until they are sold at specified prices and to have the distributor act as an exclusive agent, meaning it would not carry any other publisher's materials. Justice McReynolds in a 7–2 opinion held that the contract was not a violation of the Clayton Act, and the exclusive agency did not violate the FTC Act if done in an orderly development of business and without an unlawful motive, as was the case here. He also said that the courts are the ultimate determiners of unfair competition and that they can look at the record of a case to see if there were any material facts not reported by the FTC. The Court ruled the same way later that year in a case against four companies who leased equipment to retailers, who in turn had to use the product it produced when they used that equipment. The Court felt that those who give time, skill, and capital should have large freedom of action in the conduct of their affairs.[6]

In 1927 the Court upheld a Section 4 triple damage suit against a manufacturer who refused to sell to a company at dealers' discounts, which violated Section 2 of the Sherman Act as it was an attempt to monopolize. An interesting holding of the case was that one does not have to prove the actual cost of doing business in order to calculate damages.[7] Four years later, in 1931, came the aforementioned decision that led to the passage of the Wheeler-Lea Amendment. The Court ruled against an FTC attempt to stop a company that made a product from advertising it as a cure for obesity. The Court said that the company did not represent the product as being scientific, and no competition was injured.[8] The FTC was able to win two cases in 1934. One involved a trade name that was misleading and that caused both confusion and prejudice to retailers, architects, builders, and consumers (the product was a type of lumber),[9] and the other involved a manufacturer who made a product (candy) that contained material attractive to children in each package. The problem was that the package explained that either the price or the amount of candy was affected by chance. It was also inferior in size and quality to their other candy. The Court found it unfair competition even if there was no fraud or deception.[10] Two years later the Court found no violation of Section 3 of the Clayton Act when automobile manufacturers made dealers agree not to sell, offer for sale, or use in repairs second-hand or used parts not manufactured or authorized by the manufacturer. It felt the arrangement did not substantially lessen competition nor create a monopoly.[11]

Significant government victories and losses in the Supreme Court are listed below:

Government Federal Trade Commission and Clayton Act Cases in the Supreme Court, 1920–1959:
Government Victories:

1. *FTC v. Beech-Nut Packing Company*, 1922.
2. *FTC v. Winsted Company*, 1922.
3. *FTC v. Algoma Lumber Company*, 1934.
4. *FTC v. R. F. Keppel & Brothers, Inc.*, 1934.
5. *Corn Products Refining Company v. FTC*, 1945.
6. *FTC v. A. E. Staley Manufacturing Company*, 1945.
7. *FTC v. Cement Institute*, 1948.
8. *FTC v. Morton Salt Company*, 1948.
9. *Standard Oil of California v. United States*, 1949.
10. *FTC v. Motion Picture Advertising Service Company*, 1953.
11. *United States v. duPont and Company*, 1956.
12. *FTC v. Simplicity Pattern Company, Inc.*, 1959.

Government Losses:
1. *FTC v. Gratz*, 1920.
2. *FTC v. Curtis Publishing Company*, 1923.
3. *FTC v. Sinclair Refining Company*, 1923.
4. *FTC v. Raladam Company*, 1931.
5. *Standard Oil Company v. FTC*, 1951.
6. *Automatic Canteen Company of America v. FTC*, 1953.

The 1940s and 1950s

In 1945 the FTC was successful in breaking up two basing-point schemes. Basing-point is a system in which the companies involved will only sell at delivered prices, which avoids giving firms located near a consuming center an advantage in obtaining business. The delivered prices were the sum of the base price added to the cost of transportation to the destination, regardless of the origin of the shipment or the actual freight cost. The steel industry was one of the first to utilize the practice, although these two cases involved the glucose industry. In the first case, the Court found Section 2 of the Clayton Act plus the Robinson-Patman Act violated because the allowance of discounts to purchasers of by-products was a substantial threat to competition, as were the advertising discounts that were given because they were not on terms proportionally accorded other purchasers.[12] In the second case, the Court said there was no good-faith effort to meet competition, the FTC can decide that fact, and the fact that competitors are also doing it does not justify price discrimination.[13]

The following year, 1946, the Court awarded triple damages under both Section 4 of the Clayton Act and Section 7 of the Sherman Act, and allowed an injunction to be issued under Section 16 of the Clayton Act against film distributors plus those who owned or controlled theaters in a city. They had conspired to prevent an owner of motion picture theaters from showing pictures until after the preferred theaters had shown them, a violation of Sections 1 and 2 of the Sherman Act. An interesting facet to this case was that the plaintiff could not prove what his earnings would have been over a five-year period under fully competitive conditions, and the Court said that the wrong-doer should bear the risk of the uncertainty in computing the damages he has created.[14] Two years later, in 1948, the FTC won two cases. In one, the Court decided that Section 5 of the FTC Act and Section 2 of the Clayton Act and the Robinson-Patman Act were violated by seventy-four corporations who were acting in concert through a multiple basing-point system, resulting in price discrimination that was not made in good faith to meet the equally low price of a competitor.[15] In the other, a company was selling with quantity discounts that were not justified by cost savings. The Court found there was a reasonable possibility that the discrimination harmed competition because certain merchants had to pay more since they could not qualify for any discounts because they could not purchase the amount necessary.[16] The next year, 1949, the government won a Clayton Act Section 3 suit against a company that made contracts under which independent dealers had to purchase exclusively from the company all requirements of one or more of the products they marketed. Since these agreements accounted for 6.7 percent of the company's total sales in a seven-state area, the Court felt that competition was foreclosed in a substantial share of the line of commerce affected.[17]

In 1951 the Court did not find Section 2 of the Clayton Act plus the Robinson-Patman Act violated by a company that sold to four large customers in a city more cheaply than it sold to small customers. The Court accepted the defense that it was doing so in order to retain each of the four as a customer, and was, in good faith, meeting the lawful price of a competitor, even if it resulted in competition being injured, destroyed, or prevented.[18] Two years later, in 1953, the FTC was more fortunate and won a case against a company under the FTC Act. The company had made exclusive contracts with 40 percent of its customers in an area, and, together with three other companies, had 75 percent control nationally. The Court found unfair competition, but did not end the contracts totally. Instead, the Court said the contracts could be for only one year (the majority of them had been from one to two years).[19] That same year the FTC lost a case, with the Court finding no violation of Section 2 of the Robinson-Patman Act by a large buyer of products who received as much as one-third lower price than others. The Court felt that the burden of proof in these cases is on the government to show that there was no cost justification for the practice or any other defense, or that the buyer knew that those defenses were not present in this case.[20]

In an interesting 1956 case, the government was successful in using Sections 7 and 15 of the Clayton Act to make a company divest itself of stock it had purchased between 1917 and 1919. The problem was that the company made automotive finishes and fabrics, among other things, and the stock was in an automobile company. The Court held that there was a reasonable possibility of restricting commerce or tending to create a monopoly in that line of commerce.[21] Three years later, in 1959, the FTC was able to win a Section 2

Clayton and Robinson-Patman Act case against a company that discriminated in favor of larger customers by furnishing them services and facilities not given smaller customers on proportionally equal terms. The Court said that since these customers were competitors, neither the absence of competitive injury nor the presence of cost justification can be a defense.[22]

The First Forty Years in Retrospect

It is possible to see something of a pattern in the first four decades of Supreme Court decisions interpreting the Federal Trade Commission, Clayton, and Robinson-Patman Acts. Each act attempted to do something about business activity intended to subvert the forces of competition. The Federal Trade Commission brought almost all the government's cases, leaving the Justice Department to concentrate on the Sherman Act. It won two-thirds of them, despite the Supreme Court justices who were, at least until the mid-1950s, inclined to prevent too much government interference in the economy. This shows both the strength of many of the government's cases, along with the accompanying attempts by business to circumvent the market. One other pattern deserving of mention is the reluctance of businesses to take advantage of the Clayton Act and bring suits themselves. The fact that they won the few suits they brought should have indicated that it was a viable way to proceed. However, they were on the whole enjoying prosperity in the 1920s, fighting a depression in the 1930s, fighting a war in the 1940s, and again enjoying prosperity in the 1950s. As the adage goes, why knock a good thing? Whether that would continue will be the focus of the look at the next four decades of the enforcement of these three statutes.

Significant private suits in the Supreme Court are listed below:

Private Federal Trade Commission and Clayton Act Cases in the Supreme Court, 1920–1959:
Victories for Plaintiffs:
1. *Standard Fashion Company v. Magrane-Houston Company*, 1922.
2. *Eastman Kodak Company v. Southern Photo Company*, 1927.
3. *Bigelow v. RKO Radio Pictures, Inc.*, 1946.
Loss by Plaintiff:
Pick Manufacturing Company v. General Motors Corporation, 1936.

The Turbulent 1960s

The Federal Trade Commission and Clayton Acts, along with the latter's Robinson-Patman and Celler-Kefauver Acts, found their way to the Supreme Court in a great many cases during the 1960s. In theory it was an ideal time to bring these cases, because the Court was often dominated by its liberal wing, which is usually more agreeable to government intervention in the economy and to the attempt to try to curb the abuses of big business. That fact, together with the Democratic administrations through most of the decade, meant that suits would be initiated and that business would be in for a severe fight if, indeed, those cases ever found their way to the Court. It would also seem the appropriate time for businesses to use the laws against each other in suits for triple damages as well as for injunctive relief.

The decade started with the FTC victorious in two 1960 cases. In one, the Court agreed that Section 2 of the Clayton and Robinson-Patman Acts was violated by a company whose broker reduced his commission from 5 percent to 3 percent in order to meet the bid of a favored buyer. The company, accordingly, reduced its price only for that buyer in that and subsequent sales. The Court held that one cannot make any allowance in lieu of brokerage to the other party in a transaction. The fact that the buyer was unaware was immaterial, and it did not matter whether it was done from the broker to the buyer directly or, as in this case, indirectly through the seller.[23] In the other case the Court again found a violation of Section 2 of the Clayton and Robinson-Patman Acts by a company that reduced its prices in one area of the country (around a city). That is primary line discrimination, even though all competitive purchasers paid the same price. One does not have to show prices either below cost or unreasonably low in order to prove that a firm was trying to eliminate competition and get a monopoly. The price difference broke the law.[24] One year later, in 1961, the Court found no violation of Section 3 of the Clayton Act in a contract made between an electric company and a coal company in which the former agreed to buy all its coal from the latter for the next twenty years. However, when the price of coal rose, the coal company repudiated the contract, claiming it broke Section 3. The Court disagreed and made the company honor the contract, saying that the coal company was responsible for only 1 percent of the coal produced and supplied by seven hundred coal suppliers in that area. Therefore, the contract did not foreclose a substantial volume of competition.[25]

The following year, in 1962, the government won two cases. In the first, Section 7 of the Clayton Act and the Celler-Kefauver Act was used to stop a merger between two shoe companies, one of which was the nation's third largest retailer and fourth largest manufacturer, with the other the eighth largest retailer and twelfth largest manufacturer. It was an industry in which the top four manufacturers produced 23 percent of the nation's shoes. The result would be a lessening of competition in retail sales, particularly in cities of over 10,000 population.[26] In the second, Section 2 of the Clayton Act was used to stop the price discrimination being practiced by a company selling milk in a metropolitan area. It sold more cheaply to two chains than it did to 1,322 independent grocery stores, but could not show actual cost savings.[27] The next year, 1963, the government won three more cases. In the first the Court found Section 2 of the Clayton and Robinson-Patman Acts violated by a company giving only one of its independently owned retailers in a particular region a lower price than it gave any others, so that retailer could meet the price reductions of a competitor. The Court said that the good-faith meeting of competition in order to practice price discrimination must be done with your own competitor, not someone else's.[28] In the second, the Court found Section 3 of the Robinson-Patman Act violated by a company selling goods in a metropolitan area at unreasonably low prices for the purpose of destroying competition or eliminating a competitor. The Court found no legitimate commercial activity by the company's practice.[29] In the third case, Section 7 of the Clayton Act and the Celler-Kefauver Act were used to block a merger between the second and third largest commercial banks in a metropolitan area. At least 30 percent of the relevant market would be in the hands of the bank after the merger, and it would increase concentration in the banking industry in the area by one-third, resulting in a substantial lessening of competition.[30]

In 1964 the government continued its streak with four more victories. First, Section 7 of the Clayton Act was used to stop the acquisition by a natural gas company of one of the two major interstate pipelines serving that part of the country, due to the probability of substantially lessening competition there.[31] Then Section 7 of the Clayton Act was again used, this time to stop a company that was the largest in its field from acquiring the ninth largest one, which was also the fourth largest independent. The merger would have a probable anticompetitive effect in a oligopolistic industry (that produced aluminum conductors), where the prevention of increased competition was important. The merger resulted in a substantial lessening of competition.[32] Then a joint venture was broken up because it might well have eliminated any prospective competition between the two companies. The Court felt that the presence of a potential competitor having the capability of entering an oligopolistic market may be a substantial incentive to competition.[33] Finally, Section 7 of the Clayton Act was again used to stop the acquisition of the third largest producer of glass containers by the second largest producer of metal containers. In the combined container field, six companies dominated, with the acquiring company being number two and the acquired company number six; the two combined held 25 percent of the market. The Court felt that when there was a trend toward concentration, any further concentration should be stopped, and in a highly concentrated industry, even slight increases should be prevented.[34]

In 1965 the government won two more cases. In one, the FTC used Section 5 of the FTC Act to stop a deceptive television commercial. The Court felt that great weight must be given to what the FTC says constitutes a deceptive practice, especially deceptive advertising. The misrepresentation of any fact, so long as it materially induces a purchaser's decision to buy, is a deception prohibited by the law.[35] In the other, Section 7 of the Clayton Act was used to make a company give up another company it had acquired, because the acquiring company tried to induce reciprocal buying of the acquired company's products by the former's suppliers. Since this was an oligopolistic industry, the Court said there was a probability of substantially lessening competition.[36] Similarly, one year later the government won twice again. In one case, Section 7 of the Clayton Act and the Celler-Kefauver Act were used to stop a merger of two grocery stores in a metropolitan area. The problem was that they were two of the largest and most successful in a market characterized by a steady decline in the number of small grocery companies, and by a significant absorption of small firms by larger ones. The Court said that this was a market exhibiting a marked trend toward concentration, and the merger would probably destroy competition in the future.[37] In the other, Section 7 of the Clayton Act was used to stop a merger of the tenth largest beer brewer in the country with the eighteenth, which resulted in the former becoming number five with 4.49 percent of the market. The Court felt this was an industry that was rapidly becoming more concentrated and thus the merger would injure competition.[38]

In 1967 the Court used Section 7 of the Clayton Act and the Celler-Kefauver Act to make a company divest itself of the assets of a company it had obtained ten years earlier. The acquiring company, dominant in several areas, decided to extend its product line by merging with the other company, which was number one in its area. The acquired company's area was an oligopolistic industry, and the substitution of a powerful acquiring firm for the smaller dominant firm might reduce the competitive structure of the industry by dissuading the smaller firms from competing aggressively, resulting in a more rigid oligopoly with the acquiring firm as the price leader. The Court also felt the merger tended to raise the barriers to new entrants because of the acquiring firm's large advertising budget, thus, the merger eliminated that firm's likely entrance into that market as a potential competitor.[39] That same year the Court upheld Section 2 of the Clayton and Robinson-Patman Acts as well as Sections 1 and 2 of the Sherman Act being used against three companies engaged in predatory pricing to get rid of a local competitor in a city. The Court said that the law can be used against price discrimination that erodes competition as well as that which does it immediately. In this case there was a drastically declining price structure.[40]

The impressive string of government victories came to a halt in a 1968 case in which the FTC tried to use Section 2 of the Clayton and Robinson-Patman Acts against a chain of supermarkets, charging the company with unlawfully inducing suppliers to engage in discriminatory pricing and sales promotion activities while not giving these benefits to wholesalers who would sell to its retail competitors. The Court felt the government could only act against discrimination between customers competing for resales at the same functional level. The responsibility should, in cases such as this, be on the supplier to make promotional allowances available to the reseller. It was not up to the defendant company to do that.[41] That same year the Court upheld a Clayton Act Section 4 triple damage suit, as well as a Section 5 charge. That section states that a final judgment or decree in a government antitrust suit is prima facie evidence in a private suit. The suit charged that a company's practice of leasing and refusing to sell its major machines was illegal monopolization, and that it overcharged when it did lease. The defense was that the company leasing the machines simply passed the illegal charges on to its customers in the form of higher prices, but the Court disagreed, saying that the possibility of recoupment that way is not relevant. It is not a valid defense, and the company was guilty of breaking the law.[42] The very busy 1960s concluded the next year with a case in which the Court upheld Section 2 of the Clayton and Robinson-Patman Acts against a company charging higher prices to an independent wholesale and retail distributor than it did its branded dealers. The suit had an interesting twist, in that a wholesaler had sold to a subsidiary that had sold to its subsidiary, and it was the latter that was a competitor of the plaintiff.[43]

Significant government victories and losses in the Supreme Court are listed below:

Government Federal Trade Commission and Clayton Act Cases in the Supreme Court, 1960–Present:
Government Victories:
1. *FTC v. Henry Brock and Company*, 1960.
2. *FTC v. Anheuser-Busch, Inc.*, 1960.
3. *Brown Shoe Company v. United States*, 1962.
4. *United States v. Borden Company*, 1962.
5. *FTC v. Sun Oil Company*, 1963.
6. *United States v. National Dairy Products Corporation*, 1963.
7. *United States v. Philadelphia National Bank*, 1963.
8. *United States v. El Paso Natural Gas Company*, 1964.
9. *United States v. Aluminum Company of America*, 1964.
10. *United States v. Penn-Olin Chemical Company*, 1964.
11. *United States v. Continental Can Company*, 1964.
12. *FTC v. Colgate-Palmolive Company*, 1965.
13. *FTC v. Consolidated Foods*, 1965.
14. *United States v. Von's Grocery Company*, 1966.
15. *United States v. Pabst Brewing Company*, 1966.
16. *FTC v. Procter & Gamble Company*, 1967.
17. *Ford Motor Company v. United States*, 1972.
18. *United States v. Falstaff Brewing Corporation*, 1973.
19. *California Dental Association v. FTC*, 1999.
Government Losses:
1. *FTC v. Fred Meyer, Inc.*, 1968.
2. *United States v. General Dynamics Corporation*, 1974.
3. *Great Atlantic & Pacific Tea Company, Inc. v. FTC*, 1979.

The 1970s to the Present

Since the 1960s were unusually busy with these cases, a slowdown seemed likely, and it began in the 1970s and continues through the present. The government did win a case in 1972 when the Court upheld a Section 7 Celler-Kefauver Act suit against the nation's number two automobile manufacturer who had bought the assets of an independent manufacturer of spark plugs. Prior to the acquisition, the automobile company was the number one purchaser of plugs from independents. The Court held that the acquisition of the assets and the trade name might substantially lessen competition.[44] The government won again the next year when Section 7 of the Clayton Act was used to make the country's fourth largest beer producer divest itself of the largest seller of beer in a regional market. The Court said the acquiring company was a potential competitor to the acquired one, even though it would not have been a new entrant to the market. Its position on the edge of a market exerted a beneficial influence on the market's competitive condition.[45] One year later, in 1974, the government lost a Clayton Act Section 7 case it brought against a deep-mining coal company that had acquired a strip-mining company. The Court said there was not a substantial lessening of competition, as the acquired company did not have sufficient reserves to make it a significant competitive force. It could not compete effectively for long-term contracts.[46]

In 1977 the Court dismissed a Clayton Act Sections 4 and 7 suit brought against one of the country's two largest bowling equipment manufacturers who was also the largest operator of bowling centers. It had acquired some bowling centers that had defaulted in their payments for bowling equipment, but a regional operator of bowling centers claimed injury due to the acquisitions. The Court, however, said the regional company would have suffered the same loss had the acquired centers secured refinancing or had they been bought by someone else, and that the company was trying to get damages for profits it would have received had the acquired centers been closed.[47] That same year the Court denied a Clayton Act Section 4 suit, as well as a Sherman Act Section 1 suit, against manufacturers who had sold to specialized contractors, who in turn sold to general contractors who then sold to state and local governments. The latter alleged price-fixing and wanted triple damages. However, the Court refused to use the pass-on theory by an indirect purchaser. It would create a serious risk of multiple liability for the defendants. There would be massive multiparty litigation involving many distribution levels and including large classes of ultimate consumers remote from the defendant. Therefore, only direct purchasers have standing to bring triple damage suits.[48] One year later, in 1978, the Court did allow a foreign nation to bring triple damage suits.[49] The following year the Court ruled against the government's attempt to use Section 2 of the Clayton and Robinson-Patman

Acts against a large supermarket chain that made a deal with a dairy company to supply it with private label milk in a metropolitan area, then solicited other dairy companies to do the same. It then went back to the first company and told them to make a better offer, which they did. The Court said that since the dairy company was just meeting competition, the supermarket company was not liable.[50]

There were three suits of note in the 1980s. A 1983 case found Section 2 of the Clayton and Robinson-Patman Acts violated by the selling of a product to a wholesaler in one state at a higher price than to one in a neighboring state, without proof that competition was being met.[51] In 1986 the Court dismissed a Section 2 Robinson-Patman Act and Sections 1 and 2 Sherman Act case against twenty-one Japanese corporations or Japanese-controlled American corporations by a U.S. manufacturer of color television sets. The claim was that, over a twenty-year period, the companies had conspired to drive American firms from the market by predatory pricing. The Court held that these types of conspiracies are speculative in that they must sustain substantiated losses in order to recover uncertain gains. In this case the alleged conspiracy was implausible because it had not succeeded. The firms had not, despite the period of years, been able to dominate the market here, at least to the extent of being able to reap monopoly prices.[52] In that same year, the Court turned down a Clayton Act Section 16 request for an injunction by the fifth largest beef packer in the country to stop a proposed merger of the second and third largest companies. The Court felt the merger did not constitute a threat of antitrust injury.[53]

Four more cases appeared in the 1990s, two of which came in 1990. In one, the Court ruled against a Clayton Act Section 4 triple damage suit that was accompanied by a Sherman Act Section 1 claim. One company sued another because the latter encouraged its dealers to match the prices of independents, causing the sales of the company bringing the suit to drop. However, the Court found no antitrust injury. The losses did not flow from the harmful effects on dealers and consumers. Cutting prices to increase business is often the essence of competition, and the prices were above predatory levels.[54] In the other case, a Section 2 Robinson-Patman Act suit was upheld. It was brought against a company that sold gasoline to independent retailers in a metropolitan area but also sold to two distributors and that gave the latter substantial discounts. Both distributors eventually sold the gas at retail and their sales volumes increased while the other stations declined. The Court felt that the discount was illegal because it was not tied to the supplier's savings or the wholesalers' costs.[55]

In 1993 a case concerned a fight within the tobacco industry itself. It was a Section 2 Clayton and Robinson-Patman Act suit brought by one company against another, and they were two of the six firms that dominate the concentrated industry. It involved an allegation of predatory pricing. The Court dismissed the suit, holding that the laws are applicable only if price discrimination threatens to injure competition, and that predatory pricing schemes, in general, are implausible, and are even more improbable when they require coordinated action among several firms.[56]

In 1999 the Court rendered a decision favorable to the Federal Trade Commission. The case was *California Dental Association v. Federal Trade Commission*,[57] and the issue was whether the FTC had jurisdiction over the advertising guidelines the group issued to its members. The agency said those guidelines violated Section 5 in that they restricted two types of truthful, nondeceptive advertising: price advertising, particularly discounted fees, and advertising relating to the quality of dental services. A unanimous Court speaking through Justice Souter held that the FTC Act did give the agency jurisdiction over an association that provides substantial economic benefit to its for-profit members, even though the association itself was a nonprofit one.

Significant private suits in the Supreme Court are listed below:

Private Federal Trade Commission and Clayton Act Cases in the Supreme Court, 1960–Present:
Victories for Plaintiffs:
1. *Utah Pie Company v. Continental Baking Company*, 1967.
2. *Hanover Shoe v. United Shoe Machinery Corporation*, 1968.
3. *Perkins v. Standard Oil Company of California*, 1969.
4. *Pfizer, Inc. v. Government of India*, 1978.
5. *Falls City Industries, Inc. v. Vanco Beverage, Inc.*, 1983.
6. *Texaco, Inc. v. Hasbrouck*, 1990.
Losses by Plaintiffs:
1. *Tampa Electric Company v. Nashville Coal Company*, 1961.
2. *Brunswick Corporation v. Pueblo Bowl-O-Mat, Inc.*, 1977.
3. *Illinois Brick Company v. Illinois*, 1977.
4. *Matushita Electric Industrial Corporation v. Zenith Radio Corporation*, 1986.
5. *Cargill, Inc. v. Montfort of Colorado, Inc.*, 1986.
6. *Atlantic Richfield Company v. USA Petroleum Company*, 1990.
7. *Brooke Group, Ltd. v. Brown and Williamson Tobacco Corporation*, 1993.

WHAT DOES IT ALL MEAN?

As with the Sherman Act, it is sometimes difficult to understand the significance of the Federal Trade Commission, Clayton, Robinson-Patman, and Celler-Kefauver Acts, as well as the Supreme Court decisions interpreting them. Again, an obvious reason for that has been the steady decline of cases since the end of the 1960s. As mentioned with regard to the Sherman Act, courts in general and the Supreme Court in particular have become conservative in nature due to appointments by conservative presidents, resulting in a reluctance to interfere in business activities. Government staff in charge of antitrust prosecutions, such as the Justice Department and the Federal Trade Commission, take their lead from the president, and therefore do not bring many cases. Another pattern follows: The government has had just one major suit (1999) under these statutes reach the Supreme Court since the end of the 1970s. The other suits that have reached the Court since are private ones, and those bringing them lose about two-thirds of the time, making the filing of these suits even less likely. Ironically, private suits were seldom brought in the 1960s, when the chances of winning were better, but that might have been because the government was taking care of the situation. Both the Justice Department and the Federal Trade Commission were bringing cases and were winning almost every one they brought. Presidents and their administrations were vigorous in bringing cases, and the Supreme Court, with its liberal bent, was highly receptive to the government's position. Since history tends to be cyclical, the days of the big antitrust suits might return, but it will take changes in executive and judicial thinking for that to happen. As mentioned previously, perhaps the Microsoft case is an inkling of what might be ahead.

SUMMARY

The Federal Trade Commission Act as well as the Clayton Act and its amendments were passed to try to eliminate the gaps in the Sherman Act. To a large extent they succeeded, mainly due to administrations that were eager to use the laws, and the Supreme Court's willingness to interpret them the government's way. This chapter has attempted to trace the evolution of the Court's interpretation of these laws in a chronological fashion in order to better understand the evolutionary role of laws and to show the development of patterns in their interpretation. As has been apparent, the Supreme Court justices do not mechanically apply the law to the case, due to an element of subjectivity. The justices have their political, social, and economic values, and these, by their nature, play a role in decision-making, as does the time frame in which the decisions are given (i.e., conservative times, more liberal times, a healthy economy, an economy marred by high inflation or a recession, or even national emergencies). Thus, decisions of the Court must be looked at in their various settings, and the chronological approach is helpful. One other fact that should be apparent is that laws are seldom 100 percent precise. That is because most major laws are a result of compromise, which means that differing ideas are included in them. The lack of precision, in turn, gives the justices more room to interpret the laws as they think most proper. The fact that many laws are imprecise is good, because the resultant flexibility renders the law adaptable to changing situations without the necessity of amending or rewriting the law. In any event, antitrust history is important in any examination of the role of government in our economy. If there is an impetus for a revival of antitrust activity, it might come from the enormity of the mergers taking place recently. As will be seen in later chapters, these megamergers, both within industries and cutting across industries, might just force the government, however reluctantly, to bring some suits. Whether the courts will respond favorably to these suits is another matter. Certainly the current Supreme Court is not very receptive to the government taking an active role in the economy.

QUESTIONS FOR DISCUSSION

1. Why was the Wheeler-Lea Amendment needed?
2. Why was the Robinson-Patman Act needed?
3. Why was the Celler-Kefauver Act needed?
4. What procedural changes did the Hart-Scott-Rodino Act enact?
5. Is it important that the FTC brought most of the pre-1960 Clayton Act cases instead of the Justice Department?
6. Why did private parties not bring many cases under the FTC and Clayton Acts (pre-1960)?
7. With the government winning almost every case since the start of the sixties, why has it stopped bringing FTC and Clayton Act cases?
8. Why have private FTC and Clayton Act suits not fared well before the Supreme Court in recent years?
9. Is the Federal Trade Commission still an important agency?
10. Is the Clayton Act still an important law?
11. Are megamergers something to be concerned about?
12. Do you foresee a renewal of antitrust activity?

RECOMMENDED READING

Langran, Robert W. *The Supreme Court: A Concise History*. New York: Peter Lang Publishing, Inc., 2004.
———. *The United States Supreme Court*. 5th ed. Needham Heights, MA: Pearson Custom Publishing. 2004. Chapters 5–15.
Schnitzer, Martin. *Contemporary Government and Business Relations*. 4th ed. Boston, MA: Houghton Mifflin Co., 1990. Chapters 6 and 8.

NOTES

1. 253 U.S. 421 (1920).
2. *FTC v. Beech-Nut Packing Co.*, 257 U.S. 346 (1922).
3. *Standard Fashion Co. v. Magrane-Houston Co.*, 258 U.S. 346 (1922).

4. *FTC v. Winsted Co.*, 258 U.S. 483 (1922).
5. 260 U.S. 568 (1923).
6. *FTC v. Sinclair Refining Co.*, 261 U.S. 463 (1923).
7. *Eastman Kodak Co. v. Southern Photo Co.*, 273 U.S. 359 (1927).
8. *FTC v. Raladam Co.*, 283 U.S. 643 (1931).
9. *FTC v. Algoma Lumber Co.*, 291 U.S. 67 (1934).
10. *FTC v. R. F. Keppel & Brothers, Inc.*, 291 U.S. 304 (1934).
11. *Pick Manufacturing Co. v. General Motors Corporation*, 299 U.S. 3 (1936).
12. *Corn Products Refining Co. v. FTC*, 324 U.S. 726 (1945).
13. *FTC v. A. E. Staley Manufacturing Co.*, 324 U.S. 746 (1945).
14. *Bigelow v. RKO Radio Pictures, Inc.*, 327 U.S. 251 (1946).
15. *FTC v. Cement Institute*, 333 U.S. 683 (1948).
16. *FTC v. Morton Salt Co.*, 334 U.S. 586 (1948).
17. *Standard Oil of California v. United States*, 337 U.S. 293 (1949).
18. *Standard Oil Co. v. FTC*, 340 U.S. 231 (1951).
19. *FTC v. Motion Picture Advertising Service Co.*, 344 U.S. 392 (1953).
20. *Automatic Canteen Company of America v. FTC*, 346 U.S. 61 (1953).
21. *United States v. duPont and Co.*, 353 U.S. 586 (1956).
22. *FTC v. Simplicity Pattern Co., Inc.*, 360 U.S. 55 (1959).
23. *FTC v. Henry Brock and Co.*, 363 U.S. 166 (1960).
24. *FTC v. Amheuser-Busch, Inc.*, 363 U.S. 536 (1960).
25. *Tampa Electric Co. v. Nashville Coal Co.*, 365 U.S. 320 (1961).
26. *Brown Shoe Co. v. United States*, 370 U.S. 294 (1962).
27. *United States v. Borden Co.*, 370 U.S. 460 (1962).
28. *FTC v. Sun Oil Co.*, 371 U.S. 505 (1963).
29. *United States v. National Dairy Products Corporation*, 372 U.S. 29 (1963).
30. *United States v. Philadelphia National Bank*, 374 U.S. 321 (1963).
31. *United States v. El Paso Natural Gas Co.*, 376 U.S. 651 (1964).
32. *United States v. Aluminum Company of America*, 377 U.S. 271 (1964).
33. *United States v. Penn-Olin Chemical Co.*, 378 U.S. 158 (1964).
34. *United States v. Continental Can Co.*, 378 U.S. 441 (1964).
35. *FTC v. Colgate-Palmolive Co.*, 380 U.S. 375 (1965).
36. *FTC v. Consolidated Foods*, 380 U.S. 592 (1965).
37. *United States v. Von's Grocery Co.*, 384 U.S. 270 (1966).
38. *United States v. Pabst Brewing Co.*, 384 U.S. 546 (1966).
39. *FTC v. Procter & Gamble Co.*, 386 U.S. 568 (1967).
40. *Utah Pie Co. v. Continental Baking Co.*, 386 U.S. 685 (1967).
41. *FTC v. Fred Meyer, Inc.*, 390 U.S. 341 (1968).
42. *Hanover Shoe v. United Shoe Machinery Corporation*, 392 U.S. 481 (1968).
43. *Perkins v. Standard Oil Company of California*, 395 U.S. 642 (1969).
44. *Ford Motor Co. v. United States*, 405 U.S. 562 (1972).
45. *United States v. Falstaff Brewing Corporation*, 410 U.S. 526 (1973).
46. *United States v. General Dynamics Corporation*, 415 U.S. 486 (1974).
47. *Brunswick Corporation v. Pueblo Bowl-O-Mat, Inc.*, 429 U.S. 477 (1977).
48. *Illinois Brick Co. v. Illinois*, 431 U.S. 720 (1977).
49. *Pfizer, Inc. v. Government of India*, 434 U.S. 308 (1978).
50. *Great Atlantic & Pacific Tea Co., Inc. v. FTC*, 440 U.S. 69 (1979).
51. *Falls City Industries, Inc. v. Vanco*, 460 U.S. 428 (1983).

52. *Matsushita Electric Industrial Corporation v. Zenith Radio Corporation*, 475 U.S. 574 (1986).

53. *Cargill, Inc., v. Montfort of Colorado, Inc.*, 479 U.S. 104 (1986).

54. *Atlantic Richfield Co. v. USA Petroleum Co.*, 495 U.S. 328 (1990).

55. *Texaco, Inc. v. Hasbrouck*, 496 U.S. 543 (1990).

56. *Brooke Group, Ltd. v. Brown and Williamson Tobacco Corporation*, 509 U.S. 209 (1993).

57. *California Dental Association v. FTC*, 526 U.S. 756 (1999).

SOCIAL REGULATION OF BUSINESS

6

Government and the Consumer

In a market economy, consumer sovereignty is an important institution because consumption is supposed to be the basic rationale for economic activity. As Adam Smith said, "Consumption is the sole end and purpose of all production; and the interest of the producer ought to be attended to only as far as it is necessary for promoting that of the consumer."[1] Production is the means; consumption is the end. On the one hand, those producers that effectively satisfy the wants of consumers are rewarded by large monetary returns, which in turn enable them to purchase the goods and services they require in their operations. On the other hand, those producers that do not respond to the wants of consumers will not remain in business long.

Freedom of choice is linked to consumer sovereignty. In fact, a basic rationale that is offered for the existence of a market economy is the freedom of choice it offers to consumers.[2] They are free to accept or reject whatever is produced in the marketplace; thus they are paramount to the operation of a market economy, since production has to be oriented toward fulfilling their desires. It is assumed that consumers are capable of making rational decisions, and in an economy dominated by the existence of a large number of buyers and sellers, this assumption has some merit.[3] But parity between consumers and producers does not exist in the complex world of today. Consumers are confronted with many products and not enough information to make rational choices.

CONSUMER PROTECTION

For many years the relationship between buyer and seller was governed by the common-law concept of caveat emptor, "Let the buyer beware." Thus, in an argument between the buyer and seller over the purchase of a horse that turned out to be lame, the burden of proof was on the buyer to convince a judge or jury that the seller deliberately misrepresented the condition of the horse before it was purchased. There had to be a legal precedent before the buyer could prove his case. Otherwise, it was assumed that both buyer and seller were equally knowledgeable when it came to horse-trading. If one was not, that was his misfortune.

Two things happened that eventually led to consumer protection laws. The first was the Industrial Revolution, which provided a wide variety of manufactured products ranging from cars to refrigerators. The average person—in fact, even the most intelligent—did not have the ability or the time to be an expert on the intricacies of the many products that industry produced. Second, the advantage passed to the producers because they were able to take the initiative in changing the techniques of production that increased the volume and variety of consumer goods. They were also able to develop skilled marketing techniques, including advertising, that influenced the consumer's choice of goods. It can be argued that the purpose of advertising is to entice consumers into buying products they do not need.

The Consumer Movement

Consumer movements have not been as strong or exercised as much influence in the United States as other movements, such as the civil rights and environmental movements of the 1960s. Consumers are much more numerous and harder to organize than environmentalists, nor do they have the fervor. Generally, consumers coalesce around a particular issue, such as automobile safety. Then when laws are passed, the issues tend to disappear. The occasional identification of consumer interests, however, does not eliminate their frequent conflicts with producers over a wide variety of areas, ranging from false or misleading advertising to product safety. There has been an increase in the number of consumer groups in the United States in recent years. Examples are the National Consumer's League and Consumers Union.[4] They have expanded the policy area of consumerism.

Consumer movements have been much stronger in Europe than in the United States. The oldest type of consumer organization is the cooperative, which originated in Rochdale, England, in 1844. European cooperatives handle a significant volume of retail trade. They obtain their capital from members on the basis of a fixed return. American cooperative experience has been far more limited. The efficiency and low profit margins of American grocery chains and supermarkets have provided stiff competition to cooperatives and have weakened their appeal to consumers. While they have had some success, it is limited to certain areas of the country.

The laws protecting consumers are of an infinite variety, but it is possible to divide them into three main categories. The first category includes laws designed to protect consumers from the adulteration, misbranding, or mislabeling of food, drugs, and cosmetics.[5] The second category includes laws designed to protect consumers from unfair competition, such as false or misleading advertising or various forms of product misrepresentation. These laws generally involve some form of disclosure. An example is the Consumer Credit Protection Act of 1968, which requires banks to provide information on the true rate of interest charged to borrowers. The third category of consumer protection laws involves product safety. Their purpose is to protect consumers from the harmful use of products. Implicit in product safety legislation is that the concept of consumer sovereignty is inadequate if there are external costs in a product's consumption.

CONSUMER PROTECTION AND THE LAW

Pure Food, Drugs, and Cosmetics Legislation

State and local government provisions against product adulteration or fraud have a long history. Sanitary regulation, inspection of weights and measures, and the like were established functions when the country was created. With relatively local self-sufficiency, particularly in food, local regulation protected the public reasonably well. However, development of mass transportation and the improvement of food processing techniques made the problem of consumer protection more complex. State legislation against the adulteration of food and drugs began in Virginia in 1848 and Ohio in 1853. It spread to most of the other states during the remainder of the century. But interstate competition prevented any state from raising its standards far out of line with other states and made federal regulation necessary.

The Pure Food and Drug Act of 1906

The Pure Food and Drug Act of 1906 was adopted only after several decades of public concern about food adulteration and patent medicine fraud. Pure food bills were first introduced in Congress as early as 1890, but were opposed by business interests. However, public sentiment for protection increased, which eventually led to the passage of the act. There were several factors that were responsible for the increase in public interest, not the least of which was the publication of *The Jungle*, a book written by Upton Sinclair in 1906[6] that described business practices in the meat-packing industry in Chicago. Companies were alleged to have used chemical substances to hide the odor of spoiled meat that was sold to the public. The companies were also supposed to have used coloring substances to make the meat look fresh. The book was an immediate bestseller.

President Theodore Roosevelt, who read the book,[7] ordered an immediate investigation of the meat-packing industry, and a pure food bill that had been bottled up in committee took a new lease on life and was passed. The Pure Food and Drug Act of 1906 is considered to be the first significant piece of consumer protection legislation in the nation's history. Its main provisions are as follows:

1. The Federal Food and Drug Administration was formed to administer and enforce the provisions of the act.
2. The law prohibited the sale in interstate commerce of adulterated or misbranded food and drugs. Adulteration was defined as the hiding of damage or inferiority through the use of artificial covering or coating, the addition of poisonous or other deleterious ingredients injurious to health, and the inclusion of decomposed or diseased animals in vegetable substances.
3. Food and drugs were considered misbranded if their packages or labels bore statements that were false and misleading, or if one was sold under the label of another. Food was regarded as misbranded if its weight or measure was not plainly shown, as were drugs if their packages or labels bore false claims of their curative powers.[8]
4. Criminal sanctions were provided, with a fine of up to $200 for a first offense and $300 or one year in prison for subsequent offenses.
5. Forfeiture of adulterated or misbranded products upon their entry into interstate commerce was used as a remedy to prevent public injury.

The Food and Drug Act was, for the most part, largely ineffective. Its administration was hampered by inadequate congressional appropriations. Political pressure was placed on the Food and Drug Administration to weaken its enforcement of the law. It did have some successes, notably in barring the sale of dangerous products to the public, and in the area of product liability. Its remedies were weak. Fines were small, and juries were reluctant to convict local manufacturers.

The Food, Drug, and Cosmetics Act of 1938

The rationale for the passage of this act was a resurgence of public interest in consumer protection that developed during the Depression of the 1930s. A number of books were published that exposed various consumer abuses, including false or misleading advertising. The FDA itself exhibited products that it had seized. Filthy, decayed, and insect-infested food was displayed for the public to see. Pictures of women blinded, disfigured, or paralyzed from the use of patent medicine were shown. The catalyst for the passage of the Food, Drug, and Cosmetics Act occurred when consuming a product called

Elixir Sulfanilamide that had been marketed without ever being tested for toxicity killed almost one hundred persons.[9]

The Food, Drug, and Cosmetics Act expanded consumer protection in the following ways:

1. It enlarged the range of affected products to include cosmetics and therapeutic devices.
2. It broadened the definition of adulteration and misbranding. Food was defined as adulterated if it contained any poisonous or deleterious substances, or if it was prepared under conditions that might result in contamination with filth or injury to health.
3. A food sold under another name had to be marked clearly as an imitation, and foods bearing proprietary names had to be labeled with the common or usual name of the product.

However, recent years have witnessed increasing litigation and problems within the drug industry. In 2004, pharmaceutical Warner Lambert, whose parent company is Pfizer, pled guilty to the promotion of unapproved uses of the drug Neurontin, and agreed to pay some $430 million in fines and civil damages.

Drug Amendments of 1958 and 1962

The Food, Drug, and Cosmetics Act of 1938 was amended by the Delaney clause of 1958, which prohibits the addition to food of any substance known to produce cancer in any form, dosage, or under any set of circumstances.[10] The act was also amended in 1962 to extend the authority of the FDA, particularly in the area of drugs. The reason for this amendment came from hearings held in 1959 by the Senate Antitrust and Monopoly Subcommittee. It was argued that drug companies devoted inordinate time and research to the development of patented new drugs that represented only a minor modification of existing formulas. The companies would then exploit the patent protection through expensive promotion campaigns in which extravagant claims for these drugs were impressed on doctors and consumers.[11] Most drug innovations were characterized as socially wasteful.[12]

Thus, it was apparent that accurate information about new drugs would be provided only if the federal government regulated the manufacturers' claim of effectiveness. The primary feature of this amendment is that a manufacturer must prove to the satisfaction of the FDA that a drug must have the curative powers the manufacturer claims for it. No drug can be put on the market unless approved by the FDA, which can also remove a drug from the market if it has evidence that the drug carries a threat to health.

The Medical Device Amendment of 1976

Concern over medical devices, particularly the Dalkon Shield, led to this amendment to the Food, Drug, and Cosmetics Act of 1938. The Dalkon Shield was an Intra-Uterine Device (IUD) that was used for birth control.[13] It was a copper device shaped like a coil that was inserted into a woman's uterus. It caused a number of health problems among women, including infertility, scarring, and infection. This amendment gave the FDA the right to require premarket safety testing of medical devices. It exempted medical devices that had been on the market prior to its passage, including breast implants, which have created problems for some women. However, if the FDA believes an exempted product is dangerous, it can require manufacturers to prove its safety. In 2005, the FDA issued a number of medical device recalls, including 206,000 intravenous pumps made by Baxter Healthcare and pacemakers made by Guidant Corp.[14]

Other Food and Drug Laws

The Meat Inspection Act of 1907 was a companion to the Food and Drug Act of 1906. It prohibited the use of adulterants to hide meat decay or to color meat. It also provided that the Department of Agriculture must inspect the slaughtering, packing, and canning plants that ship meat in interstate commerce. The Wholesale Meat Inspection Act of 1967 amended the 1907 act. It is designed to force states to raise their inspection standards to those of the federal government. The Poultry Products Inspection Act of 1957 gave the Department of Agriculture the right to inspect poultry sold in interstate commerce. The Wholesale Poultry Act of 1968 offers federal government aid to the states so that they can establish their own inspection program. In drugs, the Public Health and Service Act of 1944 gave the FDA the authority to ensure the safety of vaccines, blood, serum, and other biological products. The Nutrition, Labeling, and Education Act of 1990 requires the agency to develop nutrition labeling for packaged food items, and the Generic Drug Enforcement Act of 1992 permits it to oversee the generic drug industry.

THE FOOD AND DRUG ADMINISTRATION

The FDA is a regulatory agency that exists within the executive branch of government as a part of the Department of Health and Human Services. It possesses quasi-legislative and quasi-judicial powers, as all regulatory agencies do. The power to make rules and regulations has been delegated to these agencies by legislative fiat. The only important difference between an agency rule and a law enacted by a legislative body is that the rule may be slightly more susceptible to attack because it was not made by elected officials. They can also implement policy or legislation through a process of initiating and settling cases. For many types of cases, the procedures are carefully outlined: Hearings are often prescribed, records are required, and so on. Furthermore, there are often elaborate provisions for judicial review.

All regulatory agencies, including the FDA, as agents of Congress, reflect group demands for positive action. They are not supposed to be judges like the courts; rather, they are supposed to be activists and initiate policy in accordance with their policy interests. For example, when the FDA ferrets out deceptive practices involving food, drugs, and cosmetics either through its own investigation or through information gained from an outside source, it initiates action in the name of the FDA against the party involved. It then adjudicates the very case it initiates. If the case reaches a formal hearing and goes to a hearing examiner for an initial decision, it is not at that point subject to FDA control. But after the examiner renders the decision, the FDA may reverse it. The result is that the FDA can control the decisions rendered in almost all the cases it initiates.

The FDA and Diet Pills

Many Americans resort to the use of diet pills as an easy way to lose weight, and numerous remedies are on the market. One such remedy is called Pondimin, the brand name for fenfluramine, which was manufactured and sold by American Home Products and its subsidiary Wyeth-Ayers Laboratories. It also sold a companion drug called Redux. Fenfluramine had been sold since the 1970s but became widely used in the 1990s when doctors prescribed it in combination with phentermine. When taken alone, phentermine was never associated with health problems and it remains on the market.

However, in 1997 the FDA pushed for the withdrawal of Pondimin and Redux, citing a study that linked the drugs to potentially fatal health problems. A 36-year-old woman named Debbie Lovett sued American Home Products and Wyeth-Ayers Laboratories over health problems she contended were caused by the drug she had taken for more than three months starting in October 1995. Her attorney argued before a jury that Lovett suffered from fatigue and shortness of breath and probably would need surgery to replace heart valves as her ailment progressed. Lawyers for American Home Products argued that Lovett was seeking compensation for a health condition she had before using the drug and said her weight was a bigger problem than the drug. A jury in Canton, Texas awarded her $23 million in damages, but a settlement was reached out of court.[15]

The Lovett lawsuit was only one of many brought against American Home Products, which agreed in January 2000 to pay up to $4.8 billion over 16 years to settle claims for more than three thousand consumers who took the weight-loss drug.[16] The agreement would establish a $1 billion fund for medical tests to check for heart damage for anybody who took the drug and to provide treatment if necessary. An additional $2.3 billion would be used to pay damages to those who now suffer or later develop moderate to severe heart valve problems. Payment, based on age and severity of condition, would range from $500 to $1.4 million. Those with less severe problems could get more money later if their condition worsens. Lest we forget, up to $429 million would go to the plaintiffs' lawyers.

The 1994 Dietary Supplement Health and Education Act regulates dietary supplements as foods, not drugs. Thus, such supplements are considered safe until proven otherwise, and there is no required testing for safety. The FDA can act if there is evidence to show that the product is unsafe or harmful, and can pursue action against manufacturers that make unproven claims. In 2004, the FDA issued warning letters to 23 companies distributing Androstenedione, a dietary supplement, requesting that they prove its safety. There are also labeling requirements, but no regulations regarding dosage, standards of quality, or potency. Also in 2004 dietary supplements containing ephedra, which has been suspected in 155 deaths, have been banned.

DISCLOSURE

A second area of government involvement in consumer protection is the various forms of disclosure such as advertising and product warranties. This area is rather broad, but generally the practices that come under its purview are covered by Section 5 of the Federal Trade Commission Act of 1914, which gives the FTC the right to prevent unfair competition practices, including those that affect consumers adversely. A rather common practice over the years has been false or misleading advertising. But advertising is only one area of the entire subject of disclosure. There are various product-labeling requirements designed to protect consumers against misrepresentation and fraud. There are also laws designed to protect consumers against excessive credit charges. Finally, there are laws that cover the terms of consumer product warranties.

Advertising

The rationale for advertising is that for markets to work effectively, buyers must have accurate information about the quality and the characteristics of products offered for sale. Otherwise, markets are unlikely to enable consumers to make purchases maximizing their welfare within the limits of their resources. As a result of the increases in the complexity and variety of products and the value of people's time, there has been a major shift from consumer to seller in the comparative advantages of supplying consumer product information. But this increased reliance on sellers for information about products does not mean the information provided will be truthful. A seller's general purpose is to provide information that, if believed, will induce consumers to buy this product in preference to other sellers' products. The first demands for the control of advertising came at the turn of this century as a result of the false claims made by the many charlatans who populated the food and drug industries. Although the early postal laws were meant to deal with the wholesale distribution of false advertising by mail, it was not until 1914 when the Federal Trade Commission Act was passed that broad federal legal weapons against false or misleading advertising came into existence. As mentioned earlier, Section 5 of the act declared that unfair methods of competition in commerce were unlawful. Its intention went deep, for it authorized the FTC to proceed against various forms of antisocial business conduct over and above the unfair practices proscribed by the Sherman and Clayton Acts; for example, price-fixing and group buyouts.

The FTC did make an attempt to prosecute consumer fraud, but the courts generally took the side of the advertiser. For example, in 1931, the Supreme Court overturned an FTC ruling that Raladam, the manufacturer of Marmola, cease and desist from representing its product as a remedy for obesity. The Court found misrepresentation common among vendors of such nostrums and concluded that no damage had been done to Raladam's competitors.[17] The Court held that in the absence of proof to such an effect, the FTC could not act against consumer fraud. This decision led to proposals to amend the original Federal Trade Commission Act, which eventually led to the passage by Congress of the Wheeler-Lea Amendment of 1938.

The Wheeler-Lea Amendment

A Supreme Court justice once said about pornography that he couldn't define it, but he would know it if he saw it. The same can be said for deceptive advertising. The legal definitions of deceptive advertising are rather abstruse. The Federal Trade Commission Act contains a general prohibition of deceptive advertising and a definition of false advertising that makes clear that false representations are illegal and that failure to disclose material facts can be illegal. The FTC has used the following criteria in determining whether an advertisement is illegal.[18] An advertisement is illegal if:

1. it deceives a significant number of customers;
2. a false presentation or omission relates to facts important to consumers in their purchasing decisions, and

3. a false implication relates to facts that consumers use in their purchasing decisions.

Deceptive advertising can be harmful to the public interest for two reasons.[19] First, it harms consumers by causing them to have false beliefs about the nature of the products being advertised and thereby causes consumers to make different purchasing decisions from those they otherwise would have made. For example, a consumer may buy Product A because it promises to make him or her a better athlete, even though Product B is the better product. Second, it can be argued that, apart from its immediate bad consequences, deceptive advertising can lower the general level of trust essential to the proper functioning of a free market economy. Consequently, there is a strong feeling against deception even though it does no immediate harm.

Enforcement Procedure

The FTC has one standard procedure by which it can act to prevent deceptive practices such as false or misleading advertising. It can make a formal complaint against a company engaged in deceptive practices. The company, which is the respondent or accused party, is given an opportunity to enter into a consent settlement without formal litigation. If the respondent decides to contest the complaint, the matter is set for trial before an administrative law judge or hearing examiner, appointed by the FTC. The Commission and the respondent each are represented by their own attorneys. At the conclusion of the hearings, the judge issues his or her findings and an initial decision, which, if it goes against the prosecution, can be appealed to the full commission. The respondent can also appeal if the decision is against him or her.

Sweepstakes Advertising

Getting rich is an integral part of the American dream, and since the founding of our country, there have been many ways in which Americans have tried to do it. One way was to trade whiskey to the Native Americans for valuable furs that could be sold in Europe. Another way was to prospect for gold, first in California and then in Alaska. This required very hard work, and few people struck it rich. But as America became prosperous, more civilized ways developed to make a person wealthy. One way was to speculate in the stock market, but the problem is that you have to put up your own money with the risk that the stock market can crash. One can also play the lottery for a dollar or two. Then there are sweepstakes, such as the ones sponsored by the American Family Publishers and Publishers Clearing House. These sweepstakes sponsors send out form letters insinuating that the recipients of the letters have won the grand prize; never mind that approximately 200 million such letters are sent out with each mailing.[20]

Sweepstakes, particularly the ones run by American Family Publishers and Publishers Clearing House, have come under fire, and rightfully so, because their mailings are very misleading. The fine print is hard to find, and many people assume they have won.[21] In fact, over a two-year period a Virginia man won $1 million, $3.5 million, $5 million, and $11.2 million from Publishers Clearing House. At least, that is what the letter said. The only problem was that the money never materialized. There is also the inference that your chances are enhanced if you buy the magazines the publishers push. Some thirty-two states and the District of Columbia have initiated class-action suits against American Family Publishers, and twenty-six states have initiated class-action suits against Publishers Clearing House. On March 2, 2000 a settlement was reached whereby American Family Publishers agreed to pay $1.23 million in damages.[22] In New York the company agreed to pay $60 each to 12,000 New Yorkers who bought the magazines believing that would enhance their chances of winning.

Criticisms of Advertising

Advertising has been criticized for several reasons. First, it relies on psychological needs that play on human emotion rather than reason. An example would be alcohol and cigarette advertising that play on a person's desire to feel grown-up or to fit in. However, both contain powerful addictive drugs, which are a source of pleasure but also can damage one's health. Other ads play on the desire to achieve economic and social status. Second, children are also influenced by advertising to consume certain products that can be harmful. They are often led to consume a product because some sports hero or movie star endorses it.[23] Sometimes it can be a fictitious character such as Joe Camel, who supposedly became as recognizable as Mickey Mouse to children under the age of ten in the days before tobacco advertising was regulated. The ad, which was sponsored by R. J. Reynolds, portrayed a hip camel with a baseball cap on backwards and a cigarette hanging out of his mouth. The implication was that it is cool to smoke.

Labeling

Labeling of products is the second area of disclosure. It is designed to protect consumers from product misrepresentation. An example would be the claim by a clothing manufacturer that its men's suits are 100 percent wool when they are not. In 1939 Congress passed the Wool Products Labeling Act that requires that most products containing wool must show on the label the percentage of wool and other fibers used. The Fur Products Labeling Act of 1951 was passed to protect consumers against the mislabeling of furs, such as rab-bit fur being called mink. Manufacturers are required to attach labels to a garment showing the true name of the animal that produced the fur and indi-cating whether the fur is bleached or dyed. The Textile Fiber Products Identi-fication Act of 1958, which covers the labeling of textiles and fibers, protects consumers by requiring a disclosure on the label and in advertising of the exact fiber contents of all textile fibers other than wool marketed in interstate commerce.

Other Labeling Laws

The Flammable Fabrics Act of 1954 was passed as a result of deaths that had occurred when clothes, such as evening gowns, caught on fire.[24] The act requires that clothing labels contain notice that the product is highly flam-mable. Then there is the Cigarette Labeling and Advertising Act of 1965, which requires that cigarettes sold in interstate commerce be packaged and labeled with the warning that cigarettes can be injurious to health. The Poison Prevention Act of 1970 is designed to keep unsafe products from being used by children. Some drugs may also be required to carry the notice that their use may be habit-forming. Still other drugs must state on their label that they are not to be taken by pregnant women without first consulting a physician. Recently, U.S. consumers have called for labeling on genetically-modified foods, which are so identified in other countries; however, to date there has been no action by the FDA or Congress.

Credit

In the old days, Americans were accustomed to putting aside sufficient sav-ings in order to purchase homes, cars, appliances, clothes, and vacations. But all that began to change in the 1920s when charge accounts were introduced by companies such as Sears Roebuck and Montgomery Ward. Credit cards were introduced in the 1960s and 1970s, so Americans no longer had to post-pone self-gratification. Just about anything could be purchased by using credit cards. Banks, to remain competitive, also made credit easier to obtain. However, consumer information as to the terms of credit was incomplete, so it was difficult to make a rational choice between various alternative forms of loans. Today, most consumers are constantly bombarded by advertisements from banks and other lending institutions for credit cards that supposedly offer a low interest rate.

For many years, state laws regulated consumer credit activities. But the lack of uniformity among such laws, coupled with the need to protect con-sumers against fraudulent or unfair practices, led to the enactment of a num-ber of federal laws. One of the most significant of these laws is the Consumer

Credit Protection Act, more commonly known as the Truth-in-Lending Act (TILA), which was passed in 1968.

TILA/TISA

The Truth-in-Lending Act (TILA) of 1968 is a disclosure law designed to force creditors to inform consumers of the actual cost of credit. It requires that lenders disclose to borrowers basic information about the cost and terms of credit by providing every borrower with a separate disclosure statement. It regulates transactions in which a borrower puts up his or her home as collateral. A purpose of credit disclosure is to encourage competition in financing by making borrowers more aware of specific charges and other relevant credit information, thus enabling them to shop for the most favorable terms of credit. TILA also prohibits the issuance of a credit card except in response to an oral or written agreement. Under TILA, consumers can sue dishonest lenders for damages of $100 to $1,000. Companion legislation, the Truth in Savings Act (TISA) requires disclosure about interest rates and fees, and prohibits misleading or inaccurate advertising for checking and savings accounts.

Fair Credit Reporting Act of 1970

The Fair Credit Reporting Act requires consumer-reporting companies to provide consumers with information in his or her file to verify whether the credit is accurate or inaccurate. The purpose of the act is to protect the privacy of consumers against the issuance of credit reports that may contain erroneous information. It expressly obligates every consumer-reporting agency to report only accurate and up-to-date information to creditors who would seek information about the creditworthiness of consumers. Anyone seeking this credit information must identify themselves and certify the purpose for which they are seeking this information. However, there is a two-year statute of limitations from the point of violation, i.e., the issuance of a credit report. In 2001, the Supreme Court unanimously ruled in *TRW, Inc. v. Andrews* that the two-year limitation may only be waived in extreme circumstances.[25]

Fair Debt Collection Practices Act of 1977

This act limits the ways in which a debt collector can deal with a debtor. Overt force or other forms of coercion were often used to force debtors to pay their debts. The act limits the ways in which the debt collector can communicate with a debtor. The collector cannot communicate with the debtor at the debtor's place of employment where such communication is prohibited by the employer. The debt collector can only communicate with the debtor during certain hours of the day.[26] The act permits the cessation of communications between the debt collector and debtor if the latter in writing notifies the collector that he or she refused to pay the debt.

The Credit Card Disclosure Act of 1988

This act requires banks, department stores, and other issuers of credit cards to disclose clearly their interest rates, fees, method of calculating interest charges, and the grace period before interest charges begin to accrue. The act specifically aims at bulk mail credit card solicitations to potential consumers that do not disclose application fees. The act makes it easier for consumers to shop around for lower interest rates. The Equal Credit Opportunity Act prohibits discrimination against loan applicants based on race, sex, age, marital status, religion, national origin, or receipt of various types of government assistance. Under the 2003 Fair and Accurate Credit Transactions Act, companies must adopt rules for the proper disposal of consumer report information and records.

Warranties

A warranty under common law is a promise that affirms a fact or makes an affirmation related to the goods being sold. Since a warranty involves a promise, it becomes part of a contract.[27] Warranties are of two types—expressed and implied. Only the seller can give an express warranty. For example, any affirmation of a fact or a promise that relates to the goods creates an express warranty that the goods will match the fact or the promise. An implied warranty is automatically present in the contract unless it is surrendered by the buyer or excluded by the seller. An example of an implied warranty is a warranty of title by the seller. This ensures the buyer that no one can assert a hidden claim to the goods that is superior to the claims of the buyer.

The Consumer Product Warranty Act of 1975

This act was passed because consumers had become increasingly dissatisfied with product warranties, and had to resort to the courts for redress. Generally, this dissatisfaction centered on such problems as the purchase of a product that turned out to be a "lemon," delays in making repairs, excessive labor charges, the failure of companies to honor guarantees, unscrupulous service operators, and consumers' total lack of power to enforce compliance. The act's major provisions may be divided into two categories, which are as follows:

1. The first category pertains to consumer warranty provisions. To increase the product information available to consumers, prevent deception, and promote competition in the marketplace, any warrantor offering a written warranty must disclose the terms of the warranty in easily understood language.

2. The second category extended the Federal Trade Commissions' consumer protection powers to prescribe rules and regulations for deceptive practices. It was given the authority to move against local consumer abuses when state or local protection agencies were ineffectual. With respect to defective warranties, the FTC was given the power to seek injunctions against offenders and to represent itself in litigation. In addition, the FTC can initiate civil suits against offenders that knowingly engage in an act or practice determined to be unfair or deceptive.

THE FEDERAL TRADE COMMISSION

The Federal Trade Commission Act of 1914, as mentioned in chapter 6, created the Federal Trade Commission, an independent regulatory agency consisting of five members, each holding office for seven years. Section 5 of the act empowers the FTC to prevent unfair methods of competition and unfair or deceptive acts or practices in or affecting commerce. Originally, Section 5 was used to stop practices before they developed into violations of the antitrust laws. However, it has been interpreted to go further than the antitrust laws do to reach unfair business practices, whether or not they have an impact on competition. The current aim of the FTC's enforcement activities under Section 5 is both to protect fair competition and to assure that the consumer is not subjected to unfair or deceptive practices, without regard to their effect on competition. The responsibilities of the FTC can be broken down into two main categories—antitrust and unfair and deceptive business practices. The FTC is responsible for enforcing the following antitrust laws:

Antitrust Laws
1. The Clayton Act of 1914, specifically Section 2, which pertains to price discrimination; Section 3, which prohibits the use of tying contracts and exclusive dealership arrangements when they lessen competition; Section 7, which pertains to mergers and acquisitions; and Section 8, which pertains to interlocking directorates.
2. The Robinson-Patman Act of 1936, which amended Section 2 of the Clayton Act.
3. The Celler-Kefauver Act of 1950, which amended Section 7 of the Clayton Act.
4. The Hart-Scott-Rodino Antitrust Improvements Act of 1976, which requires advance notice of proposed mergers.

The FTC is responsible for monitoring unfair and deceptive business practices in the following areas:

Unfair and Deceptive Practices
Advertising
1. The Wheeler-Lea Amendment to the Clayton Act, 1938
Labeling
1. The Wool Products Labeling Act of 1940
2. The Fur Products Labeling Act of 1951
3. The Textile Fibers and Product Identification Act of 1958
4. The Cigarette Labeling and Advertising Act of 1965
5. The Fair Packaging and Labeling Act of 1966
Credit
1. The Truth-in-Lending Act of 1968
2. The Fair Credit Reporting Act of 1970
3. The Fair Debt and Collection Practices Act of 1977
4. The Credit Card Disclosure Act of 1988
Warranties
1. The Consumer Product Warranty Act of 1975

The FTC receives consumer complaints regarding fraud and abuses. Tele-marketing used to be one such set of complaints. In 2003, the FTC added the administration of the national "Do-Not-Call" registry to its responsibilities, with hopes that it will result in a reduction of nuisance telemarketing calls to consumers. The FTC received 635,173 complaints in 2004; of these 246,570 were identity theft complaints and 388,603 were fraud complaints. The top categories of consumer fraud complaints for 2004 include:

Internet Auctions—16 percent
Shop-at-Home/Catalog Sales—8 percent
Internet Services and Computer Complaints—6 percent
Foreign Money Offers—6 percent
Prizes/Sweepstakes and Lotteries—5 percent
Advance-Fee Loans and Credit Protection—3 percent
Business Opportunities and Work-at-Home—2 percent
Telephone Services—2 percent
Other (miscellaneous)—12 percent[28]

The Identity Theft Penalty Enhancement Act of 2004

The Identity Theft act amends U.S. code to establish penalties for identity theft. It created a separate crime of "aggravated identity theft" which is sub-ject to imprisonment of between two and five years. Aggravated identity theft includes abuses by employees at financial institutions, government agencies, and other institutions collecting personal information. In addition, courts may not provide probation, reduced or concurrent sentences for those found guilty of identity theft. The law acknowledges the increasing prevalence of identity theft. In 2004, the FTC issued its report, *National and State Trends in Fraud and Identity Theft.* The report estimates that 9.9 million people fell victim to identity theft in 2002, resulting in an overall cost to businesses and consumers of $53 billion. As many as 27.3 million consumers may have fallen victim to identity theft during the period 1998–2003.[29]

PRODUCT SAFETY

Until the 1960s, national product safety legislation consisted of isolated statutes designed to remedy specific hazards existing in a narrow range of product categories. Moreover, enforcement authority was divided among a number of federal agencies. For example, the Flammable Fabrics Act of 1953 was passed after serious injuries and deaths had resulted from the ignition of clothes made from synthetic fibers. Enforcement measures by the FDA include cease-and-desist orders, seizures of offending goods, and criminal penalties of a year's imprisonment, or fines of up to $5,000 for willful violations. The Bureau of Standards establishes tests of flammability. A 2006 FDA rule said that all mattresses sold after July 2007 must meet a new fire-resistant standard that limits the speed and intensity with which a flame can spread. Other examples of product safety laws and the agencies responsible for their enforcement are as follows:

1. The Federal Hazardous Substances Labeling Act of 1960 mandates warnings on the labels of potentially hazardous substances such as cleansing agents and paint removers. This act is administered by the Food and Drug Administration.
2. The Child Protection Act of 1966, also administered by the Food and Drug Administration, prevents the marketing of potentially harmful toys.
3. The National Traffic and Motor Vehicle Safety Act of 1966 concerns automobiles that include such features as an impact-absorbing steering wheel and column, safety latches and hinges, safety glass, and impact resistant gasoline tanks and connections. This act comes under the jurisdiction of the National Highway Traffic Safety Administration. Tires must be labeled with the name of the manufacturer or retreader and with certain safety information, including the maximum permissible load for the tire.
4. The Public Health Smoking Act of 1970 extends warnings about the hazards of cigarette smoking, and the Poison Prevention Packaging Act of the same year authorized the standards for child-resistant packaging of hazardous substances.

The Consumer Product Safety Act of 1972

One of the most important laws to be passed in a long time is the Consumer Product Safety Act. Fragmentation of legislation and generally ineffective controls over product hazards prompted the federal government to introduce new product safety legislation to protect the consumer. The act was a result of congressional findings that unsafe consumer products were widely distributed, and hence consumers were frequently unable to anticipate and guard against the risks entailed in their use. Findings before the Senate Committee on Commerce indicated that more than 20 million people were injured by consumer products annually.[30] Of that total, 110,000 people were permanently disabled, and 30,000 lost their lives. The annual cost to consumers was around $5.5 billion. It was estimated that 20 percent of those injuries could have been prevented if the manufacturers had produced safe, well-designed products.

The origins of the Consumer Products Safety Act are in the common law in that the manufacturer or seller is liable for injuries to a buyer or others caused by a defective or hazardous product. The common law imposes liability on a broad group of people involved in the marketing process, including suppliers, wholesalers, and retailers. Liability is assumed for injuries to the consumer when the results of such injury are reasonably foreseeable, regardless of whether the product itself is dangerous or harmful. A consumer need not prove that a manufacturer was guilty of negligence.

Provisions of the Consumer Product Safety Act

The Consumer Product Safety Act is broad in scope and affects those consumer products not already regulated by the federal government. When compared to earlier consumer-oriented legislation, the act not only possesses more effective legal and administrative sanctions, but also allows application of safety standards. Its basic provisions are as follows:

1. It created a five-member Consumer Product Safety Commission that functions as an independent regulatory agency. A major function of the Commission is the gathering and dissemination of information related to product injuries. In addition, the Commission was empowered to create an advisory council of fifteen members to provide information on product safety.
2. Section 14 of the act requires manufacturers to conduct a testing program to assure their products conform to established safety standards. After the products are tested, a manufacturer must provide distributors or retailers with a certificate stating that all applicable consumer product safety standards have been met. Section 14 also holds the manufacturer accountable for knowing all safety criteria applicable to the product and requires that safety standards be described in detail.

3. The Consumer Product Safety Commission also can require the use of specific labels that set forth the results of product testing. This requirement has a significant impact on the production process in which the design of new products must conform to federal safety standards that are formulated at various governmental and independent testing stations.
4. Section 15 requires a manufacturer to take corrective steps if he or she becomes aware that a product either fails to comply with an applicable consumer product safety rule or contains a defect that could create a substantial product hazard. The manufacturer has to inform the CPSC of the defect. If, after investigation, the Commission determines that a product hazard exists, the manufacturer—or distributor or retailer, for that matter—may be required to publicize the information to consumers.

In addition to the Consumer Product Safety Act, the Consumer Product Safety Commission is responsible for the administration of the following acts:

1. The Flammable Fabrics Labeling Act of 1954
2. The Refrigerator Safety Act of 1956
3. The Hazardous Substance Act of 1964
4. The Poison Prevention Packaging Act of 1970

Automobile Safety Regulation

Before the 1960s the automobile industry was largely unregulated. However, this changed dramatically during the 1960s when Ralph Nader wrote his book, *Unsafe at Any Speed*,[31] which dealt with what he called dangerous designs in American cars, particularly the Corvair produced by General Motors. Helped by General Motors' response, which was to hire investigators to find damaging evidence against him, Nader became the leader in a consumer movement that catalyzed around a demand for safer cars. Federal safety standards promulgated in the 1960s involved accident avoidance, crash protection, and post-crash survivability. Accident avoidance standards were set for braking systems, tires, windshields, lamps, and transmission controls. Occupant protection standards included requirements for seat belts, head restraints, and high-penetration resistant windshield glass. Exterior protection standards included the absorption capacity of front and rear bumpers. These and other standards are presented in table 6.1.

The National Highway Traffic Safety Administration

The National Highway Traffic Safety Administration (NHTSA) was created in 1966 to set safety standards for automobiles and other types of motor

vehicles. It has the authority to establish minimum safety standards for automobiles, trucks, and their accessories. It also has the right to set standards for
fuel economy and emissions, and it regulates the safety and performance of
new and used automobiles and trucks. It has initiated such safety features as
air bags, safety belts, collapsible steering columns, and penetration-resistant
windshields, and it has the power to order the recall of defective products. It
administers state and local community grant programs, and it conducts
research and development of new automobile safety techniques.

Costs of Automobile Safety Standards

Using the automobile industry as an example, there are both costs and benefits of safety standards. The costs of safety standards are the original cost of
meeting them as well as the costs of complying with them after the companies have had sufficient time to redesign the vehicles to accommodate the
standards at the lowest cost.[32] There is the cost of variable inputs required to
produce such safety devices as seat belts, padded dashboards, and other interior protection devices. There is also the cost of external production devices,
including the installation of safer, more durable bumpers. An important part
of safety standards cost is the fuel penalty that motorists have to pay as a
result of the weight added to cars, which is due in part to bumper standards.

The automobile industry had to meet additional safety standards by 1999.
Dual air bags were required. An antilock brake system that would keep cars
from skidding had been proposed. Beginning with 1997 models, all cars had
to have stronger side guards that required thicker padding. More roof padding

Table 6.1   Safety Standards for Passenger Cars

Standard	Effective Date
Occupant protection in interior impact	1968
Door locks	1968
Impact protection for driver from steering control	1968
Seat belt assemblies	1968
Windshield wiping system	1968
Head restraints	1969 (updated 2000)
Child seating system	1971
Flammability of interior materials	1972
Side door strength	1972
Roof crash resistance	1973 (updated 1999)
Frontal offset crash resistance	1997
Seat performance in rear impacts	1998
Side impact protection	1999
Advanced air bag safety	2000

Source: Robert W. Crandall, Howard K. Gruenspecht, Theodore E. Keeler, and Lester B. Lave, *Regulating the Automobile*. Washington, D.C.: The Brookings Institution, 1986, p. 47. (with updates from NHSTA)

was required to provide head protection. Cleaner exhaust had been mandated. Already, government regulations had eliminated 95 percent of pollutants out of car exhaust. However, catalytic converters that clean exhaust do not work until they get hot. Cold-start pollution had to be cut beginning with 1996 car models. This required the introduction of either a preheated catalyst or a converter.

Benefits of Automobile Safety Standards

Benefits accrue to persons and to society as a whole as a result of safety standards. One obvious benefit is the reduction in the number of injuries and fatalities caused by automobiles and other forms of auto-related accidents. There has been a reduction in the number of highway fatalities even though the population of the United States today is larger than it was when most of these safety standards were implemented. The reductions can be attributed in part to improved safety standards for automobiles, but also in part to other factors such as driver education and the 55-mile-per-hour speed limits.[33] Table 6.2 presents deaths and death rates from motor vehicle accidents for selected time periods.

Product Liability

The United States is a litigious society, which explains why it has more lawyers than the rest of the world combined. One area of litigation is product liability, which is a part of tort law. This field of the law is concerned with compensating one person for harm caused by the wrongful conduct of another. Courts impose monetary liability on firms whose products have caused personal injury. Liability originally depended on showing that a firm

Table 6.2   Deaths and Death Rates from Motor Vehicle Accidents, 1970–2002

Year	Number of Deaths (thousands)	Rate per 100,000 Population
1970	54.6	26.9
1980	53.2	22.5
1990	46.8	17.9
1995	43.4	15.9
1998	43.5	15.4
1999	43.0	15.3
2000	43.0	14.9
2001	43.7	14.8
2002	44.0	14.8

Source: Statistical Abstract of the United States 2004–2005. Washington, D.C.: U.S. Government Printing Office, 2004, p. 697.

had acted negligently, which meant it had failed to exercise that degree of due care as would be reasonably expected in similar circumstances. However, liability has become stricter in that the fault or negligence of the manufacturer is irrelevant; it is now imposed if the product is defective and the defect is unexpected by the consumer and causes injury.

MacPherson v. Buick Motor Company

Prior to this landmark case, privity of contract governed the relationships between buyer and seller. It meant that a plaintiff could sue only when he or she had a legally binding contract with the defendant. Thus, if a manufacturer caused the product defect, the consumer had no right to recovery because the consumer's contract was with the retailer, not the manufacturer. *MacPherson v. Buick* changed all this.[34] MacPherson, the owner of a Buick automobile, was injured when a defective spoke in a wheel broke when he was driving. He sued the company but it denied responsibility for two reasons. First, it had not produced the wheel, but had purchased it from a supplier; so if liability is attached to the defect in the wheel, the supplier should be the liable party. Second, Buick claimed lack of privity in that MacPherson had purchased the car from a dealer, not from Buick.

However, Buick's arguments were rejected by the Court. The decision ended the privity of contract requirement in product liability cases. Regardless of any contractual obligations, the Court held the manufacturer liable for injuries caused by its product. After this decision, product liability became a subset of tort law rather than contract law. The significance of the case is that plaintiffs in a suit can go directly to the manufacturer and bypass any intermediary, such as a retailer or wholesaler. They have to prove fault, which means that adequate warnings or reasonable safety features have not been provided.

Each year thousands of Americans sue manufacturers in a broad array of industries, alleging they were injured by unreasonably dangerous products including asbestos, drugs, medical devices, cars and trucks, toxic chemicals, and toys. Almost all plaintiffs settle out of court. Of the small proportion who go to trial, more than half win damage awards—multimillion dollar sums in a few cases. Nevertheless, the whole process can be expensive. In total, U.S. injury claims cost $152 billion in 1994. The U.S. tort system is the most expensive in the world. As a percentage of GDP, it takes up 2.2 percent, two and one-half times the average of industrial countries. Of every dollar awarded by the courts, less than half goes to victims.[35] It can prove to be very expensive to business firms. Insurance rates go up and bankruptcy can result.

Tort Law

Product liability is a part of tort law, which is concerned with a body of private wrongs. Tort law has evolved over hundreds of years to support the protection of an individual's rights with respect to persons and property. In addition, tort law is based on common law and, consequently, the rules vary from state to state. There are three areas of tort law—intentional tort, negligence, and strict liability. An example of an intentional tort would be physical assault by one person against another person. Negligence would involve a careless act that injures a person. An example would be leaving a pair of roller skates on a sidewalk where someone might trip over them. Strict liability carries negligence one step further. An example would be someone undertaking a hazardous activity by which it is foreseeable that injury can result.

Negligence   Many product liability suits, including the aforementioned landmark case of *MacPherson v. Buick*, are based on negligence. Negligence can be said to exist when certain conditions are met, one of which is foreseeability, which addresses the likelihood that something will happen in the future. Second, there must be causation. When an injured person alleges negligence in a product liability damage suit, there must be a close causal relationship between the negligence and the injury. For example, in *MacPherson v. Buick*, a judge held the Buick Motor Company liable for the defective wooden spoke that caused the accident because it was negligent when it had not properly inspected the wheel before it was put on the car. However, if a plaintiff has not been harmed, the defendant is not liable.

Strict Liability   Strict liability is liability for an action simply because it occurred, not because it is the fault of the person who must pay. For example, a person builds a dam with the intent of creating a fishpond. The dam breaks and the water floods a neighbor's property, causing extensive damage. The person who built the dam is liable. Business firms can be held liable for defects even though they may have been unaware of their existence at the time their products were produced. This was the case in *MacPherson v. Buick*. They are also liable for failure to warn consumers of a known danger commonly faced when using a product. The application of strict liability varies from state to state and from court to court.

Compensatory and Punitive Damages   What is the basis for damage awards in a tort law suit? There are two types of damages—compensatory and punitive. The most common type of damage is compensatory damage, which is a sum of money that will place a person in the same economic position that he or she would have attained had the contract been performed. An injured person may recover only the damages that he or she could reasonably foresee. Punitive damage is damage that a court may award in order to deter the defendant from further wrongdoing. The average amount of damages has risen since 1995, but the number of cases has remained constant. Median jury awards for defective products have risen from about half a million in 1993 to over $1.8 million in 1999, not including punitive damages. The following case involves the use of compensatory and punitive damages. As the case indicates, states differ in their application of tort law to damage awards. Some states place a cap on the amount of money that can be awarded in punitive damages, while other states do not.

BMW of North America Inc. v. Ira Gore Jr.[36]

In January 1990, Dr. Ira Gore Jr. purchased a black BMW sports sedan for $40,750.88 from a BMW dealer in Birmingham, Alabama. After driving the car for approximately nine months, and without noticing any flaws in its appearance, Dr. Gore took the car to "Slick Finish," an independent detailer, to make the car look "snazzier than it normally would appear." Mr. Slick, the proprietor, detected evidence that the car had been repainted. Convinced that he had been cheated, Dr. Gore brought suit against BMW of North America, the American distributor of BMW automobiles, the German manufacturer, and the Birmingham BMW dealership. He asked for $500,000 in compensatory damages.

At trial BMW acknowledged that it had adopted a nationwide policy in 1983 concerning cars that were damaged in the course of manufacturing or transportation. The top, hood, trunk, and quarter panels of Dr. Gore's car had been repainted at BMW's preparation center at Brunswick, Georgia. The damage to the car had been caused by exposure to acid rain during the transit from the manufacturing plant in Munich, Germany, to the preparation center in Brunswick, Georgia. BMW's policy was that if the cost of repairing the damaged exceeded 3 percent of the car's suggested retail price, the car was placed in company service for a period of time and then sold as used. If the repair cost did not exceed 3 percent of the suggested retail price, the car was sold as new without advising a dealer that any repairs had been made. The cost of repairing Dr. Gore's car was $601.37, or 1.5 percent of the purchase price.

A jury returned a verdict finding BMW and the Birmingham dealership liable for compensatory damages of $4,000 and assessed an additional $4 million in punitive damages.[37] BMW filed a post trial motion to set aside the punitive damages award. It argued that its disclosure policy was consistent with the laws of thirty-five states defining the disclosure obligations of car manufacturers. It also argued that its disclosure policy had never been adjudged unlawful before this case was filed. The motion was denied, BMW then appealed to the Alabama Supreme Court, which reduced the punitive damage award to $2 million. It found that the amount of punitive damage had been improperly computed because similar sales in the other states involved different jurisdictions.[38]

The case was then appealed to the U.S. Supreme Court, which ruled that the $2 million punitive damage award was excessive. The court was concerned that BMW was being punished for an activity that was lawful in other states. It held that an award of punitive damages could be grossly excessive. It then set three guidelines by which reviewing courts could determine whether punitive damages were excessive. The first guideline is the degree of reprehensibility of the defendant's conduct.[39] The second guideline is the ratio between the plaintiff's award of compensatory damages and the amount of the punitive damages. The third guideline is the difference between the punitive damage award and civil or criminal sanctions that could have been used. The court found that BMW's conduct was not sufficiently reprehensible to justify such a large award, and the punitive damage was five hundred times the amount of the compensatory damage. The case was remanded to the Alabama Supreme Court, and Gore was awarded $50,000.

THE PHARMACEUTICAL INDUSTRY

The Pharmaceutical Industry in the United States has been the focus of intense consumer action during the past few years. The United States is the world's largest pharmaceutical market, showing revenues of $235.6 billion in the year 2004. It represents almost 50 percent of the global market for pharmaceutical. The world market is dominated by giants such as Pfizer, with 9.3 percent of the global pharmaceutical market, and GlaxoSmithKline, with 6.3 percent.[40] Chief among the complaints against the pharmaceutical industry has been prescription drug pricing.

Prescription drug pricing has risen in the United States to the extent that many seniors and uninsured Americans find the costs prohibitive. This has driven some consumers to purchase prescription drugs from Canada and Mexico, where prescription costs are lower than in the United States. The Food and Drug Administration has issued an advisory against purchasing drugs outside the United States, citing concerns about storage and packaging. However, Canadian sources protest that the drugs are exactly the same as those available in the United States. The FDA has threatened action under the Federal Food, Drug, and Cosmetic Act of 1938, as amended in 2004. The recent amendments would bring action against sales of drugs out-of-country if they are found to be adulterated or sold without proper prescription. House Bill 753 has been introduced, and is currently in committee, which would regulate internet pharmaceutical sales.

Medicare Reform Act of 2003

Senior citizens represent a particularly powerful lobby in the United States, and thus Congress has been more receptive to their concerns regarding the costs of prescription drugs. To deal with such concerns, Congress passed the Medicare Reform Act in 2004, also known as the Prescription Drug Bill. In November 2003, Congress narrowly passed the Medicare Reform Bill, also known as the Prescription Drug Bill. The compromise bill was passed in the Senate (54–44) with an estimated cost of $400 billion over ten years; however, estimates have now ballooned to $724 billion. Drug coverage will be provided through a complex formula that has left many seniors baffled. Depending upon the state, Medicare recipients may have up to forty prescription drug plans to choose from, with variations in the types of drugs covered.[41]

Detractors suggest that the main beneficiaries will be the pharmaceutical industry and the insurance industry. However, early indicators suggest that the legislation may have failed to stem the rise in prescription drug costs. A recent GAO study found that costs for both Medicare and non-Medicare consumers rose by almost 25 percent between 2000 and 2004.[42] The AARP Public Policy Institute conducted a study for the year ending in March 2005, which demonstrated an average price increase of more than 6 percent on 195 brand name drugs used by older adults. This rate doubled the Consumer Price Index for the same period.[43]

Litigation—Ernst v. Merck

The pharmaceutical industry has also experienced major recalls and lawsuits; the year 2002 witnessed a record number of recalls. Most recently, action has been taken on NSAIDS, a class of painkillers used in treating arthritis. Popular NSAIDS such as Vioxx, Bextra, Celebrex, and the over-the-counter drug Aleve have been found to increase risks for heart disease and stomach problems. While the FDA has allowed this class of drugs to remain on the market, Pfizer has voluntarily removed Bextra from the market, and Merck has voluntarily withdrawn Vioxx, based upon its own studies that the drug increased the risk of heart attack. Merck has faced a series of lawsuits from customers who allege that Vioxx resulted in death.

In 2002, plaintiff Carol Ernst sued Merck, alleging that her husband Robert died from a heart attack after taking Vioxx. Ernst, a healthy 59-year-old who ran marathons, took Vioxx for eight months prior to his death. In 2005, a Texas jury found in favor of Ernst, and awarded both compensatory and punitive damages of $259 million.[44] Merck is appealing the verdict. In a second lawsuit, *Humeston v. Merck*, a New Jersey jury ruled in favor of Merck. The company faces some 6,400 additional lawsuits, but thus far has indicated that it will go to trial on each case.[45]

Prescription Drug Advertising

Drugs such as Vioxx have raised increasing concerns about Direct to Consumer (DTC) advertising. The American Medical Association has called for further study about the impact of DTC advertising. Proponents suggest that it serves a valuable purpose in educating consumers about health care issues. However, prominent lawmakers such as Senate Majority Leader Bill Frist, (himself a physician) have called for a two-year waiting period on the advertising of new drugs, so that the risks of these drugs can be fully demonstrated. Frist has expressed concerns that DTC advertising "leads patients to demand from their doctor drugs that they may not need or, even worse, that might expose them to risks they didn't know about."[46] In November 2005 the Food and Drug Administration held hearings on whether or not it should issue rules on DTC advertising; however, new rules are not likely until 2006.

The FDA has issued standards for clarity of print ads as well as broadcast ads, however, in 2003 there were only eighteen FDA reviewers to scrutinize the 37,000 drug ads and promotional materials submitted. Thus, campaigns are sometimes over before agency watchdogs can spot a misleading advertisement. The FDA may seize drugs or take violators to court, however, the Bush administration has made proposed sanctions pass a new review by the FDA general counsel. The goal for review is fifteen days, but it has ranged from thirteen to seventy-eight days. A notice of violation letter directs the drug company to suspend or correct advertising containing false or misleading information or omitting information about risks and benefits. Warning letters for repeat offenders may seize drugs or request an injunction against the company. From 1997 to 2001, forty-four notice of violation letters and two warning letters were issued; between 2001 and 2003, ten notice of violation letters and zero warning letters were issued.

The FDA has issued new rules for labeling of prescription drugs. As of 2004, drug manufacturers must suspend the use of small print and utilize layman's terms in warning labels. Labels for hormone replacement therapy must mention the risks for breast cancer, heart attacks and stroke, as well as Alzheimer's disease and dementia. Antidepressants must warn of the increased risk of suicide.

Concerns have also arisen about the FDA's regulatory capacity with respect to prescription drugs. The office that approves new drugs has over 1,000 employees; by contrast, the Office of Drug Safety has 1,000. The FDA is understaffed and underfunded when compared with the USDA, with a $1.7 billion budget for 2004 compared to USDA's $74 billion. Additionally, the FDA is limited in its ability to force drug manufacturers to take drugs off of the market unless the Secretary of Health and Human Services declares an imminent health risk. Drug companies pay the FDA a "user fee" for faster turnaround on new drug applications under the 1992 Prescription Drug User Fee Act. And the level of FDA scrutiny on drug testing allows companies to be selective in what they report to the agency. The FDA has also come under fire for its regulation of medical devices such as defibrillators, blood-oxygen monitors, and artificial hips. Such issues have led to concerns that the FDA is "asleep at the wheel" when it comes to regulating the pharmaceutical industry.[47] To address these concerns, in 2005, the FDA created an independent board, the Drug Safety Oversight Board, which will monitor pharmaceuticals once they are on the market. The board will make recommendations regarding information to post on the government's Drug Watch website, and will create a drug safety web page with up-to-date research on the latest drugs.

SUMMARY

One of the fundamental tenets supporting a market economy is consumer sovereignty, which is based on the idea that ultimate decisions as to what will be produced rest with the consumer. This presumes that consumers have the information necessary to make rational choices in the marketplace. If this is true, consumer expenditures guide resource allocation into chosen products. But in a complex modern society, it is difficult for consumers to have the expertise necessary to distinguish among many products. In addition, consumers are led by advertising to make product choices on the basis of subjective factors. Therefore, laws have been passed to protect consumers against those practices considered harmful to their interests. These laws cover a wide variety of areas ranging from pure food and drug laws to disclosures on credit and warranties on products sold to the public. Tort law also pertains to consumer protection.

QUESTIONS FOR DISCUSSION

1. What is meant by consumer sovereignty? Are consumers really sovereign?
2. What is considered false or deceptive advertising?
3. There are costs as well as benefits in consumer protection legislation. Discuss.
4. Are some beer, wine, liquor, or tobacco ads misleading? What specifically is misleading?
5. Should caps be placed on punitive damage awards?
6. The state of California has proposed a fifty-cent tax increase per package of cigarettes sold. What impact do you think this will have on cigarette consumption?
7. Should companies producing alcoholic beverages be held liable for deaths resulting from alcohol consumption?
8. Should fast-food companies be held responsible for deaths that can be related to the consumption of high-calorie foods?
9. What is the difference between compensatory and punitive damages?
10. Why is *MacPherson v. Buick* considered a landmark case?

NOTES

1. Adam Smith. *The Wealth of Nations.* New York: The Modern Library, 1937, p. 38.

2. There was no freedom of choice in the former communist countries. Resources were allocated by central economic planning.

3. This is called pure competition, an ideal market situation that rarely exists.

4. The Consumer Federation of America is the most important consumer group.

5. The doctrine of breach of warranty affords remedies for misrepresentation that can be extended beyond the retailer as far back as the manufacturer.

6. Upton Sinclair. *The Jungle.* New York: Doubleday and Page, 1906.

7. Some 1.5 million copies of the book were sold during its printings.

8. There were all sorts of ads in the newspapers of that time period that claimed curative powers for their products.

9. Carol Ballentine. "Taste of Raspberries, Taste of Death: The 1937 Elixir Sulfanilamide Incident." *FDA Consumer Magazine.* U.S. Food and Drug Administration, 1981.

10. In 1970 all cyclamate-sweetened soft drinks were banned from the market. This was based on tests made on rats showing that they developed bladder cancer when given strict doses of cyclamates.

11. Sam Peltzman. *Regulation of Pharmaceutical Innovation: The 1962 Amendment.* Washington, D.C.: American Enterprise Institute, 1974.

12. The waste was said to result from product differentiation in an imperfect market permeated by physicians and consumer ignorance.

13. The device was made by the A. H. Robins Co. of Richmond, VA.

14. Medical Device Recalls. U.S. Food and Drug Administration. www.accessdata.fda .gov/scripts/cdrh/cfdocs/cfTopic/medicaldevicesafety/recalls.cfm

15. *The Roanoke Times*, Friday, August 20, 1999, p. 2.

16. Julie Appleby. "Diet Drug Maker Settles for $4.8 billion." *USA Today*, Thursday, February 24, 2000, p. 1.

17. FTC v. Raladam Co., 283 U.S. 643 (1931).

18. Lewis W. Stern and Thomas L. Fovaldi. *Legal Aspects of Marketing Strategy: Antitrust and Consumer Protection Issues.* Englewood Cliff, N.J.: Prentice-Hall, 1984, pp. 371–72.

19. Thomas L. Carson, Richard E. Wokutch, and James E. Brown Jr. "An Ethical Analysis of Deceptive Advertising." *Journal of Business Ethics* (Winter, 1985), pp. 99–101.

20. Two hundred million letters multiplied by the amount of money that could be won comes out to $200 trillion, which is five times the GNP of the world.

21. An elderly man, thinking that he had won the grand prize, flew to Tampa to claim it. He was going to give the money to his children. Dreams often die hard.

22. *The Roanoke Times*, Monday, February 28, 2000, p. 2.

23. Wheaties cereal used to be called "The breakfast of champions." It was endorsed by professional athletes who implied that they owed their success to eating Wheaties.

24. In Selma, Alabama, several women were burned to death when a Christmas tree caught fire, setting their billowy gowns on fire.

25. TRW, Inc. v. Andrews, 534 U.S. 19.

26. He or she cannot call before 8:00 A.M. or after 9:00 P.M.

27. Both federal and state laws on warranties conform to the Uniform Commercial Code (UCC), which follows common law theory that a product, when sold, carries with it the promise that it is fit for common use.

28. FTC Releases Top 10 Consumer Complaint Categories for 2004. *Federal Trade Commission.* February 1, 2005. www.ftc.gov/opa/2005/02/top102005.htm.

29. Federal Trade Commission Overview of the Identity Theft Program: October 1998–September 2003. Federal Trade Commission. September 2003.

30. U.S. Senate Committee on Commerce, *Hearing of National Commission on Product Safety,* 91st Cong., 2nd Sess., 1972, p. 37.

31. Ralph Nader. *Unsafe at Any Speed.* New York: Pocket Books, 1966.

32. Cadillac, to meet government rules, came out with a V-8-6-4 engine in 1981. To save gas, it shut down pairs of cylinders automatically as the car got to cruising speed. But it bucked, misfired, and lacked power, and was discontinued.

33. This is no longer in effect. The limit is now up to each state to determine.

34. MacPherson v. Buick Motor Co., 217 N.Y., 382, 111 N.E. 1050 (1916).

35. *USA Today,* Thursday: June 27, 1996, p. 13A.

36. Supreme Court of the United States, Syllabus, *BMW of North America, Inc. v. Gore,* No. 94-896. Decided May 20, 1996, pp. 1–27.

37. The amount was based on the evidence that between 1983 and 1990, BMW had sold 983 repainted cars in the United States as new, including 14 in Alabama. This number was multiplied by the $4 thousand in compensatory damage awarded to Dr. Gore to arrive at $4 million.

38. When the original $4 million verdict was returned, BMW instituted a nationwide policy of full disclosure of all repairs, no matter how minor.

39. The Supreme Court described reprehensible conduct as consisting of the following: Crimes marked by violence or threats of violence; trickery and deceit; intentional malice; repeated engagement in unlawful conduct; bad faith actions; and deliberate false statements or concealment of evidence of improper motives.

40. Global-Pharmaceuticals. "Datamonitor Industry Market Research." May 1, 2005. *Business and Company Resource Center.* galenet.galegroup.com

41. Robert Pear. "Confusion is Rife about Drug Plan as Sign-Up Nears." *New York Times,* November 13, 2005. www.nytimes.com/2005/11/13/national/13drug.html

42. Price Trends for Frequently Used Brand and Generic Drugs from 2000 through 2004. GAO-02-779, Government Accountability Office. August 2005. p. 4.

43. Average Price Increase of Brand-Name Drugs More then Doubles CPI. *AARP Public Policy Institute.* April, 2005. www.aarp.org/health/affordable_drugs/brandname_drug_prices_double_cpi.html

44. Ernst et al. v. Merck & Co. Inc., No. 19961-BH02, District Court of Brazoria County, Texas.

45. Merck Wins New Jersey Jury Trial Over Pain Drug Vioxx. *Bloomberg.com,* November 3, 2005.

46. Matthew Davis. "Controversy over U.S. drug Adverts." *BBC News online.* August 16, 2005. news.bbc.co.uk/1/hi/business/4154598.stm

47. Jennifer Barrett Ozols. "FDA Has Been Asleep at the Switch." *Newsweek.* November 21, 2004. www.msnbc.msn.com/id/6513892/site/newsweek/

7

Employment Policy

The rationale for government intervention in employment and education is that equal employment opportunity is considered to be a basic right of the American democratic process—everyone should have the same opportunity to achieve material success. When opportunity is equal, competition and market forces determine one's worth in the marketplace. The idea behind equal employment opportunity is that if everyone is given the same or substantially the same starting position in a race, the winners will have to achieve their rewards through merit rather than through any favored position. Reward would be based on merit, and the result would be the creation of a meritocratic society.[1] Logically, if everyone is given the same opportunity and there is no discrimination based on sex, age, or other factors, the rewards should be distributed fairly uniformly.

However, the problem is that a number of impediments hinder achieving true equality of opportunity. Clearly, discrimination on the basis of sex, color, religion, or any criterion outside of professional qualifications prevents any genuine equality of opportunity. And equality of opportunity is only part of the future, for opportunity is linked to the distribution of income. In part, income inequality is based on differences in people's abilities; sometimes, however, it is based on sex, race, and age, which have little or no relationship to ability. Income inequality can also be based on the distribution of wealth, the great bulk of which is held by those who are in the upper 5 percent of income earners in the United States.[2]

INCOME DISTRIBUTION IN THE UNITED STATES

Income inequality is greater in the United States than in any other major industrial country, and it has increased in recent years. From 1980 to 2002,

135

the top 20 percent of American families saw their incomes—measured in terms of purchasing power—increase while the bottom 80 percent of families saw a decrease. From 1950 to 1978, all income groups gained as the American economy grew. It was a time when unskilled assembly-line workers, with little if any education beyond a high school diploma, were able to achieve a middle-class standard of living. U.S. firms had very little competition from abroad and foreign wages were not a factor that affected U.S. wages. But all of this began to change during the 1970s when foreign competition began to catch up with U.S. companies.

Faced with this competition, U.S. manufacturers turned to technology to increase productivity, substituting machines for people wherever possible. Companies began to eliminate thousands of workers from their payrolls, sometimes more than half the industrial labor force. As manufacturing employment decreased, employment in the service industries was growing faster than in any other sector, often providing jobs without benefits such as health insurance. Moreover, the competition for jobs increased in the 1980s, as those who were born during the post-World War II era began entering the labor force. Women, too, entered the labor force in large numbers. The technological revolution that hit the manufacturing sector then reached the service sector, replacing bank tellers with automatic teller machines and telephone operators with automatic switching equipment.

From 1980 to 2002, there was a decline in real income for the bottom 80 percent of the families and a gain for the top 20 percent.[3] The lowest one-fifth of families had their share of income reduced from 5.3 percent in 1980 to 4.2 percent in 2002.[4] Conversely, the share of income received by the top 20 percent of families increased from 41.1 percent in 1980 to 47.6 percent in 2002, and the share of income received by the top 5 percent of families increased from 14.6 percent in 1980 to 20.8 percent in 2002. Income inequality was greater for black and Hispanic families in 2002 than it was for white families.

Table 7.1 presents the share of income of families by race for 2002. As the table indicates, more blacks and Hispanics are concentrated in the lower levels of income, while whites are concentrated in the higher levels of income. Over 67 percent of black and Hispanic families made less than $50,000 a year, while 54.6 percent of white families made more than $50,000 a year.

Demographic Characteristics of Income Distribution

A more complete analysis of income distribution in the United States reveals disparities based on the demographic characteristics of sex, race, and age. Some forty years after the Civil Rights Act of 1964, income distribution shows disparities related to each of these characteristics, and has created a

Table 7.1   Money Income of Families: Percent Distribution by Income Level, Race, and Hispanic Origin (Constant 2002 Dollars)

	White	*Black*	*Hispanic*
Under 15,000	8.1	20.8	16.7
15,000–24,999	10.6	16.4	18.3
25,000–34,999	11.4	14.7	16.0
35,000–49,999	15.3	15.7	16.7
50,000–74,999	21.3	15.8	17.2
75,000–99,999	14.3	8.6	7.7
100,000 and over	19.0	8.0	7.5

Source: U.S. Department of Commerce, Bureau of the Census, *Statistical Abstract of the United States, 2004–2005*. Washington, D.C.: U.S. Government Printing Office, 2004, p. 446.

demand for government policies, such as affirmative action, that attempt to reduce these disparities.

Sex

One of the defining movements of the past century has been the struggle for gender equality, led mostly by women. It was not until the twentieth century that women were given the right to vote in the major industrial countries. Women in all countries earn less than men. Moreover, 70 percent of those who live in poverty throughout the world are women, and the rate of illiteracy is much higher among women.[5] In India, for example, two-thirds of the population that is illiterate are women. In many countries women have few legal rights regarding marital relations, the division of property, or land tenure. In some countries men can divorce their wives but not the other way around; also, it is difficult for the women to get any form of alimony.[6]

The percentage of American women who have entered the labor force has increased dramatically in recent years. In 1950, 31.4 percent of women worked; by 1970, it had increased to 42.6 percent; and by 2003, 59.6 percent of all women were employed. The most dramatic increase in employment involved married women with children. In 1960, 18.6 percent of women in the labor force were married women with children; in 2003 it was 69.2 percent.[7] In 1980, 61.5 million males were employed compared to 45.5 million females; in 2003, 78.2 million males were employed compared to 68.3 million females.[8] Many women today have more financial responsibility than in the past because more of them are single heads of families. In 2003, for example, one out of every six women who worked was a single mother with a family to raise.

Two things have happened as more women have entered the labor force. First, there has been a shift in employment by occupations as more women are entering occupations once considered the preserve of men. The percentage of women who have entered such high paying professions as engineering, law, and medicine has dramatically increased. Second, wages of women relative to men have also shown an increase. In 1950 the pay ratio of women to men was 48.6 percent. Between 1960 and 1980, there was little change in the ratio, which was 60.7 percent in 1960 and 60.2 percent in 1980. In 1990 the ratio was 71.6 percent and in 1997 it was 79 percent.[9] Women's pay in some of the higher paying professions has shown little gain or has decreased.

There are several reasons that women have not made income gains relative to men's income. For one thing, women by the thousands have flocked to such lucrative professions as law and medicine, thus increasing the supply of workers. In fact, the medical profession is reputed to be overcrowded, and the AMA has asked medical schools to decrease admissions.[10] Another factor is discrimination. Women are often given the lower-paying jobs and are denied promotion. Home Depot, the home improvement chain, was accused in a class-action suit of putting women behind cash registers instead of putting them on the sales floor where they could earn commissions and get promoted.[11] Third, there is networking, or contacts, that have been built up by men over an extended period of time, and that works to their advantage in employment.

Race

In the case of blacks and other minorities, income differences can be explained in part by overt discrimination. Over an extended period of time, blacks have been systematically denied the same educational opportunities as whites, which is reflected in occupations and earnings of blacks. A majority still work in lower-pay, low-skill jobs. There has also been discrimination in hiring and promotion policies toward other minority groups. Hispanics are an example. Often the discrimination is indirect, as in testing that, although it can be a legitimate device to find out something about employee aptitudes and qualifications, may be culturally biased in favor of certain types of job applicants. Blacks and other minorities have often been unable to obtain jobs commensurate with their training. There has been some narrowing of the income gap between white and Hispanic household median income over the last 30 years; conversely, the gap between white and black household median income has widened. In terms of purchasing power, the median income of all groups has declined since 2000.

CIVIL RIGHTS LAWS

Civil rights are extremely important in the litigious world of today and have their historical background in the first ten amendments of the U.S. Constitution. Persons are protected in the free exercise of their speech, are free to choose or not to choose a religion, can peacefully assemble, and may petition their government for a redress of grievances. They also have the right to keep and bear arms, the right to be free of unreasonable searches and seizures, and the right to a jury trial. These rights are bestowed by the government upon the people. Coupled with civil rights are natural rights to which a person is entitled because he or she is human and that cannot be taken away by government.[12]

History of Civil Rights Laws

The first civil rights laws had their origin in the Civil War. After the battle of Antietam, which was fought in September 1862, President Lincoln issued the Emancipation Proclamation that freed the slaves. After the war was over, several constitutional amendments were passed that had a direct impact upon the treatment of blacks, The Thirteenth Amendment in 1865 abolished slavery; the Fourteenth Amendment in 1868 was designed to prevent southern states from passing discriminatory laws against blacks; and the Fifteenth Amendment in 1870 was designed to prevent race discrimination in voting. The Civil Rights Act of 1866 was passed by Congress to protect blacks from employment discrimination and the Civil Rights Act of 1875 was designed to protect them against discrimination in housing and transportation. It provided for a fine of up to $1,000 or imprisonment of up to one year for violation.

The civil rights laws had very little impact on improving the lot of blacks, particularly in the South. Resentment against the North increased during the period of reconstruction. Southern states passed Jim Crow laws designed to segregate blacks. The concept of separate but equal accommodations came out of the *Plessy v. Ferguson* case of 1896, which legitimized segregation.[13] This ruling provided the foundation for making segregation legal. There were separate schools for whites and blacks, separate accommodations, and separate facilities such as toilets and drinking fountains. *Plessy v. Ferguson* was eventually reversed by the *Brown v. Board of Education* case of 1954 in which the Supreme Court ruled that the separate but equal doctrine followed by the states had resulted in unequal education facilities for blacks.[14] But other forms of discrimination against blacks and other minorities continued to exist.

The Civil Rights Act of 1964

Title VII of the act specifically deals with discrimination in employment. It is designed to protect individuals from job discrimination on the basis of race, color, sex, religion, or national origin. It prohibits discrimination with respect to compensation, contract terms, and conditions or privileges of employment. The most common Title VII claims involve failure to hire, failure to promote, discipline, discharge, pay discrimination, and sexual harassment. It applies to employers who have fifteen or more employees for each working day in each of twenty or more calendar weeks per year. The act also created the Equal Employment Opportunity Commission (EEOC) to handle claims of employment discrimination. The responsibility of EEOC was subsequently extended to apply to the Age Discrimination in Employment Act (ADEA), the Americans with Disabilities Act (ADA), and the Equal Pay Act. Title IX prohibits discrimination on the basis of sex in educational programs receiving government financial assistance. The Civil Rights Act was amended in 1991 to strengthen certain provisions left ambiguous by court rulings. Presently the EEOC receives about 75,000 complaints per year, and averages 400 cases filed. The number of complaints has gone down for the last three fiscal years (75,428 in 2005) and the average complaint took 171 days to process. Only 21.5 percent had a favorable outcome for the individual.

The Age Discrimination in Employment Act of 1967 (ADEA)

The poet Byron once wrote, "The days of our youth are the days of our glory." No society in the world believes that more firmly than Americans, who are firmly committed to the pursuit of youth. The notion that older people lose their mental faculties and are unable to perform as well as younger workers is not uncommon in the American workplace. The workforce is aging, with nearly half of all workers over the age of 40. Employers have often refused to hire and promote workers and have also fired them, all on the basis of age. The Age Discrimination in Employment Act (ADEA) is designed to prohibit discrimination based on age. It protects workers who have reached the age of forty and older. It applies to employers with at least twenty employees for each day of twenty or more calendar days. The number of complaints under ADEA has risen—from 14,141 in 1999 to 19,921 in 2002. From 1999–2003, complaints increased a total of 35 percent.

The Americans with Disabilities Act of 1990 (ADA)

This act, extends the provisions of the Rehabilitation Act of 1973 to private employers, makes it unlawful to discriminate against a qualified individual with a disability. A person is said to have a disability if he or she has a physical or mental impairment that substantially limits or restricts a major life activity such as hearing, seeing, breathing, performing manual tasks, walking, or caring for oneself. The act mandates that employees make reasonable accommodations for the disabled. Reasonable accommodation is any change that is necessary to permit a worker to do the job. It may involve modifying equipment or making the workplace readily accessible to persons with disabilities. It also may mean part-time or modified work schedules. ADA applies to all employers, including state and local governments, with fifteen or more employees.

Bona Fide Occupational Qualification (BFOQ)

Exceptions to employment laws may be made on the basis of a bona fide occupational qualification (BFOQ); however, the courts have interpreted this narrowly. In terms of safety, the courts have allowed an employer to limit its recruiting and hiring for certain types of individuals when either the safety of the public or the employees are involved. BFOQ exemptions are given when it can be shown that being a member of a particular group is necessary for serving in a given job, such as an acting job, that may require a person to be a male or female. An exemption may also be given for jobs that involve legitimate privacy concerns. An example would be the hiring of a female attendant for a women's locker room in a health club. Religion can sometimes be used as a BFOQ; an example would be teaching at a religious school where teaching involves the propagation of certain religious beliefs.[15]

Other Laws Forbidding Workplace Discrimination

There are several other antidiscrimination laws that fall under the purview of the Equal Employment Opportunity Commission. The Equal Pay Act of 1963 requires equal pay for men and women doing the same job. The Vocational Rehabilitation Act of 1973 requires federal contractors to take affirmative action in hiring qualified individuals with disabilities. The Pregnancy Discrimination Act of 1978 forbids discrimination against women if they decide to have a child. The Civil Rights Act of 1991 broadens the scope of federal antidiscrimination law. It makes clear that Americans employed abroad by U.S.-owned or U.S.-controlled firms can avail themselves of the protection of Title VII of the Civil Rights Act of 1964 and ADEA, unless compliance with these laws violate the host country's laws. It broadened the categories of victims who can seek compensatory and punitive damages. The Family and Medical Leave Act of 1993 protects job rights of employees who can take up to twelve weeks leave for family reasons such as childbirth.

Employment Discrimination—Disparate Treatment and Disparate Impact

Employment discrimination claims brought under Title VII of the Civil Rights Act of 1964 have been approached through the use of two legal theories—disparate treatment and disparate impact. Under the disparate treatment theory, an employer may be liable if he or she impermissibly differentiates among employers or applicants or treats some unfavorably based on their race, sex, religion, or national origin. While the burden of proof is on the plaintiff to prove disparate treatment, if a case is established, the employer must prove that the actions were nondiscriminatory.

McDonnell Douglas v. Green[16]

Green, a civil rights activist, alleged that he was discharged for racially motivated reasons. McDonnell Douglas Corp. responded that they had discharged Green for conducting "illegal activities," i.e., protesting. The Supreme Court ruled that Green had a right to rebut McDonnell Douglas by proving that their explanation constituted a racially motivated pretext. This case therefore established the four elements for establishing a case of discrimination based upon disparate treatment:

> In a private, non-class-action complaint under Title VII charging racial employment discrimination, the complaint has the burden of establishing a prima facie case, which he can satisfy by showing that (i) he belongs to a racial minority; (ii) he applied and was qualified for a job the employer was trying to fill; (iii) though qualified, he was rejected; and (iv) thereafter the employer continued to seek applicants with complainant's qualifications.[17]

Watson v. Fort Worth Bank and Trust[18]

In 1988, Clara Watson, a black employee at the Fort Worth Bank and Trust, tried without success to obtain several promotions. The bank relied on the subjective judgment of a supervisor as to who would receive promotions. Watson filed a lawsuit but a trial court dismissed the action after finding that Watson had failed to prove racial discrimination under the standards of disparate or unequal treatment. Under disparate treatment, an employer may be liable if he or she impermissibly differentiates among employees on the basis of their race, sex, color, religion, or national origin. Watson argued that disparate impact should have been applied in her case and eventually the case went to the Supreme Court, which ruled in her favor.

While the disparate treatment approach aims at the elimination of discrimination that is usually intentional, disparate impact is designed to eliminate racially neutral employment policies that have a disproportionate impact on members of a protected class and that cannot be justified by legitimate business considerations. The employment practice may appear neutral, but it is not. The focus is on the effect of an employer's practices, not the intent of establishing these practices. Key Supreme Court cases addressing disparate impact are *Griggs v. Duke Power* and *Albemarle Paper v. Moody*.

Griggs v. Duke Power[19]

In 1971, Griggs, a black worker, applied for a semiskilled job at the Duke Power Company. However, the requisite for the job was a high school diploma or, in lieu of that, he could take the Wonderlic and Bennett tests that measured intelligence and mechanical aptitude. If he scored at the same level as whites with a high school diploma, he could get the job. In North Carolina, fewer blacks than whites had received a high school education, so blacks were limited to the lowest paying jobs. Griggs and other blacks argued that the educational requirements screened them from getting the better-paying jobs that whites were getting. The Supreme Court ruled that there was no satisfactory relationship between the educational requirements and job performance.

Disparate impact focuses on the effects of an employer's practice, not the intent in establishing those practices. To establish proof of disparate impact, statistical analysis can be used. Two types of statistical evidence—pass/fail comparisons and population/workforce comparisons—have frequently been introduced as evidence in disparate impact cases. To establish a prima facie claim of disparate impact discrimination, a plaintiff must prove that a particular practice adversely affects employment opportunities of one group of workers as compared to the effect the same practice has on the opportunities of other groups. The four-fifths rule is often used, where a plaintiff can demonstrate that an apparently neutral procedure results in selection rates of less than 80 percent of a protected class. The employer may counter by suggesting that the practice is a business necessity (to be distinguished from a BFOQ); that it is a valid procedure for selection, training, hiring, firing, etc. A plaintiff may then challenge by suggesting that a less discriminatory procedure may be applied.

Class-Action Employment Suits

A class-action suit is a lawsuit filed by a group of people who have a grievance against a particular company. It is less expensive to file than an individual lawsuit. Class-action suits may be filed when it can be demonstrated that employer practices were applied pervasively to whole classes of employees. While settlements for employees are typically lower, class action suits can focus high-profile attention on particular company practices. Corporations subject to class-action employee suits in recent years include Shoney's, Cracker Barrel, and WalMart. An example is the Mitsubishi Motors sexual harassment case.

Mitsubishi Motors Manufacturing Company of America v. EEOC

In April 1996 the Chicago office of the Equal Employment Opportunity Commission (EEOC) filed a class-action suit against Mitsubishi Motors Manufacturing Company of America (MMMA), a subsidiary of Mitsubishi Motors Corporation of Japan, charging it with condoning sexual harassment

Table 7.2   Employment Discrimination Class-Action Settlements, 1992–2004

Date of Settlement	Company	Amount	Class Description
11/04	Abercrombie and Fitch	$40 million	Latino, African-American, Asian and women applicants claiming discrimination in hiring
11/00	Coca Cola	$192.5 million	2,000 workers claiming discrimination based upon race
1/00	USIA/Voice of America	$508 million	1,100 women denied employment
9/97	Home Depot	$87.5 million	25,000 women claiming discrimination in promotion
3/97	Texaco	$172 million	1,500 past and current African-American employees claiming race discrimination
11/96	Chevron	$7.4 million	800 current and former female employees alleging sex discrimination in promotions and salaries
10/96	Southern California Edison	$18.2 million	2,500 African-American employees alleging race discrimination
10/94	Albertson's, Inc.	$29.4 million	Women and Hispanics claiming race and sex discrimination
6/94	Denny's	$54 million	4,500 people alleging race discrimination
4/94	Lucky Stores	$107.2 million	14,000 women alleging sex discrimination
1/93	Shoney's	$133 million	African-American employees alleging race discrimination
10/92	State Farm	$250 million	Sex discrimination

Source: Jeffrey A. Norris, President, Equal Employment Council, Washington, D.C., May, 1997, unpublished data, updated by author.

of women workers at its plant in Normal, Illinois. EEOC alleged that as many as seven hundred women were harassed for years while plant managers did nothing. The suit claimed the breasts, buttocks, and genitals of female assembly-line workers were groped and fondled, obscene remarks were made, and sexual graffiti covered the walls. Separately, a private lawsuit in the Peoria, Illinois, federal court was brought by twenty-nine women alleging sexual harassment at the MMMA plant. The suit contended that other workers retaliated against women, and that company officials tried to intimidate them.

The company retaliated against EEOC by staging a rally outside their Chicago office to protest the class-action suit. It shut down its production line for a day and offered all employees who wanted to participate a free lunch and a trip aboard one of the thirty-nine buses it rented for the occasion. An estimated 3,000 workers attended the rally. The purpose of the rally was to counter what the company said was a politically motivated lawsuit by the federal government. Wages at the Mitsubishi plant were quite high for that area of Illinois, averaging better than $30,000 a year. Lawyers representing the company alleged that one of the twenty-nine women had a pattern of promiscuous behavior.

Conversely, EEOC contended that MMMA made no effort to cooperate during the investigation that began in April 1994. Apparently the company refused to let EEOC representatives interview management-level personnel accused of harassment. Requests for interviews with witnesses of sexual harassment were also turned down. Companies under investigation usually make an effort to improve their practices so that they are in compliance with the law. However, MMMA did not. Moreover, the company was not interested in settling out of court. Eventually public pressure caused MMMA to try to settle the case. Although sexual harassment is common in Japan, it is not considered important. What was important to top management executives in Tokyo was the effect that a high-level lawsuit would have on the sales of Mitsubishi products in the United States.

Sexual Harassment

Sexual harassment is a form of discrimination and falls within the statutory prohibitions against sex discrimination. It is covered by the Civil Rights Act of 1964. Title VII, which prohibits discrimination on the basis of ascriptive characteristics such as sex in any employment condition, also includes behavior that has an adverse effect on the work environment. This has come to include any verbal, nonverbal, or physical behavior that has an adverse effect on work conditions. It is divided into two categories, the first of which is quid pro quo harassment, and the second of which is a hostile work environment. Quid pro quo harassment involves the exchange of sexual favors for some type of employment benefit, such as a promotion or pay raise. A hostile work environment can be created by one's coworkers, supervisors, or clients who ask for dates, post suggestive pictures, or make lewd gestures or remarks.

Quid Pro Quo Harassment

Williams v. Saxbe serves as an excellent example of quid pro quo sexual harassment.[20] The plaintiff in *Williams* was an employee of the Department of Justice. She brought an action under Title VII of the Civil Rights Act of 1967, claiming that her supervisor made sexual advances toward her. She accused her supervisor of retaliatory conduct in response to her refusal to submit to his sexual requests. Ultimately, she was fired. A court ruled that her supervisor was in a position to hire, fire, or promote her, or at least to influence others who had that influence over her. If she denied her supervisor's requests her position would have been jeopardized, as it was. The super-

visor's retaliatory action of firing her represented a sanction only an employer
can impose, and such employer behavior violated Title VII of the Civil Rights
Act.

Hostile Work Environment

The first major case that came under the category of hostile work environment was *Meritor Savings Bank v. Vinson.*[21] The plaintiff, Michelle Vinson,
was employed as a teller-trainee and was promoted. Eventually she took an
excessive number of days of sick leave and was fired. She then brought action
against the bank, claiming her supervisor had sexually harassed her. She
claimed that she had complied with his demand for sex because she was
afraid she would lose her job. She also contended that he fondled her in front
of other employees, and exposed himself to her in the women's bathroom.
Vinson asked for injunctive relief as well as compensatory and punitive damages against her supervisor and the bank, alleging unwelcome sexual
advances created a hostile work environment in violation of Title VII.

There were countercharges by the supervisor and the bank. One was that
Vinson dressed provocatively, and another was she had engaged in sexual
fantasies. The bank stated that if her supervisor had sexually harassed her, it
was unknown to the bank and was engaged in without its consent or approval.
In addressing the issues, a district court labeled Vinson's relations with her
supervisor as voluntary and said that it had nothing to do with her employment advancement. It also found that, even if the supervisor had harassed
Vinson, Meritor was not liable for his action, and held that evidence of Vinson's dress and personal fantasies was admissible. The court ruled in favor of
Meritor. Vinson then took the case to an appeals court, which ruled in her
favor. The Supreme Court upheld the court of appeals, finding that Vinson's
voluntary sexual relationship was not a defense to a sexual harassment case.
The decision strengthened the hostile environment theory of sexual harassment.[22]

Ellison v. Brady—The Reasonable Woman Standard[23]   In this case,
Kerry Ellison worked for the IRS. Sterling Gray, who worked near her, kept
pestering her for dates and wrote her love notes. She filed a complaint with
her employer alleging sexual harassment. Gray was counseled, told to leave
her alone, and was transferred to another location. Eventually, he was brought
back without Ellison's knowledge. She requested a transfer, which she got,
and then filed suit. An appellate court ruled that a hostile work environment
must be judged from the perspective of the victim—in this case, the reasonable woman. This meant that the victim's feelings must play an important
role in identifying a series of actions as sexual harassment. The mere pres-

ence of an employee who has harassed a coworker may constitute a hostile work environment.

Harris v. Forklift Systems[24]   As the only female supervisor in her company, which sold and leased forklifts, Teresa Harris tried to get along with her male counterparts. She attended some of their beer-drinking parties at a bar after work, exchanged dirty jokes, and incorporated into her vocabulary some of the off-color language the men used. But in 1987, after two years on the job, she quit and filed a lawsuit accusing her boss of ignoring her requests to stop sexually harassing her. He used crude language and sexual innuendos toward her in front of other men. He also allegedly dropped things on the floor and made her pick them up; suggested to her that she should dress in a way that would expose her legs and breasts; and asked her if she had sex with clients in order to get their business.

She claimed that this sexual harassment caused her to drink excessively and to cry all the time. The lawyer for her boss claimed she put herself in this position by conducting herself as "just one of the boys." Her boss claimed he was just joking and she should not have taken him seriously. A district court found that his conduct did not constitute a hostile work environment; even though his comments were offensive and abrasive, they were not serious enough to affect Harris's well being. A reasonable woman manager under like circumstances would have been offended, but his conduct would not have affected her performance. Moreover, the court ruled that Harris was not subjectively so offended that she suffered psychological damage. The decision went to an appellate court, which upheld the decision.

The case then went to the Supreme Court, which decided in her favor. The ruling has affected every workplace in the nation and defined, once and for all, the point at which sexual comments and tasteless jokes on the job constitute sexual harassment. In the past, many federal courts have required women to demonstrate how they have been psychologically injured. They have had to prove that the conduct was so severe that it altered the victim's work conditions and produced a hostile work environment. The Supreme Court decision has changed this.

Oncale v. Sundowner Offshore Services[25]   Joseph Oncale was a roustabout who worked on an oil rig off the coast of Louisiana. He was constantly sexually harassed by his boss and coworkers. He was sexually assaulted and threatened with rape. He filed a sexual harassment lawsuit against the company, Sundowner Offshore Services, but a lower court ruled that Title VII of the Civil Rights Act of 1964 only covered harassment of women by men, and harassment of men by women, but not same-sex harassment. In this particular case, the Supreme Court ruled that the Title VII provision applied even when the victim and the harasser were of the same sex. The case was remanded back to the Louisiana court that originally heard the case.

Violence Against Women Act of 1994

Violence in the workplace is of increasing concern in the United States. Much of the violence is directed against women. A remedy is the Violence Against Women Act (VAWA) that was passed in 1994 after nearly four years of hearings and extensive debate concerning the pervasive nature and widespread effects of violence against women. As a result of the hearings, Congress determined that a comprehensive federal approach was called for to stem the increase in gender-motivated violence and to address a perception that this type of violence was not as serious as other crimes. Gender-motivated violence was determined to be a hate crime; and guidelines for determining hate crimes included the following:

1. language used by the perpetrator;
2. the severity of the attack including mutilation;
3. the lack of provocation;
4. previous history of similar incidents;
5. the absence of any other apparent motive, such as robbery.

VAWA has two major provisions:

1. It authorized $1.6 billion in federal spending over a six-year period to aid state and local attempts to reduce violence against women, including money for education and prevention, battered women's shelters, and a national domestic violence hotline.
2. Title III of the act provides a civil rights remedy. It is statutorily limited to violent crimes committed because of gender or on the basis of gender, and due, at least in part, to hate based on the victim's gender. A crime of violence is defined as an act or series of acts that would constitute a felony if the conduct presents a serious risk of physical injury to another person. The person injured may sue for compensatory and punitive damages, and injunctive and declaratory relief.

Affirmative Action

Affirmative action means active efforts by employers to correct any racial, sexual, or other minority imbalance that may exist in a labor force. The general principle behind affirmative action is the accordance of preferences for groups that have suffered discrimination in the past. It is far more comprehensive than simple employment discrimination, which may involve only one member of a protected class. It requires employers with federal contracts to evaluate their workforces, to analyze their employment needs, and to actively solicit minority employees. Affirmative action programs must meet certain minimum requirements in which the burden is on the employer. A program must contain certain basic information. For example, the workforce must be analyzed to determine where minorities are being underused, why they are being underused, and how this situation can be corrected.

The principle of affirmative action goes back much further than the civil rights legislation of the 1960s and extends well beyond questions involving ethnic minorities or women. In 1935 the Wagner Act prescribed affirmative action as well as cease-and-desist remedies against employers whose anti-union activities had violated the law. Thus, in the landmark *Jones and Laughlin Steel* case, which established the constitutionality of the act, the National Labor Relations Board ordered the company not only to stop discriminating against employees who were union members, but also to post notices in conspicuous places announcing they would reinstate back pay to unlawfully discharged workers. Had the company been ordered merely to cease and desist from economic retaliation against union members, the effect of its past intimidation would have continued to hamper the free choice of election guaranteed by the Wagner Act.[26] Affirmative Action was initially established by Executive Orders, and has now been incorporated into the Civil Rights Act of 1991 and the Americans with Disabilities Act.

Executive Orders

An executive order can be issued by the president of the United States requiring that a certain action be taken. There are limits within which it can be done. For example, it can be challenged by Congress as a usurpation of its powers. Executive orders issued by Presidents Lyndon Johnson and Richard Nixon declared it a matter of public policy that affirmative action must be taken to rectify discrimination against minorities. President Johnson issued Executive Order 11246 in 1965, which stated that in all federal contracts or in any employment situation that uses federal funds, employers have to prove they have sought out qualified applicants from disadvantaged groups, and must hire preferentially from minority group members when their qualifications are roughly equal to those of other applicants.

Executive Order 11375, which was issued by President Johnson in 1967, banned discrimination in federal employment on the basis of race, sex, color, and national origin. Directors of federal agencies were required to draw up a positive program of equal employment opportunity for all employees, and to hire more women and minorities at all levels. Affirmative action was eventually extended to universities, and each school with federal contracts was asked to provide information on the number of women and minority members in each position, academic and nonacademic. They were also required to set specific goals for increasing the number of women and minorities in each position.

Executive Order 4, issued by President Nixon in 1971, is the basis for most affirmative action programs. Under this order, affirmative action is required from all employers who hold federal contracts. The type of affirmative action employers must take is determined by the nature of the federal contract they hold. A written affirmative action program, demanded by the Office of Federal Contract Compliance (OFCC) regulations, applies to all nonconstruction contractors and subcontractors of the federal government and to agencies of the federal government that employ fifty or more employees and have a contract in excess of $50,000 a year. All business firms or government agencies that meet these criteria must file a written affirmative action program that contains a statement of good faith efforts to achieve equal employment opportunity. Such efforts must include an analysis of deficiencies in the use of minorities, a timetable for correcting such deficiencies, and a plan for achieving these goals. Revised Order 14, issued by the Labor Department in July 1974, gave approval to the procedures that federal agencies must use in evaluating government contractors' affirmative action programs. Among other things, contractors must list each job title as it appears in their union agreements or payrolls, rather than listing only job groups as was formerly required. The job titles must be ranked from the lowest paid to the highest paid within each department. Further, if there are separate work units or lines of progression within a department, separate lists must be provided for each unit or line, including unit supervisors. For lines of progression, the order of jobs in the line through which an employer can move to the job must be indicated. For each job title, two breakdowns are required. Besides the total number of male and female jobholders, it is necessary to have the total number of male and female jobholders in each of the following groups: Blacks, Hispanics, Native Americans, and Asians.

Application of Affirmative Action

Affirmative action is very controversial. It has come under criticism for several reasons. The first involves Title VII of the Civil Rights Act of 1964, which was supposed to create an employment-neutral playing field by prohibiting discrimination based on race, sex, religion, color, or national origin. The intent of Congress in passing the act was reasonably explicit. It did not force employers to achieve any kind of racial balance in their workforce by giving any kind of preferential treatment to any individual or group.[27] Critics of affirmative action suggest that it goes far beyond this intent by requiring preferential treatment, even though laws specify its application to equally qualified candidates. The second criticism involves the problem of fairness when it comes to admission to colleges or to medical and law schools. The plaintiff in the *Bakke* case argued that he was denied admission to medical school even though his grades were higher than those of minority students who were admitted.

United Steelworkers Union v. Weber[28]   The United Steelworkers Union and Kaiser Aluminum entered into a voluntary agreement covering an affirmative action plan designed to eliminate racial imbalance in the Kaiser plants throughout the country. Black hiring goals were set in each plant equal to the percentage of blacks in the respective labor forces. In the Gramercy, Louisiana, plant, 39 percent of the area workforce was black but only 18 percent of the plant workers were black, and only 2 percent of black workers held craft positions. Kaiser established a goal for the plant whereby it was required that 50 percent of openings in craft-training positions be reserved for blacks. Brian Weber, who applied for a position, was turned down. Arguing that he had seniority, he charged reverse discrimination. The case went to the U.S. Supreme Court, which in 1979 upheld the quota system for the training program.

A number of other affirmative action cases followed *Weber*. In 1984, the Supreme Court upheld the seniority system in the *Stotts* case.[29] In the New York Sheetmetal Union Case of 1986, the justices upheld by a 5–4 vote a federal court order for a local sheetmetal workers' union in New York to meet specific minority hiring requirements of 29.23 percent.[30] In the same year in the *Cleveland Firefighters* case, it upheld a decision by a lower court settlement between the City of Cleveland and minority firefighters that called for the promotion of one minority for one white, with the intent of increasing to a certain percentage the number of black officers in each rank.[31] These and other cases delineated several factors that are important in determining whether or not an affirmative action plan that involves preferential treatment complies with Title VII of the Civil Rights Act of 1964.

1. An affirmative action plan should be remedial in nature. If an employer's workforce is imbalanced, an affirmative action plan can be justified.
2. A plan should not exclude all nonminorities. In the *Weber* case, the Supreme Court emphasized that a 50 percent minority admissions quota did not create a bar to nonminorities.
3. An affirmative action plan should be temporary. Once the goals have been met, the plan should be discontinued.

Minority Set-Asides

Minority set-asides are an area of affirmative action designed to provide preferential treatment for women- and minority-owned businesses. In addition to the federal government, state and local governments have similar programs of set-asides for preferred groups. The rationale for these programs is to encourage more women and minorities to become involved in business, and to prevent discrimination that is often based on factors that have little to do with efficiency. In some cases, these businesses may be awarded contracts by federal agencies without competitive bidding.

City of Richmond v. J. A. Croson Co.[32]   In 1989 the U.S. Supreme Court ruled against a minority set-aside program that had been established by the City of Richmond. It had set aside 30 percent of construction funds for minority contractors. A contractor, J. A. Croson Co., had bid on a city contract but was rejected on the grounds that it had not made sufficient efforts to find minority subcontractors. It argued that it had made a good faith effort but was unable to find qualified minority subcontractors. The Court, by a 6–3 decision, found the Richmond ordinance unconstitutional. Justice Sandra Day O'Connor, in writing the key opinion, argued that affirmative action programs could be justified only on the evidence of prior discrimination. She stressed that this discrimination must be specific and identifiable and this the city had failed to prove. She also held that the plan was not narrowly tailored to fit a specific disadvantaged group; it was too broad-based in its preference.[33]

Adarand Constructors, Inc. v. Pena[34]   This case involved a challenge to a federal program that granted special treatment to minority subcontractors. A large construction company received a contract to build highways in southern Colorado. It requested bids to build guardrails. Two subcontractors made bids, one white-owned and one minority-owned. Adarand, the white-owned company, made a bid that was $1,700 lower than the bid of the other company. The contract went to the other company because the main contract was with the federal government, which provided a 10 percent bonus to the contractor if it used a minority contractor. In this case, the Supreme Court decided in favor of Adarand, holding that all racial classifications, used by whatever level of government, must conform to strict scrutiny standards.[35] It ruled that only affirmative action plans that would respond to provable past discrimination would be legal.

Affirmative Action and Education

In no one area has affirmative action become more controversial than in college education. The main issue is over the use of race in college admissions and the use of different and lower selection criteria for minority applicants. Supporters of affirmative action argue that different admission policies are necessary to ensure that students of all backgrounds have access to a college education in order to create cultural diversity. However, proposals to roll back affirmative action have increased. Opponents of the use of racial preferences in admission won in California with Proposition 209. A major affirmative action case involved a white teacher who was laid off, rather than an equally qualified black teacher.[36]

Cheryl Hopwood v. Texas[37] In 1992 hundreds of students were denied admission to the prestigious University of Texas School of Law. However, four of the applicants, including Cheryl Hopwood, sued, charging that the University of Texas had discriminated against them on the basis of their race in violation of the Fourteenth Amendment and Title VII of the Civil Rights Act of 1964. The plaintiffs challenged the admissions process used by the University of Texas in which Mexican Americans and African Americans were admitted pursuant to a different and lower standard for admittance than other students. Under the 1992 admissions system, a nonpreferred applicant could have a substantially higher Texas Index score and be denied admission while a preferred minority with a lower TI could be admitted. Preferred minority applicants were color coded and reviewed by a separate minority subcommittee, while all other applicants were reviewed by the regular admissions committee.

A district court upheld the concept of UT's affirmative action program, based on the idea that obtaining educational benefits from a racially and ethnically diverse student body is a sufficiently compelling reason to support the use of racial classifications.[38] It held that the plaintiffs had to show that they would have been admitted to the law school if a constitutionally permissible admissions system had been in place. It found the plaintiffs had failed to show this, awarded them $1.00 each in nominal damages, and ordered that they be allowed to reapply to the law school without further costs. However, the Court, in justifying the rationale for affirmative action for admission to the law school, stated that the approach was flawed because UT failed to give comparative evaluation to all applicants.

The university appealed this part and the case went to the Fifth Circuit Court of Appeals, which ruled that any consideration of race or ethnicity by the law school for the purpose of achieving a diverse student body is not a compelling interest under the Fourteenth Amendment. The Fifth Circuit majority relied on two Supreme Court decisions, *City of Richmond v. J. A. Croson Co.* and *Adarand v. Pena*, for the contention that modern equal protection has only one compelling interest, namely, remedying the effect of past discrimination. It removed diversity as a compelling interest for the use of racial classification. It declared that only past discrimination could be remedied by the use of racial classifications.[39]

Grutter v. Bollinger and Gratz v. Bollinger[40] Two cases challenging the affirmative action policies of the University of Michigan may have had the farthest reaching impact on the future of affirmative action. Grutter, a white woman student, applied for admission to the University of Michigan's law school, but was rejected. She discovered that other minorities with lower admissions scores had been accepted. Gratz, also a white woman, applied for undergraduate admission to the University of Michigan and was rejected. She, too, discovered that minorities had been accepted ahead of her. Gratz's case addressed a complex point system utilized by the University, in which not only minorities, but also legacies (students whose parents attended Michigan), athletes, and others received additional points on their entrance application. The Michigan system had been considered a model for other universities.

The outcomes of the cases have been considered a "split decision" on affirmative action. In *Gratz*, the court ruled that the complex point system was unconstitutional, and has caused Michigan to revisit its admissions system. In *Grutter,* the court upheld the University's affirmative action system. The upshot of both cases is that affirmative action policies are still permissible, but under "narrowly tailored" conditions. Justice Sandra Day O'Connor, in writing the majority opinion, perhaps signaled the sunset of affirmative action:

> It has been 25 years since Justice Powell first approved the use of race to further an interest in student body diversity in the context of public higher education. Since that time, the number of minority applicants with high grades and test scores has indeed increased. See Tr. of Oral Arg. 43. We expect that 25 years from now, the use of racial preferences will no longer be necessary to further the interest approved today.[41]

State Fair Employment Laws

Federal laws pertaining to employment practices are not the only laws that affect employers; there also are state laws. In fact, federal laws are often designed to stimulate activity by the states under their existing laws. The Civil Rights Act of 1964 directed the EEOC to defer to the states for a reasonable time when there is a charge of discrimination. A number of local governments also have antidiscrimination laws. Almost all states provide for an administrative hearing and the judicial enforcement of orders of an administrative agency or officials, and carry penalties for violating the laws. State laws apply to all employers, unions, and employment agencies located within a state without being restricted to those engaged solely in intrastate operations. The Supreme Court has upheld this application of state laws to interstate employees.

State laws vary in their coverage but generally prohibit discrimination on the basis of race, sex, age, and national origin, unless a necessary occupational requirement. Apart from laws governing the practices of business firms, many states have separate laws requiring equal pay for equal work by male and female employees. These laws are limited to eliminating discrimination in wage differences and do not touch other forms of job discrimination. In addition to the equal pay laws, discrimination in compensation based on sex also is barred, either specifically or by implication, in states that include sex bias in their unemployment practice laws.

Recruitment and Testing of Workers

Laws concerning the recruitment and testing of workers also affect employers. In advertising for workers, it is unlawful for an employer to print or publish an advertisement related to employment that expresses a preference based on sex, except when sex is a necessary requisite for employment. Somewhat similar requirements have been applied to application forms with respect to race, though it quickly became apparent that if there were no records concerning race, there would be insufficient statistical evidence on which to prove discrimination or the lack of it. Thus, the EEOC had to grapple with the fact that the logical time and place to gather certain significant information about a person's qualifications is also the time when there is the greatest likelihood of discrimination in recruitment and hiring.

Employment Interviews

In hiring workers, employers can run afoul of Title VII of the Civil Rights Act of 1964 or other legislation regulating employment practices. One of the greatest areas of potential problems is in the employment interview, since virtually all employers use it. There are basically three types of questions that are illegal. First, it is illegal to ask questions about race, sex, or age in the employment interview unless they are relevant to the job. Second, questions asked of one group but not another are generally illegal. An example would be that asking a woman how many children she has without asking the same question of male applicants is usually illegal. Third, questions that would have an adverse effect on employment should not be asked unless they are job related. Table 7.3 provides examples of questions that can and cannot be asked.

Testing

Certain personnel problems confronting businesses are quite subtle. The entire area of testing is an excellent example of how genuine efforts at compliance with civil rights laws can still be construed as noncompliance. Courts have held that inquiries into a prospective employee's criminal record would be racially discriminatory unless the inquiry and the answer it was designed to elicit were somehow directly related to the total assessment of the employee. The same is true of all other types of preemptive testing and standards, such as aptitude tests, IQ tests, and educational achievement tests. That there was no intent to discriminate does not matter.

Other Employment Laws

There are other important employment laws that are worthy of note. One is the Family and Medical Leave Act of 1993, which is designed to provide job

Table 7.3   Pre-Employment Interviews: What Is Lawful and What Is Unlawful

Question	Lawful	Unlawful
Name	First, middle, last—use of any name necessary for checking previous work experience	Requirement of prefix Mr., Ms., Mrs. or inquiries about names changed by marriage or divorce
Height and Weight		Questions are unlawful unless there is a BFOQ
Religion	Only questions based on BFOQ	Questions not based on BFOQ
Age	Questions as to whether or not applicants meet minimum/ maximum age standards	How old are you? Birth date
Marital Status	Whether person can meet specific work schedules, or responsibility that would interfere with work	Whether person is single, married, divorced, or engaged; number and ages of dependent children; all questions related to pregnancy.
Photograph	May be required after employment	Requirement that applicant attach photo
Criminal Record	Have you ever been convicted of a crime?	Have you ever been arrested?
Credit Rating		All questions regarding credit ratings, charge accounts, or other indebtedness
Military History	Military experience of relevance to the job	Type of discharge, military discipline record
National Origin	Languages applicant speaks, reads, or writes	Birthplace of applicant; how foreign languages were learned

Source: Jeffrey A. Norris, President, Equal Employment Opportunity Council. (Washington, D.C., May 1997) unpublished data.

security for workers who have to take leave to care for a child, spouse, or other relatives. Unlike similar laws in the European countries that provide paid leave, often for up to one year, American workers can only take unpaid leave. The second act is the Occupational Safety and Health Act of 1970, which is designed to reduce the number of injuries and fatalities incurred in the workplace.

The Family and Medical Leave Act (FMLA)

FMLA, which is under the jurisdiction of the Department of Labor, covers public employers of any size and private employers with fifty or more employees during each of twenty or more calendar workweeks in the current or preceding calendar year. Employees eligible to take leave under the act must have worked for an employer for at least twelve months and for at least 1,250 hours immediately preceding the commencement of any leave taken under the act. An eligible employee can take a total of twelve workweeks unpaid leave during any twelve-month period for the birth of a child; adoption; the care of a child, spouse, or parent; and a serious health problem that would make him or her unable to perform the job. Eligible employees can use any accrued vacation or personal leave for FMLA purposes.[42]

The Occupational Safety and Health Act (OSHA)

OSHA covers most employers and employees, including agricultural workers, nonprofit organizations, and professionals. The purpose of the act is to assure safe and healthful working conditions for men and women. It requires employers to comply with safety and health standards promulgated by OSHA. In addition, every employer is required to furnish for each of his or her employees a job free from recognized hazards that cause or are likely to cause death or serious injury. Recognized hazards are defined as those that can be recognized by the common human senses, unaided by testing devices, and those that are generally known in the industry as hazardous. Further, a firm can be penalized only if an inspector has cited the unsafe condition and the employer has refused to correct it in the specified time. In 2001, 4.9 million workers were injured on the job, and 8,786 died.[43] In 2003, OSHA increased oversight on repeat offenders, to include follow-up inspections and mandatory safety consultants for problem employers.

Mine Safety

With some deaths of coal miners in 2006, the Mine Safety and Health Administration has been criticized for its low fines for mining company violations. The maximum fine of $60,000 was levied only twelve times from 2001–2005, and the median fine was $27,584.

SUMMARY

In recent years, the focus of government regulation has been on the achievement of social goals. An example is the regulation pertaining to the employment of women and members of minority groups. In 1964 the Civil Rights Act was passed to prevent discrimination based on race, color, sex, religion, or national origin. Other acts were passed to prevent discrimination based on age and disability and to provide equal pay for equal work. Executive orders in 1965 and 1967 introduced the idea of affirmative action, which has come to be associated with the hiring and promotion of more women and minorities. Sexual harassment has also become an important workplace issue. It is a form of discrimination and falls within the statutory provisions against sex discrimination.

QUESTIONS FOR DISCUSSION

1. What is quid pro quo sexual harassment?
2. Affirmative action is a very controversial subject. Discuss the arguments for and against it.
3. Discuss the difference between disparate impact and disparate treatment in employment.
4. What is the reasonable woman defense?
5. Why is the case of *Oncale v. Sundowner Offshore Services* significant?
6. Discuss some of the questions that can and cannot be used in employment interviews.

RECOMMENDED READING

Bennett-Alexander, Dawn D. "Same-Gender Sexual Harassment: The Supreme Court Allows Coverage Under Title VII." *Labor Law Journal*, no. 4, April 1998: 927–940.

Katznelson, Ira. 2005. *When Affirmative Action was White: An Untold History of Racial Inequality in Twentieth-Century America.* W. W. Norton & Company.

Lavelle, Marianne. "The New Rules of Sexual Harassment," *U.S. News and World Report* July 6, 1998: 30–31.

Silvi, John Anthony. 2004. *The Death of Affirmative Action: The Proposed Model for the Candidate Selection Process into Law School.* PublishAmerica.

NOTES

1. Daniel Bell. On Meritocracy and Equality. *The Public Interest*. Vol. 29 (Fall 1972): 18–21.

2. U.S. Bureau of the Census. *Statistical Abstract of the United States: 2004–2005.* Washington, D.C.: October 2004, p. 447.

3. *Statistical Abstract of the United States 2004–2005.* p. 447.

4. This percentage has remained relatively stagnant since 1996, while that of the highest 5th continued to grow.

5. United Nations Development Program. *Human Development Report 2004.* New York: Oxford University Press, 2004, p. 220.

6. Jodi L. Jacobson, *Gender Bias: Roadblock to Sustainable Development.* Washington, D.C.: World Watch, September 1992.

7. *Statistical Abstract of the United States 2004–2005.* p. 377.

8. *Statistical Abstract of the United States 2004–2005.* p. 373.

9. *Statistical Abstract of the United States 2004–2005.* p. 411.

10. The mean income of all physicians in 1995 was $182,400, which was down from the two previous years.

11. Barbara F. Reskin and Heidi I. Hartmann, eds. *Women's Work, Men's Work: Sex Segregation on the Job.* Washington, D.C.: National Academy Press, 1996, pp. 27–41.

12. Daniel Bell. *The Cultural Contradictions of Capitalism.* New York: Basic Books, 1976, p. 275.

13. *Plessy v. Ferguson*, 163 U.S. 540 (1896).

14. *Brown v. Board of Education*, 347 U.S. 483 (1954).

15. *Abrams v. Baylor College*, 805 F. 2d 528 (5th Cir. 1980).

16. *McDonnell Douglas v. Green*, 411 U.S. 792 (1973).

17. *McDonnell Douglas v. Green*, 411 U.S. 792 (1973). p. 802.

18. *Watson v. Fort Worth Bank and Trust*, No. 86-6139 S.C. (1988).

19. *Griggs v. Duke Power Co.*, 401 U.S. 424 (1971).

20. *Williams v. Saxbe*, 413 F. Supp. 654 (D.C. Cir. 1976).

21. *Meritor Savings Bank FSB v. Vinson*, 106 S. Ct. 2399 (1986).

22. Maria Morlacri, "Sexual Harassment Law and the Impact of Vinson," *Employee Relations Law Journal*. 13, Winter 1987/88: 501–513.

23. *Ellison v. Brady, Sec. of the Treasury*, 924 F. 2d 872 (1991).

24. *Harris v. Forklift Systems, Inc.*, 114 S. Ct. 367 (1993).

25. *Oncale v. Sundowner Offshore Services*, 118 S. Ct. 75, 1998.

26. Harry A. Millis and Emily Clark Brown. *From the Wagner Act to Taft-Hartley.* Chicago, IL: University of Chicago Press, 1950, p. 97.

27. U.S. Equal Employment Opportunity Commission. *Legislative History of Titles VII and XI of Civil Rights Act of 1964.* Washington, D.C.: U.S. Government Printing Office, 1969, p. 3005.

28. *United States Steelworkers Union v. Brian Weber*, 61 U.S. 480 (1979).

29. *Firefighters Local Union No. 1784 v. Stotts*, U.S. No. 82-206 (1984).

30. *Sheetmetal Workers of N.Y. Local 28 v. EEOC*, 54 USLW 3596 (1986).

31. *IAFF v. Cleveland*, 54 USLW 3573 (1986).

32. *City of Richmond v. J. A. Croson Co.*, 488 U.S. 469 (1989).

33. *City of Richmond v. J. A. Croson Co.*, 57 Law Week 9132 (January 23, 1989).

34. *Adarand Constructors, Inc. v. Pena*, 115 S. Ct. 2097 (1995).

35. Under this standard, only affirmative action plans that respond to specific, provable past discrimination and that are narrowly tailored to eliminate such bias would be legal.

36. White teacher Sharon Taxman claimed her school board violated her rights when it made a racially based decision to lay her off rather than an equally qualified black teacher. She eventually got her job back and was compensated through a settlement with the NAACP.

37. *Texas v. Hopwood*, 116 S. Ct. 2581 (1996).

38. *Hopwood v. Texas*, 861 F. Supp. 551, 557-63 (W. D. Texas 1994).

39. *Hopwood v. Texas*, 78 F. 3d 932, 937 (5th Cir. 1996).

40. *Grutter v. Bollinger*, 539 U.S. 306 (2003); *Gratz v. Bollinger,* (02-516) 539 U.W. 244 (2003).

41. *Grutter v. Bollinger*, 539 U.S. 306 (2003). www.law.cornell.edu/supct/html/02-241.ZO.html

42. The act requires employers to post notices regarding the FMLA at the work site. An employer's failure to do so can result in fines up to $100 per offense.

43. These figures exclude casualties from the September 11 attacks.

8

Environmental Protection

One of the major areas of social regulation of business is environmental protection. In fact, pollution control costs are by far the most important regulatory costs imposed on business. There are not only the incremental costs of such items as emission control devices and paperwork costs, but also the secondary effects such as opportunity costs, changes in productivity, and costs of regulation-imposed delays. An example of an opportunity cost would be money spent in cleaning up the environment that could have been spent in modernizing industrial plants to meet foreign competition. There is also the economic cost of lost jobs when a plant shuts down as a result of environmental compliance costs.

Why are these costs imposed upon business? The major reason is because of health benefits. Pollution, whether it is air, water, noise, or any other type, causes problems. Air pollution increases the mortality rate and respiratory ailments, particularly among older people. There is also a relationship between air pollution and the incidence of lung cancer. Outbreaks of infectious diseases have been traced to contaminants in municipal water supplies and certain chemicals in water supplies have been linked with increased rates of cancer.

Another reason to try to curb pollution is that it can have an adverse effect on economic activities. Agricultural production can be harmed by rising acidity in the soil. Lowered water control standards have had an adverse effect on commercial fishing production.

Finally, there are aesthetic benefits to curbing pollution. Air and water pollution can cause odors and tastes that affect people's ability to function well. Oil slicks on a beach or fish killed by a chemical spill are unpleasant, as is noise pollution. Pollutants that are visibly unpleasant can have an adverse effect on property values.

TYPES OF POLLUTION

Pollution of the environment is not a recent phenomenon, either in this country or around the world. In the United States it is a by-product of industrialization, which was stimulated by the Civil War. Examples of environmental problems are numerous. One that has received some attention in recent years is radon, an odorless, colorless radioactive gas produced by the decay of uranium in rocks and soils, and a major cause of lung cancer. Manufacturers have made radon detectors so that people can see if their homes have a problem.

Greenhouse Gases and Global Warming

The environmental problem that has received the most attention worldwide lately has been the so-called greenhouse effect, wherein the earth has been getting warmer. The eleven warmest years on record (since 1880) have all been since 1990 (twelve since 1987). 2005 was the warmest (58.3 degrees Fahrenheit), followed by 1998, 2002, 2003, 2001, and 2004. There was a one-degree increase in the twentieth century, 1.44 degrees from 1905–2005, and 1.08 degrees from 1975–2005. The average global temperature in 1880 was 56.60 degrees and in 2005 it was 57.96 degrees. It has been rising steadily since 1960. A leading cause is carbon dioxide from the burning of fossil fuels such as oil, coal (half of the electricity generated in the United States and 40 percent in the world comes from coal), and natural gas. The carbon from the fuel meets the oxygen from the air and the resultant carbon dioxide accumulates in the atmosphere. Another cause is from gases such as chlorofluorocarbons, although the United States banned most imports of them as of January 1, 1996. These and other gases come from a variety of sources, such as vehicle exhausts and industrial solvents. Greenhouse gas emissions in the United States, such as carbon dioxide, methane, and ozone, rose 12 percent in the 1990s.

The first large-scale increase in carbon dioxide levels came with the clearing of North American and European forests. Then, after a period of stability, the levels began to rise when coal was used for steam power in locomotives, factories, and ships, followed by oil, which surpassed coal as the world's leading primary energy source in the mid-1960s. One of the factors in the greenhouse effect is that since 1960 the number of automobiles worldwide has increased more than twice as fast as the population. Added to this is the burning of the Amazon rain forest, which began in earnest in the 1980s and continues today.

What happens when the gases such as carbon dioxide, methane, nitrous oxide (which collectively make up some 80 percent of the gases), sulfur hexafluoride, hydrofluorocarbons, and perfluorocarbons are released into the atmosphere? They act like the glass in a greenhouse, in that they let in the sunlight but trap the heat. About one-half of the sun's energy, solar radiation, is absorbed by the earth and converted into heat, which is then trapped, especially by carbon dioxide. The gases absorb rather than reflect the infrared radiation that produces heat. As the heat rises from the earth's surface, it strikes molecules of carbon dioxide and other gases, setting them vibrating. The gas molecules reflect some of the heat back to earth, which intensifies the warming or greenhouse effect. As more heat is trapped, the earth's overall temperature rises. If the troposphere (sea level to ten miles up) gets moisture (and water vapor is a greenhouse gas), the warming could accelerate. Water vapor, in fact, makes up 98 percent of the gases. Without the water vapor and the other gases such as carbon dioxide and ozone, the earth would be 61 degrees Fahrenheit colder. The warming is greater at night than during the day, is greater in winter than in summer, and is greater near the Arctic than near the equator. The Arctic sea ice is the lowest since measurements started in 1978, the largest ice shelf is breaking up, and the amount of sea ice floating is at a record low level. It shrank in Summer 2005, for the fourth year in a row, to what was probably its smallest size in at least a century of record keeping, continuing a trend toward less summer ice. The average minimum area from 1979 until 2000 was 2.69 million square miles, and the new summer low was 20 percent below that. It appears to be heading toward becoming self-sustaining, as the increased open water absorbs solar energy that would otherwise be reflected back into space by bright white ice. An international study predicts that the Arctic sea ice will disappear by the end of the century, causing the extinction of polar bears and some seal species, high risk for indigenous peoples, and the rising sea levels could threaten coastal areas. Coral reefs and other ecosystems already close to tolerance for heat and climate change could die off. Also, the Antarctic ice sheet is breaking, and if it moves it could cause sea levels to rise fifteen feet or more. It is breaking up faster than it can be replenished by interior snowfalls. Unless some action is taken to curb these gases, predictions have been made that the average temperature will rise another three to seven degrees Fahrenheit in the future. Most of the members of the United Nations have ratified protocols to cut down on greenhouse gases but, even if all comply, it would not be until around the years 2050 to 2070 that recovery would take place. In 2005 scientists said that the earth is absorbing far more heat than it is giving off. Evidence of global warming can be found in the dwindling sea ice, plants that are thriving in warmer climates and turning sparsely vegetated tundra into shrub land, and fire and insect outbreaks fostered by warmer temperatures that are assaulting northern forests.

The next question is, why is it so important to curtail the use of these gases? First, in addition to the problems mentioned previously, the melting of the polar ice cap due to the warmth can produce more icebergs that can endanger shipping. Also, water expands when heated, and oceans have risen some four to ten inches this century. Countries that are already adversely affected by flooding will have more flooding. In addition, the warming produces hotter and drier summers, which hurts farming and could cause crop failures. Tropical diseases could follow the rising mercury. The increase in warmth could also affect the world's wildlife, such as birds, that have adapted to the climate in which they are located.

In 2001, at a United Nations Conference in Shanghai, an Intergovernmental Panel on Climate Change made the most comprehensive study yet of the problem and unanimously approved a report predicting severe droughts, floods, and violent storms over the next century because air pollution is causing surface temperatures to rise faster than anticipated. The average temperatures will rise 10.4 degrees over the next 100 years and the earth will warm by 2–10 degrees by 2100. Ice caps will melt and raise sea levels by as much as 34 inches, causing floods. Also there will be droughts, more frequent storms due to climate extremes, and diseases. It will be the most rapid change in 10,000 years and more than 60 percent higher than the same group predicted less than six years before.

Kyoto Protocol

The greenhouse effect problem has been compounded by the fact that carbon dioxide stays in the atmosphere for a century, on average. One result of all this is that the nations of the world have decided to try to do something about the problem. In 1992, at the United Nations Framework Convention on Climate Change (Earth Summit) held in Rio de Janeiro, Brazil, attended by 166 nations including the United States, an agreement to limit harmful climate change was signed. Each country must submit periodic reports, and the third one submitted by the United States in 2002 said global warming is harmful and blamed fossil fuel burning, which supplies 90 percent of the world's energy needs, and also mentioned other effects such as substantial disruption of snow-fed water supplies, loss of coastal and mountain ecosystems, and more frequent heat waves. The developed nations pledged to reduce emissions of greenhouse gases by the year 2000. However, some countries, such as the United States, are falling short of that target. Therefore another conference on climate change, sponsored by the United Nations, met in Kyoto, Japan in December 1997. More than five thousand delegates represented some 159 nations, and the United States signed the document at an international conference held in Buenos Aires, Argentina, in November 1998. The goal now for the United States is to reduce emissions of carbon dioxide, two-thirds of which comes from cars and households, by 7 percent of 1990 levels by the year 2012. Other nations and regions of the world have their own goals and timetables ranging from 2008–2012. A conference with more than 170 countries was held at The Hague in 2000 to try to implement Kyoto but it failed. However, rules for Kyoto were adopted in 2001 in Marrakech, Morocco, at a conference attended by 164 countries. Most of the countries have approved them, and they came into effect on February 16, 2005, when 55 of the countries included the group responsible for at least 55 percent of the heat-trapping emissions for industrial countries in 1990. The United States, the world's largest emitter of heat-trapping gases, was not one of them, although power plants that burn fossil fuels are responsible for emitting (along with cars and trucks) much of the nation's nitrogen oxide (urban smog—ozone), sulfur dioxide (acid rain), carbon dioxide (climate change) and mercury (poison). The nation's air that is smoggy enough to violate federal health standards is rising (new smog standards were set in 2004).

The problem, in addition to meeting goals and timetables, is that not everyone is committed to them. For example, some members of the U.S. Congress have declared themselves against this goal for various reasons (it must be ratified by the Senate) and despite a campaign promise in 2000 to support the Kyoto Protocol President Bush formally rejected it in 2001. In 2004 there was a two-week UN conference on climate change in Buenos Aires and the United States blocked efforts to begin more substantive discussions. Instead, an agreement was reached to hold one workshop in 2005 to exchange information. The Bush administration favors the term "climate variability" rather than "climate change." A panel of scientists has opposed the Bush policy on global warming, saying too much emphasis is put on costs as opposed to having any substance. In a 2004 report to Congress, federal research indicated that emissions of carbon dioxide and other heat-trapping gases are the only likely explanation for global warming since 1970 (natural shifts in the output of the sun and other factors were responsible from 1900–1950). Also, accumulating emissions pose newly identified risks to farmers, as carbon dioxide promotes the growth of invasive weeds far more than it stimulates the crops and it reduces the nutritional value of some rangeland grasses. In 2005 132 mayors representing 29 million people in 35 states joined a bipartisan coalition to fight global warming on the local level. They pledged to have their cities meet the Kyoto Protocol (reduction in heat-trapping gas emissions to levels 7 percent below those of 1990) by 2012. Thus the future of the greenhouse effect is still uncertain.

Air pollution is a consistent problem in the United States. A 2004 study showed that 30,000 people die from it each year in the United States. The top 100 electric power companies emit 70 percent of sulfur dioxide pollution, although because of regulations there has been a significant decline in both sulfur dioxide and nitrogen oxide, which is a positive step because they contribute to smog, acid rain, and increased heart and lung diseases. However, carbon dioxide, which is unregulated (dealt with on a voluntary basis) has risen, and it raises temperatures plus causes violent weather. Power companies are responsible for one-third of the emissions due to coal-fired plants.

The EPA in 2004 said that all or parts of 474 counties (over 150 million people) either have air that is too dirty or contributing to neighboring counties' inability to meet federal air standards for smog-causing ozone. It causes respiratory diseases, and is especially damaging to children and people with asthma. The deadline for meeting air quality standards (85 parts per billion of ozone from 120) plus air sampling over an eight hour period, not one hour, range from 2007 to 2021. 2,668 counties had met the standards and 19 states had all counties in compliance. Also in 2004 the EPA said that almost one-third of all Americans live in 225 counties (20 states plus D.C.) that do not meet the 1997 standards for microscopic particles of pollution (car exhausts, wood-burning stoves, and power plants) that cause thousands of premature deaths a year (the sooty chemical particles are so small they can lodge deep in the lungs if inhaled). They have to develop plans in three years to bring the counties into compliance by 2010 or face the loss of federal highway money. Even partial compliance by 2010 would prevent 15,000 premature deaths a year, 75,000 cases of chronic bronchitis, 20,000 cases of acute bronchitis, 10,000 hospital admissions for respiratory and cardiovascular diseases, and loss of 3.1 million days worked.

Other Types of Pollution

There are, of course, other types of environmental problems, not the least of which is the depletion of the earth's ozone layer. That layer protects living organisms by using up ultraviolet and other high-energy forms of radiation through a cycle of chemical reactions. When the layer is weakened, ultraviolet radiation interacts with genetic material. The result is an increased incidence of skin cancer. What causes the depletion of the ozone layer? The chief culprits are freons, which are gases commonly used as solvents, refrigerants, and aerosol propellants. Freon reacts with ozone by converting it to atmospheric oxygen, thereby reducing the amount available to interact with ultraviolet radiation. Besides skin cancer in both humans and animals, there is a possibility that the depletion of the ozone layer might lower crop yields. Warmer temperatures also cause ozone layer depletion. There is a hole over Antarctica caused by the depletion that is the size of Europe. The use of ozone-depleting substances is down, but it is still a problem.

Another environmental problem is acid rain, caused by acid deposition in the atmosphere. What happens is that sulfuric acid and nitric acid are oxidized, the former primarily by coal-fueled electric utilities, the latter primarily by motor vehicles and electric utilities. Also, a variety of volatile organic compounds are released during petroleum refining, chemical manufacturing, and with the use of paints and solvents, and they too oxidize into acid rain. The problem, of course, is that when the acid rain falls to earth it affects metals, paint systems, stones, and other materials sensitive to it. It can affect the growth of forests, and it may affect agricultural growth. Acidic soil makes trees more vulnerable to climate changes, and acidic buildups in forests wash into waterways by erosion and spring runoff. Aquatic organisms can be damaged when acid rain falls into lakes and streams. Sulfur emissions are down in the United States, but are expected to triple in Asia by 2010.

Pesticides are yet another environmental problem, as they are hazardous to some forms of life and their misuse can cause environmental contamination. Humans can ingest them because some may get into food products. DDT, which is now banned in the United States, is the classic example; it got into streams and lakes, poisoning fish and the people who ate them. Any pesticide that is water-soluble can get into food crops, which are then consumed by humans. One of the biggest problems with pesticides is their increased use by developing countries; misuse can not only affect those who live there but those from the industrialized countries, since the pesticides can be reimported as residues on food. The U.S. government was concerned enough about the pesticide problem to unanimously pass a law in 1996, the Food Quality Protection Act, tightening the regulation of pesticides and imposing tougher rules to curb the risks for children. The EPA must apply a margin of safety ten times larger than the limits it previously set on cumulative exposure to traces of the chemicals. In 1999, in the first regulations intended specifically to protect children, it banned most uses of a pesticide applied widely for years on fruits and vegetables, and tightened restrictions on another. In 2006 an Environmental Protection Agency (EPA) rule said that researchers no longer will be allowed to include children and pregnant women in all studies not conducted or supported by a federal agency, that examine the effects of pesticides to help set federal standards, and would establish an independent oversight panel to ensure that all studies submitted to the agency were conducted ethically and followed internationally accepted protocols for human testing. The panel includes medical ethicists and experts in chemical tests and excludes anyone with connections to the agency or chemical companies. The rule applied to the toxicity tests involving humans that were currently before the agency at the time as well as all those in the future.

Hazardous waste, both solid and toxic, creates another environmental problem. Solid waste includes garbage, disposable cartons, and other items emitted by consumers. The problem is what to do with it in our increasingly consumptive society. Landfills are full, and incineration can cause pollution. People in the United States have endorsed the concept of recycling, but some recyclers have more material than they can handle. As for toxic waste, various by-products of industrial production cause that. For example, nitrous acid is released by the production of fertilizers, and usually disposed of in barrels that are buried in the earth. The barrels, unfortunately, can sometimes leak and cause pollution. Another example is wastewater from factories and sewage treatment plants, because it includes such toxic substances as heavy metals, including lead and mercury. They, in turn, have been responsible for the decimation of oysters, lobsters, and crabs in some places such as the Chesapeake Bay.

Mercury

Mercury is an especially difficult problem. A 2003 study found that 8 percent of American women were over the EPA recommended level, and it was fourfold higher among women who ate three or more servings of fish in a ten-day period. In 2004 the EPA monitored 35 percent of our lakes, 24 percent of our total river miles, 75 percent of our coastal waters, and all the Great Lakes, and said that fish in virtually all our lakes and rivers were contaminated with mercury. One in twelve women of childbearing age have unsafe levels and more than 600,000 children born each year are at risk. Nineteen states put all their lakes and rivers under statewide advisory for fish consumption the Food and Drug Administration advises pregnant or nursing women and children not to eat too much of certain fish, and in 2003 48 states issued warnings. In 2004 55 percent of the fish in our lakes and reservoirs were above the safe limit for women of average weight who ate fish twice a week, and it was 76 percent for children of average weight under three years of age. A 2004 study found that coal-fired plants were responsible for 41 percent of mercury emissions (more than 90,000 pounds a year) and up to 80 percent in some parts of the country. The level of mercury emissions from human causes did fall 45 percent in 1999 from 1990, and the Bush administration wants to reduce emissions 29 percent by 2010 and 69 percent by 2018. The Clean Air Act, however, calls for 90 percent by 2008.

Still More Kinds of Pollution

A potential problem in the environmental area is the possibility of a nuclear accident with the accompanying radiation danger. The meltdown of the nuclear power plant in Chernobyl in the former Soviet Union has been the biggest accident thus far, with a number of fatalities among workers who were employed at the plant as well as radiation damage that extended to neighboring countries, with contaminated milk as one example.

Perhaps the most important of all environmental problems is deforestation, because trees provide oxygen and prevent soil erosion. The major forests of the world are the tropical rain forests, and those of the Amazon River and equatorial Africa have been disappearing at an alarming rate. Half the world's tropical rain forests have been destroyed in the past one hundred years. One side effect is that wildlife populations native to the regions are in danger of becoming extinct or, at the very least, endangered. (These wildlife populations are further endangered by illegal wildlife trade, which garners $2–3 billion per year.) Also, since the deforestation occurs in very poor areas of the world, the leaching of the soil, the polluting of water supplies, and the land becoming less arable reduce the little food supply that exists. Another item of worry associated with deforestation is the disappearance of the carbon sink, which is anything that absorbs and retains carbon dioxide. Oceans are one type of sink, but so are forests and soils. When deforestation occurs, the trees are not there to absorb the carbon dioxide and so it goes into the atmosphere, helping to cause the greenhouse effect.

As can be seen, pollution is a global problem that transcends national boundaries and from which no country is immune. Water pollution is a good example. In the United States, whether looking at drinking, swimming, or fishing, and whether looking at streams and rivers, lakes, or estuaries, waters are impaired. In the 1970s most pollution came from sewage treatment plants or factories; now it comes from fertilizer running off farm fields and motor oil washing across highways. Every eight months nearly four million gallons of oil run off streets and driveways into our waters, which equal the *Exxon Valdez* spill. The largest EPA fine was levied in 2003 against a pipeline company that spilled 1.45 million gallons of oil into waterways. More than 60 percent of coastal rivers and bays have been degraded by nutrient runoff, which damages seagrass, kelp beds, coral reefs, and spawning ground for fish. It creates a dead zone in the Gulf of Mexico each year the size of Massachusetts. Congress appropriates money for dams, irrigation projects, and river dredging, and the Army Corps of Engineers will then alter the course and level of rivers to make them more navigable for barges, supply drinking water to cities and irrigate farms, but at the same time river bottoms are gouged of vital grass and more riverbanks are buried under concrete. The government does match other money for the protection of wetlands and will restore waterways, plant native trees, and acquire land that is home to endangered species, especially migratory waterfowl. In 2001 23 percent of the United States' oceans and coasts were too dirty for swimming, fishing, and supporting marine species, and in 2004 the U.S. Commission on Ocean Policy said that pollution, overfishing, and poor management have put North American oceans (U.S. has 3.4 million square nautical miles) in serious peril.

Overfishing is also an issue. Some 30 percent of our nation's fish populations are overfished, which increases the number being driven to extinction and invasive species are crowding out native ones in coastal waters. In recent years the government has declared West Coast groundfish fishing an economic disaster due to overfishing and poor ocean conditions. Nine species were declared overfished, some fisheries were closed, and the groundfish fleet was cut by one-third. In 2005 two councils of federal fishing regulators recommended to the National Marine Fisheries Service that a permanent ban on trawl fishing be imposed on waters off the Alaska coast and off the West Coast in order to protect coral beds, kelp forests, rocky reefs, and other sensitive fish habitats. The federal government claims jurisdiction of the waters off our coasts from 3 miles to 200 miles.

Worldwide, billions of people lack access to safe, clean water for drinking and sanitation, and contaminated water kills millions of people each year. Each year about 15 million children under five die from polluted water. Agriculture needs fresh water. By 2015 the UN wants to reduce in half the number of people lacking clean water. By 2025 half the world's people are expected to be thirsty. Then there is pollution of the seas. People who traverse waters, whether they are recreational boaters, people who fish, or even those who operate ocean-going ships, have dumped their garbage overboard. The resultant debris entangles many different marine species, and some species even ingest it. In addition, persons on land can dump pollutants into rivers that eventually make their way to the sea. Finally, a combination of marine pollution plus overfishing can cause a declining food supply.

Although not usually thought about, there is also a problem of noise pollution and the public health hazards associated with it.

Another point that should be apparent is that pollution comes from many sources. For one thing, the simple matter of population density means there will be more waste created in those areas. Just in the United States, more than half the people live in 1 percent of the total land area, and two-thirds live in 9 percent of the area. Along with the density, there is widespread affluence in Western industrial society. Two cars per family is common, which means that many cars are junked each year, along with other items such as bottles and cans. People want creature comforts. Even something such as air conditioning can lead to environmental pollution. The following is a summation of major environmental problems today:

1. Radon
2. Greenhouse effect and air pollution
3. Acid rain
4. Pesticides
5. Hazardous waste—solid and toxic
6. Mercury
7. Nuclear accidents
8. Deforestation
9. Water pollution and overfishing
10. Noise pollution

Industry does have its share of responsibility. Steel was one of the industries that polluted places, such as Lake Erie, with its wastes. Even something as innocuous as changing the way steel is made lessened the demand for scrap metal, which in turn lessened the incentive for junk dealers to salvage old cars, which in turn led to the problem many cities face of having to dispose of old automobiles. The governments of the world share some of the blame, as they have often been lax in disposing of sewage and solid wastes and have ended up polluting rivers and the air. Many cities operate their own public utilities and have polluted, as has the federal government with some of its facilities.

SOLUTIONS TO POLLUTION

What can governments do to help solve the many environmental problems? They can regulate by such methods as legislation and the requiring of licenses, permits, and registration, along with zoning. An advantage of regulation is that similar standards are established for all business firms. A disadvantage is that it could lead to rigidities and might be unwieldy and inefficient. Governments could also try levying emission charges, such as taxes or fees, against polluters. Subsidies to business firms to defray the cost of compliance with pollution control standards are another possibility. Examples of subsidies are tax credits to compensate for the cost of buying pollution abatement equipment, outright cash payments to reduce the level of pollution, accelerated depletion allowances to let business firms write off the cost of pollution control equipment in a shorter time than usual, and property tax exemptions on pollution control equipment by state and local governments. Although subsidies sound good, they do have disadvantages, such as less pressure on a firm to find alternate ways of dealing with pollution. Subsidies are also financed out of general tax revenues, which violates the principle of equity because not all taxpayers are involved with the making or consuming of those products. All these approaches can be used in combinations; they are not mutually exclusive.

Major Environmental Laws

How has the U.S. government responded to the problems affecting the environment? It has passed many laws over the years to try to handle the various issues. The following is a list of some of the major U.S. environmental laws:

1. 1899 Refuse Act
2. 1924 Oil Pollution Act
3. 1948, 1956, and 1972 Water Pollution Control Acts and Amendments
4. 1963 and 1970 Clean Air Acts and Amendments
5. 1965 and 1970 Water Quality Acts

6. 1967 Air Quality Act
7. 1970 National Environmental Policy Act
8. 1972 Noise Control Act
9. 1973 Endangered Species Act
10. 1975 Energy Policy and Conservation Act Amendments
11. 1976 Toxic Substances Control Act
12. 1976 Resource Conservation and Recovery Act
13. 1980 Comprehensive Environmental Response, Compensation, and Liability Act
14. 1984 Hazardous and Solid Waste Amendments
15. 1986 Emergency Planning and Community Right-to-Know Act
16. 1990 Global Change Research Act
17. 1992 Safe Water Drinking Act Amendments plus 1996 Safe Water Drinking Act Renewal
18. 1996 Magnuson Fishery Conservation and Management Act
19. 1996 Food Quality Protection Act
20. 2000 Beaches Environmental Assessment and Coastal Health Act
21. 2003 Healthy Forests Restoration Act

The 1899 Refuse Act prohibited the discharge of waste materials into navigable waters. The 1924 Oil Pollution Act forbade the discharge of oil into coastal waters, and the 1948 Water Pollution Control Act authorized the Public Health Service to coordinate research, provide technical information and, on request from the states involved, provide limited supervision of interstate waterways.

Congress then turned its attention to air pollution in 1955 by authorizing technical assistance to states and localities and setting up a research program. In 1956 the Water Pollution Control Act, amended in 1961, 1965, 1966, and 1970, considerably extended federal involvement, both regulatory and financial, in water pollution.

Congress then returned to air pollution with the 1963 Clean Air Act, which gave states grants to improve pollution control programs and to provide for federal enforcement in interstate pollution cases. It also expanded federal research, particularly in connection with pollution from motor vehicles and from the burning of coal and fuel oil, and it emphasized the need for controlling pollution from facilities operated by the federal government. The act was amended in 1965 to authorize federal regulation of motor vehicles through standards that became effective in 1968. It was amended again in 1966 to broaden the federal aid program, making grants available for state and local control programs. Meanwhile, in 1965, Congress revisited water pollution by passing the Water Quality Act, which created the Water Pollution Control Administration that was almost immediately transferred to the Department of the Interior. Then Congress went right back to air pollution with the 1967 Air

Quality Act that directed the Department of Health, Education, and Welfare (the agency handling air pollution problems) to delineate broad atmospheric areas for the entire country, as well as air quality control regions. It continued and strengthened most of the provisions of the earlier laws and provided for special studies of jet aircraft emissions, the need for national emission standards, and labor and training problems. It also established the Presidential Air Quality Advisory Board.

With all the previously discussed laws and with the problem of two agencies trying to coordinate their enforcement, President Nixon in 1970 sent a reorganization plan to Congress to create an independent agency to handle all environmental problems. Congress approved the plan and the Environmental Protection Agency was created in the executive branch. Besides air and water pollution problems, the EPA was given other environmental problems that had been in various agencies, such as studies on the effects of insecticides and pesticides, and the creation of tolerance norms for pesticide chemicals.

Now that the EPA was in place, Congress passed probably the most important of all federal laws governing pollution, the 1970 Clean Air Act. Among other points, the act required that new cars be virtually pollution free by 1975, and specified that emissions of hydrocarbons and carbon monoxide gases had to be 90 percent less than levels permissible in 1970. When automobile manufacturers had difficulty meeting the requirement due to costs, the date was pushed to 1981. The manufacturers also had to offer a 50,000-mile warranty on emission control devices, and the law established strict controls for fuel additives.

In addition to the automobile sections, the law also set national standards for air pollution, with the states being required to establish programs to meet the national standards within four to six years. The EPA was authorized to set both primary and secondary standards for pollutants. The primary ones were to promote human health with an added margin of safety for the most vulnerable, such as the elderly and infants. The secondary standards were to prevent damage to such things as crops, visibility, buildings, water, and materials.

The law also directed the EPA to determine maximum emission limits for plants and factories on an industry-by-industry basis. States could then use these as guidelines for more specific restrictions for individual factories. If any region violated any standards, the states there had to limit new construction of pollution sources until the air was brought up to federal standards. Any company wanting to build a plant there had to install equipment that limited pollution to the least amount emitted by any similar factory elsewhere in the country. The EPA is required to reevaluate its standards every five years.

The year 1970 also saw the National Environmental Policy Act, by which developers, loggers, etc. must describe in detail the impact the proposed project will have on the environment and come up with measurements to minimize it, and another Water Quality Act that extended federal control standards to oil and hazardous substance discharges from onshore and offshore vessel facilities. However, the big law affecting water was the 1972 Water Pollution Control Act, which amended the previous acts in that field. Included in the law is a requirement that manufacturers monitor discharges at point sources of pollution and keep records of the results of their efforts to reduce water pollution. Both the EPA and the state may inspect the records. The law also extended federal control to all navigable waters. When there is a violation, the EPA can issue an order requiring compliance or notifying the state of the problem. If the state does not begin appropriate enforcement within thirty days, the EPA can issue a compliance order requiring the violator to comply with a conditional or limited permit, or it can bring a civil action or begin criminal proceedings. Finally, the law (as did the Clean Air Act) gives citizens the right to bring suits to enforce standards in the U.S. district courts.

The year 1972 found the government finally passing a law in the field of noise pollution, realizing that noise can be a danger to the health and welfare of the population, particularly in urban areas. Human blood pressure and heartbeat can be adversely affected, and sustained noise can cause permanent injury. Accordingly, the Noise Control Act sets noise emission standards for a wide variety of product categories. Specifically, it targets aircraft noise, sonic booms, railroads, and motor carriers, as well as newly manufactured products that have been identified as being major sources of noise. These standards were to be established for all products identified as major noise sources within eighteen months of the law's passage, with public health, safety, and welfare as the goal.

As with both the Clean Air and Water Pollution Control Acts, criminal sanctions under this law range from fines of up to $25,000 per day of violation, or imprisonment for up to one year, or both, for the first offense. Subsequent offenders are liable for fines of up to $50,000 for each day of violation or for imprisonment of up to two years, or both. Each additional day of violation constitutes a separate offense.

Also as with the other two laws, citizens may sue in federal district courts. In addition, citizens may sue both the administrator of the EPA and the administrator of the FAA for alleged failure to perform their duties under the law. The law provides for technical assistance to be given state and local governments to develop and enforce noise standards, and it also authorizes labeling requirements for any product that emits noise capable of adversely affecting the public health and welfare or that is sold on the basis of its effectiveness in reducing noise. When a product is labeled, purchasers or users must be informed of the level of noise the product emits or its effectiveness in reducing noise, whichever may be the case.

In 1975 Congress passed the Energy Policy and Conservation Act Amendments, setting corporate average fuel economy standards for new cars produced in the United States that required car companies to achieve a sales-weighted, fleet-average economy of 27.5 miles for cars and 21.6 miles for SUVs and other light trucks in the 1985 model year.

Congress followed this in 1976 with the Toxic Substances Control Act, which gave the EPA broad regulatory authority over chemical substances from before their manufacture to their disposal. The EPA had to make an inventory of approximately 62,000 chemical substances then in use, and the EPA has to be notified before any new chemical substances are manufactured although the law requires little, if any, lab testing for the 18,000 approved since then (chemicals in pesticides, foods, and drugs do require tests). The EPA can require testing of any it believes may pose a "reasonable risk" to human health or environment—it usually asks the companies to conduct them. It can restrict use only if the risks are not outweighed by economic and social benefits for each way the substance might be used. There is a ninety day screening process for new chemicals, but when they are compared with the old ones the safety data on the latter can be limited. In addition, companies were given recordkeeping, testing, and reporting requirements so that the EPA can assess the relative risks of chemicals and regulate them.

Another 1976 law was the Resource Conservation and Recovery Act, which requires the safe disposal of hazardous wastes. Regulations define hazardous waste and establish standards for their generation and transportation. Owners and operators of facilities that treat, store, or dispose of hazardous wastes must get a permit, and a waste generator has to prepare a manifest for hazardous wastes that tracks the movement of the wastes from the point of generation to the point of disposal. If a waste is hazardous, it must be properly packaged and labeled.

The Comprehensive Environmental Response, Compensation, and Liability Act was passed in 1980 and created a $1.6 billion fund (Superfund) for the cleanup of both spills of hazardous substances and inactive waste disposal sites. This was followed in 1984 by the Hazardous and Solid Waste Amendments to try to protect groundwater. The amendments place restrictions on the treatment, storage, and disposal of hazardous waste in land-management facilities. They provide new regulations for underground tanks that store liquid petroleum and chemical products. They also created new and more stringent requirements for land disposal facilities that existed then and that will be created. The EPA also had to develop standards before November 1986, governing the burning of hazardous waste fuel mixtures. Finally, the amendments require producers and distributors of hazardous waste fuels to place a warning label on the invoice or bill of sale.

In 1986 Congress passed the Emergency Planning and Community Right-to-Know Act. Under it there was created a Toxic Release Inventory, and industry must report on an annual release or off-site transfer of some three hundred toxic chemicals. Any company breaking the law can be sued. After that came the Clean Air Act Amendments of 1990 to update the 1970 Clean Air Act. Among other provisions, communities can not only sue polluters but they can seek a portion of the fines. Also in 1990 the Global Change Research Act requires a report to Congress every four years on the consequences of climate change.

Congress next focused on drinking water and, in the 1992 Safe Water Drinking Act Amendments, made water suppliers monitor eighty-eight regulated contaminants, whereas in 1986 it was twenty-three. Then in 1996 Congress renewed the Safe Water Drinking Act. It set $7.6 billion in grants and low-interest loans over a seven-year period to help communities upgrade drinking water systems, plus it gave state and local officials more leeway in regulating contaminants. However, consumers must be given more information about any significant contaminants in their local supply.

Also in 1996, Congress passed a new Magnuson Fishery Conservation and Management Act. It defines overfishing and it gave the Secretary of Commerce one year to determine which fisheries are overfished or nearly so. For those that are overfished, the relevant fishery management council must develop a plan to stop the overfishing and enact a plan to rebuild the fish stock in twelve months. Fishery managers can no longer use short-term financial considerations to legitimize setting exploitation rates above what scientists consider to be ecologically sustainable in the long run. The law defines "bycatch," setting new national standard obligating councils to manage all fisheries so bycatch of nontarget species is minimized. It includes fish thrown overboard dead because they were the wrong size or species to be of no economic value to the fisher. The North Pacific Council must reduce these annually for four straight years. Finally, in order to halt the privatization of fisheries, there were to be no individual transferable quota programs for the next four years.

In 2003 the Healthy Forests Restoration Act reduced environmental reviews, limited lawsuits that delay some logging projects, and authorized spending $900 million to pay for thinning of less profitable smaller trees.

International Agreements and Conferences

Since pollution is global, there have been many international agreements, especially with regard to ocean pollutants. The following is a list of some of the major international environmental agreements and conferences:

1. London Dumping Convention
2. Barcelona Convention
3. Cartagena Convention
4. 1959 Antarctic Treaty plus 1982 Convention and 1991 Environmental Protocol

5. 1987 UN Montreal Protocol on Substances that Deplete the Ozone Layers
6. 1989 Basel Convention on Hazardous Waste plus 1995 Amendment
7. 1992 Rio de Janeiro Earth Summit
8. 1992 Kyoto Conference on Climate Change
9. 1994 UN Convention to Combat Desertification
10. 1994 Law of the Seas Convention
11. 1995 Treaty on Overfishing
12. 1996 Global Treaty on Chemicals
13. 1998 Buenos Aires Conference on Implementing the Kyoto Pact
14. 2000 Conference at The Hague on Implementing the Kyoto Pact
15. 2000 Johannesburg Conference plus 2001 Stockholm Convention on Persistent Organic Pollutants
16. 2001 Marrakech Conference on Implementing the Kyoto Pact
17. 2001 UN Conference in Shanghai on Climate Change
18. 2002 UN Conference in Johannesburg on Sustainable Development
19. 2003 UN Environmental Conference in Kenya
20. 2004 UN Conference in Buenos Aires on Climate Change

The London Dumping Convention came into force in 1975 and regulates wastes loaded on ships with the express intent of dumping them at sea. The agreement prohibits the dumping of certain substances, such as mercury, DDT, PCBs, oil, and certain plastics, and requires special permits for certain other wastes, such as low-level radioactive waste. The Regional Seas Program of the United Nations Environmental Program encourages countries to develop regional action plans. One example is the Barcelona Convention, which prohibits the dumping of certain substances, such as mercury and radioactive wastes, into the Mediterranean. Another would be the Cartagena Convention, to which the United States belongs, and which is designed to reduce petroleum contamination of the Caribbean Sea and to control land-based sources of marine pollution.

There are also international agreements pertaining to the Antarctic seas. The Antarctic Treaty of 1959 prohibits use of the continent for nuclear explosion, and the Convention of 1982 requires a comprehensive ecosystems approach to controlling the use of living marine resources. Restrictions on harvests must protect the species being harvested and other species that depend on the harvested species for food. In 1996 the United States ratified the environmental protocol that had been signed in 1991 by 26 nations. It provides for more vigorous treatment for sewage, an end to incineration of waste and to open disposal, increased mandates for removal of waste altogether, and a fifty-year ban on mining for oil, gas, or any other mineral.

The 1987 UN Montreal Protocol on Substances that Deplete the Ozone Layers was a treaty eliminating many ozone-depleting substances used to produce such items as cut flowers, smoked ham, and honey, although it could take as long as fifty years to be fully implemented. A pesticide, methyl bromide, was added to the list during the administration of the first President Bush, with industrialized nations having to cut its use until a 2005 ban, and developing countries having the ban in 2015. However, in a 1999 meeting in Nairobi, Kenya of 181 nations, the United States tried for broad exemptions. At that time 72,000 tons of it was used worldwide, with the United States using 25,000 of those tons. We asked to be allowed to use 10,000 tons. In 2004 in Montreal, the United States and 10 other countries dropped a request for a cut of 40 percent, saying they will do 35 percent (30 percent is the target) with anything over 30 percent coming from existing stockpiles, not new products. A total of 17,700 tons was approved for use in 2005, which was supposed to be the final year of its use by those countries. However, in a 2005 meeting of 189 nations in Montreal, thirteen nations were given approval to use more than 14,300 tons of it (nearly 20 percent less than in 2005) in 2006, with the United States using more than half of it.

The 1989 Basel Convention which took effect in 1992 and which the United States has not ratified regulates overseas shipment of hazardous waste to developing nations that have few environmental safeguards or facilities, and a 1995 amendment would ban the shipments. The 1994 UN Convention to Combat Desertification was signed by 120 nations and addresses the problem of encroaching deserts caused by drought, too much grazing, poor irrigation, agricultural practices, and tree clearing. 1994 also found the Law of the Seas Convention take effect with more than 100 nations (United States has not ratified it). It regulates economic activity in the oceans by such points as letting nations establish exclusive economic zones along their coasts (sole rights to fishing, drilling, mining, and other commercial activities), guaranteeing safe passage through waters controlled by other nations, and creating international agencies to regulate seabed mining and arbitrate disputes. A treaty in 1995 signed by 100 countries regulates overfishing of migratory species such as cod, pollock, and tuna. A 1996 global treaty ended United States and European production of many chemicals that destroy the ozone layer.

In 2000 in Johannesburg 122 nations agreed on a global ban on twelve highly toxic chemicals not used in developing countries, such as PCBs, dioxins and furans (toxic by-products of burning and industrial production), organic DDT and other pesticides, that have been linked with cancer, birth defects, and other genetic abnormalities. The following year in Stockholm 151 nations including the United States signed it at a convention in Stockholm and it had to be ratified by 50 nations (the United States has not ratified it). It took effect in 2004. Nine of the twelve chemicals were banned as soon as the treaty took effect. Electrical equipment containing PCBs is allowed until 2025 as long as there are no leaks, and the treaty can be expanded to include other chemicals. Industrialized nations pay about $150 million a year to help developing countries use cleaner but costlier options.

In 2002 there was another UN conference in Johannesburg, this time dealing with sustainable development. The countries reached an agreement to protect marine ecosystems from overfishing by commercial trawlers and to replenish fish stocks by 2015, to substantially increase the global share of renewable energies (solar and wind) but with no targets, that locals should share in any benefits western companies can gain by exploiting natural resources there, to actively promote corporate responsibility (but not legally binding), and to help get affordable energy to 2 billion people who have no access (but 80 percent of energy comes from fossil fuels).

The mercury problem was addressed by the 2003 UN environmental conference in Kenya attended by 130 nations. It endorsed a global crackdown on pollution caused by mercury, but the United States blocked efforts for binding restrictions on its use. The conference said much of the mercury comes from coal-fired plants and plants that make chlorine and caustics often used in detergents. The mercury falls to the ground near the source ("hot spots") can damage human fetuses, can cause brain damage to babies and children under six years of age, and therefore women, children, and fetuses are most at risk. Mercury also comes from fish, occupational and household uses, dental fillings, and some vaccines. The nations said they would assist countries in devising methods for cutting emissions from coal-fired power stations and incinerators that are absorbed by algae and eaten by fish. Mercury can cause development problems and can affect the brain, kidneys, and liver. It travels throughout the world at a far greater rate than was previously known. It is also used in small-scale mining of gold and silver and in thermometers, fluorescent lamps, and some paints. The conferees agreed to meet again in South Korea in 2005.

COSTS OF POLLUTION

Because pollution control is costly, sometimes a cost-benefit analysis is used to see if the benefits outweigh the costs. This is a point at which environmentalists and businesses often disagree. The EPA, conscious of the problem, has introduced the "bubble concept," which is based on the idea that it is often possible to reduce emissions of a given pollutant from one source far less expensively than from another. Thus, a "bubble" is placed over a plant or geographic area, and private decision makers are allowed to decide the standard for the area at the lowest cost.

Businesses will try to shift the cost of pollution control forward to consumers in the form of price increases, backward to stockholders in the form of lower dividends, or to the workers in the form of lower wages. If the demand for a product is inelastic, meaning there are few, if any, close substitutes and the product is inexpensive, the consumer will pay the higher price. On the other hand, if the demand for a product is elastic, the consumer will not pay the higher price and revenue will fall. Also, the more competitive a market is, the more difficult it will be for firms to pass pollution abatement costs on to consumers. In an oligopoly, however, a firm can move in concert with other oligopolistic firms or follow a price leader. A monopolist has more leverage and more opportunity to push the cost of pollution control onto the consumer by simply readjusting output on the demand curve for the product and by charging a higher price. In the case of natural monopolies, such as power companies, pollution control costs are reflected in higher rates to consumers.

Although jobs are created in the pollution abatement industry, that increased employment may be offset by the closing down of plants that cannot comply with the cost of cleaning up the environment. Businesses also find a problem with the regulatory infrastructure that has been built up in the federal and state levels of government to administer pollution control laws. In addition, government is making an effort to control other areas that are in some way related to environmental pollution, such as land use, energy, and urban transportation. All directly affect business operations.

Businesses sometimes have to pay fines when they violate the environmental laws. For example, Wal-Mart paid a $1 million dollar fine in 2001 and a $3.1 million fine in 2004 for violating the storm runoff provision of the 1972 Clean Water Act, and in 2003 under that same law the EPA imposed a $34 million fine on Colonial Pipeline Co. for gross negligence (seven oil spills). Exxon-Mobile did pay $1.1 billion for the 1989 oil spill, but that was damages, not a penalty.

Under the Clean Air Act, Dominion Resources in 2003 agreed to pay $1.2 billion over 12 years to clean up eight coal burning power plants. In 2005 Illinois Power, due to violating the "new source review" provisions of that same law, agreed to spend $500 million on new pollution controls and paid $9 million in fines, the largest penalty imposed on a power company for excessive emissions, and had to reduce overall levels of sulfur dioxide and nitrogen oxides by 54,000 tons a year. It also had to spend $15 million to work on the harmful effects of past emissions. Also in 2005 a settlement was reached with ConocoPhillips in which it paid civil fines of $4.5 million, will spend more than $525 million for technology upgrades on nine refineries (10 percent of the nation's refining capacity) in seven states to comply with new source review, and will spend $10 million on other environmental projects, all of which should lead to annual reductions of 47,000 tons of harmful emissions. The settlement was the largest of thirteen that the government negotiated since the EPA started enforcing the rule in 1998. Over half the refining industry is in compliance, with annual reductions of more than 250,000 tons of nitrogen oxide (smog) and sulfur dioxide (soot), and all this was achieved without suits. However, there are suits against operators of power plants for similar violations, some of which have resulted in settlements, covering less than 10 percent of the industry.

THE SUPREME COURT AND POLLUTION

Once in awhile a pollution case reaches the Supreme Court. In the 1992 case of *New York v. United States*[1] Justice O'Connor, in a 6–3 decision, upheld parts of a 1985 federal law that provided financial incentives to states to find places to store low-level radioactive waste. However, the part that made the state the legal owner of all such waste within its borders if it had not met its disposal needs by January 1, 1996, was struck down. Along with the ownership, the state would assume all legal liability for any harm caused by the material. O'Connor thought it was a violation of the Tenth Amendment, which gives the states and their people the power over anything not expressly given the federal government in the Constitution nor prohibited to the states. She felt that Congress might not simply commandeer the legislative processes of the states. The federal government may not conscript state governments as its agents.

In 1994 the case of *Oregon Waste Systems, Inc. v. Department of Environmental Quality of the State of Oregon*[2] found the Court looking at the touchy issue of solid waste disposal. Oregon decided to charge $2.50 per ton on in-state disposal of solid waste generated in other states, but only 85¢ on that generated within Oregon. A 7–2 decision by Justice Thomas said that what Oregon was doing was unconstitutional because it discriminated against interstate commerce and did not advance a legitimate local purpose that could not be adequately served by reasonable nondiscriminatory alternatives.

Another 1994 case, *Chicago v. Environmental Defense Fund*,[3] involved the important issue of what can be dumped in ordinary landfills. The 1976 Resource Conservation and Recovery Act states that any toxic residue created by burning household and industrial waste in municipal incinerators must be treated as hazardous waste and not be dumped in ordinary landfills. Instead, it requires storage in specially constructed leak-proof sites and other handling that can be more expensive than conventional waste disposal. Chicago was charged with breaking the law by using landfills not licensed to accept hazardous wastes as disposal sites for the ash left after the incinerator. However, the city cited a 1984 amendment entitled Clarification of Household Waste Exclusion and said it should be exempt from the law because, in addition to household waste, it also burned nonhazardous industrial waste. Justice Scalia, however, in a 7–2 opinion, ruled against Chicago, saying that Congress had not created an exemption for the ash. He cited the plain meaning of the law rather than the law's history or the EPA's view of the law to support his conclusion (the EPA was supporting Chicago).

Still another 1994 case, *C. & A. Carbone, Inc. v. Clarkstown*,[4] involved a town that had a solid waste transfer station. In order to finance its cost, the town guaranteed a minimum waste flow, and then passed an ordinance requiring all nonhazardous solid waste within the town to be deposited at the station. That meant that a recycler had to bring nonrecyclable residue to the transfer station and pay a fee. Rather than do that, Carbone shipped it out of state. In a 6–3 opinion, Justice Kennedy said the ordinance violated the commerce clause because it regulated interstate commerce. It drove up the cost for out-of-state interests to dispose of their solid waste, and it deprived out-of-state businesses of access to the local market. It also discriminated against interstate commerce by favoring a single local proprietor. He said the town could still do uniform safety regulations, and it could still subsidize the facility through general taxes or municipal bonds. The decision was important in that more than half the states had some type of flow control.

Also in 1994 came *PUD No. 1 of Jefferson County v. Washington Department of Ecology*.[5] The law involved was the 1972 Clean Water Act, and the issue was whether the state could impose a minimum stream flow requirement in order to protect a river's fishery when it gave permission to build a hydroelectric project. Justice O'Connor, for a 7–2 Court, upheld the state, saying that a state may impose conditions necessary to enforce a designated use in its water quality standard, and it is not limited to discharges. In this case it was necessary to enforce the designated use of the river as a fish habitat. A project must be consistent with the designated use and the water quality criteria, and a sufficient lowering of the quantity of water could destroy all of a river's designated uses. Also, a reduced stream flow can constitute water pollution. Any difference between water quality and quantity is artificial because, in many cases such as this, they are related. She also said this is consistent with EPA regulations.

In an important environmental case in 2000, *Friends of the Earth v. Laidlaw Environmental Services (TOC), Inc.*,[6] Justice Ginsburg in a 7–2 opinion upheld the ability of private plaintiffs to invoke the citizen suit provisions of the federal environmental laws to bring lawsuits to stop pollution.

A 2001 case, *Solid Waste Agency of Northern Cook County v. Army Corps of Engineers*,[7] found Chief Justice Rehnquist writing a 5–4 decision holding that the 1972 Clean Water Act, which requires a permit from the Corps to build landfills affecting U.S. waters, including lakes, wetlands, and ponds, and a 1986 refinement of the law dealing specifically with migratory birds, does not apply to seasonal pools used by migratory birds because they are not navigable waters that Congress intended to protect. Thus the suburban Chicago localities may build the landfill atop some 500 acres (including about 17 acres classified as wetlands) of abandoned gravel pits that at times fill with water to become seasonal ponds used by migratory birds.

Also in 2001, in *Whitman v. American Trucking Associations, Inc.*,[8] a unanimous decision by Justice Scalia upheld the way the government sets air quality standards under the Clean Air Act. Specifically, the EPA uses public health and safety benefits in determining the standards, and need not consider financial cost (cost-benefit analysis), although it can consider it in its instructions for implementing the rules. The agency did not take too much power from Congress in its 1997 ozone (ground-level that causes smog) and soot (fine airborne particles) standards. The Court did, however, strike down the agency's policy for implementing new ozone rules, which would have applied it in regions of the country, chiefly metropolitan areas, which had not met the previous standard, because it ignored a section of the law that restricted its decision-making authority. The EPA had to rectify various ambiguities and come up with a more reasonable interpretation of the law.

In 2004 in *Alaska Department of Environmental Conservation v. EPA*,[9] a 5–4 decision by Justice Ginsburg upheld the EPA's authority to insist that factories and power plants use the best available antipollution technology and to block construction of those that do not. In this case, the state had accepted the technology the world's largest zinc mine proposed to use, but because it was less efficient than a costlier alternative the EPA overruled the state and the Court said that Congress had expressly endorsed an expansive surveillance role for the EPA which the agency properly carried out.

In the 2004 case of *Engine Manufacturers Association v. South Coast Air Quality Management District*,[10] an 8–1 decision by Justice Scalia held that the district, which regulates air quality in four counties in southern California in and around Los Angeles, issued regulations in 2000 and 2001 that conflicted with the Clean Air Act by forcing fleets of vehicles to meet stricter antismog standards. The regulations required new taxis, garbage trucks, school buses, city buses, airport shuttles, and other vehicles to use alternative fuels such as natural gas or be equipped with extra-strict pollution controls. He said the federal law allows the federal government to dictate pollution limits for cars and trucks, but does not allow for local standards for vehicle emissions.

Although not relating directly to pollution, the Court has also decided a couple of cases dealing with the 1973 Endangered Species Act, a law passed by Congress to try to make the environment safe for wildlife. In the 1992 case of *Lujan v. Defenders of Wildlife*,[11] the group went to court over the Interior Department's interpretation of the law as being limited to domestic projects only. Justice Scalia, 6–3, said the group lacked standing to bring the case, but then 7–2 upheld the Department's interpretation of the law. Then in 1995, in *Babbitt v. Sweet Home Chapter of Communities for a Greater Oregon*,[12] Justice Stevens in a 6–3 decision upheld regulations issued under the law that prohibited modifying any habitat when it would impair an endangered species' ability to breed, feed, or find shelter, even on private land. This particular case involved loggers and the spotted owl. Stevens felt the Secretary of the Interior's actions were reasonable, given Congress's clear expression in the law to protect endangered and threatened wildlife. The word "harm" as used in the law naturally encompasses habitat modification that results in actual injury or death, and he would defer to Congress in this matter.

THE ENVIRONMENT AND THE GOVERNMENT IN THE TWENTY-FIRST CENTURY

The Years of the Bush Administration

The Bush administration in 2001 backed off a campaign pledge to regulate carbon dioxide emissions from power plants, and abandoned the Kyoto Protocol despite the National Academy of Scientists telling Bush that global warming is on the rise, mostly due to humans. It tried several times for a law allowing drilling in the Arctic National Wildlife Refuge, finally getting it in the 2006 budget bill. It scrapped the phaseout of snowmobiles in Yellowstone and Grand Teton National Parks, but it did impose new pollution regulations for them and ATVs and off-road motorcycles and put a limit of no more than 1,140 per day there plus on the highway connecting them. It briefly dropped a Clinton proposal to cut the permissible level of arsenic in drinking water by 80 percent, and it scuttled the Clinton ban on new roads and timber harvesting in 58.5 million acres (one-third) of roadless national forests (the ban was opposed by logging, mining, and drilling interests even though half the nation's 190 million acres of forest are open to them). A 2001 National Energy Report recommended weakening enforcement actions against large utility companies. In May 2001, executive orders were issued reminding agencies to consider the energy implications (supplies and prices) of environmental and other regulatory actions, and created an interagency task force to accelerate the time it takes to review corporations' applications for permits for energy-related projects (power plants) and exploration of oil and gas in public lands. The Bureau of Land Management has greatly increased the number of drilling permits. The Interior Department rescinded a measure requiring hard-rock miners to post cleanup bonds to ensure that they do not leave behind Superfund sites, and the administration reversed a regulation that gave the Secretary of the Interior the right to veto permits for mining on public lands if it would cause substantial and irreversible harm to the community.

In 2002 the administration weakened several rules designed to protect thousands of streams, swamps, and other wetlands from destruction through the Clean Water Act despite opposition from the EPA and the Fish and Wildlife Service. It is therefore somewhat easier for developers, mining companies, and others to qualify for nearly automatic "general permits" to develop and fill wetlands.

In 2004 the EPA put forth a rule applying to companies whose smokestack emissions are not monitored under specific EPA rules, telling them that it will not require pollution checks more than twice every five years, because that is what the Clean Air Act requires and it could not do more than the law mandates. In that same year, although federal laws force federal agencies to survey for rare species in Pacific Northwest forests and establish buffers to protect them, the administration eliminated it in the Northwest Forest Plan. Also in 2004 the EPA put forth new regulations regarding haze in 156 national parks and wilderness areas in 35 states (Congress in 1977 amended the Clean Air Act to address it). In the east the haze is primarily due to sulfur particles from sulfur dioxide from power plants, whereas in the west it is from nitrates, dust, and soot.

In 2005 the EPA issued new guidelines, replacing those nearly twenty years old, to assess chemicals that might cause cancer, taking into account for the first time the likelihood that children may be more vulnerable to exposure than adults. However, the OMB will allow outside groups to challenge scientific conclusions before they become part of the new guidelines.

Superfund

The Superfund, started in 1980, has been running into monetary problems this century that has hurt in the cleanup effort. In 2003, for example, the fund ran out of money and ten projects were left unfinished that year. The budget is used to conduct investigations, enforcement, litigation, engineering studies, and cleanup, but money has declined in inflation-adjusted dollars since 1993, and cleanup costs are higher. In addition, less money than requested has been given to regional EPA offices and for many long-term projects. About two-thirds of sites not on federal property are cleaned up with money from the responsible companies (70 percent paid by companies, 30 percent by taxpayers). However, if companies balk, the EPA pays the cost and then collects from the company plus three times the cost. A problem is what to do about orphan sites. They were originally funded by taxes on some companies, including chemical and oil, but Congress let that expire in 1995 and starting in 2004 the money comes from general tax revenues. There is a backlog of sites with no money for them, and there are about 500 new sites per year. It is estimated that as much as 355,000 sites could require cleanup over the next three decades at a cost of $250 billion. From 1992–1996 there were 70 cleanups per year, and from 1997–2000 there were 85. However, the current administration averages about 40. As for the EPA proposing sites to clean up, in 2002, out of some 1,200 sites, it proposed doing 9, in 2003 it proposed 14 sites, and in 2004 11 sites, all of which were less than half that of Clinton's second term. One bright spot is that in 2003 the Superfund law was upheld against a charge that it violated due process by not conducting hearings before issuing an administrative order, and sites must be cleaned up by the parties responsible, which in this case were General Electric and some 75 sites.

Trading Emissions

In 2002 the government allowed power plants to trade emissions of sulfur dioxide by placing electronic monitors on smokestacks. Companies that pollute too much must pay $2,000 plus inflation for each extra ton, and buying a scrubber is a multimillion dollar investment. Congress initially withheld some trading allowances (it drops each year) to be sold for $1,500 each plus inflation. The EPA withholds 3.8 percent of the allowances for an annual auction. Companies are allowed to purchase (trade) allowances from competitors that cleaned up more than they had to for $100–200 apiece, which gives them the right to pollute. The problem is that sulfur dioxide has effects on such things as: (1) health—the formation of tiny particles that aggravate respiratory diseases; (2) cars and buildings—acid rain; (3) forests—dissolves aluminum in the soil, poisoning trees; (4) fish—dissolved aluminum clogs fish gills.

Clean Air Act and New Source Review

Under a 1977 New Source Review regulation for the Clean Air Act, businesses that make significant (beyond "routine" maintenance) modifications or improvements in older plants must also install modern pollution controls. It affects some 17,000 coal burning plants and refineries, chemical plants, and pulp and paper mills. But, a 2003 rule lets them modernize without the regulation as long as the cost of replacement is less than 20 percent of the cost of essential production. Plants that have installed state-of-the-art pollution controls are assured that for ten years they will not have to install more effective equipment even if they expand or change operations in a way that results in greater pollution. Plants with numerous pollution sources may increase pollution for some of them as long as overall plant-wide air emissions are not increased. Also, greater leeway is allowed in calculating pollution to reduce the likelihood that new controls will be required. The Clean Air Act says that older plants do not have to have the kind of emission controls new plants need to have but only if they do not expand or make changes that significantly increase smokestack emissions. The EPA dropped investigations of fifty power plants for Clean Air Act violations, despite having found serious ones, saying it will only investigate power plants in violation of the new, more lenient standards.

New EPA Rule on Air Pollution

Although air pollution citations have plummeted since 2001, in 2005 the EPA announced the Clean Air Interstate Rule to cut air pollution in 28 Eastern states plus the District of Columbia. The goal, when the regulations go fully into effect in 2015, is to reduce emissions of nitrogen oxides, which create ground-level ozone, buy more than 60 percent from 2003 levels and to reduce sulfur dioxide, which forms soot, by more than 70 percent (the Clean Air Act generally requires five years to reach such goals). How? The cap-and-trade system, under which the EPA allots emissions credits state by state that the states then allocate to the utilities. A utility that has aggressively reduced its emissions can sell or trade credits to a utility in any state that has not acted so quickly. Utilities will have to spend up to $50 billion to upgrade power plants in the next decade with scrubbers and other antipollution equipment. The EPA says the rule will result in up to $100 billion in annual health benefits.

Lawsuits

Thirteen states brought a suit concerning the new EPA rule on the changes in the New Source Review regulation, saying it was in violation of the Clean Air Act, but a Court of Appeals ruled against them in 2005. In 1999 several states and environmental groups formally petitioned the EPA to regulate carbon dioxide, methane, nitrous oxide and hydrofluorocarbons that spill out of the tailpipes of new motor vehicles, in order to control greenhouse gas emissions, but in 2003 the agency rejected the petition, saying that it lacked the statutory authority to act because the emissions do no direct physical damage to people, plants, or animals. Twelve states, three cities, American Samoa, and environmental groups then sued the EPA for violating the Clean Air Act by not regulating the emissions, characterized as a pollutant under the Act, but in 2005 a Court of Appeals rejected the suit, saying the EPA had administrative discretion not to order reductions in the emissions, calling it a justifiable policy judgment. Some states and the National Resources Defense Council have also sued the EPA for failure to protect children from pesticide residue in food (fruits, vegetables, and nuts) by waiving a requirement that residue standards 110 times stricter than those considered acceptable to adults be established.

In 2004 the National Marine Fisheries Service division of the National Oceanographic and Atmospheric Administration of the Commerce Department, (which earlier in the year proposed including fish bred in hatcheries along with those in the wild in calculating whether a salmon species is endangered), ruled out the possibility of removing up to fourteen federal dams on the Columbia and Snake Rivers to protect eleven endangered species of salmon and steelhead, even as a last resort (there are eight dams on the lower stretch of the two rivers). Five years earlier the Clinton administration had allowed for it if all other measures failed, but twice courts ruled against that, with the later decision in 2003 finding that the policy was too vague and did not go far enough to protect the fish. However, in 2005 a federal judge ruled that the administration had arbitrarily limited and skewed its analysis and thus had shirked its duty to ensure that government actions were not likely to jeopardize the survival of the species. The government had contended that the harm could be remedied over the next ten years by $6 billion in improvements to the dams, including spillways. The judge cited fundamental flaws in the Service's opinion, including the distinction, drawn for the first time, between harm to the fish resulting from the dams' existence and the harm resulting from the operation of the dams. The Service had said that the dams were an immutable part of the landscape, and its obligation to fish under the Endangered Species Act extended only to those actions it could control.

Water Pollution

The EPA Inspector General has said the computer system used to track and control water pollution is obsolete, full of faulty data and does not take into account thousands of significant pollution sources. It will take about three years to fix, but only if the funding is there (the EPA gets about two-thirds of what it needs). The system used is a permit one called the National Discharge Elimination System to try to make waterways clean enough for fishing, swimming, etc. The computer system is supposed to allow federal and state governments to check a facility's (64,000 of them) monthly discharge against its allowable amounts. However, mining and oil industries and developers can discharge pollutants undetected. New categories have been added to the Clean Water Act, such as overflowing sewers (the Clinton administration proposed increased controls over them) and discharges from large livestock operations. Thousands of permits expire every year without being renewed, the backlog to be issued has been reduced slowly, and tens of thousands of pollution sources have not been listed in the EPA's database. The EPA grants permits only after considering how much pollution is already flowing into a watershed, but without comprehensive data it is almost impossible. The system now does manual input of data. A proposal advanced would be to defer for two years the permit requirement for certain activities of oil and gas producers.

In the area of overfishing, the Fisheries Service in 2005 proposed fishing guideline revisions involving the timetable that fishery managers are supposed to meet in restoring depleted stocks. As the law now stands, managers must act to restore stocks within ten years, unless doing so is biologically impossible. Under the new rules, managers have the amount of time it would

take stocks to rebound if there were no fishing, plus the time it takes the species, on average, to reach spawning age. The proposed changes also call for
managing fish in stock assemblages (stocks that live together, have the same
life histories and are caught with the same fishing gear), but that could lead
to seriously overfishing some minor stocks.

New Power Plant Regulations on Mercury Emissions

In 2005 the administration said that new power plant regulations to begin
in 2010 would cut mercury pollution from electric utilities nearly in half by
2020 (the current level is 48 tons per year, which will become 31.3 tons in
2010, 27.9 tons in 2015, and 24.3 tons in 2020). They are the first mercury
controls on the 450+ coal-burning power plants (since the late 1990s the
EPA has regulated mercury dumped in water and air from municipal waste
and medical waste incinerators). A cap and trade approach, already used for
acid rain pollutants, can be used. During the first five years the plants can rely
on incidental cuts from scrubbers to reduce fine particles from sulfur dioxide
(soot and acid rain) from 10 million tons to 3.2 million tons and from chemical processes to reduce smog-forming ground-level ozone from nitrogen
oxides from 4 million tons to 1.7 million tons. After that they are expected to
find ways to specifically reduce mercury. 40 percent of human-caused mercury emissions come from power plants in 30 states. Smokestack hazards,
especially to children and developing fetuses, eventually end up in rivers and
lakes, absorbed by fish. The rationale used to reverse a 2000 stance on this
issue is that it is not like most toxic air pollutants (asbestos, chromium, lead)
that cause cancers and neurological disorders, but rather it is more like smog
and acid rain pollutants. It is a neurotoxin that builds up in fish tissue and
those who eat them, and is harmful to pregnant women because of the devel-
opmental effects on fetuses. A report from the Congressional Research Service in 2005 said that mercury emissions can be cut in half within fifteen
years without direct pollution controls, using the market trading plan, but
reducing emissions by 70 percent by 2018, the administration target date,
would be unlikely until 2030.

Diesel Emissions

In 2004 the administration put the first limits for diesel emissions for trucks
and off-road vehicles (the Clinton administration had done the same for
trucks and buses and the standards took effect in 2002 after surviving a challenge in federal court—full compliance by 2007). There was no legal challenge to the new regulations. Big diesel vehicles like tractors, bulldozers and
other off-road vehicles, locomotives, barges, etc. (a set of regulations for
locomotives and marine engines is under development) emit more soot than

the nation's entire fleet of cars, trucks, and buses. Full compliance must be done by 2012. Refineries must produce cleaner burning diesel fuel and engine-makers must cut diesel emissions. The goal is to reduce polluting sulfur in diesel fuel by 99.5 percent by 2013 (the sulfur not only leads to soot but prevents newer engine technologies from reducing the level of other pollutants) and to require many types of diesel engines (construction, farm, and other industrial equipment—bulldozers, tractors, and portable generators) to burn cleaner by reducing nitrogen oxide (smog) by 2013, which should reduce the level in the air by 738,000 tons annually and the level of soot by 129,000 tons once the current fleet of engines is retired. Non-locomotives and marine vessels must reduce sulfur content to 500 parts per million by 2007 and to 5 parts per million by 2010. Locomotives and boats have until 2012 (it was 3,400 million at the time of the regulation). Thirty thousand deaths are caused each year by soot, and by 2030 it should be reduced to 9,600 a year. It will cost about $1.5 billion a year for the first 27 years, but will save from $16 billion to $80 billion a year from prolonged lives and avoided health-care costs. It could prevent 12,000 premature deaths and 15,000 heart attacks each year.

In 2005 the EPA proposed regulations that for the first time would set limits on air pollution from stationary diesel engines, like those that run factories and power plants. They are scheduled to be phased in over ten years and would apply to engines that go into service after the rules are put into effect, to those manufactured after April 2006, and to old engines that undergo modification or reconstruction. They would have no bearing on the 600,000 engines currently in operation. The agency estimates that by 2015 there would be annual reductions, compared with current levels, of 68,000 tons of pollutants known to cause respiratory problems. The substances specifically mentioned in the rules are nitrogen oxides, particulate matter, sulfur dioxide, carbon monoxide, and hydrocarbons. The regulations reflect a consent decree from a 2003 lawsuit by a group that sought to force agency officials to set a deadline for regulations that had been considered by the agency since 1979 but never completed. The new standards would go into effect in three stages, leading to 81,500 cleaner-burning engines by 2015.

Defense Department

The Defense Department controls 28 million acres of land and uses some of it for combat exercises and weapons and munitions testing. Due to that, it won exemptions in 2003 and 2004 from parts of the Endangered Species Act and the Marine Mammal Protection Act, and it is trying to exempt military activities for three years from parts of the Clean Air Act. It also controls 140 of the nation's 1,240 toxic Superfund sites (has added almost no new sites to the list unlike the three previous administrations) and is seeking partial exemption from the Superfund law and from the Resource Conservation and Recovery Act governing toxic waste. It is also trying to revise a directive that mentions "environmental security" and instead wants to emphasize national defense. The military has more Superfund sites, groundwater contamination, illegal discharges, and failure to meet EPA regulations than any other industry. Appropriations for cleanups are slightly lower in the Bush administration than in Clinton's even though estimates for cleanups at closed bases have far exceeded current spending. The army did settle a case in Alaska, promising to restrict firing during twice-yearly bird migrations and while cleanup activities are underway in the marsh. It also agreed to monitor to determine if toxic constituents of explosives were seeping into water beyond the base. Another problem area for the Defense Department is the redeployment of fighter jets versus environmental controls, such as the Navy wanting to simulate carrier takeoffs and landings near a wildlife refuge. All the environmental laws do contain waivers for national emergencies.

Forest Service

In 2004 the Forest Service issued new rules, environmental management systems, that overhauled the guidelines for managing the nation's 155 national forests and made it easier for regional forest managers to decide whether to allow logging, drilling, or off-road vehicles. They relaxed long-standing provisions on environmental reviews and the protection of wildlife on 191 million acres of national forests and grasslands. They also cut back on requirements for public participation in forest planning decisions. The forest managers and the Forest Service will have increased autonomy to decide whether to allow logging roads or cell phone towers, mining activity or new ski areas. The rules seemed to go against protection for native animals and plants found in the 1976 National Forest Management Act (regional managers had to show environmental sensitivity in decisions on how the national forests would be used).

The supervisors of the individual forests and grasslands will shape forest management plans, and the effects will be subject to independent audits, which could be by other Forest Service employees and/or outsiders. The supervisors are appointed by the Forest Service to manage national forests and report to regional managers. They will now be allowed to approve plans more quickly for any particular forest use—recreation, logging, grazing, etc., and to adjust plans with less oversight. They must comply with the requirements of the 1969 National Environmental Policy Act, but a new proposal gives them new direction on what kind of environmental review constitutes compliance. The supervisor would be making the call as to whether a particular plan must undergo a full environmental impact statement, a more modest review, or no formal review.

Secrecy

In 2002 the White House ordered a chapter on climate change deleted from the EPA's annual report on air pollution trends. In 2003, as the EPA was finishing a broad assessment of environmental problems, the White House ordered so many changes in the global warming chapter that the Administrator yanked all but a few paragraphs. Also, the EPA has been told not to provide cost-benefit analyses to senators sponsoring bills that compete with the administration's proposals, even though such information has been routinely furnished in the past. The administration relies more on administrative action than on legislation and has been accused of trying to pressure or ignore its scientists at the EPA and the Fish and Wildlife Service. Political appointees aggressively police scientific work that could form the basis of new regulations.

In 2005 it was reported that the Chief of Staff for the White House Council on Environmental Policy (who resigned two days after the report surfaced) repeatedly edited government climate reports from the Climate Change Science Program (coordinates government climate research) in ways that played down links between greenhouse gases and global warming. He would remove or adjust descriptions of climate research that government scientists and their supervisors had already approved, and in many cases the changes appeared in the final reports. They tended to produce an air of doubt about findings that most climate experts say are sound. The problem is that before taking the position in 2001 he was the "climate team leader" and lobbyist at the American Petroleum Institute and had no scientific training, and two days after resigning his government position he took a job with Exxon Mobil.

SUMMARY

As can readily be seen, environmental protection is a complex problem of the utmost magnitude. That pollution is a problem is a given, and most persons are highly supportive of regulations to assure a safer environment. Differences do exist as to the magnitude of some of the problems, as well as how best to solve the problems. It would seem best to err on the side of believing a problem is serious and imminent rather than believing the problem is more trivial and far in the future. The damage done by pollution is difficult to undo, so to catch it before it reaches a catastrophic level makes sense indeed. The government has done a lot in this area, but there is more that needs to be done both at the national and international levels.

QUESTIONS FOR DISCUSSION

1. Has the issue of environmental protection become overstated?
2. Which environmental problem is the most pressing?
3. Are our laws adequate to handle the pollution problem?
4. Should polluters be made to pay emission charges?
5. Should taxpayers bear some of the burden of protecting the environment?
6. Has the Supreme Court generally been supportive of environmental protection?
7. Has the current Bush administration been supportive of environmental protection?

RECOMMENDED READING

New York Times. Many articles over the years dealing with the environment.
Schnitzer, Martin. *Contemporary Government and Business Relations*. 4th ed. Boston, MA: Houghton Mifflin Company, 1990. Chapter 13.

NOTES

1. 505 U.S. 144 (1992).
2. 511 U.S. 93 (1994).
3. 511 U.S. 328 (1994).
4. 511 U.S. 383 (1994).
5. 511 U.S. 700 (1994).
6. 528 U.S. 167 (2000).
7. 531 U.S. 159 (2001).
8. 531 U.S. 457 (2001).
9. 540 U.S. _____ (2004).
10. 541 U.S. _____ (2004).
11. 504 U.S. 555 (1992).
12. 515 U.S. 687 (1995).

IV

DEREGULATION OF BUSINESS

9

Deregulation of Transportation

There has been a noticeable trend since the mid- to late 1970s toward getting the government out of the area of regulating business. In order to understand this trend, one must first examine the reasons behind regulation and whether or not those reasons were accomplished. As previously noted, the government first regulated a business when, in 1887, the Interstate Commerce Act created the Interstate Commerce Commission to regulate railroads. The railroads had brought regulation upon themselves with such practices as rate discrimination, including charging more for short hauls than for long hauls, and deviating from published tariffs. Since it was the farmers and small businesspersons who were most adversely affected, they organized into the Grange movement and took control of the legislatures of several Midwestern states, passing laws regulating rates. The problem was, however, that most of the railroads engaged in these practices were interstate in nature, and the Supreme Court in the 1886 case of *Wabash, St. Louis, and Pacific Railway Company v. Illinois*[1] invalidated an Illinois law that had forbidden railroads to charge more for a short haul than for a long haul. Since the law affected all railroads, including those in interstate commerce, Justice Miller thought it unconstitutional as our Constitution gives Congress the power to regulate interstate commerce, not the states—thus, the creation the following year of the ICC.

GOVERNMENT REGULATION

Railroads

The Interstate Commerce Act made it unlawful for railroads to charge a higher rate for short hauls on shipments on the same line in the same direction. Schedules of freight rates and passenger rates had to be made to prevent

195

discrimination against shippers, and rate increases could be made only after advance public notice of ten days had been given. In 1906 the Hepburn Act gave the ICC jurisdiction over pipelines and express companies, and in 1910 the Mann-Elkins Act gave the ICC jurisdiction over telephone, telegraph, and cable and wireless companies engaged in interstate commerce.

Despite this promising beginning, the ICC had a rocky early few years, thanks to a highly conservative, probusiness Supreme Court. In the 1896 case of *Cincinnati, New Orleans, and Texas Pacific Railway Company v. Interstate Commerce Commission*,[2] the Court, speaking through Justice Shiras, held that the ICC was not given any authority in the law creating it to fix rates. It could only fact-find. The following year, in *Interstate Commerce Commission v. Cincinnati, New Orleans, and Texas Pacific Railway Company*,[3] Justice Brewer held that the ICC had no power over rates whatsoever. Ratemaking is a legislative matter and Congress could not delegate it to an agency in the executive branch. Also in 1897, in *Interstate Commerce Commission v. Alabama Midland Railway Company*,[4] the Court held that when federal circuit courts heard appeals from ICC rulings, they need not accept the facts as presented by the ICC. This voided a provision in a law that held that the courts were limited to the facts as presented by the ICC. The rationale was that when a court hears a case in equity, as in these appeals, it must always be able to investigate facts anew. The reason this decision was detrimental to the ICC was that railroads would withhold key facts at the ICC hearing, and then when the decision went against them they would present these facts at the circuit court. Based on these new facts, the ICC decision would look foolish and would be overturned by the Court, lowering the esteem of the ICC in the minds of the general public.

The Court finally changed its attitude toward the ICC with its 1907 decision in *Illinois Central Railroad Company v. Interstate Commerce Commission*[5] in which it said it would not investigate the facts anew in an appeal. Whatever the facts were as presented by the record in the case, that was what the Court would use. That was followed by the 1910 case of *Interstate Commerce Commission v. Illinois Central Railroad Company*,[6] in which Justice White ruled that the Court would defer to the policymaking power of the ICC. As long as the ICC had the power to rule the way it did, the Court would not overturn the ruling just because it disagreed with the wisdom of the policy.

In the 1914 *Shreveport Rate Cases*,[7] Justice Hughes even allowed the ICC to change the allowable rate charged by an intrastate train and set by that state's railroad commission. The state was Texas, and the reason the ICC became involved was that an interstate railroad (Louisiana to Texas) and the Texas railroad were serving the same region in east Texas. However, their rates were different. The ICC was allowing the interstate railroad to charge a higher rate. Since that hurt the interstate railroad's ability to attract riders, the ICC had two alternatives. It could lower the rate of the interstate railroad, which it would not do because it was convinced the rate was fair, or it could raise the rate of the Texas railroad. It did just that, and the Court upheld the ICC, saying that the ICC could regulate those intrastate rates which, as in the case at point, directly affected interstate commerce. Congress, in 1920, passed the Transportation Act that reaffirmed that decision, and in the 1922 case of *Railroad Commission of Wisconsin v. Chicago, Burlington & Quincy Railroad*,[8] Chief Justice Taft for a unanimous Court upheld it. He said that the Commission is supposed to see that a national railway system is achieved, and it is also supposed to assure that the railroads get a fair return. Therefore, the law was constitutional.

Trucks, Buses, and Airlines

In 1935 Congress passed the Motor Carrier Act that gave the ICC jurisdiction over trucks and buses engaged in interstate commerce. These common carriers could operate only under a certificate from the ICC, and rates and fares had to be published and not be discriminatory. These were minimum rates that had to be filed with the ICC, which could prescribe minimum (but not maximum) rates. The ICC also enforced safety standards. Private carriers were only under the ICC for such matters as hours of service for employees, safety, and equipment. Brokers for motor carrier routes had to be licensed by the ICC. However, Congress took away much of the ICC's regulatory power with the 1980 Motor Carrier Reform Act, the 1980 Staggers Rail Act, and the 1982 Bus Regulatory Reform Act. The ICC itself was abolished during the administration of President Clinton, although the government does have a safety agency for motor vehicles called the Federal Motor Vehicle Safety Administration, and there is a Federal Railroad Commission to oversee the nation's railroads.

Meanwhile, in 1938 Congress decided to regulate the airline industry. It had already, in 1934 and 1935, given the postmaster general the power to regulate schedule frequencies, departure times, stops, speed, load capacities, etc., for airmail. But the Civil Aeronautics Act created the Civil Aeronautics Board and gave it regulatory authority over entry, routes, rates, airmail payments, and subsidies of common carriers. The CAB would issue a certificate of convenience and necessity for an air carrier to serve a particular route. Rates had to be approved and published by the Board, which also had control over pooling, combinations, intercorporate relations, and abandonment of service, although it had no control over security issues. Two years later an executive order by President Roosevelt created the Civil Aeronautics Authority to maintain the national airway system, to plan and administer the airport program, and to enforce safety, licensing, and traffic control regulations. However, Congress, in 1978, passed the Airline Deregulation Act eliminating the CAB by 1985 and ending economic regulation by then. The hope was to allow existing interstate carriers to enter new markets, and to make it easier for new firms to enter the air transportation industry. In addition, domestic airlines were allowed to cut or raise fares in single markets until, on January 1, 1983, all regulations on fares were eliminated.

The government did not get out of the airline business altogether. The Federal Aviation Administration, successor to the Civil Aeronautics Authority, can order design changes in airplanes, and the National Transportation Safety Board can recommend safety improvements. The intent of deregulation was to promote competition among air carriers, so that consumers would be better served.

Major Federal Transportation Laws:
1887   Interstate Commerce Act
1906   Hepburn Act
1910   Mann Elkins Act
1935   Motor Carrier Act
1938   Civil Aeronautics Act
1978   Airline Deregulation Act
1980   Motor Carrier Reform Act
1982   Bus Regulatory Reform Act

Characteristics of Regulation

In order to better understand the movement to deregulate, which was not confined to the transportation industry, one must first understand the mechanics of regulation. Regulation began with the transportation industry and later spread to such industries as communications and electric and gas services, all classified under the general category of public utilities. The rationale was that these industries must charge fair, nondiscriminatory rates and render on demand satisfactory service to the public. On the other hand, the utility generally is free from direct competition and is permitted, although not assured, a fair return on its investment. The reasoning behind singling out utilities for regulation is because they are considered to be natural monopolies (i.e., they offer a single service or a limited number of services, they are localized, and direct competition would be uneconomical). They are usually very capital intensive as there is a high ratio of fixed assets to total assets, and their fixed costs do not vary with output. The expenses of many utility companies, particularly those in the gas and electric fields, decrease as the size of the plant increases, although there is a minimum beyond which the average total costs would begin to increase should the plant grow larger. A relatively small plant would have higher average costs than a larger plant. When the government regulates the price charged by a utility, it is greater than the marginal cost, as it is equal to the average total cost. In other words, the utility is allowed to cover all its costs and earn a normal profit. The marginal cost price would be the socially optimum one, the one that maximizes society's welfare. However, that is not used because the utility might not be able to cover average costs and thus it would lose money, or it might make too much money if the demand increases.

Critics of regulation had several points to make. One was that the regulatory agencies began to act more in the interest of the firms they were regulating than in the public interest. Another was that there was too much regulation by the commissions. Still another was that there was a blurring of the principle of separation of powers, as the same people in the agencies made the rules, brought action against offenders, and served as judges. On the other hand, some commissioners were thought to be too far removed from actual fact-finding, with the result that they never heard testimony even though they had to make the decisions. A final criticism related to prices because, if the price allowed to be charged was below the market price, those who were not able to buy from the regulated firm would be paying more for the substitute product. Also, since firms that are regulated do not compete on the basis of price, the only thing that distinguished one company from another was service, a criticism particularly levied at the airline industry. Perhaps surprisingly, it was the more liberal element in our society that, for the previously discussed reasons, began openly to call for deregulation in the mid-1970s. When the conservative element joined in, the deregulation movement was assured of success. The only questions remaining were which industries to deregulate and to what extent. A general distrust of big government was reflected in this movement, and it was to extend into the 1980s and beyond. One area especially hit by deregulation in the early 1980s was the banking industry, and another one that is ongoing is the communications industry.

DEREGULATION

Railroads

What has the effect of deregulation been in the transportation industry? In 1998 Laidlaw, Inc., of Canada, bought Greyhound Lines, Inc. for $470 million in a merger of bus companies, and in 2000 Volvo got the truck division of Renault (which includes Mack Trucks in the United States) for $1.5 billion. Both trucking and railroad rates have dropped significantly, and railroad employment has also dropped significantly, although for those who remain, salaries and fringe benefits have risen. The biggest impact of deregulation in the railroad industry, however, as with industry in general lately, has been the number and size of the mergers that have taken place. The end result is that in just a forty-year period, from 1955–1995, the number of railroads in the United States, excluding local lines, fell from 126 to 11. In fact, the Surface Transportation Board was created in 1996 to review railroad mergers. Among the larger mergers were the joining of the Union Pacific and Southern Pacific railroads into one, the Union Pacific, for $3.9 billion (it also has the Chicago Northwestern railroad), and the joining of the Burlington Northern and Santa Fe railroads. The STB in 2000 did turn down the proposed merger of the Union Pacific with the Canadian National Railway Co., and in 2001 came up with new rules for the six remaining (there used to be around 30) rail freight companies with more than $250 million in yearly revenues. They cannot merge without written assurances that combining operations will actually increase competition and would not interrupt existing service. Other big railroads are the Soo Line and the Illinois Central. However, the biggest completed merger was the 1997 acquisition of Conrail by CSX and Norfolk Southern railroads for $9 billion. A background study as to how these railroads evolved is illuminating.

CSX railroad traces its origins to the first American railroad, the Baltimore and Ohio, started in 1827. It was bought in 1962 by the Chesapeake and Ohio railroad, which had begun as Virginia's Louisa railroad in 1836. The B&O and the C&O got the Western Maryland railroad in the late 1960s, and all three became subsidiaries of the Chessie System in 1973. Meanwhile, the Seaboard Coast Line had been formed by combining Virginia's Portsmouth and Roanoke railroad, started in 1832, with the Atlantic Coast Line railroad, formed in the late 1800s from several southern railroads. In 1980, the Chessie System and the Seaboard Coast Line merged to form CSX. Besides being a railroad, CSX owns Sea-Land Services, Inc., which is an international container-cargo carrier with some 100 ships; American Commercial Lines, Inc., which has 3,200 barges and 116 towboats that navigate our inland rivers; an intermodal services company; a logistics company; and the Greenbrier resort.

Norfolk Southern railroad can trace its origins to the Norfolk railroad, an eight-mile Virginia line formed in 1838 that later became part of the Atlantic, Mississippi, and Ohio railroad, which in 1881 became the Norfolk and Western Railway Company. That railroad bought the Virginian Railway in 1959 and the New York, Chicago, and St. Louis Railway in 1964. Meanwhile, the Southern Railway Company, begun in 1827 as the South Carolina Canal and Railroad, started our first regularly scheduled passenger train in 1830. In 1982 it merged with Norfolk and Western to form the Norfolk Southern. The latter also owns North American Van Lines (a major moving van company), and Pocahontas Land Corporation (an owner of coalfields).

Conrail owes its beginnings to an 1831 railroad, the Mohawk and Hudson, which joined with nine others in 1853 to form the New York Central Railroad. Its major competitor for years was the Pennsylvania Railroad, formed in 1846. When railroads started having financial difficulties because of competition, the two giants merged in 1968 to form the Penn Central Transportation Company, which went bankrupt in 1972. The federal government set up Conrail in 1973 to take over the freight operations of the Penn Central and five other railroads; it began operations in 1976. The federal government sold its holdings in it in 1987. It was the largest freight railroad in the eastern part of the United States. One can easily see why CSX and Norfolk Southern both wanted Conrail, and why they thought it best to buy it jointly rather than engage in a price war.

Amtrak

One other point of note is that the federal government in 1971 also created a corporation formed from 18 railroads to handle the passenger service of Penn Central, namely Amtrak, and that is still a government corporation. However, under the 1997 Amtrak Reform and Accountability Act, the railroad cannot use government funds (which has totaled some $29 billion in operating and capital subsidies) to cover operating expenses after 2002. In 1999 Amtrak said that, beginning in the year 2002, it would give passengers free rides when its service falls below national standards for customer treatment, late trains, and the condition of railcars.

Amtrak's principal problem is persistent lack of funds. For example, it goes through 46 states but very few of them pay subsidies and therefore contribute very little to Amtrak's budget. In addition, although the government has put billions of dollars toward intercity rail infrastructure, it has put much more into highways and aviation. Amtrak is billions of dollars in debt, and it was able to get a $1 billion loan from the government in 2002, $1.05 billion in 2003 (wanted $1.2 billion), $1.2 billion in 2004 and again in 2005 (wanted $1.8 billion each year).

Another difficulty for Amtrak is that it only owns 730 miles of track, and the rest of the 21,000 miles it uses is owned by freight companies, which are required to give Amtrak priority but lack of rail capacity and more slow-moving freight traffic are difficulties. Freight traffic density has increased greatly. Amtrak pays bonuses to both freight and commuter lines to give it greater priority.

Safety

In 2005 the Transportation Department inspector general said that the four biggest railroads (Union Pacific, CSX, Burlington Northern and Santa Fe, and Norfolk Southern) suffer from substantial and systematic safety problems. The report said that the Federal Railroad Commission stresses partnership over punishment, and its Safety Assurance and Compliance Program tries to fix safety problems through committees of union representatives and railroad managers. They are unable to reduce the overall accident rate among most of the biggest railroads and, after declining for a number of years, grade-crossing accidents were up sharply in 2004. Also, safety defect ratios rose at three of the top four railroads. The Union Pacific was the worst even though it paid relatively more money in fines. There are fewer than 450 inspectors for 230,000 miles of rail, and the report required a new regulatory strategy within ninety days.

Conclusion

Has deregulation accomplished its objectives in the railroad industry? Since rates are lower, one would think so. However, because of the many mergers there are very few railroads remaining, thus not as much competition as critics of regulation had sought to achieve. Perhaps many of the merged railroads would have failed but for the mergers. Then too, there are always local railroads to give interstate railroads competition. Nevertheless, it seems the mergers have gone beyond what is optimum for the economy and for the consumers, and that corporate greed is the controlling factor. In other words, the rich get richer. The ones who benefit the most are the directors and officers of the merged companies, together with the stockholders. Too many workers lose their jobs or are urged to take early retirement, and with fewer and fewer railroads there is less competition, and less competition, in the long run, usually means higher rates. Perhaps the railroad industry is an anomaly. A look at the result of airline deregulation should help provide an answer.

Airlines

When airlines were deregulated, the major airlines were at a severe cost disadvantage. New entrants were able to use nonunion and smaller crews on their aircraft, which gave them a cost advantage over the major airlines with union contracts. Despite this advantage, most of the new entrants went broke: some 150 in the 1978–1986 period. The ones that survived generally took advantage of the opportunities now available to them and radically changed their routes and prices in order to attract passengers. The new airlines currently have some 20 percent of the market.

One method used to change route structure was the creation of hubbing, when airlines create hubs at one or more airports in about a dozen cities. They then schedule flights from these airports in banks, meaning that a number of flights come into an airport within a short period of time and a number leave a short time later. There are many gates at an airport that are utilized by the hub airlines; passengers enjoy the comfort of nonstop flights to their destinations and they accumulate frequent-flier miles with those airlines. This is an efficient use of facilities and enables an airline to provide service on routes that were previously unserved. In addition, these hub airlines sometimes affiliate with commuter carriers in order to serve smaller markets. Some have developed multiple hub systems and have become regional and even national in scope. Besides not having to change airlines in the middle of a journey, there is less layover time with hubbing because airlines no longer stop at several cities to fill planes. In addition, since planes now fly with a higher percentage of seats filled, fares as a whole are lower.

However, as with most things, there is a downside—if one or two airlines dominate a particular hub, there is the potential of a monopoly with resultant higher fares. In fact, hub airlines dominate in the cities where passengers pay the highest air fares (unless Southwest Airlines is present). A 2001 Department of Transportation study found predatory pricing at the hubs. The major airlines cut fares and increase service on routes with new entrants, then reverse it once a smaller company is driven away or put out of business. The most common tactics are to reduce fares and bracket the small carrier's flights with multiple ones of their own, double frequent flier miles on a given route, and double commissions to travel agents who sell tickets on that route. For corporations with contract fares (discounts for buying a certain number of tickets per month) the airlines give them no discounts if they use the new carrier. The discount carriers that have survived have been making inroads and, according to the Department of Transportation, air travelers save billions of dollars a year by using them.

Since deregulation took effect, on the average, ticket prices have fallen, particularly for long-distance flights (flights over 400 miles are up) and in the big-city markets. They did rise 2 percent in the first half of 2005, and 7 percent in the second half. They have increased in short-distance markets (flights under 400 miles are down) and the number of passengers for short-distance flights has decreased. They have the alternatives of automobiles, trains, buses, and smaller planes. Those who do fly short distances, even though their fares have risen, are usually paying for the true cost of the service.

Since deregulation, most of the complaints that arise are about service. In 2004 air travel complaints rose 27 percent. Now that air transportation has become so affordable that most people can fly, terminals have become crowded. The number of passengers flying has increased so much since deregulation (it has more than doubled) that there is a burden on terminal facilities and on the use of airplanes. The number of airline departures increased greatly after deregulation. This, in turn, has resulted in delays because, to accommodate travelers, airlines offer more flights at the peak periods. This puts a strain not only on the services supplied by the airports, but also on the services provided by one or more of the Federal Aviation Administration control centers who guide the aircraft through the sectors under their control. A 2004 FAA study showed that at least forty-three airports need to add capacity in the next fifteen years, and five are already too crowded (Philadelphia, LaGuardia, Newark, Atlanta, and O'Hare). Other reasons for delay are weather and mechanical problems. Weather, indeed, is responsible for the majority of airplane delays. One point to keep in mind is that the Department of Transportation, in compiling service complaints, only reports complaints dealing with "on time" (more than 15 minutes late) and baggage for domestic flights, and only complaints made to it, not to the airlines. Other complaints involve canceled flights or flights diverted to another airport, flight information displays saying "on time" when the flight was delayed more than 20 minutes, and inaccurate flight announcements made by airlines. The major airlines did reduce their flights for a while after September 11, 2001, which did ease traffic and delays. Today more people than ever are flying. 20.5 percent of flights were delayed in 2005, the highest since 23.9 percent in 2000. The FAA aims for an 82 percent "on time" arrival figure, and because O'Hare was so far below this the agency made an agreement with the airport, which took effect in November, 2004, to cut 37 peak hour arrivals.

In 1999 the major airlines issued guidelines for better service. They said they would now tell customers of the lowest fares available, notify them of known delays, support an increase in the baggage liability limit (the Department of Transportation said it was doubling to $2,500 the minimum liability on lost, damaged, or delayed baggage), allow reservations to be held without payment for twenty-four hours, give prompt refunds, accommodate disabled passengers, and meet customer needs during long aircraft delays. There was much pressure on the airlines to take such steps as the previous winter, during a storm, passengers were forced to sit seven or more hours in planes on runways without food and other services. If the airlines had not issued the guidelines, Congress might have imposed some regulation on them.

The annual Airline Quality Rating survey for 2004 measured the 16 major airlines that carried at least 1 percent of the 630 million who flew domestically, for service (complaints rose 20 percent while there was only a 3.3 percent growth in passengers), "on time" record (78 percent, down from 82 percent in 2003), lost luggage (4.83 bags lost, stolen, or damaged for every 1,000 passengers, which was more than in 2003) and consumer complaints (also more than in 2003), and found only 4 of 14 that were rated in both years had improved. The number of passengers "bumped" (denied boarding due to lack of seats) was 0.87 per 1,000 passengers, up from 0.86 in 2003. The seven largest carriers employed 12 percent fewer people than the year before. The Christmas holidays were especially bad in that delays and cancellations inconvenienced more than 500,000 passengers. Comair canceled all its flights that weekend due to bad weather and computer problems, and US Airways' baggage system failed, according to the survey, due to poor planning and poor labor relations

Another factor to consider in airline deregulation is safety, and airline fatality rates have fallen since deregulation. That could be the result of many factors, including better technology. One area in which there are more near-accidents since deregulation, however, involves small private planes or military planes. Near-collisions involving only commercial airlines are a very small percent of the total. In examining our traffic control system, the problems, rather than being due to deregulation, are due to federal budgetary constraints. These have slowed FAA regulatory processes and procurement, have eliminated many expert technical personnel (who take more rewarding jobs in industry), and have prevented modernization of traffic control equipment. In 2005 the National Transportation Safety Board said that close calls between jets happens with alarming frequency on the nation's runways (as many as thirty serious near collisions each year) and federal regulators need to find better ways to curb the problem.

Mergers and Other Agreements

This brings one to the final factor to be considered in airline deregulation and, as with railroads; it is the great increase in mergers. With several airlines going bankrupt and with the increase in mergers, the airline industry has become an oligopoly. Airlines do have to have the approval of the Department of Transportation in order to merge. The 1985 revision of the Federal Aviation Act sets two standards for the DOT when it evaluates proposed mergers. One is the antitrust standard, which holds that any merger that would violate Section 7 of the Clayton Act by substantially lessening competition in any region of the United States must not be approved unless DOT finds the anticompetitive effects are outweighed by the public interest due to benefits accrued from meeting increased transportation needs. The second is the public interest standard, which holds that DOT must determine whether or not a merger is in the public interest. In addition to DOT approval, the Antitrust Division of the Justice Department must be notified of proposed mergers, and usually participates in airline merger hearings. However, the final say belongs to DOT, and it has approved mergers to which the Justice Department was opposed.

Some of the 18 mergers consummated in the mid-1980s include US Airways getting Piedmont Aviation, Northwest getting Republic, Delta getting Western, Texas Air getting Eastern, Frontier, and People's Express, and TWA getting Ozark. In 1991 Delta got most of Pan American. Many of the former largest carriers have disappeared. In 1998, Northwest bought a controlling stake in Continental for $519 million. They merged their flight schedules and frequent-flier programs, but maintained separate identities and managements. In 2001, a bankruptcy court judge said that American Airlines could do a $200 million emergency financing plan for TWA, clearing the way for an auction. It then bought it for $742 million and assumed $3.8 billion of debt. Worldwide, in 2003 Air France and KLM (The Netherlands) merged, and in 2005 in the United States, US Airways (7th largest carrier) and America West (8th largest carrier) merged and will fly under the US Airways name.

In addition to mergers, several U.S. airlines have entered into alliances with other airlines, including foreign ones. They include the Star Alliance, started in 1997, OneWorld Alliance (1999), and SkyTeam (2000). These alliances have an immunity from the antitrust laws that allow them to set rates, schedules, and fares together; pool frequent-flier programs; share employees and airport space, and jointly purchase food, fuel, etc. They also code share all flights, which means they appear in travel agency computers as if they were operated by just one airline, which in turn helps to market their connecting services. Passengers need to book only one ticket and check in baggage once, regardless of how many times they change carriers. Domestically, United and US Airways code share with each other, and Delta, Northwest, and Continental do the same among themselves. In 2003 American Airlines and British Airways decided to code share for two years.

The major carriers have increased their market share since deregulation, and ease of market entry is not present in the industry except for short-distance hauls in low-density markets. For the denser markets, air carriers require time and must absorb sunken costs to obtain gate space and establish patronage. The problem of airport access is crucial, whether it be gates, slots, ticket counter space, or restricted access to an airport in the form of noise regulation, because the increase in the problem means that new airlines are hampered in their ability to enter markets. As for establishing patronage, that can be difficult when competing against carriers that offer frequent-flier programs that effectively increase the cost of switching carriers. One result is that in several major cities the bulk of the traffic is controlled by one or two airlines.

Revenue Problems

Airlines were greatly hurt financially by the September 11, 2001 disaster. The Air Transportation Stabilization Board was created that year (it ends in 2006) to try to help, and immediately extended $10 million in loan guarantees and $14.99 billion in cash. Congress appropriates money for the agency. However, the only two airlines of note rescued were America West and Frontier. Six airlines got $1.6 billion each, but more than half were turned down. US Airways has gotten the biggest package of loan guarantees—$900 million in 2003, plus cash, and was in bankruptcy for a while. In 2004 it got revised loan terms plus it could draw a portion of the $750 million the board agreed it could use to run its operations. ATA Airways and Aloha Airlines also got them but filed for bankruptcy. The only other big airline to apply for the guarantees was United, and it was turned down three times and was in bankruptcy (it came out in 2006). American, Continental, Delta (in bankruptcy), and Northwest (in bankruptcy) decided not to undergo the extensive scrutiny and hand over the stake the board demanded in return for aid, and Southwest did not apply because it remained profitable.

One other point worth noting is the amount of money the government has spent on transportation security since the 9/11 Transportation Security Administration has been created. And the government has spent over $15 billion for airline security, but only $250 million for mass transit, and in view of terrorist attacks on mass transit systems in Madrid in 2004 and London in 2005 some people think the government should spend more on mass transit security.

THE SUPREME COURT

The Supreme Court did render an interesting decision in 1995 concerning frequent-flier programs. The case was *American Airlines, Inc. v. Wolens*,[9] and the airline had modified its frequent-flier program retroactively. The state of Illinois challenged this as both breach of contract and consumer fraud. A 6–2 decision written by Justice Ginsburg held that the breach of contract law could be used since that simply holds parties to their agreements which, in turn, advances the market efficiency that the Airline Deregulation Act was designed to promote.

However, in a 7–1 split, she disallowed the use of the consumer fraud law as that controls the primary conduct of those fully under it, which is not the case with airlines. Breach of contract, on the other hand, deals with private obligations; thus the difference between the two laws.

The Court also rendered a decision in 2004 in the case of *Olympic Airlines v. Husain*.[10] It held in a 6–2 decision by Justice Thomas that an airline is liable, in this case for $1.4 million, for the death of a 52-year-old passenger who had an asthmatic reaction to cigarette smoke because a flight attendant repeatedly refused to move him farther from the smoking section. The flight attendant's refusal constituted an "accident" under the Warsaw Convention, a treaty governing airline liability, because it was external and unexpected and was a link in a chain of causation.

SUMMARY

Has airline deregulation worked? Fares have fallen; air safety, particularly with the major airlines, has improved; more people are traveling by air, and congestion could be reduced if fewer flights were put at peak times; profits are up. But there is a downside, and that is the reduction in airlines due, in part, to so many mergers. If the antitrust laws were vigorously enforced, and if authority to administer them were transferred from the Department of Transportation to the Justice Department, airline deregulation would indeed be a success. Now, however, with an oligopolistic industry, one must be concerned with the fact that it is very difficult for new carriers to enter the market and compete effectively, which in turn makes it easier for the established carriers to act in concert on fares, with competition, as in days of regulation, mainly in services rendered to passengers. More competition would make deregulation truly a success.

All in all, deregulation of transportation, whether it be trucks, buses, railroads, or airlines, has been a mixed bag. The lowering of rates is impressive, but the number of mergers is disturbing, especially in the railroad and airline industries. With less and less competition come the dangers associated with oligopolies, not the least of which is higher prices. The government should be more vigilant with the antitrust laws and not so quick to approve mergers. Not everything big is bad, but competition is healthy and the transportation industry, since deregulation, has become less competitive.

QUESTIONS FOR DISCUSSION

1. What are the major arguments for regulating transportation?
2. What are the major arguments for deregulating transportation?
3. Has railroad deregulation worked?
4. Has airline deregulation worked?
5. Do you agree with the elimination of the ICC?
6. Are the many mergers in the railroad and airline industries good for the economy?
7. Should the government financially help out Amtrak and the airlines?

RECOMMENDED READING

Cohen, Jeffrey. *Politics and Economic Policy in the United States.* Boston, MA: Houghton Mifflin Company, 1997. Chapters 10 and 11.
Schnitzer, Martin. *Contemporary Government and Business Relations.* 4th ed. Boston, MA:
Houghton Mifflin Co., 1990. Chapter 14.

NOTES

1. 118 U.S. 557 (1886).
2. 162 U.S. 184 (1896).
3. 167 U.S. 479 (1897).
4. 168 U.S. 144 (1897).
5. 206 U.S. 441 (1907).
6. 216 U.S. 452 (1910).
7. 234 U.S. 342 (1914).
8. 257 U.S. 563 (1922).
9. 513 U.S. 219 (1995).
10. 540 U.S. ——— (2004).

10

Deregulation of Financial Institutions

One of the major industries to be affected by the movement to deregulate is that of financial institutions, especially banks. This is a field that had been highly regulated, and for good reason. Alexander Hamilton, our first secretary of the treasury, thought it would be in this country's best interest for Congress to charter a Bank of the United States. The national government would transact business through this bank and therefore avoid dealing with state banks, some of which were not that sympathetic with what the national government was doing. The problem was that chartering a bank was not one of the powers expressly given to Congress in Article 1, Section 8, of the Constitution, which lists what Congress can do. Hamilton, however, argued that the final clause of that section says that Congress can make all laws "Which shall be necessary and proper for carrying into Execution the foregoing powers," and since Congress was expressly given the powers to tax, regulate commerce, and coin money, surely it could charter a bank to help facilitate those powers. Although such luminaries as James Madison and Thomas Jefferson disagreed with that interpretation, Congress passed the bill and President Washington signed it into law in 1791. The Bank had a twenty-year charter and, when it expired, Congress waited five years before chartering the second Bank of the United States, also for twenty years. Since it was competition for state banks, some states passed laws restricting branches of the Bank in their states.

One such state was Maryland, and it imposed a tax on the branch in Baltimore. McCulloch, the cashier, would not pay, and a case ensued that eventually reached the Supreme Court. Chief Justice Marshall wrote the unanimous opinion in the 1819 case of *McCulloch v. Maryland*[1] upholding the law creating the Bank and echoing Hamilton's old arguments concerning the necessary and proper clause. He also said that states could not tax the Bank because it would be useless to allow Congress to charter a bank if a state could negate that power by a destructive tax. Marshall reiterated that decision five years later in another unanimous decision, *Osborn v. Bank of the United States.*[2] Here he also allowed an Ohio state official to be sued for damages, as he had collected the tax there despite knowing that it was unconstitutional.

The second Bank ran into opposition from President Jackson, who vetoed a bill to extend its charter and, upon winning reelection in 1832, proceeded to take all the federal money out of the Bank and put it in various state banks. We went without a national bank until the Civil War, when Congress passed the 1864 National Banking Act enabling the national government to charter national banks. These banks issued notes that circulated as currency. Since state banks had their own notes, Congress, in 1866, decided to impose a 10 percent tax on them, which effectively drove that competition out of existence. The Supreme Court had already said, in the 1837 case of *Briscoe v. Bank of Kentucky,*[3] that state banks were different from the state itself; this enabled them to issue notes that circulated as currency (states themselves are prohibited by Article 1, Section 10 of the Constitution from issuing bills of credit). Thus, it had no problem in the 1869 case, *Veazie Bank v. Fenno,*[4] upholding the tax, since it was not on the state itself but on a bank. It said also that a tax is not invalid simply because it is too high, and that it would not look into the motive behind a statute. It would only look to see if the statute is consistent with the Constitution. The Court said that the statute might not even be considered as a tax, but rather part of Congress's power to control the currency.

The power to control the currency was also the basis for the Court upholding the right of Congress during the Civil War to pass three Legal Tender Acts authorizing greenbacks to be used as money for all purposes, even for debts incurred prior to the passage of the Acts. The Court had at first said no, in the 1870 case of *Hepburn v. Griswold,*[5] as it felt the law took away property without due process, a Fifth Amendment violation. But the next year, in the *Second Legal Tender Cases,*[6] the Court reversed itself due to the addition of two justices to the Court.

REGULATION OF BANKS

The system of national banks seemed to work for a while, but soon much of the power in the banking business fell into the hands of a few large banks, especially in the eastern part of the country. When President Wilson took office he wanted to change that and, as a result, Congress in 1913 passed the Federal Reserve Act, creating our present structure. It divided the country into twelve districts, each one having a Federal Reserve Bank. All national banks had to become members of the system; state banks had the option of joining it. The notes issued by the Federal Reserve Banks were to circulate as currency and a Federal Reserve Board was created to oversee the operation. Again, this seemed to work, but along came the Depression and with it the failures of many banks. When Franklin Roosevelt was elected president in 1932, one of the first actions he took upon being inaugurated the next year was to declare a moratorium on bank operations. Congress then passed an Emergency Banking Act providing for the inspection of banks and the reopening of licensed solvent banks.

In order to try to stimulate inflation, Roosevelt took the country off the gold standard. Congress then passed a joint resolution that canceled any clause in any private contracts or government bonds that called for payment in gold. The Supreme Court, in the 1935 case of *Norman v. Baltimore and Ohio Railroad Company*,[7] upheld the section of the Resolution regarding private contracts, as Congress has the power to regulate the currency and thus can say what is legal tender. However, in the companion case of *Perry v. United States*,[8] the Court felt that Congress could not do the same with government bonds as the government had pledged its word to pay in gold when people bought the bonds. After saying this, the Court turned around and refused to allow the suit, holding that the difference between the amount Perry would have received in gold and the amount he actually would receive from the bond was so negligible that he suffered no real damages and thus had no standing to bring a suit.

Roosevelt now got Congress to further regulate the banking industry. The 1933 Glass-Steagall Act created the Federal Deposit Insurance Corporation to guarantee bank deposits in all banks in the Federal Reserve System, originally up to $2,500 and now up to $100,000. Commercial banks had to give up their securities affiliates and to abstain from investment banking, and a limit was placed on the investment securities that member banks could have in their investment portfolios. Federal Reserve Banks were required to supervise the member banks' use of credit, and an Open Market Committee, composed of twelve members including five of the twelve Federal Reserve Bank presidents, was created to control commercial bank policies. In 1935 Congress further regulated the industry with the passage of the Banking Act, by which the old Federal Reserve Board was dissolved. It was replaced by a Board of Governors, composed of seven members appointed by the president, with Senate approval, for fourteen-year terms. The president also designates who will be the chair and the vice-chair, with Senate approval, for four-year terms. The Board was given broader power over the federal funds (discount) rate, which is the interest rate banks with excess reserves charge other banks needing overnight loans to meet reserve requirements, and over the reserve requirements of banks, which are assets a bank must hold and not lend out. Each Reserve Bank must restate its discount rate every two weeks with the approval of the Board. One other federal agency of note is the National Credit

Agency Administration, which charters and supervises federal credit unions and insures deposits there plus in many state credit unions.

Since the FDIC insures deposits for its member banks as well as for any other savings associations or commercial banks who want to participate, it needs to finance itself with semiannual assessments on each insured bank, based on the volume of the bank's deposits. It also receives income from investing the fund's balances. Another function of the FDIC is to supervise state-chartered banks that are not members of the Federal Reserve System.

One power the FDIC does not have is to close a bank. A chartering authority can only do that, which would be a state banking commission for a state bank or the Office of the Comptroller of the Currency, which charters and supervises national banks. Once a bank is closed, however, the FDIC is appointed receiver and is responsible for settling the affairs of the bank. The FDIC seldom had to worry about bank failures until the 1980s came along, but at that time the number of failures and their cost became significant enough to cause concern. In fact, one part of the 1982 Garn-St. Germain Act expanded the authority of the FDIC to arrange mergers between healthy and failing banks, and the 1987 Competitive Equality Banking Act expanded the options available to the FDIC to deal with failed banks.

The option employed most by the FDIC to deal with failed banks is called a purchase and assumption contract. Under it, a buyer comes forth to purchase all or some of the failed bank's assets and to assume its liabilities. This is usually done by having the FDIC invite a number of possible buyers to a bidder's meeting, with the highest bidder getting the bank.

There are other options available to the FDIC. One is a deposit payoff, with the FDIC paying depositors the full amount of their insured claims and beginning to liquidate the assets of the failed bank. Those whose deposits are not insured, as well as other creditors, get receiver's certificates under which they get a proportionate share of the collections received on the bank's assets.

Another option is a bridge bank, by which the FDIC keeps the bank open briefly until prospective purchasers have had enough time to assess the bank and make a reasonable offer for it. The bank retains much of its value and there is less community disruption.

Yet another option is the insured deposit transfer; the insured deposits and secured liabilities are transferred to another bank and the FDIC pays that bank sufficient cash to cover those liabilities. The acquiring bank, in turn, generally purchases some of the failed bank's assets.

Finally, there is open-market assistance, wherein the FDIC gives the bank money before it closes. The amount covers the difference between the estimated market value of the bank's assets and its liabilities. Private investors then provide new capital.

The reason the FDIC does mostly purchase and assumption is that it does not disrupt the community too much when another bank moves right in for those who had been doing business with the failed bank. There might not even be a delay as the one bank will close at the end of a business day and the new bank will open the next day, with just a new name on the building.

When banks were first regulated, they were not allowed to conduct interstate business. However, in 1970 Congress changed that, except for deposit taking, and at the same time narrowed the definition of a bank to include only those institutions that both accepted deposits and made commercial loans. That enabled bank holding companies and others to establish an interstate network of consumer financing corporations, mortgage companies, etc., that were not regulated because they either did not accept deposits or they did not make loans. The 1982 Garn-St. Germain Act allowed bank regulatory agencies to permit the acquisition of failing banks across state lines. In 1994 federal limits on interstate banking were repealed.

With the movement to deregulate picking up steam in the late 1970s, with consumer groups complaining that interest ceilings placed by the government were discriminatory against small savers, such as the elderly, and with technological changes occurring that banks could not install due to regulatory constraints, the time was right to deregulate banking. With interest rates fluctuating wildly at that time, people were turning to other institutions to invest their money at higher rates, such as money market funds.

Congress attempted to make banks more consumer-friendly with the passage of some legislation. In 1978 the Electronic Fund Transfer Act was passed. Among its provisions was one which said that if an ATM or debit card or password was lost or stolen, the financial institution must be notified within two business days, in which case the loss is limited to $50 or the amount of the unauthorized transfer, whichever is less. However, one who waits longer to report it could be liable for losses up to $500, and if one waits longer than 60 days after receiving the bank statement the bank does not have to reimburse for any transfers after that. Once one notifies the bank, under most circumstances the liability is limited from then on. The law also said that people must be told about ATM fees and other matters. If an ATM owner imposes a surcharge for using its machines, it must disclose the amount and allow the user to cancel the transfer. Finally, if a hacker gets a debit card and password and uses it to transfer funds from a bank account, there is no liability if the owner did not lose either one and if the owner notifies the card issuer within 60 days of the date the bank mailed the statement with the error. If one does lose either the card or the password and an unauthorized withdrawal is made, the person must notify the bank within two business days and the liability will be $50 or the transfer amount, whichever is less.

In 1987 Congress passed the Expedited Funds Availability Act that set the maximum time periods that financial institutions may hold funds deposited by check before making the money available for withdrawal. Then in 2004 Congress passed the Check Clearing for the 21st Century Act (Check 21), which says that banks must accept and process substitute checks (high quality paper reproductions created from electronic images of both sides of an original check) as the legal equivalent of original paper checks, and everyone must treat substitute checks as the legal equivalent of original checks. Banks had to provide notices to consumers explaining the law and indicate that substitute checks will speed up the check clearing practices. Customers can get expedited recrediting if the bank improperly charged the account for a substitute check, and customers must show that producing the original check, or a better copy of it, is necessary to determine the validity of the charge to the account. Claims must be made within forty days of delivery of the relevant bank statement, or the date when the substitute check is made available to the customer, whichever is later.

BANKING DEREGULATION

The result of the previously discussed events was the 1980 Depository Institutions Deregulation and Monetary Control Act. The law provided for the gradual elimination of interest rate limitations, although it also put all banks under the reserve requirements of the Federal Reserve system, even though the amount that had to be kept in reserve was lowered. All banks were allowed to offer checking services, negotiable order of withdrawal (NOW) accounts, and automatic transfer systems (ATS) accounts. Mutual savings banks could transact deals with business customers, and state usury laws could not be used to hinder agricultural, business, and mortgage loans (at that time, the prime rate was above the usury rate that many states allowed). At the same time Congress was easing restrictions states were doing the same. For example, Pennsylvania in 1982 allowed banks to merge with each other.

Once deregulation occurred, there was a substantial increase in the level of interstate banking, and computer advances such as the electronic funds transfer system (EFTS) were adopted, especially by bigger banks. However, non-bank institutions expanded into the financial services industry, with services such as consumer, business, and commercial mortgage loans. Money market funds were there for deposits. There were virtually no limitations anymore on entry and expansion into the field, the scope, and the nature of the activities, or on geographic expansion. As a result, in 1996, for the first time, the amount of money deposited at federally insured commercial banks was less than the $3 trillion invested in mutual funds.

Unfortunately, banks began to fail in large numbers. There were many reasons for it. One of the most important was the depressed economic conditions in a particular region of the country. When the price of oil dropped precipitously, real estate prices dropped in the oil-producing states. Banks that had loaned money on real estate could not recoup their losses by selling real estate. The same thing happened in the agricultural states. When an agricultural recession hit in the early 1980s, farm prices dropped, farmers could not pay off their loans, their mortgages were foreclosed, and the banks, which now had the farms, could not sell them.

Other banks failed when they made loans to less-developed countries, such as Mexico; when oil prices dropped, Mexico had all it could do to pay the interest on the loans, much less the capital.

Yet another factor was fraud and insider abuse, including outright criminal conduct. The FDIC has published a list of warning signs to be used as aids to examiners and auditors to try to spot these, and some FDIC examiners receive special training focusing on criminal motivation and early detection in spotting these things.

Deregulation has also played a part. The banking system has had to adjust to dramatic changes, and the increased level of competition has placed new pressures on bank management. The more sophisticated and complicated the decisions become, the more chance there is for a wrong choice, which adversely affects the safety and soundness of the bank. The technological changes have also added pressures to the industry, as the advances in the delivery of services have increased competition. There are startup and maintenance costs, which are a fixed cost that smaller banks find difficult to cover, and if those banks are in depressed agricultural areas, as so many are, the result can be failures.

One tactic banks have used to try to get more money is to increase their fees, and the percentage of revenue received by commercial banks from fees has risen greatly over the years. The rest of their income is from loans.

THE CASE OF SAVINGS AND LOANS

The savings and loan industry somewhat parallels the commercial banking industry. In 1932 Congress passed the Federal Home Loan Bank Act to improve the mortgage system and provide home-financing institutions better able to serve borrowers. Twelve federal Home Loan Banks were created; they raise money by issuing debentures or bonds guaranteed by the United States. They then make loans to member institutions on the security of mortgages. All federal savings and loan associations must be members, and others may join on the purchase of bank stock and by conforming to the system's regulations. The member institutions make mortgage loans to homeowners.

The Federal Savings and Loan Insurance Corporation insures the deposits of those in the system, up to $100,000 per deposit for individual accounts, as does the FDIC for commercial banks. However, when savings and loan institutions failed at comparatively high rates in the 1980s, Congress decided to recapitalize the FSLIC with the passage of the 1987 Competitive Equality

Banking Act that created the Financial Corporation capitalized from the earnings of the Federal Home Loan Banks. The Financial Corporation then raises
funds in the long-term credit markets, which it invests in FSLIC stock. The
FSLIC, in turn, can use the proceeds, in addition to its other income, to close
insolvent savings and loans. It can also use cash to try to prevent closing or
to restore normal operations.

The savings and loan industry was deregulated with the same laws that
deregulated the commercial banking industry. One was the 1980 Depository
Institutions Deregulation and Monetary Control Act, which gradually eliminated limitations on interest payments and which expanded the authority of
the savings and loan associations into the consumer loan business. The other
was the 1982 Garn-St. Germain Act that permitted savings and loan associations to have a much greater access to commercial loans by allowing them to
invest up to 55 percent of their assets in such loans. States were passing similar deregulatory legislation because, as in the commercial bank field, inflation
was running in double digits in the 1970s and the savings and loans were
stuck with old 5 and 6 percent mortgages at a time it cost them more to borrow. Depositors looked elsewhere because they could earn higher interest in
money market accounts.

Why did so many savings and loans fail? One reason was poor management; with deregulation the banks were able to do almost anything with their
money. Managers loaned money for practically any purpose, and not all of
the loans were fiscally sound. Also, there was some evidence of corruption
on the part of certain managers. Another factor was economic in nature, in
that many of the failed banks were in the Southwest, particularly in the oil-
producing states. Yet another factor was loose state regulation. Laws were
passed to attract deposits that were used to fund high-risk and poorly under-
written investment schemes. The end result was a lot of repossessed real
estate from failed savings and loans, and electronic runs by which wealthy
investors transferred their funds by computers from a problem savings and
loan to other areas of investment.

The upshot of all this was the creation of the Office of Thrift Supervision
to try to coordinate the bailout effort and to supervise federally and state
chartered savings banks, and the creation of the Resolution Trust Corporation
to auction off the assets of any remaining insolvent savings and loans. It has
auctioned off billions of dollars worth of real estate and loans backed by real
estate, but it has also cost into the billions for the government to do this,
which means, in turn, that the taxpayers are footing the bill. In order not to
have so many failures again, the government now requires banks to keep four
percent of their assets, and if the assets drop to less than two percent the bank
is taken over by the government.

Major Federal Financial Institutions Laws:
1791 and 1816 Laws creating the first and second Banks of the United States

Civil War years: Three Legal Tender Acts
1864   National Banking Act
1866   Tax on state bank notes
1913   Federal Reserve Act
1932   Federal Home Loan Banking Act
1933   Emergency Banking Act
1933   Joint Resolution canceling gold payments
1933   Glass-Steagall Act
1935   Banking Act
1978   Electronic Fund Transfer Act
1980   Depository Institutions Deregulation and Monetary Control Act
1982   Garn-St. Germain Act
1987   Competitive Equality Banking Act
1987   Expedited Funds Availability Act
1989   Financial Institutions Reform, Recovery, and Enforcement Act
1999   Repeal of Glass-Steagall
1999   Gramm-Leach-Bliley Act
2004   Check Clearing for the 21st Century Act (Check 21)

MERGERS

It is apparent that the partial deregulation of the banking industry is only one of several factors that helped cause so many bank failures in the 1980s. However, one more recent phenomenon needs to be examined and, as with transportation deregulation, it is the great number of large mergers that took place in the 1990s. Thousands of banks have been eliminated since 1990. Banks feel they have to do it, as they now account for only 15 percent of the loans made in the United States. Mergers are facilitated by branch banking, as large banks can create branches by mergers with smaller banks. Also, if a bank wishes to offer a new form of service, a merger can be the easiest way to acquire the facilities. Then too, economies of scale are a motive, as spreading overhead costs over a larger volume of business reduces unit costs. Finally, mergers allow banks to increase their capital base, which allows them to make larger loans. Of course this is not a one-way street; small banks might want to merge to avoid failure and because they are sometimes are at a disadvantage in attracting skilled management personnel.

Bank holding companies are very important, as they control not only a high percentage of commercial banks but they dominate branch banks. While the number of banking companies in this country has dropped significantly, the number of branches and automated teller machines (ATMs) has sharply risen.

An example of the enormity of some mergers in the 1990s is the 1991 merger of Chemical Banking Corporation with Manufacturers Hanover Corporation, with combined assets of $135.5 billion. The 1995 merger of Chase

Manhattan Bank with Chemical followed this for $10 billion, making Chase Manhattan the country's largest bank at that time but costing 12,000 jobs. In 1997 NationsBank, one of the country's largest, announced it would buy Barnett Banks, the largest in Florida, for $15 billion. Also in 1997, Banc One and First USA merged, with a value of $7.9 billion, which moved Banc One higher on the list among credit card issuers. 1997 also saw Morgan Stanley, which does investment banking; combine with Dean Witter, Discovery and Company, which does retail stocks, to form at that time the country's largest securities firm. The year 1998 saw the then two biggest bank mergers in the United States announced the same day. NationsBank, the third largest bank then, bought BankAmerica, the fifth largest bank then, to become at that time the country's second largest bank—BankAmerica. The price for the merger was $61.6 billion. NationsBank had started as NCNB (North Carolina National Bank) and had become one of the country's biggest; it had even gotten into investment banking with its 1997 purchase of Montgomery Securities. BankAmerica had also gone into investment banking in 1997 with its purchase of Robertson Stephens.

Not to be outdone, Banc One, the eighth largest then, merged with First Chicago, the ninth largest then, to become the country's fourth largest bank at that time, just ahead of J. P. Morgan. The price for the merger was $29.6 billion, and once more Banc One moved even higher among credit card issuers.

Later in that year, Wells Fargo was bought by Norwest, the then eighth and ninth largest, for $34.4 billion, making Wells Fargo the country's seventh largest bank at that time (Wells Fargo had a few years earlier acquired First Interstate Bancorp for $11.6 billion, with some 7,200 people losing their jobs).

1998 also saw the largest merger in terms of financial services involving banks. The two companies were Travelers Group and Citicorp and the amount was $72.6 billion. Citicorp at that time was the country's second largest bank and owned Citibank, which was the world's largest issuer of credit cards. Travelers was a multifaceted company selling life insurance and annuities, property and casualty insurance, did consumer loans, commercial credit, and credit cards, and did investing services through Salomon Smith Barney (it had Smith Barney, and in 1997 acquired Salomon, known mostly for bond investments, for $9 billion). It underwrote stock, municipal bonds, and American and international debt offerings. The new company is called Citigroup. In 2005 the company did sell its Travelers Life and Annuity Business to Met-Life for $11.5 billion, and unloaded its asset management unit to Legg Mason in an asset swap of $3.7 billion.

In 1999 there were still more mergers. Fleet Financial Group acquired Bank of Boston for $15.9 billion, creating the then eighth largest bank in the country and preeminent in New England and was called FleetBoston Corporation.

Next came the largest takeover of a U.S. institution thus far by a foreign financial concern. Deutsche Bank of Germany paid $10.1 billion for Bankers Trust, creating at that time the world's largest commercial financial institution, with assets of about $1.55 trillion (Deutsche is Germany's biggest bank, and Bankers Trust was this country's ninth largest).

The 1990s decade of mergers did not come to a halt when the 2000 decade arrived. In 2000 Firstar Bank acquired US Bancorp for $21.1 billion and retained the bank's name. Also in 2000 J. P. Morgan was acquired by Chase Manhattan, the then number two bank, for $33.6 billion and the company is called J. P. Morgan Chase. It then acquired Bank One in 2003 for $58 billion. Also in 2003, Bank of America, the number three bank (but number one in deposits), acquired FleetBoston for $48 billion. Then in 2005 Bank of America acquired MBNA, the third largest issuer of credit cards, for $35 billion and became the country's largest issuer of credit cards, with some 20 percent of the market (the 10 largest companies control 87 percent). In 2005 mergers were only half of those in 2004, the second least active year in a decade.

One of the best case studies of bank mergers would be to examine what has happened in the Philadelphia area, where commercial banking in the United States began in 1782. Since Pennsylvania allowed banks to merge, there are no longer any good-sized banks based in Philadelphia. Out-of-city-based or out-of-state-based banks have acquired them all, and the end result is that a handful of banks now dominate the nine-county Philadelphia area. The largest is Wachovia, based in Charlotte, North Carolina. It traces its Philadelphia connection to 1986, when Industrial Valley Bank was sold to Fidelcor, which two years later was sold to First Fidelity, which in 1996 was sold to First Union, a combination worth about $5.4 billion. That, by itself, only made First Union number four in the region. What made it number one was its 1997 acquisition of the previous number one, CoreStates, the last remaining Philadelphia-based big bank, for $17.1 billion, the largest ever bank merger at that point, and made First Union the then sixth largest bank in the nation. CoreStates had been number one due to mergers of its own. It had been known as Philadelphia National Bank but changed its name in 1983. In that same year Central Penn Bank was sold to Meridian Bank, and then in 1990 CoreStates bought First Pennsylvania Bank followed by buying Meridian in 1996, a $3 billion value. Then in 2001 First Union bought Wachovia for $14.3 billion and kept the latter's name. In 2004 Wachovia acquired South Trust Bank for $14.7 billion.

Among the other big banks in the region is PNC, based in Pittsburgh. It can trace its roots in the Philadelphia area to 1983 when Provident Bank merged with Pittsburgh National Bank, and the result was PNC Bank. That same year Continental Bancorp, Inc. was sold to Midlantic, which in 1996 was sold to PNC Bank. Another bank is Citizens, based in Rhode Island (but owned by Royal Bank of Scotland), which bought Mellon Bank in 2001 for $2.1 billion. In 1983 Mellon had bought the Girard Bank, and in the period from 1989–1992 it bought the bank PSFS.

Those three banks along with three others have a large part of the Philadelphia regional market, and this situation is largely a result of the deregulation of financial institutions. It does not make for a great deal of banking competition in the Philadelphia area. What is even more disconcerting is the fact that there is not one Philadelphia-based bank left among the big banks, whereas there were at least eight or nine of them when the decade of the 1980s began.

REPEAL OF GLASS-STEAGALL

Late in 1999 Congress repealed the Glass-Steagall Act, under the premise that American companies will be enabled to compete better in the new economy. Under the new law, banks will be able to affiliate with insurance companies and securities concerns with far fewer restrictions. It will also be more difficult for industrial companies to control a bank, as prior to the new law a number of commercial enterprises had been permitted to open savings associations known as unitary thrifts. One controversial provision in the new law allows mutual insurance companies to move to other states to avoid payments they would otherwise owe policyholders as they reorganize their corporate structure. This preempts the laws of many states that required the state's consent before such relocations. These companies can now simply move to states with more permissive laws and set up a mutual holding company.

What is the bottom line for the deregulation of financial institutions? Surely there are more financial services available than ever, only some of which are banks. This is a positive result. On the other hand, the decrease in the number of banks is alarming. Many failed, and many have been taken over by big banks through mergers. This decreases the amount of choice available to consumers. Banks have even been helped by some Supreme Court decisions.

BANKS AND THE SUPREME COURT

In the 1978 case of *First National Bank of Boston v. Bellotti*,[9] a 5–4 opinion by Justice Powell struck down a Massachusetts law that had banned banks and businesses from trying to influence the outcomes of political referenda. He thought it an abridgement of free speech. In that same year, in *Marquette National Bank of Minneapolis v. First of Omaha Service Corporation*,[10] Justice Brennan wrote the unanimous decision that a national bank can charge out-of-state credit card customers an interest rate allowed by the bank's home state, even if it was higher than that permitted by the state where the card-holder resides. Then in 1994, in *Central Bank v. First Interstate Bank*,[11] Justice Kennedy, in a 5–4 opinion, said that banks cannot be sued just because they had, as had the bank in this case, delayed in conducting an independent review of the property securing some bonds while serving as a trustee, and the bonds had defaulted. He thought the 1934 Securities Exchange Act did not permit such suits. In 1996, in *Smiley v. Citibank*,[12] a unanimous opinion written by Justice Scalia held that national banks could charge any late-payment fee permitted by their home state, regardless of whether the fee violates the law of the state where a cardholder lives. Citibank does its credit card operations from South Dakota, which has no cap. Since the Comptroller of the Currency said that the late fee is a form of interest, the Court, in light of the *Marquette* decision, accepted that interpretation as reasonable and thus ruled for the bank.

Also in 1996, the government was taken to task by the Court in the case of *United States v. Winstar Corporation*.[13] At issue was the $120 billion tax-payer bailout of the failed savings and loans through the passage of the 1989 Financial Institutions Reform, Recovery, and Enforcement Act. Under the act, paper assets of banks were converted into liabilities. Unfortunately, that caused two of three savings and loans to fail because the three had been induced by regulators to assume huge liabilities to salvage other savings and loans. Justice Souter, in a 7–2 opinion, held that the government knowingly went back on its word through accounting changes that made the savings and loans insolvent. He felt that the three contracts promised that the government, not the savings and loans, would assume the financial risk of any regulatory changes that might deprive the savings and loans of favorable accounting treatment. The bottom line was that the savings and loans could not meet the minimum capital requirements. The government's contention was that the contracts did not provide insurance against a legislative change, but Souter said that position was fundamentally implausible. He stated that it would have been madness to enter into them without that guarantee, for their very existence would have been in jeopardy from the moment the agreements were signed. He thought that this was a case of ordinary contract law, and that the government's arguments were at odds with its own long-term interest as a reliable trading partner. When the savings and loans were failing, the government urged the good ones to take the others over, stating that the liabilities would be carried on the books as good will that would be amortized over 35–40 years. These paper assets allowed the banks to make more loans. However, the 1989 law removed intangible assets, such as good will, from those that could be counted toward a savings and loan's minimum capital requirements. The consequences were swift and severe. The government had assumed the risk of paying damages for any financial injury from changes. The law was not a public and general one, but one for government self-relief.

In the 2004 case of *Household Credit Services, Inc. v. Pfennig*,[14] a unanimous decision by Justice Thomas upheld a Federal Reserve Board rule allowing credit card issuers, in this case the MBNA Corporation, to charge interest on fees they impose on customers who exceed their credit limits. The fees are imposed separately from finance costs and are listed as separate purchases that accrue interest charges. The Board had issued the rule because the 1968 Truth-in-Lending Act requires lenders to disclose credit terms, but does not say whether over-limit charges must be included in the finance charge.

PRIVACY

Congress, concerned that banks and other financial institutions, including tax preparers, travel agents, and some department stores, had been giving information about consumers in an indiscriminate way, passed a law in 1999 to attempt to impose a remedy. It is the Gramm-Leach-Bliley Act, and under it these institutions must tell consumers how they are using their information, and it bars the institutions from sharing some of that information with outside companies but permits information-sharing among affiliated companies.

SUMMARY

In conclusion, one must be concerned about the rise in bank mergers because with a lessening of competition come all the dangers associated with oligopolies. One can sense that already, with the number of banks that are not only raising their existing fees but starting to impose fees for services that previously were free, such as having an in-person transaction at the bank rather than doing it by automation. If that is a portent of things to come, one must indeed worry that banking deregulation has unleashed a potential problem for consumers, especially those of limited means.

An illustration of how countries, including the United States, are concerned about global banking is an agreement reached by 102 countries in 1997, which took effect March 1, 1999. They decided to knock down barriers to financial firms, namely banks, securities firms, and insurance companies. The amount covered was $17.8 trillion in global securities assets, $38 trillion in global bank lending, and $2.2 trillion in worldwide insurance premiums. The point should be clear that financial markets are global in scope, and since the United States is such a key player, what we do in this country affects the world. Therefore, our deregulation of financial institutions affects people all over the world, not just our own consumers, and hopefully deregulation will prove effective. This agreement, in any event, was a positive step toward international cooperation.

QUESTIONS FOR DISCUSSION

1. Do you believe that Congress ought to be able to do things, such as chartering banks, when not expressly given the power in the Constitution?
2. Do you think that state banks should be able to issue notes that circulate as currency?
3. Do you think it proper that Congress taxed state banknotes out of existence?
4. Why has the Supreme Court consistently favored banks in its decisions?
5. Is it good that the government has substantially deregulated banking?
6. Do you see any problems with the megamergers in the financial institutions field?

RECOMMENDED READING

Schnitzer, Martin. *Contemporary Government and Business Relations*. 4th ed. Boston, MA: Houghton Mifflin Company, 1990. Chapter 15.

NOTES

1. 4 Wheat. 316 (1819).
2. 9 Wheat. 738 (1824).
3. 11 Pet. 257 (1837).
4. 8 Wall. 533 (1869).
5. 8 Wall. 603 (1870).
6. 12 Wall. 457 (1871).
7. 294 U.S. 240 (1935).
8. 294 U.S. 330 (1935).
9. 435 U.S. 765 (1978).
10. 439 U.S. 299 (1978).
11. 511 U.S. 164 (1994).
12. 517 U.S. 735 (1996).
13. 518 U.S. 839 (1996)
14. 541 U.S. ——— (2004).

11

Deregulation of Communications

The communications industry is one that has seen tremendous growth due to new technologies. Household spending on communications has jumped rapidly, mostly due to wireless phone and high-speed Internet service. The federal government first sought to regulate this field in 1910 when it placed telephone, telegraph, cable, and wireless companies engaged in interstate commerce under the jurisdiction of the Interstate Commerce Commission. However, radio proved to be such a perplexing problem that three conferences were held during the 1920s to try to bring order to an industry that was growing in a chaotic fashion. The result was the passage of the Radio Act of 1927 that established the Federal Radio Commission and placed it in the Department of Commerce. By assigning frequencies in an orderly manner, the FRC accomplished its task. However, when Franklin Roosevelt won the 1932 presidential election, he reorganized the executive branch. As a result Congress, in 1934, passed the Federal Communications Act, replacing the FRC with an independent regulatory commission called the Federal Communications Commission. The FCC is composed of five persons, appointed by the president with Senate approval, for five years each. The initial terms were staggered so that they would not expire simultaneously and, as is the practice for these kinds of agencies, no more than three of the five commissioners could come from the same political party. Besides regulating radio and later television, the FCC was also to regulate the telephone, telegraph, cable, and wireless companies that had been under the ICC. Whereas the FCC has power over such matters as services, accounts, interconnections, facilities, combinations, and finances, its power over rates is restricted as it has no control over broadcasting charges. That is left to the marketplace and the going rate can be high, as shown by what advertisers pay for spots on professional football's Super Bowl.

What the FCC does for radio and television is to assign frequencies and channels, grant them licenses to operate their stations, fix their hours of operation, and prevent interference among stations. Section 303 of the 1934 law charges the FCC with seeing that broadcasters serve the public convenience, interest, or necessity.

When it comes to rates, such as for the telephone and telegraph companies, they must file them with the FCC and make them available for public inspection. Notice must be given of rate changes. If a new rate is filed, the FCC may suspend it for a period not exceeding three months and hold hearings on its reasonableness. The burden of proving reasonableness is on the company.

TELECOMMUNICATIONS

AT&T and the Bells

The high point of government regulation of the telecommunications industry occurred in 1982 when the American Telephone and Telegraph Company, the largest in the world at that time, reached a settlement with the Justice Department in that agency's attempt to break up AT&T's monopoly of the telephone industry. AT&T divested itself of the local telephone services of its twenty-two Bell Operating Companies. They became part of seven independent holding companies: Ameritech, Bell Atlantic, Bell South, Nynex, Pacific Telesis, Southwestern Bell, and US West. AT&T also turned over to them its intrastate long-distance service. These companies, in turn, had to share their facilities with all long-distance telephone companies on the same terms, and could not discriminate against AT&T's competitors in buying equipment and planning new facilities.

On the other hand, AT&T was allowed to retain its equipment-manufacturing subsidiary, Western Electric; its research unit, Bell Laboratories; and its long-distance division (it still has about half the market for long-distance service in the United States). AT&T's stockholders retained their stock and were issued proportionate shares in the local companies. The divestiture, the largest in antitrust history, amounted to $87 billion.

Did the divestiture work? Because of new competition in the long-distance industry, prices have dropped for customers, and equipment prices have also dropped for phone companies. There has been growth in new technology, such as fiber-optic cable and fax machines. On the other hand, customers paid higher costs for equipment installation and service provided by the short-distance phone companies. Rates now seem stable, but there have been complaints about quality of service and there was, especially in the beginning, customer confusion over telephone bills.

Meanwhile, AT&T got larger in 1994 when it bought McCaw Cellular Communications for $11.5 billion, and in 1995 it split into three companies:

one for long-distance and credit card operations, one for telecommunications equipment and systems, and one for its computer unit. It also won a big Supreme Court decision in the 1994 case of *MCI Telecommunications Corporation v. American Telephone and Telegraph Company.*[1] The FCC had relieved AT&T's competitors from the need to file a listing of their rates and services. Normally, rates must be posted 120 days before they take effect. However, the FCC decided that was only for dominant carriers, so it let the others negotiate customized service agreements with big companies. The FCC thought it could do so because the law does allow it to modify any requirement, but Justice Scalia, for a 5–3 Court, held that the provision in question connotes moderate change, not fundamental revision, and rate filings are the essential characteristics of a rate-regulated industry.

What about the seven "baby Bells"? They are not small, despite the nickname, and they are not even seven. Mergers have begun to permeate the field. One of the companies, Bell South, has stayed rather constant until 2006, when AT&T announced plans to buy it for $67 billion, subject to the approval of regulators.

Vodaphone, a British wireless company, bought Airtouch in 1999, and later in 1999 Bell Atlantic and Vodaphone Airtouch (which was the world's largest wireless telephone operator) agreed to combine their U.S. wireless operations and create the nation's largest coast-to-coast network serving millions of customers and covering most of the population. In 2000 Vodaphone Airtouch bought Mannesmann, a U.S. company, for $198.9 billion.

Bell Atlantic bought a stake in Metromedia and paid it to use its nationwide fiber-optic data network for twenty years. It gave Bell Atlantic access to expensive equipment that allowed it to directly connect its customers to points across the United States, instead of using outside companies to reach some areas, and it gave Metromedia money to accelerate the growth of its network, which can be used to transmit data, voice, video, and multimedia communications here and abroad.

Mergers have occurred with most of the Bell companies. In 1997 Southwestern Bell and Pacific Telesis (also called Pacific Bell) merged to form SBC. The price was $16.7 billion. The next year SBC Communications Inc. bought Ameritech for $72.4 billion. It had also bought Southern New England Telecommunications. In 1999 it bought Comcast's cellular operations for $1.67 billion. In 2000, SBC, at the time the nation's second largest local phone company, received FCC permission to begin to offer long-distance service. In 2005, SBC, already big in local phone liners, Internet services, and mobile phones, ironically bought ATT, its former parent company (and now calls itself AT&T), for $16.9 billion and therefore got the latter's corporate telephone and data market and long-distance service.

Not to be outdone, Bell Atlantic and Nynex merged for $22.7 billion in 1997, calling itself Bell Atlantic, and the next year Bell Atlantic merged with

GTE for $71.3 billion. It is now called Verizon Communications. This created at the time the nation's largest telephone company as Bell Atlantic had local telephone service in thirteen states and GTE had local telephone service to rural areas in twenty-eight states. GTE started in 1935 as General Telephone, became General Telephone and Electric when it merged with Sylvania in 1955, and became GTE two decades later. GTE also brought to the merger long-distance service in all fifty states, regional computer networks, and World Wide Web services for businesses. Bell Atlantic folded GTE's wireless assets into its Vodaphone venture, creating one of the nation's largest mobile phone companies. GTE bought the long-distance company Sprint in the 1980s, but because the law required that Sprint stay a separate company (so that one company would not do both local and long distance), it decided to sell it in 1992. However, the 1996 Telecommunications Act dropped that provision, so GTE got back into it. Sprint, meanwhile, sold 10 percent each in 1996 to Deutsche Telekom of Germany and France Telecom. Since Bell Atlantic's local calling region was thirteen states, it could not start long-distance services in them without FCC permission. Permission was granted in 1999 to begin to offer long-distance services. Altogether, Verizon controlled millions of local phone lines (one-third of the nation's) plus millions of cellphone customers. It and SBC controlled more than two-thirds of the nation's telephone lines. Today Verizon has local and long-distance telephone service, wireless communication (it has a joint venture whereby Verizon Mobile uses the Sprint wireless network), and high speed Internet. It is the largest regional phone company, and it got even larger in 2005 when it bought MCI (was MCI WorldCom but changed the name in 2003), the second largest long-distance company, for $8.5 billion, getting its long-distance service and its business customers.

Verizon has been directly involved in two 2002 Supreme Court cases each based on the 1996 Telecommunications Act. In *Verizon Communications Inc. v. Federal Communications Commission*,[2] a 5–3 decision by Justice Souter upheld FCC rules under the Act that permitted start-up telephone companies to lease equipment at relatively low cost from the biggest phone companies. Specifically, the FCC is authorized to require state utility commissions to set the rates charged by the incumbents for leased elements on a forward-looking basis untied to the incumbent's investment, and to require incumbents to combine such elements at the entrant's request when they lease them to the entrants.

In *Verizon MD Inc. v. Public Service Commission of Maryland*,[3] an 8–0 decision by Justice Scalia held that, since the Telecommunications Act was silent on the subject, states as well as individual state commissioners can be sued in federal court for their part in bringing competition into local phone markets.

In 2004 Verizon was in yet another Supreme Court case, this one involving antitrust. A unanimous decision by Justice Scalia in *Verizon Communications Inc. v. Law Offices of Curtis V. Trinko*[4] said that even though the Telecommunications Act required local telephone companies to give competitors access to local networks, their alleged failure to provide sufficient assistance was not the basis of a recognized antitrust claim by consumers.

US West bought Continental Cablevision in 1996 for $10.8 billion. It had a media group (MediaOne) but it spun it off as a separate company in 1997 and it was bought by AT&T in 1999. US West, meanwhile, in 1998 sold its domestic wireless operation for $5.7 billion to Airtouch Communication. Vodaphone, a British wireless company, bought Airtouch in 1999 for $65.8 billion. US West, with its digital subscriber line and wireless and local phone service, then merged with Qwest Communications International with its long distance, broadband Internet data, video and voice communications capabilities, and optical fiber, for $56.3 billion and took the Qwest Communications name. Global Crossing, a Bermuda local and long-distance phone company that had also wanted US West, then acquired Frontier Corporation, a U.S. based long-distance carrier, for $1 billion.

In 2004 the FCC voted to relax the rules, called UNE-P (unbundled network element platform), that had required the remaining four Bell companies (Verizon, SBC, Bell South, and Qwest) to give their rivals access to their new, super-fast fiber-optic networks that carry voice, video, and data, at sharply discounted wholesale prices. The exemption was for crucial elements of their new high-speed Internet networks and equipment, which was a setback for companies such as AT&T, MCI, etc. It did so because of the increasing competition in the phone markets since Congress imposed the obligations on the Bells in the 1996 Telecommunications Act to lease their equipment to rivals in an effort to promote competition, and because of a series of court cases brought by the Bells that had questioned the earlier, tougher rules. However, it did preserve some discounted wholesale rates covering high-capacity lines used primarily by businesses and set by states. A lower federal court upheld the FCC's exemption for the Internet, but struck down the remaining rules and the FCC decided not to appeal.

More Mergers

There has been billions of dollars worth of mergers in the telecommunications fields beginning in the 1990s. Metromedia entered the long distance field in 1993 with a $2.5 billion merger with Resurgens Communications Group. In 1997 WorldCom purchased MCI for $37 billion. WorldCom Technologies merged with Williams Telecommunications for $2.5 billion and got 11,000 miles of fiber-optic cable network. UUNET was acquired, as it was part of MFS Communications and MFS was bought by WorldCom for $14 billion. Once it had its Internet provider, WorldCom bought CompuServe, an online service, from H&R Block for $1.2 billion. It then sold the consumer side of it (content, data bases, and subscribers) to America Online, to which it supplied the hardware network. An AOL competitor, Microsoft, bought Web TV, a net deliverer directly to television sets. There is much competition as to which company can have the leading site on the Internet. AOL in 1998 bought Netscape Communications Corporation for $4.21 billion, giving it the Netcenter Web site in addition to its own (it also gets to distribute Netscape's Internet browser software). As part of the deal, Sun Microsystems, a maker of business software and computers, would distribute Netscape's corporate software for three years. As for the rest of the Web site competition, Walt Disney Company bought Infoseek and folded it into its new portal, the Go Network. Microsoft has its MSN portal, but in 1999 a big company became even bigger. Yahoo bought Geocities, another popular site, with the latter remaining as an independent unit. Yahoo bought Broadcast.com in 1999 for $5.7 billion. The latter was the Internet's leading supplier of radio and video program. Later in 1999 Internet service providers Earthlink Network and MindSpring Enterprises merged in a $1.7 billion deal to create the then number two provider in the United States, behind AOL.

As for making computers, Compaq Computer Corporation purchased Tandem Corporation, a maker of high-end mainframes used in retailing, banking, stock trading, and telecommunications, for $2.8 billion. Then in 1998 it purchased Digital Equipment Corporation, a maker of large corporate computers, for $9.6 billion. It also had the Alta Vista Web site. In 2001 the then number two, Hewlett Packard, acquired Compaq, which was number three, for $19 billion.

AT&T

In the meantime, what is happening at AT&T? The world's largest telecommunications company bought, in 1998, Teleport Communications Group, which provided telecommunications services to businesses, and then bought Tele-Communications Inc. (TCI), the nation's number two cable television company, including TCI's stake in At Home, for $31.8 billion. By buying the former, it could bypass the wires of local phone companies, and by buying the latter, it could use those wires to offer local telephone and Internet services. At Home later bought Excite, a Web site, but went bankrupt in 2001 and Excite@Home, as it was called, was bought by new owners. AT&T then entered into a global venture with British Telecom, Britain's biggest phone company, to sell $10 billion per year of telephone, Internet, and data services to big corporate customers around the globe by the formation of a new, jointly owned company. The next year the two companies agreed to spend $1.8 billion to buy 30 percent of Japan Telecom. Meanwhile, AT&T bought IBM's global network business for $5 billion. Again in 1999, AT&T struck a deal to offer telephone service over Time Warner's cable systems in thirty-three states, making it more involved in local phone service. AT&T owns slightly more than three-quarters of the joint venture. The hope of AT&T was that consumers would want the convenience of receiving phone service on the same cable TV circuits that deliver channels, Internet access (Worldnet being their service provider), and online banking. Then AT&T purchased cable TV's MediaOne for $58 billion (MediaOne owns a 25.5 percent stake in Time Warner Entertainment, which owns most of the cable systems of Time Warner). In 2000 the FCC ordered AT&T to sell its interest in Time Warner Entertainment, which it did in 2002. Meanwhile, Comcast, another cable company that had wanted MediaOne, got the right to buy as many as 2 million MediaOne customers from AT&T for up to $9 billion. Microsoft also got into the act, paying $5 billion for about a 3 percent stake in AT&T. Because of that, AT&T agreed to use Windows CE software in some of the cable TV set-top boxes it uses to put the Internet into homes. Microsoft also bought MediaOne's 29.9 percent in a European cable operator.

The AT&T and MediaOne deal gave AT&T more than one-third of the nation's cable network for television, high-speed Internet access, and online telephone services, making it the nation's largest at that time. The end result of this is that AT&T was involved with television, the Internet, and local, long-distance, and wireless telephone services. The FCC approved the acquisition in 2000, subject to the companies selling some of their assets. AT&T tried reorganizing its structure in the early years of the twenty-first century, including selling AT&T Broadband to Comcast Corporation in 2001 for $44.5 billion. However, it was hurt by cellular phone, e-mail, and by the baby Bells who earned more from long distance because they own the local wires. AT&T then decided to no longer market its phone services to residential customers, and as mentioned previously was bought by SBC in 2005.

Cell Phones

The merger mania has appeared in the wireless cell phone area as well. In 2004, Cingular, which was number two and is owned by SBC Communications (now known as AT&T) (60 percent) and Bell South (40 percent), acquired AT&T Wireless, which was number three, for $41 billion and became number one, ahead of Verizon Wireless owned by Verizon Communications (55 percent) and Vodaphone (45 percent), Sprint and Nextel. If the AT&T and Bell South merger is approved, Cingular will be renamed AT&T wireless. Not to be outdone, Sprint proceeded to acquire Nextel for $35 billion and is called Sprint Nextel. It has a problem in competing with Cingular and Verizon in that they both sell cellular service to customers who also buy local and long-distance phone service and broadband connections, plus the former Bells are also marketing satellite television services and have started to do their fiber-optic networks to deliver video programming. Nextel had no traditional fixed-line business and Sprint has a small percentage of the local phone customers, which it plans to spin-off. However, Sprint does have contracts to connect Internet-based phone calls for some cable companies and will build a high-speed network that will let consumers send and receive e-mail messages and other data services with their handsets, as does Verizon Wireless. Sprint works with some cable companies to introduce mobile phone services, and cable companies also use its long-distance network to carry their phone calls. Cingular has a data service too, but it is more limited. Without such a service one could lose high-paying business customers. Cingular has several popular international phone plans, while Sprint and Nextel use less common technology to run their networks, which makes it more cumbersome for their subscribers to use their phones overseas. One other important company is T-Mobile, which used to be Voicestream but was bought in 2001 by the German company Deutsch Telecom for $50.7 billion, and another is Altel.

The FCC made fall, 2003, the deadline for number portability, meaning you may keep your number while switching providers, and then in 2004 approved rules it said would lead to wider availability of high-speed Internet connections on airplanes and adopted a measure to begin studying whether to remove the ban on the use of cell phones in planes. In 2005 it extended the "truth-in-billing" guidelines to cell phone bills (they already cover traditional phone service). They must be brief, clear, nonmisleading and in plain language. It is misleading to suggest that any fees in addition to the base rate for a cell phone service were caused by taxes or government-mandated charges. Such charges must be folded into the base rate so that consumers can more accurately compare costs when shopping for cell phone service.

One problem with cell phones is that when an emergency 911 number is called, they are harder to trace than with landline phones. Nevertheless, the number of cell phones that can receive music and video clips is growing quickly, and the importance of the cell phone industry is apparent in that the number of subscribers in 2004 rose 15 percent to 181.1 million (was 79.7 million in 1999) whereas landlines were down 2.8 percent to 177.9 million (was 189.5 million in 1999), which was the first time mobile users exceeded landlines. AT&T and MCI lines went from 20.9 million in June to 19.8 million in December, and all landline carriers for their residential and small business lines went from 114.6 million to 112.2 million. The FCC figures did not include Internet-based calling.

Merger Implications and Legal Issues

What are the implications of all these deals? For one, several of AT&T's competitors started a coalition in 1999 in the form of a nationwide lobbying effort to force AT&T to open its system to Internet competitors. The group calls itself Open Net. In 1999, AT&T said it would give its cable customers a choice of Internet service providers in June 2002. In addition, the entrance of foreign companies into the U.S. telecommunications industry brings a provision of the Federal Communications Act into play, because it allows no more than 25 percent foreign ownership of a U.S. telecommunications company. However, the FCC can waive it if the country of the foreign company has liberalized its own market for U.S. companies, as has Great Britain, and/or if it would help a U.S. company compete more effectively. The 1996 Telecommunications Act further complicates the situation in that it prohibits the "baby Bells" from offering long-distance service in their home territories unless they are proved open to local competition. Once that opening is there and the long-distance companies want to offer local service, the FCC can set the pricing rules, according to the Supreme Court in the 1999 case of *AT&T Corporation v. Iowa Utilities Board*.[5]

The Court, in a 5–3 decision authored by Justice Scalia, said the 1996 Telecommunications Act allowed such power to the FCC to implement the Act's local competition provisions. The Court also upheld most of the FCC's rules aimed at prohibiting local phone companies from separating parts of their network and then requiring a customer who leases those parts to pay the cost of reassembling them. It imposes unneeded costs on a competitor. The Court did strike down one FCC rule that required a local phone company to provide competitors with access to various local network elements. The Court also ruled that the FCC can impose a "pick and choose" rule on local phone companies, which allows competitors to buy or lease any service or network element under the same terms as they were provided under any previous agreement, without having to accept the entire agreement.

In a 2004 case, *Nixon v. Missouri Municipal League*,[6] an 8–1 decision by Justice Souter said that states can bar local governments from offering their own communications services. The decision hinged on a provision in the 1996 Telecommunications Act that says that states may not prohibit an entity from offering phone service, and Souter said that was not meant to include local governments, which are subdivisions of the state. Because cities have no inherent right to provide telecommunications service, only states can grant or rescind that privilege. The decision was a victory for telephone companies that objected what they considered unfair competition.

Another problem inherent in the communications explosion is the question of which companies will get the FCC licenses to provide mobile phone, paging, voice mail, and other services. The FCC decided that the fairest method would be to auction these specialized mobile radio service licenses, and it did just that in 1996. Nextel Communications was the biggest winner. It did lead to a Supreme Court case in 2003, *Federal Communications Commission v. NextWave Personal Communications, Inc.*,[7] and Justice Scalia ruled 8–1 that the FCC had no right to cancel the wireless communications licenses that a bankrupt company had won at auction and then could not pay for them. It actually did make a $500 million down payment on a $4.74 billion deal but then filed for bankruptcy in 1998. In 2004 the company gave 10 percent of the licenses back to the government and sold the rest.

An issue that constantly irritates consumers is that of telemarketers, and the 1991 Telephone Consumer Protection Act gave the FCC the power to regulate telemarketers from any industry, which culminated with the 2003 "do not call" list. Telemarketers must identify the individual or business they represent and the purpose of the call, and calls are prohibited between 9 P.M. and 8 A.M. Exempt are political groups, not-for-profits, and telephone surveys, along with parties for which the calling party has received the called party's express invitation or permission. A person must renew being on the "do-not-call" list every five years.

Another area in which Congress has gotten involved is faxes. In 2005 it passed the Junk Fax Prevention Act, eliminating an FCC rule that was going into effect that would have had recipients say "yes" before being faxed. The law allows businesses and associations to send out unsolicited faxes to those with whom they have an "established business relationship." It does not overturn the 1991 law outlawing unwanted ads from unfamiliar firms promoting investment opportunities, mortgage refinancing, or vacation packages. Those sending faxes must alert the recipients in a highly visible manner of their right to opt out of future faxes and they must abide by such requests. The law exempts nonprofits.

Internet

The Internet, with its DSL (digital subscriber line), is included in what is termed broadband, or high-speed, which also includes cable, fixed wireless, and satellite, as opposed to dial-up phone lines, which is slower. There is an emerging legal issue as to whether a search engine can sell banner ads linked to particular search keywords, including trademarked terms. Congress in 1999 passed the Anti-Cybersquatting Consumer Protection Act to prevent the abuse of other people's trademarks on the Internet.

Another legal issue is whether some smut can be kept out of e-mails. A provision of the 1996 Telecommunications Act makes it a crime to transmit an obscene communication with intent to annoy, abuse, threaten, or harass another person. All e-mail was included, even messages sent from one friend to another, and federal courts have upheld it.

One very annoying aspect of the Internet is the vast amount of unwanted commercial e-mail that is sent. Congress in 2003 passed the Controlling the Assault of Non-Solicited Pornography and Marketing Act, better known as the CAN-SPAM Act. It set national standards for the sending of such material and required the FTC to enforce its provisions. It permits e-mail marketers to send unsolicited commercial e-mails as long as it contains: an opt-out mechanism, a functioning return e-mail address, a valid subject line indicating it is an advertisement, and the legitimate physical address of the mailer. Other provisions include the formation of a national do-not-spam list, and the prohibition of certain e-mail address collection methods. In the 2005 Violence Against Women and Department of Justice Reauthorization Act there is a section called "Preventing Cyberstalking" which extends the prohibition against anonymous telephone harassment to the Internet and carries penalties of fine or imprisonment or both.

One more legal issue coming to the forefront is the practice of Internet advertising companies getting access to consumer data, raising the privacy issue. For example, in 1999 one of the advertising firms, DoubleClick, merged with Abacus Direct Corporation, a company that sold information about consumers' catalogue purchases. They used the DoubleClick name and were able to serve Internet "banner" ads to users based on what a person had purchased offline in the past. One of its chief rivals was already doing this; 24/7 Media had an agreement with Intelliquest, a marketing firm that processed product registrations for approximately 85 percent of the companies who did not do it themselves. When a customer registered a product over the Internet with a company that worked with Intelliquest and agreed to accept future marketing messages, a data file called a "cookie" was assigned to that person's browser. Intelliquest then provided 24/7 with the cookie number and the person's name and address. Even more startling is the amount of information that is available offline. Acxiom Corporation supplied customer information to marketing firms and had detailed data on 95 percent of the households in the United States, such as names, addresses, occupations, home values, and frequently hobbies, income investments, and cars. In 2002 Yahoo and Excite said it would sell the data it collects about its users. This complex issue is a long way from being resolved, and the industry is attempting self-regulation through its Online Privacy Alliance. One thing Congress did was to pass the 1998 Children's On-Line Privacy Protection Act under which Web sites, facing a maximum fine of $11,000 per violation, must obtain parental permission or notification before collecting any personal information from children under thirteen, and in 2001 three Web sites paid $100,000 in civil penalties imposed by the FTC. In 2000 the federal government said that no federal site could use cookies unless the agency demonstrates a compelling need to gather the data and the cabinet secretary must approve. In 2004 the FCC imposed the same regulations for the Internet regarding political and children's advertising as it has for broadcasting.

Another law is the 1986 Electronic Communications Privacy Act, which prohibits intercepts of electronic communications and creates liability for intentionally accessing without authorization a facility through which an electronic communication is provided, and thereby obtaining access to a communication while it is in electronic storage (temporary, intermediate, or backup). The one exception is for the person or entity providing the communications service. In 2000 Congress passed the Electronic Signatures and Global National Commerce Act, saying that digital signatures are legal and enforceable.

In 2002 Microsoft signed a consent decree with the FTC saying it will monitor Passport for 20 years, shore up security and be more truthful about what it does with its data, and agreed to an outside audit of its practices every two years. The case arose due to four problems concerning Microsoft: (1) it lied about its effectiveness to protect users' personal information such as credit card numbers; (2) it said it was safer than others; (3) it said it did not collect any personally identifiable information beyond its privacy policy; (4) it said parents had control over the information the Web site collected on children if they used the kids' Passport.

One other problem is copyright protection over the Internet. The 1997 No Electronic Theft Act extends criminal copyright law to cases where there is no clear profit motive; distributors of copyrighted works face a maximum fine of $250,000 and up to five years in prison. The 1998 Digital Millennium Copyright Act makes it illegal to circumvent copyright-protection technologies. It also told the Copyright Office to come up with a royalty payment structure for songs played on Internet radio stations. Since the Internet music providers and the record companies could not agree, the Office in 2002 said it would be 70 cents for every song heard by 1,000 listeners, retroactive to 1998. That prompted the two sides to reach their own deal, which kept the payment at 70 cents but exempted 47 percent of a Webcaster's songs, plus an option was provided; namely, Webcasters can pay royalties as a percentage of their revenue or at an hourly rate.

Along that same line, the FCC in 2002 approved digital radio, but the latter has to pay Sound Exchange due to a government-imposed performance fee for digital music, based on the number of listeners (whereas broadcast and network radio pay about 3 percent of revenue to the songwriters).

As for digital television, in 1996 Congress gave broadcasters digital TV licenses worth up to $70 billion. The next year the Balanced Budget Act required broadcasters to give up their current airwaves by 2007, or when 85 percent of the nation can receive the new digital signals, whichever comes later, and the FCC ordered that there be digital tuners on all TVs by May 1, 2002, but there was only 15 percent compliance. Therefore the FCC lent each station an extra channel, and when there is 85 percent compliance the FCC will get the broadcast spectrum for traditional TV and sell it for uses such as wireless phones. The new deadline dates were: for 35 inch and bigger screens—July 1, 2004 (with a one-year phase in period); 25 inch to 35 inch screens—July 1, 2005, (with a one-year phase in period); all the rest that are at least 13 inch screens—July 1, 2007. In 2004 a plan was proposed to reach the 85 percent target by 2009. Many stations broadcast digital to most households, but very few of the sets sold each year have the tuners.

The FCC imposed a rule in 2003 designed to limit to copying of digital

TV programs over the Internet. Programmers can attach a code, or flag, to digital broadcasts that would, in most cases, bar consumers from copying, and manufacturers of TV sets that receive digital over-the-air broadcast signals had to produce sets that could read the digital code by July 1, 2005. However, in 2005 a Court of Appeals said that perhaps the FCC had overstepped its authority, although it did not hand down a final decision.

A recent Internet innovation is Voice over Internet Protocol (VoIP), where phone calls are made over the Internet rather than over circuit-switched networks. In 2005 the FCC required Internet phone service providers, within four months, to connect their customers to the same emergency 911 capabilities as callers with traditional service. Calls will have to be routed to the caller's local 911 operations center and must provide the emergency operator with the customer's callback number and location, regardless of whether the call is being made from the customer's home or elsewhere. The Internet companies must inform their customers within that 120-day period of the capabilities and limitations of the 911 service they are being provided.

The Supreme Court rendered an important Internet decision in the 2005 case of *National Cable & Telecommunications Ass'n. v. Brand X Internet Services.*[8] The majority of high-speed Internet users do it by cable rather than the slower dial-up Internet service, and Justice Thomas in a 6–3 decision upheld a 2002 FCC rule which said that cable companies do not have to allow rivals to offer high-speed Internet access over their systems. The 1996 Telecommunications Act requires providers of telecommunications services to sell their networks on a nondiscriminatory basis. However, the FCC decided that cable Internet service is an information service rather than a telecommunications one because it combines Internet access, which is communication, with additional services, like e-mail message ability, and therefore is exempt from the law. The Court said the FCC has the authority to interpret an ambiguous statute. In response, the FCC said that telephone companies can keep their new systems (fiber-optic networks to offer video, Internet, and phone service) entirely to themselves.

Downloading

Since the Digital Millennium Copyright Act says nothing about file-sharing networks, the problem of downloading music and movies arose. Since 2002 movies can be legally downloaded for a fee, and there is a company (Macrovision) that tries to stop the pirating of movies and digital video discs (DVDs) and is teaming with Microsoft to stop music from being ripped and traded on the Net (the DVD industry is so big that several companies have joined together in rival groups to make them). Because of more sophisticated technology people can now use their computers to record satellite and Internet radio broadcasts. Overpeer has been hired by record companies to post phony tracks to discourage file swapping. It tracks and counts illegal files. Music United for Strong Internet Copyright (MUSIC) is a music industry coalition that denounces unauthorized downloading as theft in an ad campaign. Because so many people download music from the Internet (recent studies show that CD burning is the most important online subscription feature to consumers), much of it illegally by not paying for it, lawsuits have been brought for copyright infringement. A federal appeals court ruled that the Internet providers do not have to provide the names of their subscribers who illegally download the music. The law covered only those suspected of operating private Web sites, in which case a District Court clerk could issue the appropriate order. Since 2003 the Recording Industry Association of America (RIAA) has sued thousands of the users themselves (many have been settled for roughly $3,000 each), and in 2004 the federal government, using the No Electronic Theft Act, went after the leaders of a private peer-to-peer underground network which trades copies of movies, software, games, and music by searching computers in six locations. As for the services, Napster was found guilty and stopped doing it in 2001 (its assets were bought by Roxio). Five major record companies then sued MP3.com for copyright infringement. It was settled for $130 million and an agreement to license the music. In 2003 a federal judge ruled for two of the companies charged with illegal downloading (Grokster and Streamcast) but against a third, KaZaa, in a suit brought by the RIAA and the Motion Picture Association of America (MPAA). An appeals court upheld the ruling for Grokster and Streamcast, and the case went to the Supreme Court.

In 2005 in *Metro-Goldwyn-Mayer Studios Inc. v. Grokster, Ltd.*,[9] Justice Souter reversed the lower courts and unanimously held that Internet file-sharing services will be held responsible if they intend for their customers to use software primarily to swap songs and movies illegally. He said there was enough evidence of unlawful intent for the case to go to trial, as the companies were seeking to profit from their customers' use of the illegally shared files. The lower courts could find the file-sharing services responsible by examining factors such as how companies marketed the product or whether they took easily available steps to reduce infringing uses. He said the companies sought to capitalize on the online trading of copyrighted material and there was no evidence that they tried very hard to block or impede that sharing.

The telecommunications industry, including the computer field with the Internet, has grown so fast that the government seems unable to keep up with it, hence the trend toward the megamergers. In fact, Congress, with the 1996 Telecommunications Act, deregulated the industry massively by letting each company engage in whatever activity it wants, such as phone companies providing television service, short-distance phone companies getting into long-distance, cable companies providing phone service, etc. Any venture one can imagine seems legal, which means that there will probably be more mergers than before, with companies buying others in order to enter a new field.

Indecency on the Internet

There was one area, however, that the Telecommunications Act tried to regulate, but to no avail. Title V is the Communications Decency Act, which established a number of content-based restrictions on what could appear on the Internet. Among them were things deemed obscene, indecent, child pornography, and the availability of abortion services. When the American Civil Liberties Union challenged the law, the government did not try to defend the part dealing with abortion services, and the ACLU did not challenge the parts dealing with obscenity and child pornography. The case centered around indecency, namely, sending sexual communications to minors, which in the law were defined as those under the age of eighteen. Anyone convicted under the law faced a fine plus a prison sentence of up to two years. The case, *Reno v. American Civil Liberties Union*,[10] was decided in 1997, and in a 7–2 opinion (unanimous in part), Justice Stevens held the law to be an unconstitutional infringement of free speech. The law censored speech that was protected for adults under the First Amendment, and was both vague and overly broad.

Congress in 1996 also passed the Child Pornography Prevention Act, but the Supreme Court, in the 2002 case *Ashcroft v. Free Speech Coalition*,[11] struck down several of its provisions. Justice Kennedy, 7–2, said that the government could not constitutionally make it a crime to present young-looking adults as children, and could not make it a crime to advertise or promote material in such a manner that conveys the impression that it is real child pornography. In a 6–3 split he also struck down the provision that made it a crime to create, distribute, or possess "virtual" child pornography that used computer images of young adults rather than actual children. The law was not restricted to pornography and was unconstitutionally broad; so far-reaching that it had the potential to chill expression with clear artistic and literary merit. The criminal penalties under the law were as much as fifteen years in prison for a first offense and thirty years for a second, and the law placed the burden on defendants to prove the images were not of actual children (under eighteen).

Also in 2002 the Court, in an 8–1 decision in *Ashcroft v. American Civil Liberties Union*,[12] vacated a lower court ruling that had struck down the 1998 Child Online Protection Act, although it continued blocking enforcement of the law until the lower court examined its content more fully. The law provided for up to six months in prison and fines up to $50,000 a day for knowingly and unrestrictedly placing material that is harmful to minors on a Web site available to those under the age of seventeen. In order for Internet viewers to look at such material, the Web site must collect a credit card number or access code. When the case came back to the Court once more two years later, also called *Ashcroft v. American Civil Liberties Union*,[13] a 5–4 decision by Justice Kennedy again kept the order in place blocking enforcement of it until its validity can be resolved. However, he said that the government must show why the voluntary use of filters to screen out material unsuitable for children would not work as well as the law's criminal penalties. Not only are filters less restrictive, which is more in keeping with the Court's First Amendment precedents, but they can block pornography anywhere in the world, while the statute applies only to pornography posted on the Web from within the United States.

In 2003 in a 6–3 decision by Chief Justice Rehnquist in *United States v. American Library Association, Inc.*,[14] the Court did uphold the 2001 Children's Internet Protection Act which requires public libraries to install pornography filters on all computers receiving Internet access as a condition of continuing to receive federal subsidies and grants under two programs: one provides Internet access at a discount; the other gives grants for setting up and linking to electronic networks. There are no criminal sanctions in the law, and it does authorize, but not require, librarians to unblock sites at the request of adult users.

Online information services have said they would try to keep this type of material off the Internet. Even before the Congress passed its laws, CompuServe blocked access to some discussion groups, and America Online blocked the use of certain prohibited words it deemed vulgar. Both the industry and civil libertarians would rather the industry police itself than the government step in with censorship. Whether that approach will work is something only the future will tell. In 1998, the Commerce Department selected a private, nonprofit organization with nineteen international board members appointed by a committee representing various Internet constituencies: technical, business, government, and community involvement, called the Internet Corporation for Assigned Names and Numbers (ICANN), for international governance of the Internet. It assigns domain names whose owners have thirty days to reactivate when they expire.

In 2005 the United States said that it would retain oversight of the main computers that control Internet traffic. The thirteen computers serve as the Internet's master directories and tell Web browsers and e-mail programs how to direct traffic. Internet users around the world interact with them every day. The computers are in private hands but contain government-approved lists of the approximately 260 Internet suffixes, such as ".com." ICANN decides what goes on those lists. The Commerce Department has the veto power but indicated it would let go when ICANN met a number of conditions, but now it will keep control whether the conditions are met or not.

One problem on the Internet is pornographic Web sites, and ICANN announced in 2005 that it will begin negotiating with a nonprofit group called ICM Registry, which is run by representatives of adult Web sites, free-speech, privacy, and child-advocacy concerns, to resolve the commercial and technical issues, such as registration eligibility, associated with having each of those Web sites end in "xxx.com." That proposal has been put on hold. An impetus for this action is a section of the 2003 Amber Alert law called the Truth in Domain Names Act that makes it a crime to use a misleading one to deceive a minor into viewing harmful material and provides prison sentences of up to four years. Congress in 2005 passed the Family Entertainment and Copyright Act which gives legal protections to filtering technology that helps parents automatically skip or mute sections of commercial movie DVDs.

THE MEDIA

The FCC currently licenses a radio or television station for a period of eight years, which means that there must be an available frequency in order to even be granted an initial license. The Mass Media Bureau of the FCC will issue the construction permit if the applicant meets the conditions, such as U.S. citizenship, good character, and the financial ability to do it. Once the license is granted, the 1996 Telecommunications Act allows broadcasters to renew them automatically without competition as long as they have served the public interest and not seriously broken any FCC rules or federal laws. They do not have to worry about competing applications, although the FCC could renew it for less than eight years if it felt the station had a problem that would be corrected during that time.

The FCC's licensing policies were upheld by the Supreme Court in the 1943 case of *National Broadcasting Company v. United States*.[15] NBC and the other networks with chains of stations challenged some regulations that restricted their control over local stations, but the Court, speaking through Justice Frankfurter, upheld the regulations as well as the licensing policies. He felt that because there are only so many frequencies available, the FCC had to determine who should get them through licensing, and a denial of one was not a denial of free speech. The Court also upheld the FCC rule of only one radio station per owner in a particular community, a rule meant to try to prevent monopolies.

FCC and Ownership Rules

For many years the FCC imposed strict rules regarding media ownership (voting stakes of 5 percent or more), but gradually relaxed them. In 1941 the FCC said that a TV company cannot own stations that collectively reach more than 35 percent of all viewers. In 1941 it said that a radio company cannot own more than five to eight stations in one market, depending on the market's size. In 1946 it said that a company cannot own more than one of the four major TV networks. In 1964 it said that a TV company cannot own two stations in the same market if both are among the top four or if it leaves fewer than eight independently owned stations. In 1970 it limited local station ownership to two TV and six radio, or one TV and seven radio stations in large markets. In 1975 the FCC said that a company cannot own a newspaper as well as a TV or radio station in the same market. For many years it limited companies to seven AM radio stations, seven FM radio stations, and seven television stations, but in 1984 it decided to gradually eliminate the restrictions, first going to twelve each and in 1994 to twenty each. Under the 1996 Telecommunications Act, there are almost no limits. The law ordered the FCC to reconsider the rule regarding one television station per market. In 1999 it let broadcasters have two TV stations in some cities, and in 2003 the FCC relaxed the rule so that a company can own three stations in the largest cities (about twenty markets) but kept the one about not owning two of the top four stations in one city; there are 100 markets where a company can own two TV stations.

In 2003 the FCC also revised the rules on newspaper-broadcast cross-ownership and radio-TV cross-ownership so as to lift the ban in over 80 percent of the markets. In markets of nine or more TV stations there are no restrictions; in markets of three or fewer TV stations both restrictions will apply; in markets with four to eight TV stations, some kinds of cross-ownership will be permitted.

Also in 2003 the FCC said that a TV company can own stations that collectively reach 45 percent of all viewers, meaning that Fox and Viacom were within the limits. Congress responded with a law making it 39 percent, which still left both companies safe. One problem, however, is that the FCC counts audiences of UHF stations as half that of VHF stations, so that the 39 percent can become as much as 90 percent.

The FCC was also ordered to allow all but the biggest television networks (ABC, CBS, NBC, and Fox) to own more than one network, and all television networks were allowed to own cable systems, unless that would discriminate against broadcasters affiliated with that network. The FCC in 2003 declined to reinstate a rule that blocked cable companies from owning local TV stations (the law against it had been repealed by the 1996 Telecommunications Act, but it permitted the FCC to grant it on a case-by-case basis).

The deregulation in the Telecommunications Act followed by the 2003 FCC actions led to an expansion of companies engaging in areas that were previously barred to them, and also led to even more mergers in a field in which megamergers have become commonplace. As might be expected there was a backlash against the FCC's actions, and in 2003 a Court of Appeals issued an injunction against their implementation, but in 2004 affirmed the repeal of the rule prohibiting one company from owning a newspaper and a broadcast station in the same community, plus the provision that permits the FCC to regulate newspaper-broadcast ownership when needed to ensure diversity. It told the FCC to reconsider the relaxation of its rules and to rethink the numerical limits of multiple station ownership in one market plus the proposed repeal of the Failed Station Solicitation Rule, whereby the owner of a failed station had to advertise the sale of the station to potential out-of-market buyers. It said the agency had failed to adequately justify the new rules and had been arbitrary and capricious in the way it sought to relax the old ones. In 2005 the government said it would not appeal the decision. Some media groups did appeal, but the Supreme Court would not review it.

Cable

Cable has grown steadily in the United States (as has its rates), and in 2002 for the first time the number of cable prime-time viewers outnumbered those watching broadcast programming. The FCC issued rules regarding cable first in 1962 and again in 1966, but the latter was restrictive to cable in that the FCC tried to protect existing television stations from competition. The Court upheld the rules in the 1968 case of *United States v. Southwestern Cable*.[16] It felt that cable, like radio and television, should be subject to FCC rules. But the FCC soon realized that television was not being hurt by cable and began to deregulate it. Congress then passed the 1984 Cable Communications Policy Act, which allowed for local governments to handle the awarding of franchises but which put cable into the 1934 Federal Communications Act, meaning it had the same content restrictions as broadcasters, such as equal opportunity for political candidates, right of reply for personal attacks, no lottery information (later amended), and no obscenity and indecency. State and local governments also banned obscene and indecent material, but the Miami, Florida ordinance was struck down by two lower federal courts for the indecency part, and the same thing happened to a Utah law. The Supreme Court affirmed without comment. Congress later passed the 1992 Cable Television Consumer Protection and Competition Act, one part of which says that cable companies that have an ownership stake in programming must make it available to competitors, but only when the programming is distributed by satellite. There were three major parts in the law dealing with censorship, and the Supreme Court considered them in the 1996 case of *Denver Area Telecommunications Consortium, Inc. v. Federal Communications Commission*.[17] Justice Breyer, in a 7–2 opinion, upheld the provision allowing cable operators to decide whether or not to transmit indecent programming. It was private censorship, not governmental, and society has the right to keep this material away from children. However, he struck down in a 6–3 vote the provision that required cable operators that allowed indecent programming to place it all on one channel and block access to it unless a viewer requested access in advance and in writing. He thought it too broad and that there were less restrictive means to protect children from seeing this material. Also, those who requested access might fear for their reputations if the list were made public. He also struck down in a 5–4 vote the provision that allowed cable operators to censor public access channels because those channels were already closely scrutinized by the educational and governmental institutions that use them. Two others agreed with that rationale; the final two votes supported the view that public access channels are like a public forum and similar First Amendment rules should prevail.

Another part of the 1992 law concerned the so-called "must-carry" controversy that started in 1966 when the FCC said cable systems had to carry the signals of all local television channels viewed by a significant portion of a community. This was an attempt to help educational TV as well as UHF stations that were not as strong as the VHF ones. After a lower court ruled the provisions unconstitutional, the FCC revised them, but again a lower court ruled them unconstitutional. Then Congress said in the 1992 law that cable systems had to use some of their channels for local television stations. This time a lower court upheld it, the Supreme Court sent the case back for further hearings, the lower court again upheld it, and finally, in the 1997 case of *Turner Broadcasting System v. Federal Communications Commission*,[18] the Supreme Court in a 5–4 decision authored by Justice Kennedy upheld the rule. He felt that since some 40 percent of households in this country do not have cable, they must depend upon local broadcasters, but many of those broadcasters would go off the air if cable did not pick them up. He said that the rule preserved free television broadcasting, promoted a wide dissemination of information from many sources, and promoted fair competition in the television market. There was no free speech violation because it burdened no more speech than necessary to accomplish the above interests. In 2001 the FCC ruled that cable companies are required to carry only one digital channel per station, and in 2005 it upheld that and rejected a request that cable and satellite operators be required to carry multiple digital-channel offerings from local TV stations. With regard to satellite television, a 2002 law says that satellite TV must carry all local TV if they offer any local TV.

Cable companies did get a favorable decision in the 2000 case of *United States v. Playboy Entertainment Group, Inc.*[19] Justice Kennedy held 5–4 that Congress went too far in the 1996 Telecommunications Act when it included a provision that required cable operators that did not fully scramble or block adult sex-oriented programming for nonsubscribers to show those channels only between 10 p.m. and 6 a.m. It was included in the law for households that do not subscribe to the sexually explicit programming but nevertheless pick up portions of it because of insufficiently scrambled signals. Kennedy said that Congress had failed to prove that the flickering sexual images were a huge threat to children, and had failed to meet the high hurdle necessary to curb First Amendment free speech rights. He also said that parents appalled by the images that might reach their children can obtain a free blocking device to filter out the sexual content altogether.

Comcast

Comcast is the largest U.S. cable system (until the AT&T and Bell South merger is approved) as well as the largest high-speed Internet provider, and how it got that way is an interesting story. In 1988 it bought Storer Communications to become the fifth largest cable operator, and in 1994 it bought Maclean Hunter's cable operations to become the third largest. It solidified its position by buying E. W. Scripps' cable systems in 1995 and Jones Intercable in 1998. In 2000 it swapped cable systems with Adelphia and AT&T, and it became number one with its 2001 purchase of AT&T Broadband. In 2005 it, along with the second largest cable company Time Warner, acquired Adelphia, the fifth largest but in bankruptcy protection since 2002, for $17.6 billion. As part of the deal, Comcast bought back its 21 percent interest in Time Warner Cable, thus getting more customers. Meanwhile, Comcast had worked out a deal with AOL that enabled it to distribute AOL Internet service through a cable modem. Comcast gets about $38 a month from AOL for every customer, and gets a cut when a customer buys something on AOL. Those customers who have both are billed and serviced by Comcast. In addition, Microsoft can offer service and can write the software used in some of Comcast's cable boxes. Also, in 2004 Sony Corp. bought MGM's film and video library (it had some 17 percent of the available film titles) for $4.8 billion. Comcast joined Sony's consortium and said it would create several premium channels that will broadcast both Sony and MGM movies, and would also offer movies through its video-on-demand service. Comcast will compete with Verizon and SBC when they begin to provide TV service over their fiber-optic lines, and also plans to reenter the phone business (it left the cell phone business in the early 1990s). Its goal is to sell phone, cable, Internet access, and cell phone service in a single package. Comcast's major competitors are Time Warner Cable, Cox Communications, Charter Communications, and Cablevision.

Content Restrictions and Other Legal Issues

One of the most controversial areas involving the relationship of government and the media is in regard to the content of what goes out over television, radio, and cable stations. Back in 1941 the FCC said that radio stations could not do editorials, but then in 1949 it came up with the fairness doctrine that allowed stations to editorialize as long as other points of view were also aired. Stations also had to allow the right of reply to personal attacks. In the 1969 case of *Red Lion Broadcasting Company v. Federal Communications Commission*,[20] a unanimous Court upheld the doctrine. Justice White felt the doctrine promoted free speech because there were only so many licenses for broadcasters, and that scarcity meant that those without licenses must be able to have some access. This is how matters stood until 1985 when the FCC itself became critical of it; two years later a lower court told the FCC to reexamine its doctrine. The FCC then said it would not enforce the balanced programming part of it, but would enforce the personal-attack rules. This was accepted by the lower court. Congress attempted to restore the doctrine, but a veto by President Reagan was not overridden.

Another area of content restriction is the equal-opportunities part of the 1934 Federal Communications Act, which says that stations who allow a candidate running for office airtime must allow all other candidates for that office equal opportunities, and the stations have no power over censoring the material. However, when the FCC ruled that short radio and television news clips of a candidate required reply time, Congress amended the law to exclude bona fide newscasts, news interviews, news documentaries, and on-the-spot coverage of news events. That amendment was in 1959. The following year Congress made a one-time exemption so that John F. Kennedy and Richard Nixon could debate in their quest for the presidency without any minor candidates taking part. The FCC in 1975 ruled that presidential debates could be broadcast as news events if they were sponsored by a nonpartisan group, and then in 1984 said that a nonpartisan sponsor would not be required for them.

Meanwhile, Congress, in 1971, amended the 1934 law to require broadcasters to allow candidates for federal elections to purchase reasonable amounts of time for campaign purposes. When, in 1979, the three major networks refused to sell time because it was too early for the 1980 campaign for the presidency, the FCC agreed with those who were denied that time, and in 1981 the Supreme Court, in *CBS v. Federal Communications Commission*,[21] upheld the FCC. Chief Justice Burger felt the law properly balanced the First Amendment rights of all concerned: candidates, public, and broadcasters.

One problem faced by the FCC in the late 1970s was format change, with stations changing their programming to some other type. The FCC decided to allow the stations to do this, and the Supreme Court sustained the FCC in the 1981 case of *Federal Communications Commission v. WNCN Listeners Guild.*[22] Justice White saw no First Amendment problem.

In the 1934 law Congress did prohibit the broadcasting of lottery information, and in 1948 moved the prohibition to the Criminal Code, which provides for a fine of up to $1,000 or imprisonment up to one year. With the advent of state run lotteries in many states, Congress in 1988 amended the law to allow broadcasting of information about state lotteries and Indian reservations' lotteries. However, the station doing the broadcasting must be in the same state as the lottery. In the 1993 case of *United States v. Edge Broadcasting Company*,[23] the Supreme Court, in a 7–2 opinion authored by Justice White, upheld the law being used against a radio station in North Carolina near the Virginia border that broadcast ads for the Virginia lottery (North Carolina did not have a lottery). Even though 90 percent of the station's listeners were in Virginia, the Court felt that the government had an interest in substantially reducing lottery ads, and that the First Amendment affords only a limited protection of commercial speech.

The Supreme Court gave a victory to radio and television in the 1999 case of *Greater New Orleans Broadcasting Association, Inc. v. United States.*[24] Justice Stevens, for a unanimous Court, struck down a law that banned broadcast advertising for lotteries, gift enterprises, or similar schemes offering prizes dependent upon lot or chance. The problem was that Congress had amended it to allow ads for casinos on Indian reservations, state-run lotteries, or any gambling sponsored by nonprofit promoters for charitable purposes. The Court decided that the law had too many exemptions and inconsistencies and therefore could not be enforced in those states in which casino gambling is legal. It was a violation of free speech that did not sufficiently advance the government's stated interest in protecting compulsive gamblers and did not do it in the least intrusive way.

Another part of the 1934 law prohibited the broadcast of profane, indecent, or obscene material, and that was also switched to the Criminal Code in 1948. The penalty can be up to a $10,000 fine and up to two years in prison. The 1996 Telecommunications Act puts the fine up to a maximum of $500,000 for corporations that knowingly permit their television facilities to be used for illegal programming. The issue came before the Supreme Court in 1978 in the case of *Federal Communications Commission v. Pacifica Foundation,*[25] that concerned the recording called "Filthy Words" being played over the radio; in it several words regarded as objectionable by many people were repeated over and over again. The FCC banned the record, and the Court, speaking through Justice Stevens, upheld the ban. Even though those words did not meet the Court's definition of obscenity, they still were explicit enough to be regulated by the FCC because the use of the airwaves is not totally without restriction. The FCC has the obligation to protect the listeners of radio stations, especially children, from material deemed offensive by society.

The FCC, for the next few years, only took action against excessive indecency, as in this case, and actually allowed this type of material between 10 P.M. and 6 A.M. However, in 1987 it made the ban a twenty-four-hour one and broadened what was considered indecent. A lower court agreed with the expanded definition but asked the FCC to reconsider the total ban. Congress then passed a law in 1988 making the ban twenty-four hours, but the lower court suspended it until the FCC rendered its report in 1990, again endorsing the total ban. The next year the court rejected the total ban, so Congress in 1992 passed another law, this one allowing the material to be broadcast between midnight and 6 A.M. The FCC adopted a rule to that effect. The court agreed with it but moved the starting time to 10 P.M., since the 1992 law allowed public stations that finished at midnight to use the 10 P.M. to midnight period for material that was considered indecent.

In 2004 the FCC imposed the then maximum indecency fine ($27,500 per violation per station) for each of eighteen violations in a 2003 show on six Clear Channel radio stations that carried Howard Stern and proposed fining Clear Channel Communications $495,000. It also proposed fining Infinity Broadcasting (Stern's employer) $27,500 for a Stern show in 2001. Infinity had paid $1.7 million in 1995 for various Stern violations, and fines against Stern have accounted for much of the penalties proposed by the FCC since 1990. Viacom has taken over Infinity and in 2004 agreed to pay a record $3.5 million for off-color remarks by Stern and others. Clear Channel has since dropped Stern, but in 2006 he reappeared on satellite radio. He also sued CBS for breach of contract. Also in 2004 CBS stations and other broadcasting outlets were fined $550,000 for Janet Jackson's "wardrobe malfunction" during the Super Bowl half-time show. In 2005 the maximum fine for radio or TV indecency was raised to $32,500, but it does not include pay TV or pay radio.

Newspapers are much freer with regard to governmental regulation. For example, two lower federal courts said that newspapers are free to decide what advertising they wish to accept and what they do not. To see what the Supreme Court has said, one can look at the 1974 case of *Miami Herald Publishing Company v. Tornillo.*[26] A Florida law required newspapers to print replies to stories that were critical in nature, and Chief Justice Burger, for a unanimous Court, struck it down as a violation of freedom of the press.

The printed media is not completely free to do as it pleases, and a good example is the Supreme Court's 2001 decision in *New York Times Company v. Tasini.*[27] Justice Ginsburg held in a 7–2 decision that a group of newspaper and magazine publishers infringed on copyrights of freelance contributors by making their articles accessible without permission in electronic databases after publication. The electronic user retrieves, views, or downloads the individual article, divorced from its original context, whereas the 1976 Copyright Act gives the publishers, who hold a collective copyright in the entirety of each issue, the right to publish any revision of that collective work. Ginsburg said that the electronic databases are not simply the modern versions of old-fashioned microfilm, and the principle of media neutrality should protect the authors' rights. Since the mid-1990s, most publishers that use freelance work require authors to waive their electronic reproduction rights.

Although the 1996 Telecommunications Act allowed for massive deregulation of the communications field as far as structure is concerned, such as various types of companies now being permitted into other areas of communication, there still remains some content regulation for broadcasters. Admittedly, the Court will step in if the regulation oversteps its bounds, but broadcasters still must abide by some regulation. On a continuum, the printed media is the freest, followed by cable, and then by radio and television. With the public at large feeling that not everything should go out over the airwaves, the chances of much change in the situation seem remote.

Major Federal Communications Laws:
1927   Radio Act
1934   Federal Communications Act
1976   Copyright Act
1984   Cable Communications Policy Act
1986   Electronic Communications Privacy Act
1991   Telephone Consumer Protection Act
1992   Cable Television Consumer Protection and Competition Act
1996   Telecommunications Act
1996   Child Pornography Prevention Act
1997   No Electronic Theft Act
1997   Balanced Budget Act
1998   Child Online Protection Act
1998   Digital Millennium Copyright Act
1999   Anti-Cybersquatting Consumer Protection Act
1999   Radio Broadcasting Preservation Act
2001   Children's Internet Protection Act
2003   Truth in Domain Names Act (part of Amber Alert law)
2003   Electronic Signatures and Global National Commerce Act
2003   Controlling the Assault of Non-Solicited Pornography and Marketing Acct
(CAN-SPAM Act)
2005   Family Entertainment and Copyright Act
2005   "Preventing Cyberstalking" section of law

Mergers

As with the field of telecommunications, there have been so many mergers of such giant proportions in the last several years as to boggle the mind. An examination of them is enlightening and also frightening because it means there is less and less competition, thus people are less and less able to receive various points of view. For example, since 1995 the great majority of independent newspaper owners have disappeared.

Virtually all city newspapers have the same owner, and almost all the daily newspaper circulation is controlled by companies that publish two or more dailies. Newspaper companies own commercial radio and television stations. Gannett owns *USA Today,* television and radio stations, and cable franchises. There is also a trend toward concentration in the publishing industry, largely due to high advertising and publishing costs. For example, Random House has been owned since 1998 by the media company Bertelsmann AG (books, magazines, and records), there is the AOL Time Warner Book Group, Harper Collins is owned by News Corporation, Simon & Schuster by Viacom, and Penguin Putnam by Pearson. In the movie theater industry, mergers have led to theaters showing many movies under the same roof. It is difficult to find an old-fashioned theater that has only one screen.

Congress made an attempt at preserving competition in the newspaper industry by passing the 1970 Newspaper Preservation Act. It allows competing newspapers to share certain costs, such as printing and distribution, and to split certain revenues, such as advertising and circulation dollars. However, newsrooms and editorial pages would remain separate, ideally to provide diverse viewpoints. Despite this, many newspapers disappeared, mostly due to mergers. Illustrative of these mergers is the one in 2000 in which Tribune Company bought Times Mirror for $8 billion. Tribune Company owned newspapers, television stations, radio stations, the Chicago Cubs baseball team, and investments in AOL and in the WB network. Times Mirror owned newspapers and magazines. By all estimates this megamerger was an indicator of what is to happen in the future as newspapers, with their daily circulation falling, struggle for survival in this increasingly electronic age. News dealers and newsstands have increased, meaning the reading material is plentiful but the source is not.

Bookstores are also falling prey to mergers, as well as to online sellers like Amazon.com. Barnes and Noble purchased Dalton in 1986 and Doubleday in 1990. Borders purchased Waldenbooks. It is hard to find an independent bookstore.

Music

In the music business, Seagram Co. purchased 80 percent of MCA in 1995 for $5.7 billion and renamed it Seagram Universal Studios. Its Universal Music Group included several record labels. Then in 1998 the Group acquired PolyGram (which was 75 percent owned by a Dutch firm which it merged with its music division) for $10.2 billion, a sale that included several other record labels. Besides MCA records, MCA had Universal Pictures, theme parks, and a television production unit. Seagram was concentrating its efforts in the music business in order to compete with its rivals, Warner Music, Sony Music, BMG (Bertelsmann), and EMI, in terms of newly released albums, but it was purchased in June 2000 by the French company Vivendi for $34 billion, with the new name of Vivendi Universal Entertainment. The latter was eventually sold to NBC except for its Universal Music Group.

Meanwhile, Bertelsmann, the world's largest book publisher, is attempting to become bigger in the record industry through BMG, its global music company with its various record labels. It has an alliance with AOL, which gives owners of CDs from BMG artists access to the Internet, and it had joined with AT&T to create a secure system for selling digital downloads (online sales). In 2003 it merged BMG with Sony's music division to form Sony BMG. In that same year, Warner Music Group, including its publishing segment, was sold to the Bronfman Group for $2.6 billion.

In 2000, Time Warner, Sony Corporation of America, Bertelsmann Music

Group, EMI Music Distributors, and Universal Music and Video Distributors, who controlled 85 percent of the $15 billion CD market, agreed to a consent order with the FTC to stop marketing agreements that had been used to end a price war, inflate the prices of CDs, and sharply restrict the ability of retailers to offer discounts. Specifically, they could not link any future financing of advertising with prices for CDs for seven years, and for thirteen years after that they cannot impose price conditions in advertisements that are paid for by the retailers.

Radio

No company owned more than forty radio stations in 1940. Then Congress, in the 1996 Telecommunications Act, eased restrictions on ownership, and many radio stations have changed hands. The number of radio stations has increased but the number of owners has dropped. Stations owned by the two largest companies have greatly increased, as has the percent of industry revenue to the five largest companies. Four companies have approximately two-thirds of the listeners for news. The average number of music radio formats in the largest markets has grown, but many of today's top music formats overlap. In 1996 Westinghouse/CBS (now Viacom) bought Infinity Broadcasting Company with its hundreds of stations and its outdoor advertising for $4.7 billion and in 1997 it bought American Radio Systems for $1.6 billion. In 1998 Chancellor Media merged with Capstar Broadcasting creating Chancellor Media with hundreds of stations in many markets. But the largest owner of radio stations in the United States is Clear Channel with more than 1,200 stations. It had only 36 stations in 1996. In 1998 it merged with Jacor, and in 2001 it bought AMFM Inc. (the nation's second largest) for $17 billion. It was allowed to keep the clusters of stations that exceeded the caps. Its latest venture is getting into online radio. It also owns some TV stations, and it owns or operates or has a stake in thousands of outdoor billboards worldwide and hundreds of live entertainment venues.

Congress in 1999 enacted the Radio Broadcasting Preservation Act, telling the FCC to conduct tests to ensure that low-powered radio would not interfere with regular AM/FM radio. The Supreme Court also rendered a decision in 2001 that was a help to radio. In *Bartnicki v. Vopper*,[28] a 6–3 decision by Justice Stevens held that a radio host and station cannot be sued for airing a phone conversation taped illegally by a third party. They played no part in the illegal deception, the host obtained the information legally, and the subject matter was of public concern and importance, not simply newsworthy. The privacy protections of wiretap laws are designed to punish illegal conduct by those who illegally record conversations.

The Networks

Many of the independent television station owners have disappeared, largely due to mergers. The trend toward mergers in the media began in 1985 when ABC network was bought by Capital Cities. ABC also owns movie theaters and publishing companies and publishes newspapers in various cities as well as trade publications. Ten years later, Disney bought Capital Cities-ABC for $19 billion, making it at that time the second biggest media company by revenue and giving it control over television and radio stations, a film library, theme parks, television channels, movie studios, books, magazines, and movies. An even bigger merger will occur in 2004 and will be discussed later.

Not to be outdone, in 1986 NBC network was bought by General Electric, and in 1996 MSNBC (owned by Microsoft) and NBC went together in a joint venture television channel. However the big merger, to be discussed later, will not come until 2004.

That left CBS alone, until in 1995 it was bought by Westinghouse for $5.4 billion, and in 1997 Westinghouse Electric Corporation became CBS Corporation and got out of its industrial side. CBS has television stations and its cable television networks, and in 1999 it bought King World Productions, television's biggest program syndicator, for $2.5 billion. However, its biggest push was in the radio field. Again, the big merger came in 1999 and will be discussed later.

During the time the three networks were involved in these transactions, other companies were also expanding in the media field. In 1989 Sony purchased two movie studios for $4.8 billion, and in that same year two giants, Time and Warner, merged for $18 billion. That put into Time Warner's hands a television network, film and television studios, cartoons and movies, TV channels and cable systems, magazines, comic books, book publishing companies, record labels, theme parks, retail stores, and home videos.

Time Warner solidified its position as the number one media company by revenue at that time with its 1996 merger with Turner, a $7.5 billion stock deal. This brought into the company some more movie studios, movies and cartoons, and cable stations. In 1999 MGM, whose films were included in the deal, regained broadcast rights to more than 800 old MGM and United Artists films, and in 2000 made a deal with Blockbuster to show them on the Internet.

Meanwhile, in 1993, Paramount merged with a publishing company, for $553 million, making it the then second largest book publisher. The following year it merged with Viacom for $9.6 billion, and the year after that they formed the United Paramount television network (Viacom owned half of it). Viacom owns several Internet properties designed for children and music fans, theme parks, several cable channels, TV production companies, and television stations. Viacom also bought an 81 percent interest in the Blockbuster video rental chain in 1994 for $8.4 billion, but spun it off in 2004. Paramount, meanwhile, brought to the merger a movie studio, a television studio (plus one used for syndication purposes), half of USA (which it sold to Seagram in 1997 for $1.7 billion, giving Seagram the entire network), a book publishing company, amusement parks as well as the New York Knicks basketball team, the New York Rangers hockey team, and the part of Madison Square Garden where they play. It decided to sell those last three in 1994 to Cablevision Systems Corporation and ITT-Sheraton for $1.075 billion. Cablevision then bought all but 11.5 percent of them from ITT-Sheraton in 1997 for $650 million. Cablevision has a network and cable channels, 82.1 percent of Rainbow Media, and Radio City Music Hall.

As mentioned previously, Seagram wanted to concentrate in the music field, so in 1998 it sold a majority of USA (Universal cable networks and TV production) for $4.1 billion to an emerging player in the field, Barry Diller. The next year Seagram sold Diller its film studios. In 1997, USA had merged with Ticketmaster in a deal valued at $800 million, and later merged online operations with CitySearch, an online city guide. In 1999, USA expanded CitySearch by acquiring the Sidewalk online entertainment guide from Microsoft Corporation. USA Networks has other companies selling goods online and Diller became the CEO of USA InterActive plus the head of Universal Entertainment with its movie studio, music group, theme parks, television group, and resorts.

Vivendi Universal Entertainment was created in 2002 by Vivendi Universal and InterActive Corporation in connection with IAC's sale of its entertainment assets, including its cable channels. It bought the TV and film rights of USA Networks for $10.3 billion and, although giving up its stake in USA Networks, owns most of VUE InterActive (USA and Diller had the rest) and can buy 12 percent of USA Interactive. In this complicated deal, Diller also got some Vivendi stock as did another media company, Liberty Media Group, which also has some USA Network stock. In 2005 Diller sold his 5.4 percent stake in Vivendi Universal Entertainment to NBC Universal for $3.4 billion. Diller still runs IAC with its many travel, electronic retailing, ticketing, personals, and other Web sites, will spin off a couple of them into a separate company, and will take over an online search-engine maker.

News Corporation is yet another example of big media. It has Fox Entertainment and included in its holdings are a television network and channels, a news group and a sports group, a children's network, Asian and European satellite television networks, movie studios and animation studios, magazines including about 40 percent of *TV Guide*, a publishing company, newspapers, and an Internet service company for its news and sports. In 1996, Fox and Liberty Networks went in on a joint venture. Liberty Media Group was controlled by AT&T Corporation and had interests in some TV channels plus a large stake in Liberty Digital. Fox/Liberty Networks owned some cable networks, and in 1997 bought, for $850 million, 40 percent of Rainbow Programming, a unit of Cablevision that controlled the Knicks, Rangers, and the part of Madison Square Garden where they play, plus one-third ownership of the Golf Channel. Because Murdoch wanted to be a major player in the sports field, the News Corporation paid Liberty $1.4 billion to take control of the 40 percent interest in Rainbow, as well as Fox Sports Network and FX. Liberty still kept 50 percent of the venture's International Sports Programming. Liberty sold Murdoch its 40 percent stake in the Staples Center, the new arena for the Los Angeles Kings hockey team, and in 1998 Murdoch purchased the Los Angeles Dodgers baseball team (which he sold in 2004). Liberty was purchased by its shareholders in 2000 for $46 billion, and in 2003 became the sole owner of the QVC channel by buying Comcast's stake in it for $7.9 billion. Among other holdings, Liberty has a media services company, 18 percent interest in News Corp. and 19 percent in IAC, spun off its international cable holdings in 2004 into Liberty Global, and in 2005 spun off its 50 percent interest in the channel group Discovery Communications to its shareholders in a newly created organization known as the Discovery Holding Company. News Corp., meanwhile, bought Chris Craft's ten television stations in 2001 for $5.4 billion, and it got into the satellite TV business by buying DirecTV from General Motors (its Hughes Electronics Division) for $6.6 billion. It and AOL Time Warner can create and distribute TV programs. It has more subscribers than the Dish Network, in which Vivendi bought 10 percent in 2001. In 2005 it bought Intermix Media, an Internet company that runs MySpace.com, in an effort to get more involved in that medium.

Following the aforementioned mergers, the richest merger up to that time in media history happened. In 1999, Viacom bought CBS Corporation for $37.5 billion, making Viacom the then third largest media company by revenue. The new company carries the Viacom name, although the CBS name continues to identify the TV network. By virtue of the deal, CBS got a TV and film studio to provide shows for its network, and Viacom got major advertising outlets to promote its films and TV shows. One reason the merger took place was a 1999 FCC ruling that allowed companies to own more than one TV station in the same city, as long as that city had at least eight independently owned TV stations. In 2005 it decided to split into two companies: one, Viacom, has its cable networks such as MTV plus Paramount Pictures Studios (which in 2005 bought the live-action film business of Dreamworks SKG for $1.6 billion), and the other, CBS Corporation, has the CBS, UPN and Showtime CBS television networks, radio, outdoor advertising, and Simon and Schuster Publishing Company.

The new century brought with it the inevitable merger, approved by the FTC in 2000 and the FCC in 2001, of the then nation's largest online company, AOL, with the then world's leading media and entertainment company,

Time Warner. AOL paid $165 billion in what was then the biggest corporate merger ever, and the combined company was called AOL Time Warner. Time Warner will therefore be able to reach people online with its movies, music, and magazines.

That was followed by the merger of NBC and Vivendi Universal Entertainment for $13 billion which was approved by the European Commission, the FCC, and the FTC in 2004 (plus they settled with Diller due to his involvement with VUE). GE, NBC's owner, has 80 percent control and VUE 20 percent, and the title is NBC Universal. Universal Music Group was not included in the deal.

These examples of the mergers taking place in the media field should make one worry that deregulation plus antitrust laxness is creating an industry in which a few players dominate; therefore, the public is not being exposed to various viewpoints, but only to the ones preferred by those dominating the field. Where it will end is unclear, but the industry has become a highly oligopolistic one. In 2005 Sony bought MGM Entertainment and its extensive film library for $5 billion, and in 2006 Disney bought Pixar for $7.3 billion.

Diversity and Propaganda Issues

Another important issue point is the relative lack of minorities in the broadcasting industry. The FCC has a policy giving special, favorable consideration for minority ownership and participation in management for television stations, as well as a distress-sale policy in which a broadcaster faced with the loss of a license may sell to a minority-owned business at 75 percent of the station's market value, as long as that minority-owned business meets certain requirements. These were challenged in court, but the Supreme Court, in the 1990 case of *Metro Broadcasting, Inc. v. Federal Communications Commission*,[29] upheld them in a 5–4 decision authored by Justice Brennan. He stated that the policy did not violate equal protection but instead had congressional support and served the important governmental objective of broadcast diversity. Because subsequent affirmative action decisions by the Court showed that they must be narrowly tailored to meet specific problems, the future of the FCC's minority preference policy is uncertain.

One problem that appeared in 2005 is that some government agencies were circulating video news releases through commercial TV outlets. Congressional investigators concluded that prepackaged news stories created by the Office of National Drug Control Policy constituted covert propaganda, and thus the FCC issued a notice reminding broadcasters and cable operators that they must clearly disclose the nature, source, and sponsorship of the material that their audiences are viewing, and an even greater obligation if the materials deal with political or controversial issues.

SUMMARY

The field of communications affects almost everybody in the United States, whether one is speaking of telecommunications or the media. The electronic age is here to stay, and the government has had a difficult time keeping up with new technology. The 1996 Telecommunications Act saw the government retreat from its regulation of the field, although it still keeps some regulation, especially through the FCC. Nevertheless, the field has opened up and companies are taking advantage of the opening. Whether the public is best served by this approach remains to be seen, but there is no denying that fewer and fewer companies are left to serve the public in this age of communications.

QUESTIONS FOR DISCUSSION

1. Why did the radio industry ask for regulation?
2. Do you approve of the FCC having no control over broadcasting charges?
3. Are telephone company mergers good for the economy?
4. Has the deregulation of the telecommunications industry led to more competition?
5. Do you agree with the invalidation of the Communications Decency Act?
6. Are the megamergers in the media field good for the public?

RECOMMENDED READING

Carter, T. Barton, Marc A. Franklin, and Jay B. Wright. *The First Amendment and the Fourth Estate.* 9th ed. New York: Foundation Press, 2005.

Franklin, Marc A., David A. Anderson, and Lyrissa Barnett Lindsay. *Mass Media Law.* 7th ed. New York: Foundation Press, 2005.

Pember, Don R., and Clay Calvert. *Mass Media Law 2005/2006.* New York: McGraw-Hill, 2005.

Sadler, Roger L. *Electronic Media Law.* Thousand Oaks, CA: Sage Publications, Inc., 2005.

Schnitzer, Martin. *Contemporary Government and Business Relations.* 4th ed. Boston, MA: Houghton Mifflin Company, 1990. Chapters 5 and 7.

Tedford, Thomas L., Jr., and Dale A. Herbeck. *Freedom of Speech in the United States.* 5th ed. State College, PA: Strata Publishing, Inc., 2005.

Teeter, Dwight L., Jr., and Bill Loving. *Law of Mass Communications.* 11th ed. New York: Foundation Press, 2004.

NOTES

1. 512 U.S. 218 (1994).
2. 535 U.S. 467 (2002).

3. 535 U.S. 635 (2002).
4. 540 U.S. ——— (2004).
5. 525 U.S. 366 (1999).
6. 541 U.S. ——— (2004).
7. 537 U.S. 293 (2003).
8. 534 U.S. 327 (2005)
9. 545 U.S. ——— (2005).
10. 521 U.S. 844 (1997).
11. 535 U.S. 234 (2002).
12. 535 U.S. 564 (2002).
13. 542 U.S. ——— (2004).
14. 539 U.S. ——— (2003).
15. 319 U.S. 190 (1943).
16. 392 U.S. 157 (1968).
17. 518 U.S. 727 (1996).
18. 520 U.S. 180 (1997).
19. 529 U.S. 803 (2000).
20. 395 U.S. 367 (1969).
21. 453 U.S. 367 (1981).
22. 450 U.S. 582 (1981).
23. 509 U.S. 418 (1993).
24. 527 U.S. 173 (1999).
25. 438 U.S. 726 (1978)
26. 418 U.S. 241 (1974).
27. 533 U.S. 483 (2001).
28. 532 U.S. 514 (2001).
29. 497 U.S. 547 (1990).

V

GOVERNMENT AND FOREIGN TRADE

12

International Trade

The importance of international trade has been recognized by nations for thousands of years. The Phoenicians controlled the seaborne commerce of the Mediterranean 4,000 years ago, and the goods they secured from Babylon and Egypt or produced in their own shops they carried throughout the Mediterranean to Africa and southern Europe. Foreign trade flourished during the Roman Empire, and Rome itself depended on the grain it imported from Egypt and Africa. Roman traders penetrated Germany as far as the Baltic Sea, and others sought the markets of Turkestan to buy Chinese goods.[1] The Chinese were engaged in international trade even before the Romans.[2] In the fourteenth and fifteenth centuries, the Italian trading centers of Genoa and Venice carried on trade with Asia, exchanging woolen cloth and raw materials for spices.

At the beginning of the twentieth century, the United Kingdom was the world's leading trading nation and the pound was the most important currency unit in the world. Its many colonies served as markets for British goods, and it was able to import goods that were unavailable or too expensive to produce at home. But times have changed, and it is now the United States that is the world's leading trading nation, while the United Kingdom has slipped to the sixth position. Japan, which was not even in the top twenty leading trading nations in 1900, ranks third.[3] Germany, which was second in 1900, still ranks second. And China ranks fourth. The United States, Germany, and Japan were responsible for 28 percent of the world's international trade in 2003.[4]

THE RATIONALE FOR INTERNATIONAL TRADE

The basic rationale for international trade between nations is that it maximizes the interest of consumers throughout the world by giving them a wider variety of goods from which to choose. Differences in the efficiency of land, labor, and capital make it profitable for nations to specialize in the production of goods and services in which their resource situation is the most advantageous, and exchange them for the goods and services of other nations with different resource advantages. If there were no restraints placed on the movement of goods and services from one region to another, or from one nation to another, then in theory the welfare of consumers would be maximized.

Certain trade theories have been developed over a period of time to explain why the exchange of goods and services between nations is beneficial. Mercantilism was the dominant trading policy for the European countries between 1500 and 1800. To the mercantilists the important question was: What is the right policy for a government to pursue in order to increase the national wealth and the national power? The answer was a strong central government with the acquisition of colonies that would serve as markets and provide it with wealth. This theory of international trade was replaced with a new theory of international trade based on the writings of Adam Smith and David Ricardo.[5] They believed society benefited from a division of labor and commerce. Each country would do that which it did best, and free trade benefited consumers in all nations.

MERCANTILISM

The United States is a direct result of the policy of mercantilism pursued by the British. England hoped to replicate what Spain found in its conquest of Mexico and Peru in the early 1500s—gold and silver. Although it did not find gold and silver, it found other natural resources that were brought back to London.[6] The United States became a colony of England. It served as a market for British goods and exported to England goods that could not be produced there. Trade between England and its colony was regulated. American goods had to be shipped only on British ships, and British goods had to be purchased by Americans. Moreover, there was taxation without representation. England would send over its representatives to govern the colonies based on instructions of the British government.

THEORIES OF TRADE

Absolute Advantage

The theory of absolute advantage was based on Adam Smith's book, *The Wealth of Nations*.[7] His writings and those of Ricardo and others dominated Western economic thought for 150 years. Absolute advantage states that there is a basis for trade when one nation can produce a good or service more efficiently than another nation, in which case the latter should buy from the former. To put it simply, if Brazil has the resources to produce coffee more cheaply and of better quality than the United States, we should buy their coffee. Conversely, if the United States can produce automobiles more cheaply and of better quality than Brazil, they should buy our cars. By this logic each country gains by concentrating on what it does best. Resources are allocated to those areas in which they can be used most efficiently.

Comparative Advantage

The theory of comparative advantage is associated with David Ricardo, who was an important economist during the early part of the nineteenth century.[8] It holds that if one country has an advantage over another country in the production of several goods, it should produce the good in which it has the greatest comparative advantage and buy the good in which it has the least advantage from the other country. Assume that Brazil has an advantage over the United States in the production of coffee and sugar. Brazil can produce five units of coffee for every unit of coffee produced by the United States, and it can only produce two units of sugar for every unit produced in the United States. As the example below indicates, a ratio of 5 to 1 is better than a ratio of 2 to 1, so Brazil should produce coffee, and the United States has only a 1 to 2 disadvantage in producing sugar. The exchange between the countries should be coffee for sugar.

	Brazil	*United States*
Coffee	5 units	1 unit
Sugar	2 units	1 unit

Factor Endowment Theory

The factor endowment theory, which was developed by Bertil Ohlin, a Swedish economist, simply states that each nation is best equipped to produce the goods that are best related to the factors—land, labor, or capital—that are most abundant.[9] For example, Argentina and Australia, which have an abundance of land relative to labor and capital, should and do specialize in the production of agricultural and meat products. Countries that have a large amount of labor relative to land and capital should specialize in labor-intensive industries, such as clothing. China is a case in point.[10] Countries that are capital intensive should specialize in the production of goods that require a great deal of capital. Germany and Japan, with their automobile industries, would be examples of countries that are capital intensive.

National Competitive Advantage

The most recent contribution to international trade theory is the book *The Competitive Advantage of Nations*, written by Michael Porter, a management professor at Harvard, and published in 1990.[11] He proposes a paradigm to explain the dynamic relationship among a country's industries, institutions, and people that is pivotal to achieving economic advantage over other nations. He contends that the theories of absolute advantage and comparative advantage are obsolete because their emphasis on only natural resources and other factors was obsolete. Instead, his approach takes the form of a dynamic diamond whose parts push each other forward or backward. It is competition—the fiercer the better—that is likely to produce a country's success. As figure 12.1 shows, the dynamic diamond is divided into four parts, one at each point of the diamond.

1. Company Strategy, Structure, and Rivalry—the dominant environment in which firms compete shapes their ability to compete internationally. To survive competitively in their home country, firms must strive to

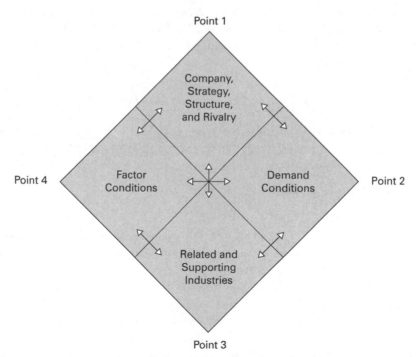

Figure 12.1. Porter's Diamond of National Competitive Advantage

Source: Michael Porter, *The Competitive Advantage of Nations*. New York: Free Press, 1990, p. 72. Reprinted with permission.

reduce costs, boost product quality, raise productivity, and develop innovative products. Firms that have been tested this way in the home market are better able to compete internationally. Further, many of the investments they have made in the home market for research and development and quality control, are transferable to other countries.

2. Demand Conditions—This includes the size of the market, sophistication of consumers, and media exposure of product. Consumer demand for convenience, utility, and affordability made the United States the first mass-market, mass-production society, and put its industry in a strong position to capitalize on subsequent demand all over the world for goods that have that quality.

3. Related and Supporting Industries—Firms that are located close to their suppliers will enjoy better communications and the exchange of ideas and inventions with them than firms that are not located close to their suppliers. Competition among these suppliers will lead to lower prices, higher quality products, and technological innovation in their inputs, in turn reinforcing firms' competitive advantage in world markets.

4. Factor Conditions—This would not only include the basic factors of land, labor, and capital but more advanced factors such as the educational level of the workforce and the quality of a nation's infrastructure. The possession of natural resources, such as oil and coal, are no longer considered the determinants of national success that they once were. The training of its workforce, innovation, and research will give a nation a competitive advantage over other nations.

Two other factors, chance and government, can also play an important role in developing a nation's competitive advantage. Chance events are occurrences that have little to do with circumstances in a nation and are outside the power of a government to influence. Wars, oil shocks, natural disasters, and political decisions by governments are examples of chance. The decision of the Japanese to bomb Pearl Harbor caused the United States to enter World War II, which benefited American industry by spurring research and development financed by government. Many products were produced during the post-war period long before they would have been produced were it not for the war. Government is another factor. Japan and South Korea are cited as examples in which government policies are responsible for their economic success.

THE INTERNATIONAL TRADE AND INVESTMENTS OF THE UNITED STATES

The international trade of the United States consists of two categories—the export and import of goods and the export and import of services. The export and import of goods is called the merchandise trade account and the export and import of services is called the invisible account. Merchandise trade covers exports and imports of automobiles, machinery, food and beverages, agricultural products, and other tangible goods. Services include health care, travel, financial services, telecommunications, transportation, and other intangibles. In 2004 U.S. exports of goods amounted to $818 billion and imports of goods amounted to $1,470 billion, for a deficit of $652 billion.

The Merchandise Trade Account

The United States is the world's largest trading nation. The total value of its exports and imports for 2004 was around $2.2 trillion, Canada was second with a total of $445 billion, and Mexico was third with a total of $307 billion. As table 12.1 indicates, the bulk of U.S. merchandise trade is with three major regions of the world—the NAFTA countries of Canada and Mexico, the European Union consisting of twenty-five European countries, and East Asia, which includes China, Japan, and the Newly Industrialized Countries (NICs) of South Korea, Singapore, Malaysia and Hong Kong, and Taiwan.[12]

One thing that is faithfully reported each month in the newspapers and on

Table 12.1   U.S. Exports and Imports, 2004 (Millions of Dollars)

	Exports	Imports
World	817,936	1,469,670
European Union	172,555	282,560
France	21,239	31,813
Germany	31,381	77,235
United Kingdom	35,960	46,402
NAFTA	299,877	411,770
Canada	189,101	255,927
Mexico	110,775	155,843
Argentina	3,386	3,745
Brazil	13,863	21,157
Venezuela	4,781	24,962
China	34,721	196,698
Japan	54,400	129,594
Hong Kong	15,809	9,313
South Korea	26,333	46,162
Singapore	19,601	15,305
Taiwan	21,731	34,617
Malaysia	10,896	28,185
Egypt	3,104	1,329
Russian Federation	2,959	11,847
Australia	14,270	7,544

Source: Industry, Trade, and the Economy: Data and Analysis. (2005) International Trade Administration. www.ita.doc.gov/td/industry/otea/ustrade.html

the national news is the U.S. trade deficit with other countries. It has been many years since it has been positive, and 2004 was no exception. The deficit for the year was $652 billion, most of which was with Japan and China. The trade deficit with Japan was $75 billion and with China $162 billion. The United States also has a trade deficit with Canada and Mexico and with the European Union, but the combined total is less than that for China. An explanation for the trade deficit with Japan is that the United States imports automobiles and automotive parts from Japan. In the case of China, which has cheap labor, the United States imports a wide variety of consumer goods from them. The trade deficit with China is due to the American appetite for cheap manufactured goods, including toys, sporting goods, and electronics.

Service Accounts

Services are another important component of international trade. They are different from merchandise trade in several ways. First, they are intangible, thus are referred to as invisibles in the U.S. current account. Second, they are usually not storable and are wasted if not used. An example would be an empty airline seat. Third, they usually require consumer participation. Payments received from tourists measure the services that American hotels and shops provide to visitors from other countries. Financial and shipping charges to foreigners measure the fees that American banks, airlines, and shipowners charge for services provided. It also works in reverse. Foreign countries receive payments from American tourists flying foreign airlines, staying at foreign hotels, and eating at foreign restaurants. The United States gains from an inflow of income from the provision of various forms of services to foreign countries, and loses from an outflow of income from the provision of various forms of services performed by other countries.

The service sector and service exports are increasing in importance in the American economy. Service jobs are expected to account for virtually the entire net gain in U.S. employment in the first decade of the twenty-first century. In 2004 service exports of $343 billion exceeded service imports of $296 billion, a surplus of $47 billion, which offset about 5 percent of the deficit in the merchandise trade account. Travel at $10 billion and passenger fares at $5 billion accounted for 0.5 percent of the total. Travel expenditures consisted primarily of the local expenditures of foreign visitors. Passenger fares and other forms of transportation services consisted of foreign purchases from U.S. firms. Royalties and license fees and a wide variety of financial, professional, and technical services amounted to $28.7 billion.[13]

Balance of Payments

Just as a country's gross domestic product is an account of all the goods and services produced within a country, its balance of payments is an account of goods and services, capital loans, gold, and other items flowing into and out of a country. A balance of payments (BOP) is similar to a business balance sheet in that each is a summary of the monetary results of economic and business activity over a period of time. In the balance of payments account, a credit (+) is any transaction that results in a monetary inflow from other countries, while a debit (−) is any transaction that results in a monetary outflow to other nations. Double entry bookkeeping assures in principle that total credits equal total debits. Table 12.2 presents an example of a BOP account. There are four categories—current account, capital account, official reserve account, and statistical discrepancy.

Current Accounts

The current account consists of four categories—the merchandise trade account, the service account, income from U.S. assets abroad and foreign

Table 12.2 Balance of Payments Account

CURRENT ACCOUNT	
Exports +	*Imports −*
Merchandise Trade	Merchandise Trade
Services	Services
Travel	Travel
Financial	Financial
Royalties	Royalties
Other	Other
Income from U.S. Assets Abroad	Income from Foreign Assets in U.S. Gifts

CAPITAL ACCOUNT	
Exports +	*Imports −*
Foreign Assets in the United States +	U.S. Assets Abroad −
Portfolio Investment	Portfolio Investment
Short-term[1]	Short-term[1]
Long-term[2]	Long-term[2]
Direct Investment	Direct Investment

OFFICIAL RESERVE ACCOUNT	
Exports +	*Imports −*
Gold Inflows	Gold Outflows
SDRs[3]	SDRs[3]
Foreign Currencies	U.S. Currencies

STATISTICAL DISCREPANCY

[1]Securities with a maturity date of one year or less—a U.S. Treasury bill.
[2]Securities with a date of more than one year—a U.S. Treasury six-month bond.
[3]Special Drawing Rights (SDRs) are credits granted by the International Monetary Fund that can be used to settle transactions between central banks.

income from U.S. assets in the United States, and unilateral transfers. As previously noted, the merchandise trade account was negative for 2004, because U.S. consumers bought more goods from abroad than foreign consumers bought from the United States. The service account was positive because the United States exported more services than it imported. The third category, income from U.S. assets abroad and foreign income from assets in the United States, is also of importance. Income takes the form of dividends, interest, and profits that are repatriated back to the United States or, if earned in the United States, sent to the home countries. The final category, unilateral transfers, involves money sent to other countries in the form of foreign aid, dividends, and other forms of income. An example would be an American living in Mexico who receives U.S. Social Security checks. In September 2005, the United States hit a record current account deficit of $166.2 billion. Economists attribute the ballooning deficit to the overvaluation of the dollar. Also, American manufacturers have failed to increase their share of the global market.

The Capital Account

The capital account consists of investment inflows and outflows into and out of a country. Inflows into a country are a + item in its capital account, while outflows from a country are a deficit (−). There are two major types of investment—direct investment and portfolio investment. Direct investment occurs when assets are acquired for the purpose of controlling them.[14] This can be done through the acquisition of an existing plant or other tangible asset, the construction of a plant or other tangible assets, or through joint ventures with other firms or countries. An example of direct investment in the United States is the construction of a plant in Alabama by the German auto firm Daimler Benz to produce the Mercedes-Benz car. This is a plus item in the American capital account because German money flows into the United States and a minus item in the German BOP.

The second major type of investment is portfolio investment, which involves holdings of intangible assets such as stocks and bonds. There are two types of portfolio investment—short-term and long-term. Short-term portfolio investment involves holdings of liquid assets with a maturity date of one year or less. Examples would be a U.S. Treasury bill, with a three months' maturity date, checking and savings accounts, and commercial paper. Long-term portfolio investments include those that have a maturity date of more than one year. Examples would involve corporate stocks and bonds, and government bonds and notes. Individuals, mutual funds, banks, corporations, and companies can own portfolio investments. The purchase of a U.S. government bond by a foreign investor is a plus item in the U.S. current account because money comes into the United States. It is also a liability in that there is foreign ownership of the bond. The foreign owner is a creditor; the U.S. Treasury is the debtor. Conversely, the American investor who buys French government bonds is a creditor and the French government is a debtor. As of 2006, the country holding the largest amount in U.S. Treasury Securities is Japan ($685 billion) followed by China, the United Kingdom, Taiwan, and Germany.

Tables 12.3 and 12.4 present a breakdown of direct investment flows into the United States by countries and areas of the world, and U.S. direct investment flows to countries and areas abroad for 2004. As the table indicates, investment flows are like trade flows in that both are from developed countries to developed countries. Europe is the main area of U.S. direct investments and the main supplier of foreign direct investment to the United States. The European Union and Canada account for around 82 percent of FDI in the United States. The greatest imbalance is in the Latin American and Caribbean area, where U.S. investment exceeds the area's investment in the United States by $20 million. Bermuda is a popular resort area, so U.S. money has been invested in the construction of hotels and condominiums. The poorer areas of the world are bypassed by world trade and investment. The entire continent of Africa, with a population of 885 million people, had less investment than Bermuda, with a population of about 64 thousand people.

Table 12.3   U.S. Direct Investment Abroad 2004 (Millions of Dollars)

Canada	22,411	Caribbean	5,062
Mexico	7,424	Bermuda	4,764
Europe	96,848	South America	1,433
Austria	303	Argentina	929
Belgium	1,310	Brazil	1,802
Denmark	375	Chile	864
Finland	373	Africa	2,663
France	9,757	Nigeria	−152
Germany	9,956	Middle East	1,369
Greece	136	Asia and Pacific	84,995
Ireland	10,449	China	4,228
Italy	3,477	Hong Kong	5,368
Luxembourg	4,533	Japan	10,690
Netherlands	12,598	Singapore	5,914
Portugal	−12	World Total	229,294
Spain	3,953	NAFTA	29,865
Sweden	1,883	European Union	60,800
United Kingdom	22,926		
Central America	7,928		
Panama	97		

Source: U.S. Department of Commerce, Bureau of Economic Analysis, "U.S. Direct Investment Abroad and Foreign Direct Investment in the U.S.," (2003) www.bea.doc.gov/bea/di/home/directinv.htm

Table 12.4 Foreign Direct Investment in the United States, 2004 (Millions of Dollars)

Canada	31,805	Central America	3,365
Mexico	1,273	Panama	1,425
Europe	41,396	Caribbean	−2,981
Austria	333	Bermuda	−1,790
Belgium	591	Latin America	384
Denmark	216	Brazil	617
Finland	63	Africa	−571
France	9,234	Middle East	508
Germany	1,545	Asia and Pacific	22,337
Ireland	−3,359	Hong Kong	−135
Italy	980	Japan	16,146
Luxembourg	−538	Singapore	840
Netherlands	6,192	Total FDI in United States	95,859
Spain	515	NAFTA	33,078
Sweden	3,394	European Union	46,406
United Kingdom	19,430		

Source: U.S. Department of Commerce, Bureau of Economic Analysis, "U.S. Direct Investment Abroad and Foreign Direct Investment in the U.S.," (2003) www.bea.doc.gov/bea/di/home/directinv.htm

The Official Reserve Account

The official reserve account reflects in part gold flows and the claims to gold among governments, for it is an accepted medium of international payment among governments. Gold movements are like short-term capital movements; they serve primarily to make up the difference in payments and receipts resulting from other international transactions. A second item included in the reserve account is convertible foreign exchange, which is exchange freely convertible into currencies such as the U.S. dollar. A third item is Special Drawing Rights (SDRs), which are credits granted by the IMF for the purpose of selling transactions among banks to settle accounts. An SDR has a value that is currently calculated daily as a weighted average of five major currencies—the dollar, mark, yen, franc, and pound. U.S. outflows of reserves represent a negative item in the official reserve account; U.S. inflows of reserves represent a positive item in the reserve account.

Statistical Discrepancy

Statistical discrepancy, or errors and omission, is the last account in the BOP accounting system. It is the balancing item that is supposed to make credit and debits equal. Its purpose is to indicate that information about offsetting debit and credit items may come from different sources. Because data from these sources differ in coverage, accuracy, and timing, the balances of payments seldom sum up as they are supposed to in accounting.

INTERNATIONAL MONETARY SYSTEMS

International trade involves the use of different national currencies, which are linked together by foreign exchange rates. An exchange rate is the number of units of one currency that must be given up to acquire one unit of another currency. For example, on a particular day, $1.00 may exchange for 10.6 Mexican pesos, conversely 1 peso would exchange for $.09. These exchange rates fluctuate daily and are determined by supply and demand factors that would affect the dollar and the peso.[15] There have been three types of international exchange rate systems, ranging from a fixed exchange rate system called the gold standard, to a mixed gold and paper standard, to the exchange rate system of today, by which some currencies are allowed to fluctuate based on supply and demand, while other currencies are either pegged or managed.

The Gold Standard

The gold standard lasted roughly from 1821 to 1931. It was a fixed-exchange rate system, by which each country defined the value of its currency in terms of a fixed amount of gold, thereby establishing fixed exchange rates among the countries on the gold standard. The key currency was the British pound sterling. For example, the U.S. Treasury was required by law to pay $20.67 for an ounce of gold, and the Bank of England was required to buy and sell gold for 4.25 pounds for an ounce of gold. The exchange rate between the dollar and the pound was $4.8665 = 1 pound, or 1 pound = 113.22 grams of gold, and $1 = 23.22 grams of gold. Dollars in paper and gold were interchangeable. Debts could be paid in either one. International trade could be financed in dollars or gold, and payments between countries could be settled either way.

The most important point about the gold standard was that the amount of money in circulation was tied to the amount of gold in circulation. Governments could only print money that was backed by gold, so basically the money supply was equal to the gold supply. A nation on the gold standard had two responsibilities. First, it had to buy and sell gold to the public in exchange for paper money at a fixed exchange rate, and second, it had to permit gold to be exported and imported without restriction. An outflow of gold from the United States to France increased the money supply in France, but decreased it in the United States. Prices would rise in France and fall in the United States. French exports to the United States would be more expensive and U.S. exports to France would be cheaper. France would buy more U.S. goods and the United States would buy fewer French goods, and gold would flow back to the United States.

The gold standard began its collapse in World War I when countries had to suspend their pledge to buy gold and sell gold at a fixed rate. After World War I, most countries readopted the gold standard in the 1920s. However, the

Depression of the 1930s finished the gold standard. Countries would no longer pledge to buy and sell gold at a fixed price. Currencies were devalued so that each nation could try to make its goods cheaper in world markets, thereby stimulating its exports and reducing its imports. But when one country devalued its currency, others would retaliate by devaluing theirs, so no one gained. International trade declined, and unemployment rates in the United States and other nations increased, creating economic conditions that helped bring about World War II.

The Bretton Woods Agreement and the Gold and Paper Standard

The rationale for the Bretton Woods Agreement, which was held in 1944, was to prevent what had happened during the 1930s. Various forms of trade restrictions and currency devaluation used by nations to improve their trade position increased unemployment and prolonged the Depression. The Bretton Woods Agreement devised a new monetary system that would serve as a substitute for the gold standard. This system, which lasted from 1945 to 1973, did as follows:

1. The dollar, which was the world's strongest currency, was made convertible into gold at $35 an ounce. Other countries could convert their currencies into dollars and acquire gold.
2. Each country fixed an exchange rate for its currency in relation to the dollar. For example, the German mark exchanged at a rate of 4 marks = $1.00.
3. It created the International Monetary Fund, which was supposed to serve as a substitute for the gold standard in that all member countries were supposed to adhere to certain rules of the game. For example, they agreed to maintain stable exchange rates, to abstain from exchange controls, and to avoid competitive currency devaluation. The IMF had the authority to lend to countries that had a deficit in their balance of payments.
4. Countries wishing to become members of the IMF had to make an initial payment of gold (25 percent) and their currency (75 percent) to the IMF.

The Bretton Woods system began to decline when the United States no longer dominated world trade. Other countries had recovered from World War II and were competing in world markets. Accelerating inflation during the Vietnam War made dollars less attractive as a medium of exchange relative to other currencies, particularly the deutsche mark (DM). In 1971, the German Central Bank revalued the DM against the dollar, and in the same year President Nixon announced that the United States would no longer buy gold at $35 an ounce. In December 1971, the Smithsonian Agreement among the central banks of ten major nations fixed the value of gold at $38 an ounce and allowed exchange rates to fluctuate + or − 2.25 percent around their new par values. The oil shock of 1973 destroyed the gold-paper standard. The oil-importing countries incurred deficits in their balance of payments and cut their ties to the dollar.

Exchange Rates Today

The IMF currently classifies exchange rates into three categories: those that are pegged to a single currency or group of currencies, those with limited flexibility, and those that float freely with minimum government intervention.

Pegged Exchange Rates

Pegged exchange rates are usually used by small countries that tie their currencies to one of the major world currencies (e.g., the dollar). Some countries, which were formerly a part of the British or French empires, tie their currencies to the pound or franc, while others tie their currencies to the U.S. dollar. An example is Argentina, which has pegged its peso at an exchange rate of 1 peso = 1 dollar. Senegal, which was once a part of the French empire, ties its currency unit to the franc.

Limited Flexibility

Currencies that have limited flexibility are commonly called managed float, which means that their currencies fluctuate within certain limits around the currency of another country. An example is the Mexican peso, which fluctuates within an upper or lower range against the value of the American dollar. Another example is the Polish zloty, which fluctuates within limits around the German mark. Managed float means that it is the responsibility of the central banks of Mexico and Poland to use monetary policy to keep their currencies within the ranges set above and below the dollar and the mark. In 2005, China abandoned its fixed rate currency in favor of a managed float system. The move was viewed favorably by the United States, which has felt that the low price of the yuan has resulted in artificially cheap Chinese goods.

Free Float

Free-floating exchange rates are determined by the forces of supply and demand. Each day the exchange rate between the U.S. dollar and the German mark can fluctuate based on supply and demand factors. Travel expenditures by American tourists in Germany would increase the demand for German marks; conversely, travel expenditures by German tourists in the United

States would increase the demand for dollars. Factors affecting the supply and demand of German marks in the determination of the dollar/mark exchange rate can be presented as follows:

Supply	*Demand*
U.S. exports to Germany	U.S. imports from Germany
Travel expenditures by Germans in the United States	Travel expenditures by Americans
German investment in the United States	U.S. investment in Germany

The U.S. Dollar

The U.S. dollar is the world's leading currency. Other currencies, such as the Argentine peso, are pegged to it. It is the dominant currency in the Eurocurrency market. Eurocurrencies are currencies deposited outside the country of issue. A Eurodollar is simply a dollar held by any bank outside of the United States, including foreign branches of U.S. banks. Eurodollars consist of 65 to 80 percent of the Eurocurrency market. The Eurodollar is heavily used for the following reasons:

1. It eliminates the cost risks of converting from one currency to another. In a trade between an American exporter and a European importer, the terms of payment are usually set at a rate in the future. The exchange rate between the dollar and the mark will change before the date is reached, either to the advantage of the American exporter or the German importer. A Eurodollar can be transferred from importer to exporter through a bank.
2. The largest volume of Eurobonds are denominated in U.S. dollars. Eurobonds are a way to raise long-term capital. They are sold outside the borrower's country. For example, a U.S. company can sell bonds in England in pounds, francs, marks, or dollars.

The dollar was the world's strongest currency unit during the last half of the decade of the 1990s. This was beneficial for the U.S. economy by reducing import prices and thus reducing the chance of inflation. A combination of interrelated factors was responsible for the strength of the U.S. dollar relative to other currencies, but particularly the mark and yen. One reason was the unsettled state of the Japanese and other East Asian economies in 1997 and 1998, which caused investors to find a safe haven for their funds. Second, the United States is regarded as the leader and most politically and economically stable of the world market economies. In order to buy U.S. assets, they must first buy U.S. dollars. The increase in demand for dollars drives up their value relative to other currencies.

INTERNATIONAL MONETARY INSTITUTIONS

The two most important international monetary institutions are the International Monetary Fund and the World Bank. Both were a result of the Bretton Woods Agreement of July 1944, which reorganized the world monetary system. As mentioned previously, it was a system of fixed exchange rates based on a modified gold standard. The agreement created the IMF to prevent the use of exchange rate devaluations, which had contributed to prolonging the Depression of the 1930s. The IMF was created to oversee the functioning of the new monetary system by promoting international monetary cooperation and by promoting a stable exchange rate system. The World Bank was created to help finance the reconstruction of Europe after World War II.[16] Its mission has expanded over time to provide loans to support the economies of the less-developed countries.

International Monetary Fund

As of November 2005, 184 countries were members of the IMF. To belong, a country has to pay a quota consisting of 25 percent Special Drawing Rights and 75 percent in the country's currency. The amount of the quota is based on the relative economic importance of the country in the world economy. Each country has voting rights based on the amount of its quota.[17] The borrowing power of each member country is based on the size of its quota. It has the right to borrow up to 25 percent of its quota, and additional amounts are subject to IMF-imposed restrictions. These restrictions would include the elimination of export subsidies, reductions in a country's money supply, and higher interest rates. A country's quota is a part of its official reserves in its balance of payments account.

Special Drawing Rights (SDRs)

Special Drawing Rights (SDRs) constitute an international reserve asset that can be used when countries incur balance of payments deficits. They were created by the IMF in 1969 and are used as a unit of account. In addition, several countries peg their currencies to the SDR. All member countries of the IMF may use SDRs to acquire foreign exchange when they have short-term balance of payments problems. For example, if Argentina has a balance of payments problem with the United States, it can use its SDRs to acquire dollars. SDRs have a value determined by the weighted value of five currencies: the U.S. dollar, the German mark, the French franc, the Japanese yen, and the British pound sterling.[18] They have a value that fluctuates daily, and they are part of a country's unilateral transfer account in its balance of payments.[19]

The World Bank Group

The World Bank Group, or World Bank as it is more commonly called, was created in 1945 as the International Bank for Reconstruction and Development (IBRD). Its original purpose was to help rebuild the war-torn economies of Europe. In recent decades emphasis has been placed on loans to less-developed countries to improve their infrastructures. Examples would be the financing of engineering and agricultural projects. Service and educational projects are also eligible for loans. Capital is provided by the countries that are members of the IBRD. Loans are made only to governments or to organizations having a government guarantee. Private business firms can bid on contracts for development projects, such as building roads, and can act as suppliers and engineers.

Other institutions that are a part of the World Bank Group include the following:

1. The International Finance Corporation (IFC): The IFC provides loans to individual business firms, with the criteria that the projects benefit the economies of the developing countries, and that they have a reasonable chance of making a profit. The IFC can make loans at conventional interest rates for a period of up to twelve years and can also purchase stock shares.
2. The International Development Association (IDA): The primary purpose of IDA is to help the poorest countries among the World Bank Group members. It, too, provides loans for development purposes at low rates of interest, or even on an interest-free basis. Loans can also be made for a period of time of up to fifty years. An example of this type of loan would be a loan to Ethiopia to improve rural water supplies.
3. The Multilateral Investment Guarantee Agency (MIGA). The purpose of MIGA is to provide political risk insurance for firms doing business in countries with a high degree of political risk.[20] It was created in 1988 to encourage direct investment in less-developed countries by offering private investors insurance against noncommercial risks, such as wars and government expropriation of property.

U.S. GOVERNMENT POLICIES TO PROMOTE EXPORTS

Since its inception, the United States has generally followed a policy of trade protection designed to protect domestic consumers against foreign competition. At first, the rationale for trade protection was based on the "infant industry" argument. American industries that were just getting started were in no position to compete against the established industries of Europe, so protective tariffs were used. Then tariffs were lowered at the request of farmers who could import farm equipment from abroad more cheaply than it could be purchased in the United States.[21] Trade protection hit its peak during the Depression of the 1930s when the Smoot-Hawley tariff was passed. The raising of the tariff against foreign goods provoked retaliation from abroad as other countries raised their tariffs on American goods, increasing unemployment here and abroad.

Governments are very much involved in international trade. In the United States, federal, state, and local governments promote international trade and investment. The federal government promotes foreign trade through the Department of Commerce and through agencies like the Export-Import Bank (Eximbank). State governments promote international trade through their development offices and trade missions. They offer various forms of subsidies to attract foreign investments. Local governments create Free Trade Zones (FTZs) to attract companies. In general, government trade policies can be divided into two types—those that are designed to promote exports and investment and those that are designed to discourage imports.

Several types of government policies can be used to promote exports. Of these, tax policies are probably the most important. A government can manipulate its tax system to grant exemptions and rates to various forms of activities, corporations, and people. Japan, for example, has exempted income earned from its exports from the corporate income tax. Favorable tax treatments of certain types of income can influence shifts in economic behavior. Governments can also promote exports through loans financed out of budget revenues or other sources. The U.S. Export-Import Bank (Eximbank) is an example. Subsidies can also be used to aid export industries or to attract foreign investment. Favorable tax treatment is one form of a subsidy.[22] Another would be rebates to exporters.

Export-Import Bank (EXIMBANK)

The Export-Import Bank (Eximbank) is a federally owned enterprise that receives its financial support from the federal budget. Its mission is to promote U.S. exports. It does this by making direct loans to exporters and by insuring and guaranteeing loans made by private lenders. Since it concentrates on areas where private financing is not available and on meeting foreign competition, its programs are generally intended to supplement private sources of credit. Direct loans extended by Eximbank are dollar credits made to borrowers outside the United States for the purchase of U.S. goods and services. Disbursements under the loan agreements are made in the United States to the suppliers of the goods and services, and the loans plus interest must be repaid in dollars by the borrowers. The purposes for which the loans can be used are the following:

1. To supplement private sources of financing when the lenders are unable or unwilling to assume the political and financial risks involved.
2. To extend credit on terms longer than those private lenders can provide.
3. To match the special terms that foreign governments provide to their exporters.

In addition, Eximbank has financial guarantee programs under which it can guarantee, backed by the full faith and credit of the United States, the repayment of credits extended by private lenders to foreign purchasers of U.S. goods and services. In this respect, the bank's role is comparable to that of the many foreign institutions that provide guarantees and insurance to help their country's exporters and safeguard them from undue risks from overseas sales. Under the financial loan authority, Eximbank can guarantee repayment by a borrower of up to 100 percent of the outstanding principal due on such loans, plus interest equal to the U.S. Treasury rate for similar debt obligations.

Overseas Private Investment Corporation (OPIC)

Political and financial risks are facts of life in the world marketplace. Political risk can apply to wars, revolutions, riots, and terrorism.[23] It can also cover default on debt payments by governments, increased taxes, and currency controls.[24] There are a number of areas of the world in which political risk is high, for example, Bosnia, Iran, Iraq, Nigeria, Rwanda, Russia, and many other countries. Financial risk refers to nonpayment of debts and currency instability. A foreign importer may default on debts owed to an American exporter.[25] Currency instability also has an adverse affect on trade. Using the East Asian currency crisis as an example, U.S. exporters doing business in Indonesia or Thailand were hurt because the values of their currencies declined in value against the dollar, making imports of American goods more expensive.

The Overseas Private Investment Corporation (OPIC) provides insurance for U.S. direct investment in less-developed countries. It is an agency of the U.S. government, and is financed out of the federal budget.[26] It provides loan guarantees and political risk insurance. It can also make direct loans and some equity investments. The types of projects assisted are those that promote economic development, such as manufacturing, fishing, mining, agriculture, and tourism. Loans are usually made to firms with sales of less than $142 million annually.

1. Direct loans are made for amounts ranging from $500,000 to $6 million. Proceeds may be used to acquire goods and services in the United States or in a foreign country.
2. Guaranteed loans can be provided to lenders, including banks and insurance companies. If, for example, an American bank lends money for a development project in Nigeria, OPIC will guarantee the loan against potential loss.
3. Equity participation on the part of OPIC can occur. It can purchase up to 30 percent of stock or bonds in U.S. companies, local companies, or joint ventures.[27]
4. Risk insurance is the largest and most important of OPIC's activities and covers expropriation, currency inconvertibility, and any form of political violence.

Foreign Trade Zones (FTZs)

In order to encourage foreign trade, many countries, including the United States, set up foreign trade zones that allow business firms to store, assemble, and display goods from abroad without first having to pay a tariff. FTZs are widely used by local governments in the United States to promote trade and create jobs. New Orleans is an example. Goods may be brought into the FTZ of the city tariff-free. Once they are assembled and leave the zone, a tariff must be paid, but not on the cost of assembly or profit. For example, a furniture maker would pay a duty only on the raw materials brought into the zone, but not on the cost of assembling the final product or on profits. A foreign automaker can bring parts to New Orleans FTZ, assemble them, and not pay a tariff until the finished product is delivered to a U.S. showroom.[28]

Foreign Sales Corporation Act (FSCA)

The FSCA was passed in 1984 for the purpose of encouraging small business firms to go into the exporting business. It allows small firms to form into foreign sales corporations (FSCs) in order to stimulate exports. There are specific benefits to be derived from the formation of an FSC. It can get a tax exemption on income earned from foreign trade. It can get a tax exemption on a portion of foreign trade income earned from the sale or lease of export property, and the performance of engineering and managerial services. There is an exemption from U.S. income taxes of up to 50 percent of earnings by small firms. To be incorporated, an FSC must conform to the following requirements:

1. It has to incorporate under the laws of a foreign country with which the United States has an agreement for the exchange of tax information, or of any U.S. possession with the exception of Puerto Rico.

2. It has to maintain an office outside of the U.S. customs territory.
3. It cannot have more than twenty-five stockholders.

TRADE PROTECTION

Government policies to promote the development of their home industries go back to mercantilism. The mercantilist nations believed that the value of exports should always exceed the value of imports. In this way, the wealth of each nation would be increased. To accomplish this objective, trade was regulated between these nations and their colonies. England would not allow its American colonies to produce steel because it would compete against British steelmakers. Only raw materials of lesser value could be sent to England; in return, the British would export finished products of more value to America, thus always having a favorable trade balance with its colonies.[29]

It can be said that Japan's economic development after the end of World War II was based on mercantilist policies. Its development was based on an export-driven strategy, by which the Ministry of International Trade and Industry promoted an industrial policy based on picking and promoting industries that could export successfully throughout the world. An example is the Japanese automobile industry that grew from the production of 32,000 cars in 1950 to becoming the world's largest automobile producers by 1980.[30] The automobile industry was helped through the provision of low-cost loans by the Japanese banks. During the early stages of its development, the automobile industry received subsidies from the government, and was protected from foreign competition by tariffs and quotas.[31]

Tariffs

The tariff is probably the most common device used by other nations to restrict foreign trade. It is simply a tax levied on foreign goods coming into a country. The result is to make imported goods more expensive than comparable domestic goods, which, of course, are not subject to the tax. The main effect of a tariff is that it raises the prices of the goods protected by it; if it did not raise prices, it would afford no protection. The sugar beet industry of the United States provides a good example of tariff protection. It is much more expensive to produce sugar made from beets than it is to import cane sugar made in Cuba and elsewhere. The end result is that American consumers pay more for sugar than they would have to in the absence of the tariff.

Import Quotas

Compared with tariffs, which have been used by countries since the days of mercantilism, import quotas are relatively new. Introduced in France in the

1930s as an antidepression measure, the import quota has become a significant part of most countries' international commercial policy. As the name implies, a quota places limits, numerical or other, on the amount of a product that can be imported. For example, one country decides to restrict its auto imports from another country to two million cars a year. An import quota is generally considered more restrictive than a tariff. With a tariff, there is still the option of buying the foreign product, albeit at a higher price, but the import quota limits even this option. Prices cannot be forced by a tariff to rise by more than the amount of the tariff, but there is no upper limit to the price increase that can result from a quota. The prices to consumers are raised, and the restrictions placed on imports take away the incentive of domestic producers to innovate and promote efficiency. The United States has imposed import quotas on China, including knit fabrics, dressing gowns and robes, bras, and most recently on cotton shirts, pants, and underwear.

The Automobile Industry and Import Quotas

In 1981, the U.S. auto companies asked Congress and the Reagan administration for quotas against the Japanese automobile industry. At stake, the U.S. auto industry claimed, was the survival of the industry and the necessity of preserving jobs. Import quotas would provide a time-out or respite, so to speak, while the auto industry could recuperate, retool, and develop new cars that could compete successfully against Japanese cars. Precedents for import quotas had already been established. Beef quotas have assisted cattle raisers, sugar quotas have kept high-cost domestic sugar cane and sugar beet growers in business, and quotas and other forms of support have been used to protect domestic steel producers from further losses to Asian and European steel producers. The Reagan administration made a compromise to reach an agreement with Japan whereby Japanese auto companies would voluntarily limit their exports to the United States. These quotas, set at 1,680,000 cars a year over a three-year period, ended in March 1984. A new quota, which raised the number of cars the Japanese could ship to the United States to 1,850,000 cars, was applied from April 1, 1984, to March 31, 1985. The allocation of import shares among Japanese automobile manufacturers was determined by the Japanese government on the basis of each company's shares of the U.S. market before the quota was imposed. The breakdown of the market was as follows:[32]

Toyota	31%
Nissan	27
Honda	21
Mazda	9

Mitsubishi	7
Subaru	4
Isuzu	1

Results of the Import Quota on Japanese Cars

The import quota had a number of results, few of which were of benefit to U.S. consumers. As the market allocation indicates, the quota benefited those Japanese auto firms that had already established a market for their cars in the United States. Toyota was assured of a market share of around one-third of the quota. Conversely, Japanese car companies that had not established a market share before the quota were virtually shut out of the U.S. car market. U.S. consumer choice was limited to a choice of the cars produced by Toyota, Nissan, or Honda, or the U.S. cars, or the cars of countries to which the import quota did not apply. However, the import quota on Japanese cars also had other effects on U.S. consumers:[33]

1. It raised the prices of both American and Japanese cars to U.S. consumers. One estimate was that the price of Japanese imports increased an average of $920 to $960 per car in the 1981–1983 period. Since restrictions were placed on Japanese cars, the companies shipped their top-of-the-line models. It was estimated that Japanese producers and their dealers benefited by as much as $2 billion a year during the quota.
2. The prices of U.S. automobiles also increased by an estimated $1,300 for each new U.S. car sold during the period 1981–1983. The estimated additional cost to consumers for new U.S. and Japanese cars was $4.3 billion in 1983.
3. One benefit of the import quota was to protect U.S. jobs. An estimated 20,000 to 25,000 jobs were saved in the automobile industry, at a cost to consumers of $160,000 a year per job.
4. Another purpose of the import quota was to enable the U.S. car companies to improve the quality of their cars. There is little evidence that such improvements were made.
5. The U.S. automobile companies increased their market shares and made record profits. In 1984, Chrysler's profits were the highest in its history. Automobile industry profits were $6.3 billion for 1983 and close to $10 billion in 1984.
6. With such profits, the automobile companies paid their executives and some employees substantial bonuses. Chairman Philip Caldwell of Ford Motor Company received a 1983 salary and bonus of $1.4 million plus $5.9 million in long-term compensation. Chrysler Chairman Lee A. Iacocca received stock options valued at $17 million.

Dumping

Dumping is simply selling a product in another country at a cost lower than its production cost. The loss is often made up by a subsidy from the government. An example is the development of the Korean automobile industry. Three Korean conglomerates were picked to produce cars for exports, and targets were set for each of them. Export prices for cars were set low, often below cost, and the government made up the difference. For example, one Hyundai model that cost $3,700 to produce was sold for $5,000 in Korea and $2,200 overseas.[34] The car was overpriced in Korea and underpriced in Southeast Asia and Latin America. The intent was to establish a market for the car in these areas by selling below cost, with the Korean government covering the loss. Hyundai was also supported by the state-owned Korean banks, which provided low-cost interest loans.

Exchange Controls

Exchange controls have been used by many countries. All importers needing foreign exchange to pay for imports can be required to obtain it from a government agency. Before approving such a request, the agency will want to know what is to be imported, whether the import competes against domestic producers, and from what country the import comes. India provides an example. Many imports were excluded from India to protect certain industries. The government set different exchange rates, depending on the importance of the import. If it were necessary for the economy, the exchange rate the government offered to importers might be 5 rupees = $1.00; if it was not important, the exchange rate might be 50 rupees = $1.00.[35] The government, not the free market, decided what was important and what was not important.

The Omnibus Trade and Competitiveness Act, 1988

The Omnibus Trade and Competitiveness Act joined the Bible and *Gone with the Wind* as one of the longest publications ever written.[36] It is 1,115 pages long and contains something for everyone. The purpose of the act is to develop coherent trade policy in dealing with countries with whom the United States has an unfavorable trade deficit, thus preventing future declines in the U.S. economy. In the past, U.S. presidents have preferred to handle trade on an ad hoc basis, with each issue left to the political and economic circumstances of the moment. But no trade dispute can be separable from many other kinds of issues. Congress wanted future presidents, beginning with President Bush, to give more weight to trade in their foreign policy and to make their performance more consistent. However, nearly all the provisions in the act give the president the right to do nothing when he (or she) considers that to be in the country's best interest.

The most important provision of the act is Section 1102, which states that the president, on finding that import restrictions of other countries have an adverse effect on the foreign trade of the United States, is to negotiate to reduce them.[37] The principal negotiation objective is to improve the provisions of GATT and nontariff measure agreements in order to define, deter, and discourage the use of unfair trade practices, including subsidies, dumping, and export targeting practices. Agreements entered into by the president are valid only if he (or she) informs Congress of his (or her) intent to enter into them. The president must also inform Congress if the United States provides reciprocal benefits under a trade agreement. Other purposes of the act are to provide increased cash assistance and job training for U.S. workers who lose their jobs as a result of foreign competition; restrictions against certain imports that threaten national security; and increased funding to improve foreign language teaching in the United States.

The General Agreement On Tariffs And Trade (GATT)

The General Agreement on Tariffs and Trade (GATT), like the World Bank and the International Monetary Fund, is a by-product of the Depression of the 1930s when the world economy collapsed. It was created in Geneva, Switzerland, in 1947, and had as its major purpose the reduction of trade barriers that had contributed to the prolongation of the Depression. To do this, member countries agreed to uphold the following principles:

1. Nondiscrimination in trade through adherence to Most Favored Nations (MFN) treatment, which means that any preferential treatment given to one country be given to all member countries. However, to assist less-developed countries in their economic development, wealthier countries may lower tariffs to these countries without lowering them for other countries.
2. Reduction of tariffs through negotiation.
3. Elimination of import quotas.
4. Resolution of differences between member countries by negotiation.

A series of negotiations called "rounds" have occurred since GATT's inception in 1947. The first rounds were concerned, for the most part, with reducing tariffs. Beginning in the 1960s, however, the focus shifted as countries began to rely less on tariffs and more on import quotas and subsidies. GATT rules had little influence over government investment policies that affected international trade or on policies concerning the protection of intellectual property rights such as patents, trademarks, and copyrights. Agricultural trade, which usually involved the use of subsidies, was another area in which GATT rules did not apply.

The Uruguay Round

The Uruguay Round involved a series of discussions among member nations that lasted from 1986 to 1995. A number of issues ranging from agricultural policy to intellectual property were discussed. Agricultural subsidies and restrictions on the import of agricultural products were a major bone of contention among nations. For example, Japan is an inefficient producer of rice. The availability of land for the production of rice in Japan is limited, so there are a large number of rice farmers cultivating small rice fields. The supply of rice to Japanese consumers is limited and expensive. It would be far cheaper to import rice from the United States but Japanese farmers, like U.S. farmers including those who produce tobacco, have political clout.[38] Japanese restrictions on the import of American rice discriminates against American rice producers and Japanese consumers who pay on the average five times as much for Japanese rice than for American rice. One of the objectives of the Uruguay Round, summarized below, is to reduce subsidies on agricultural products.

1. Agricultural liberalization: A major accomplishment of the Uruguay Round was to convert various types of subsidies into tariffs to be reduced by 36 percent over a period of time. The rice markets of Japan and South Korea, which are closed to imports, will gradually be opened over a period of time, thus providing better market opportunities for foreign suppliers. Domestic farm supports are to be reduced by 20 percent, and subsidized exports are to be reduced 36 percent in value and 21 percent in volume.[39] Countries were treated differently based on their income levels. In industrial countries, import tariffs on agriculture were to be reduced by 36 percent over a six-year period. Developing countries committed themselves to reducing their tariffs over twenty years, and less-developed countries were exempted from any commitment.
2. Services: The export of services is an area in which the United States has a trade surplus. Of particular importance is the export of such services as finance, telecommunication, and transportation. There are no international trade rules covering services, so countries protect their service industries from foreign competition. Some countries may require that their exports and imports be carried only on their own ships. Other countries may place restrictions on the provision of financial services by foreign banks.[40] The Uruguay Round sets basic fair-play principles involving nondiscrimination against services, with each country pledging openings in areas ranging from banking to entertainment. Part of the

Uruguay Round was the creation of the General Agreement on Trade in Services (GATS) that will establish rules for services that aim for nondiscrimination and market access.

3. Intellectual Property: Intellectual property rights are very important to the foreign trade of the United States because American movies, television programs, music, and various other forms of entertainment are popular overseas. When copyrights and other forms of intellectual property are infringed upon, as they are in a number of countries, income is lost to their owners. The Uruguay Round strengthened the protection granted to the owners of intellectual property. The TRIPS (Trade-Related Intellectual Property Rights) agreement was a part of the Uruguay Round. It covers such intellectual property rights as patents, copyrights, trademarks, and designs. It covers all the 123 signatory countries of the Uruguay Round. Much of TRIPS simply extends the international agreements of intellectual property that are discussed in the next section.

4. Manufacturing: The export of manufacturing is the most important item in the U.S. merchandise trade account and so is the import of manufacturing from the rest of the world. Contributing to the deficit in the merchandise trade account is the fact that we import more automobiles from Japan than we export to Japan. Tariffs, import quotas, and other devices are used to protect domestic manufacturing industries. Successive rounds have had as their objectives the reduction of these trade restraints. The Uruguay Round aimed at cutting tariffs on manufactured goods from rich countries by more than one-third. Over 40 percent of imports will enter duty-free. Tariff reductions were also set for such countries as South Korea, Thailand, and other East Asian countries. The reduction of import quotas was also a major objective of the Uruguay Round.

The World Trade Organization (WTO)

The World Trade Organization (WTO), the successor to GATT, was created by the Uruguay Round and entered into existence on January 1, 1995. It is a permanent forum for 148 member governments to address issues affecting their multilateral trade relations as well as to supervise the implementation of the trade agreements negotiated in the Uruguay Round. The WTO operates in much the same manner as GATT, while overseeing a wider variety of trade agreements.[41] It also creates a stronger dispute settlement process by having an appellate court to review interpretations of trade agreements. There are some fifteen agreements that are the responsibility of WTO. The WTO financial services agreement signed on December 13, 1997, covers countries representing 95 percent of the global financial services market. The WTO is based in Geneva, Switzerland. In 2006 it ruled that tax breaks the United States gives to some of its largest exporters are illegal as unfair subsidies. Consequently, the European Union, which brought the suit, may impose sanctions on U.S. exports.

THE UNITED STATES AS A DEBTOR NATION

The United States has had a deficit in its merchandise trade account for the period 1986–2005. The deficit reached a high of $725.8 billion in 2005.[42] Regardless of whether the dollar has been weak or strong against other world currencies, the trade deficit persists. During this period the United States imported around $4.6 trillion more of goods than it exported. Approximately 25 percent of the deficit has been with China, which has created trade tensions between the two countries. Foreign investors have grown wary of financing the U.S. deficit; however, Asian governments, particularly Japan and China, have stepped in to purchase American debt in the form of bonds. For September 2005, Japan held $687 billion in U.S. Treasury securities; China held $252 billion, and the United Kingdom held $182 billion.[43]

Today, the United States is the world's leading debtor nation and Japan is the world's leading creditor nation. A part of the debt increase can be attributed to the fact that the American dollar increased in value relative to European and Japanese currencies, making U.S. assets abroad worth less. The U.S. merchandise trade deficit has been a contributory cause of the deficit. Countries with trade surpluses can use the amounts to invest in the United States. U.S. Treasury securities are of particular importance to foreign investors because they represent one of the safest forms of investment in the world. Much of the rise in U.S. stock market prices can also be attributed to foreign investors who find U.S. stocks an attractive vehicle for investment.

SUMMARY

The balance of payments accounts of any country are a systematic record of its transactions with the rest of the world over a given period of time. The accounts include trade, services, capital movements, and unilateral transfers. Trade includes merchandise exports and imports such as machinery and foodstuffs. Services are also an important export and import. The United States has a deficit in its merchandise trade account, most of which can be attributed to an excess of imports from Japan and China over exports. Capital movements comprise the capital account and consist of direct investment and portfolio investment. International payments between countries can be made in gold and convertible foreign exchange. These payments come under the balance of payments category of official reserve accounts.

QUESTIONS FOR DISCUSSION

1. What is the purpose of the International Monetary Fund?
2. Discuss Michael Porter's theory of national competitive advantage.
3. The great bulk of American foreign trade is done with three major trading areas of the world. Discuss. Which area is the most important? Why?
4. What is a country's balance of payments? The United States usually has a negative balance of payments. Is that good or bad?
5. Discuss some of the factors that affect the supply of and the demand for American dollars.
6. The IMF currently classifies exchange rates into three categories. Discuss.

RECOMMENDED READING

Collins, S. and Graham, C. *Brookings Trade Forum: Globalization, Poverty, and Inequality.* Brookings Institution Press. 2004.
International Trade Statistics 2005. World Trade Organization. December 2005.
Trade Profiles 2005. World Trade Organization. November 2005.
World Economic Outlook: Globalization and External Imbalances. International Monetary Fund. April 2005.

NOTES

1. Stewart C. Easton, *The Western Heritage.* New York: Holt, Rinehart, and Winston, 1961, p. 112.
2. David Landes, *The Wealth and Poverty of Nations.* New York: W. W. Norton, 1998.
3. Angus Maddison, *The World Economy in the 20th Century.* Development Center for the Organization for Economic Cooperation and Development, Paris: 1989, p. 29.
4. Leading exporters and importers in world merchandise trade. WTO. 2003. www .wto.org/english/res_e/statis_e/its2004_e/its04_bysubject_e.htm
5. The building of classical economic theory can be attributed to the writings of Adam Smith and David Ricardo. It dominated economic thought of the Western world from the late eighteenth century until the 1930s.
6. Mercantilism was also used in Holland, France, and Spain. Colonial empires were built by each of these nations.
7. Adam Smith, *The Wealth of Nations.* Indianapolis: Liberty Classics, 1981.
8. David Ricardo, *The Principles of Political Economy and Taxation.* New York: E. P. Dulton and Co., 1948, pp. 82–83.

9. Bertil Ohlin, *Interregional and International Trade.* Cambridge, MA: Harvard University Press, 1933.

10. Although China is a large country, much of its land is not suitable for agriculture. Labor is plentiful, so the cultivation of rice and other agricultural products is labor intensive.

11. Michael Porter, *The Competitive Advantage of Nations.* New York: Free Press, 1990.

12. Taiwan is not recognized as a nation because of the objection of China, which considers it to be a Chinese province.

13. Bureau of Economic Analysis, Balances of Payments, 2004. Also included would be royalties from American music sold abroad.

14. A minimum of 10 percent stock ownership is the basic requisite for a direct investment.

15. For example, American college students going to Cancun for a vacation would increase the demand for pesos.

16. The World Bank and the Marshall Plan aid were responsible to a considerable degree for European recovery.

17. The International Monetary Fund has a pool of funds amounting to around $213 billion, coming mostly from the rich nations. The biggest givers are as follows: (1) United States, $37.0 billion; (2) Japan, $13.3 billion; (3) Germany, $13 billion; (4) United Kingdom, $10.7 billion; (5) France, $10.7 billion; (6) Saudi Arabia, $7.0 billion.

18. The U.S. dollar accounts for around 40 percent of the value of an SDR.

19. On November 21, 2005, 1 SDR = $1.43.

20. However, there are some countries that are not covered by risk insurance. An example would be Rwanda.

21. This was one of the causes of the Civil War. The South felt that the North was discriminating against it because the tariff compelled it to buy more manufactured goods from the North.

22. Favorable tax treatment of foreign trade takes many forms. An example would be export exemption from income taxes.

23. Kidnapping is one form of terrorism. It has been on the increase in some Latin American countries. Assassination is another form of terrorism.

24. Currency controls refers to the amount of money that can be taken into or out of a country.

25. This occurrence would involve dispute resolution that is normally covered in the contract between exporter and importer.

26. The governments of all major exporting nations would have similar arrangements.

27. A joint venture is an arrangement between two or more firms or with firms and a government to produce and sell a particular product. The partners provide capital and management expertise and share in the profits.

28. FTZs have increased in importance in the United States. They have increased from around 25 in the 1970s to 268 in 2006.

29. See the discussion of mercantilism on page 260.

30. The Japanese automobile industry dates back to the early part of the twentieth century.

31. This is also true of the South Korean automobile industry.

32. Robert W. Crandall, "Import Quotas and the Automobile Industry: The Costs of Protection," *The Brookings Review* 2, no. 4, September 1984: 11.

33. Crandall, 1984, 11–16.

34. Congress of the United States, Office of Technology Assessment, *Competing Economies: America, Europe, and the Pacific Rim.* Washington, D.C.: U.S. Government Printing Office, October 1991, pp. 329–331.

35. Since the 1990s, India has relaxed many of its trade restrictions, but still maintains some exchange controls.

36. H.R. 3, 100th Congress, 2nd session, April 20, 1988.

37. H.R. 3, 100th Congress, 2nd session, April 20, 1988. p. 23–27.

38. A very good example was the failure of Congress to pass legislation that would have raised the tax on a package of cigarettes and would have made the tobacco companies responsible for reducing teenage smoking. The tobacco lobby cited lost jobs if the law were passed.

39. These are guidelines, not categorical goals.

40. Mexico has restricted U.S. banks operating in Mexico from providing various services not offered by Mexican banks.

41. Jim Sanford, "World Trade Organization Opens Global Markets, Protects U.S. Rights," *Business America.* Washington, D.C.: U.S. Government Printing Office, January 1995: 4–7.

42. U.S. Department of Commerce, Bureau of the Census, *Statistical Abstract of the United States, 2004–2005.* Washington, D.C.: U.S. Government Printing Office, 2004, p. 814.

43. Major Foreign Holders of Treasury Securities. Department of the Treasury/Federal Reserve Board. 11/16/2005.

13

Regional Trading Blocs

Globalism and regionalism are two main currents in the world today. Technological innovation is a driving force in the world economy and has no distinctive nationality. As technology has developed, it has increasingly become an internationally marketable commodity. A globalized market for goods and services has also resulted from rapid technological developments that have greatly diminished the costs of international transportation and communication, and international trade in manufacturing products has been boosted by the trend toward convergence in per capita incomes and demand patterns of industrial countries. There has also been a globalization of financial markets in that the pool of savings is worldwide and financial intermediaries know no international boundaries. Finally, American companies increasingly think in terms of the advantages of international plant location.

At the same time, as a counter to globalization, there are also increasing trends toward regionalism. Several major economic spheres, formed or in the process of being formed, will be the focus of this chapter. The first is the European Union, consisting of twenty-five member countries.[1] Its major objectives are the free movement of people, services, and capital from one country to another; the free movement of goods through the elimination of tariffs; and the creation of a common currency, the euro. The second is the North American Free Trade Agreement (NAFTA), which includes the United States, Canada, and Mexico, with the objective of eliminating tariff barriers among the three countries. (The recently ratified Central American Free Trade Agreement (CAFTA) between the United States and six of its Central American neighbors: the Dominican Republic, Costa Rica, Nicaragua, Honduras, El Salvador, and Guatemala. The purpose of CAFTA is to lower tariff barriers between the member countries.)

There are other regional trading blocs throughout the world. They include:

- The South American Community of Nations, which consists of the countries of Argentina, Bolivia, Brazil, Chile, Colombia, Ecuador, Guyana, Paraguay, Peru, Suriname, Uruguay, and Venezuela. Its purpose is to promote freer trade among these countries by lowering tariff barriers.
- The Caribbean Community (Caricom), which consists of fourteen small, formerly British colonies in the Caribbean and South and Central America. It started out as a free trade area and later became a customs union.
- ASEAN, which includes Brunei, Indonesia, Malaysia, Philippines, Singapore, Thailand, and Vietnam. ASEAN started out as a preferential trade arrangement, granting preference margins on certain commodities. It became a free trade area in 1992.

Regional trading arrangements cover a spectrum ranging from preferential trade agreements, to economic union. These arrangements are as follows:

1. Preferential Trade Arrangements (PTA): Preferential Trade Arrangements can range from giving trade preferences to a set of trading partners to all countries covered in an agreement.
2. Free Trade Area (FTA): The North American Free Trade Agreement (NAFTA) is an example. Its objective is the eventual removal of tariffs and other trade barriers among the three countries; however, each country may establish its own trade policies with nonmember countries.
3. Customs Union (CU): A customs union is a higher level of integration. It occurs when the members of an FTA go beyond removing trade barriers among themselves and set a common level of trade barriers against outsiders. This could entail a common tariff on goods coming from other countries. It would set all trade policies for its members as a unified whole.
4. Common Market: A common market involves a higher stage of trade integration. It would not only include the free exchange of goods and services among members, but also the free movement of factors of production: labor and capital.
5. Economic Union (EU): This goes far beyond the free movement of goods, services, and the factors of production. It involves the creation of common national economic policies, including a common currency and taxes. The decision of the European Community (EC) in 1994 reflected the determination to proceed to this higher stage of integration. However, the full unification of economic policy, including the creation of a common currency, the euro, requires full political integration of all the countries involved in the economic union. Thus, the European Union involves both an economic union and a political union.

THE EUROPEAN UNION (EU)

The European Union (EU) is the largest regional trading bloc in the world. The twenty-five countries comprising the EU have about 7 percent of the world's population, but account for 30 percent of the world's gross national income and 30 percent of the world's foreign trade. Table 13.1 presents the population, per capita gross national income, and gross national income for each country. Germany and France are the two wealthiest countries, accounting for about 38 percent of the GNI of the European Union. Members of the European Union have agreed to do five things. First, by combining both political and economic integration, the members have effectively transformed themselves into one country. Second, the members will integrate their economies by coordinating their economic policies through one central bank and

Table 13.1   Population, Per Capita GNI, and GNI for the European Union

Country	Population (millions)	Gross National Income per capita (dollars)	Gross National Income (GNI) (billions of dollars)
Austria	8.1	26,720	215.4
Belgium	10.3	25,820	267.2
Cyprus	0.8	12,320	9.4
The Czech Republic	10.2	6,740	68.7
Denmark	5.4	33,750	181.8
Estonia	1.4	4,960	6.7
Finland	5.2	27,020	140.8
France	59.7	24,770	1,523.0
Germany	82.6	25,250	2,084.6
Greece	10.7	13,720	146.6
Hungary	10.1	6,330	64.0
Ireland	3.9	26,960	106.4
Italy	57.6	21,560	1,243.0
Latvia	2.3	4,070	9.4
Lithuania	3.5	4,490	15.5
Luxembourg	0.4	43,940	19.7
Malta	0.4	9,260	3.7
Netherlands	16.2	26,310	426.6
Poland	38.2	5,270	201.4
Portugal	10.2	12,130	123.7
Slovakia	5.4	4,920	26.5
Slovenia	2.0	11,830	23.2
Spain	41.1	16,990	698.2
Sweden	9.0	28,840	258.3
United Kingdom	59.3	28,350	1,680.3
EU-25	454	18,090	9,544
World	**6,271.7**	**5,500**	**34,491.5**

Source: The World Bank, *2004 World Bank Atlas*. Washington, D.C.: The World Bank, 2004, pp. 54–55.

one common currency, the euro. Third, the members will eliminate all barriers that restrict the movement of capital and labor among themselves. Fourth, the members will adopt a common trade policy toward nonmember countries. Finally, the member countries will create a free trade area by removing tariffs, import quotas, and other barriers to international trade among themselves; however, each country can establish its own trade policies toward nonmember nations.[2]

History of the European Union

The concept of a united Western Europe has been a major force since the end of World War II. The Benelux (Belgium, Netherlands, Luxembourg) customs union of 1944 was designed to remove tariffs on commodity trade among the countries. In 1950, Robert Schumann, French minister of foreign affairs, proposed that France and the Federal Republic of Germany[3] pool their coal and steel production under the auspices of a European organization that eventually became the European Coal and Steel Community (ECSC). It consisted of six countries—Belgium, France, the Federal Republic of Germany, Italy, Luxembourg, and the Netherlands—which in 1957 signed the Treaty of Rome establishing the European Economic Community (EEC) and the European Atomic Energy Commission (Euratom). The major reason for the creation of the EEC was to reduce tariff and other trade barriers among member countries. The Treaty of Rome together with the Treaty of Paris forms the Constitution of the Economic Community.[4] Between 1959 and 1979, a customs union was created. The first step was taken in 1959 when customs duties among the six countries were reduced.[5] The customs union was completed in 1968. It combined the elimination of internal barriers among the six countries with the adoption of common external trade policies toward nonmember countries. Thus, a firm from a nonmember country paid the same tariffs on exports to any member of the customs union. In 1969 at the Hague Summit, the leaders of the six countries called for an economic and monetary union and closer political ties. The European Economic Community became known as the European Community (EC), and in 1973 Denmark, Ireland, and the United Kingdom became members, raising the total to nine member countries. In 1974 the European Council was created, comprising the heads of state of each country, their foreign ministers, and key Community officials.

The European Monetary System

In 1979 a move toward an eventual monetary integration of the European Community was made through the creation of the European Monetary System (EMS), which was designed to coordinate the monetary policies of the member nations. It did two things, as follows:

1. It created the Exchange Rate Mechanism (ERM) that was designed to limit fluctuations among the EC currencies. For example, the franc could increase or decrease sharply in value against the mark. This worked to the disadvantage or advantage of the parties affected by the fluctuations of the currencies. Thus, most of the EMS members chose to participate in the ERM. They pledged to maintain fixed exchange rates among their currencies within a limit of ±2.25 percent.[6] It was the responsibility of the central banks of the member countries to keep their currencies within the range of ±2.25 percent. If German interest rates rose, then the interest rates of other countries had to rise; if German interest rates fell, the interest rates of the other countries also had to fall.[7]

2. It created the European Currency Unit (ECU). Its value was determined by a weighted "basket" of the currencies of the EC members based on the importance of their currencies in the world market. The German mark accounted for 32 percent of the value of the ECU, the French franc accounted for 20.4 percent, and the British pound accounted for 11 percent.[8] The ECU was a unit of account. It was important in international financial circles and had a value. It was used as a denomination for Eurobonds, traveler's checks, bank deposits, and loans. It also constituted bank reserves and could be moved from one bank to another. In 1992, the Maastricht Agreement created the ECU as a real currency designed eventually to replace the marks, francs, pounds, and pesos used by member nations. Eventually it became the euro.

Prelude to Maastricht

The period from 1979 to 1993 witnessed the expansion of the European Community beyond its original concept of a common market, where trade barriers would be lowered, toward a political and economic union. Greece was admitted to the EC in 1981 and Spain and Portugal were admitted in 1986. During this period, the European Commission, one of the governing bodies of the European Community, issued the White Paper on Completing the Internal Market. Its objective was to remove all trade barriers among member countries, and to promote the free movement of people, services, goods, and capital among countries. The Single European Act, confirming these objectives, was ratified in 1986 and set the goal for the creation of a single European market by December 31, 1992. Various trade barriers were removed, most passport controls were eliminated, and technical standards, which varied from country to country, were made uniform.

The Maastricht Treaty, 1991

In December 1991 leaders of the twelve EC member countries met in Maastricht, the Netherlands, to discuss the future of the EC. An agreement was worked out that would change the future of Europe. It was agreed that a common currency was required to cement a closer economic union similar to that of the United States. The advantage of a single currency would be the elimination of the exchange rate problems when the different currencies were exchanged for each other. This would benefit banking, business, and tourism. This new currency would go into effect on January 1, 1999. The treaty also laid down the framework of a future European government, with a common foreign and defense policy, a common parliament, and a common citizenship with the right to live, work, vote, and run for office anywhere within the EC. The treaty was ratified and became effective on November 1, 1993.

European Monetary Union (EMU)

The European Monetary Union is one part of the European Union. There are two major parts to the EMU which are as follows:

1. A new central bank called the European Central Bank (ECB) has replaced the central banks of the twenty-five member countries and is based in Frankfurt, Germany. It has replaced the former German central bank (Deutsche Bundesbank), which to a large extent dictated monetary policies, not only for Germany but for Western Europe. The central banks of the EU member nations have lost their former autonomy and have come under the jurisdiction of the ECB. It is very similar to the U.S. monetary system in that the Federal Reserve is based in Washington and there are twelve Federal Reserve Banks located in major economic areas throughout the United States. The ECB coordinates monetary policy for the member nations.
2. On January 1, 1999, the euro became the official currency unit for eleven members of the European Union, thus providing the world with three major currencies—the dollar, the euro, and the yen. The old currencies of these countries are no longer traded in international exchange markets around the world. European stocks and bonds are quoted in euros, and the euro is increasingly used for bank transactions, business deals, and public finances. The United Kingdom, Denmark, and Sweden opted out of accepting the euro because of public anxiety that dropping their national currencies would mean giving up too much independence. Greece did not meet the eligibility requirements.

The basic rationale for the euro was that it would eliminate the problem of currency conversion when transactions had to be made in different currencies. Tourists visiting Europe would have to exchange dollars for pounds when they were in England, pounds into marks if they visited Germany, and marks into lira if they visited Italy. These and other European currencies would fluctuate against each other daily. There was a cost in converting from one currency to another, and also a transaction risk. Contractual relationships between buyer and seller usually involve payment at some time in the future. An exporter in Germany would contract with an importer in France for payment in ninety days. By the time of payment, if the franc fell in value against the mark, the French importer would lose; if the mark fell in value against the franc, the German exporter would lose. By using the same currency unit, the euro, neither would lose.

After an auspicious start, the fate of the European Union, as well as the euro, remains a point of contestation. Supporters of the euro contend that a single currency will save Europeans $25 to $30 billion annually by eliminating exchange rate risks and the costs of exchanging different currencies. With the euro, foreign investors will have easier access to investment opportunities across a broad territory. And those investments will be priced in a single currency that is expected to be more stable than a number of different currencies. It represents the culmination of an effort that began after the end of World War II to promote peace by uniting the European economies. Finally, there are those analysts who predict that the euro will present the first serious challenge to the dollar since the dollar dethroned the British pound as the world's leading currency. There are also critics of the euro who contend that it will not solve Europe's problems, which have a high unemployment rate and numerous rules and regulations that tend to stultify entrepreneurship. There is concern over the economic soundness of the European Union, as evidenced by the outcomes of the 2005 referenda in France and the Netherlands and the 2005 election of the German premier.

The Maastricht Treaty set up several financial criteria for membership into the European Union, as follows:

1. Budget deficits had to be below 3 percent of GDP.
2. The public ratio of debt to GDP had to be below 60 percent.
3. The inflation rate had to be no higher than 1.5 percentage points above the average of the three lowest-inflation countries in the union.
4. Long-term interest rates, as a measure of inflationary expectations, could not exceed by more than 2 percentage points those of the three best performing countries.
5. Candidates could not experience devaluation in their currencies for at least two years.

Austria, Finland, and Sweden were admitted as members to the EU in 1995, bringing the total to fifteen members. (The remaining 10 members were admitted by 2004). Norway was also accepted, but Norwegian voters voted against membership on two separate occasions. In 1997 the Treaty of Amsterdam was concluded. The treaty pledged that EU members would promote higher levels of employment, increase gender equality, achieve greater environmental protection, and strengthen consumer and social policies. Other measures included creating freer movement of persons in the EU and more effective ways of combating international crime.

Political Union

The political system of the European Union will become very much like that of the United States. It consists of the Council of the European Union, the European Commission, the European Parliament, and the European Court of Justice. The functions of each component of the EU political system are as follows:

1. The European Council of Ministers: The European Council of Ministers is based in Brussels and consists of fifteen members who are selected by their home governments for a term of five years. Normally, a country's foreign minister represents his or her own country. The council presidency rotates among the members every six months. The council is the premier decision-making body of the EU but, unlike the United States where each state regardless of size has two senators, decision making in the EU is weighted toward those countries with the largest economies. In council decisions, France, Germany, Italy, and the United Kingdom have twenty nine votes each, while Malta, the country with the smallest economy, has three votes. Approval on proposals requires a unanimous or qualified vote, depending on the importance of the proposal.

2. The European Commission: Based in Brussels, the European Commission consists of twenty members selected to serve for five years. The larger countries get two members; the smaller countries get one. It has several major functions, which are as follows:
   a) It proposes legislation to be considered by the Council.
   b) It implements all EU treaties, including the Treaty of Rome.
   c) It has extensive legislative powers in implementing various internal agreements, such as the completion of the Common Agricultural Policy (CAP).

3. The European Parliament: The European Parliament is based in Strasbourg, France, and has 732 members[9] who are directly elected by their respective countries, based on population size. Germany, the largest country, has 99 members, while the United Kingdom, France, and Italy have 78 each.[10] Members are elected for five-year terms. It is a consultative rather than a legislative body. It debates legislation proposed by the Commission and forwarded to it by the council. It can propose amendments to that legislation, but they are not binding on the Commission or the council.

4. The European Court of Justice: The European Court of Justice is based in Luxembourg and comprises one judge from each country. Like the Supreme Court of the United States, the Court of Justice is the supreme appeals court for EU law. It is also somewhat similar to the Supreme Court in that member nations' courts as well as our states' courts can refer their cases to it.

5. National Governments: The legislatures of each of the twenty-five member nations implement approved proposals as their laws. They will collect taxes and commit revenues for state functions such as education and road building. The value-added tax, which is a tax levied on the value created at each stage of the production process, is the single most important tax used by the European countries.

The Treaty of Rome

The 1957 Treaty of Rome provides the legal base for the European Union. Its purpose is similar to that of the antitrust laws of the United States; namely, to provide rules of competition. The Commission enforces the Treaty. Its two major provisions are Article 85 and Article 86. Article 85 prohibits agreements, contracts, cartels, and joint activities that intend to restrict or distort competition within the EU. Price-fixing, division of markets, tying arrangements, and price discrimination are all prohibited under Article 85. It does recognize the fact that some contracts benefit consumers by improving the production or distribution of goods or by promoting product improvement. Article 86 bars one or more companies from using a dominant market position to restrict or distort trade. Prohibited abuses of dominant positions would include price-fixing and price discrimination. Either buyers or sellers can have dominant market positions. The Commission and the European Court of Justice have defined market dominance as the power to control suppliers and customers and the ability to prevent competition. Most of the fifteen countries are civil law countries, using either the Napoleonic Code (France, Spain, Portugal) or the Germanic Code (Germany, Austria). These laws will remain intact.

The Importance of the European Union to the United States

The European Union is a major foreign trade rival for the United States. It forms the world's largest trading bloc, accounting for 30 percent of the value of world foreign trade. Table 13.2 provides a comparison of the monetary value of foreign trade to the European Union and its most important rival, NAFTA. The European Union is an important outlet for American goods and services, and an important supplier of the same to the United States. In terms of foreign investment, 43 percent of U.S. foreign direct investment is in the

Table 13.2   U.S. Exports to and Imports from the European Union and NAFTA, 2000–2003 (Millions of Dollars)

Partner	Exports to the EU (millions)				Imports from the EU (millions)			
European Union	2000	2001	2002	2003	2000	2001	2002	2003
Austria	2,554	2,626	2,424	1,793	3,233	3,990	3,817	4,489
Belgium	13,960	13,524	13,343	15,218	9,931	10,129	9,835	10,141
Denmark	1,513	1,611	1,496	1,548	2,974	3,400	3,236	3,718
Finland	1,571	1,554	1,537	1,714	3,250	3,394	3,444	3,598
France	20,253	19,896	19,019	17,068	29,782	30,296	28,408	29,221
Germany	29,244	30,114	26,628	28,848	58,737	59,151	62,480	68,047
Greece	1,218	1,296	1,153	1,191	592	506	546	616
Ireland	7,727	7,150	6,749	7,699	16,410	18,539	22,388	25,841
Italy	11,000	9,916	10,089	10,570	25,050	23,824	24,290	25,437
Luxembourg	398	550	480	279	332	306	299	265
Netherlands	21,974	19,525	18,334	20,703	9,704	9,500	9,864	10,972
Portugal	957	1,258	863	863	1,579	1,556	1,673	1,967
Spain	6,323	5,811	5,226	5,935	5,731	5,192	5,678	6,708
Sweden	4,557	3,548	3,154	3,225	9,603	8,851	9,287	11,125
United Kingdom	41,579	40,798	33,253	33,895	43,459	41,397	40,870	42,667
TOTALS	164,825	159,175	143,747	150,549	220,366	220,031	226,115	244,811
NAFTA								
Canada	176,430	163,724	160,799	169,481	229,209	216,969	210,590	224,166
Mexico	111,721	101,509	97,531	97,457	135,911	131,433	134,732	138,073
TOTALS	288,151	265,233	258,330	266,938	365,120	348,402	345,322	362,239

Source: Industry, Trade, and the Economy: Data and Analysis. (2005) International Trade Administration. www.ita.doc.gov/td/industry/otea/ustrade.html

European Union countries, and over half of foreign direct investment in the United States comes from the European countries.

The United States, and for that matter Canada and Mexico, is bound to Europe by culture and history. The great majority of immigrants who came to this country during the latter part of the nineteenth century and the early part of the twentieth century came from Europe, and ties still remain. The Protestant and Catholic religions were exported from Europe to the United States. Democratic institutions exist in Europe and in the United States. Living standards in the United States and Europe are comparable, so there is a mass market for consumer goods that has promoted increased investment in Europe by U.S. business firms, and conversely by European business firms in the United States. As the European Union expands to take in more countries, its importance to the United States will increase.

THE NORTH AMERICAN FREE TRADE AGREEMENT (NAFTA)

The North American Free Trade Agreement (NAFTA) is neither an economic union nor a political union as is the European Union. It has no common monetary unit, nor does it involve the complete economic and political integration of the three countries involved—the United States, Canada, and Mexico. It is simply a free trade area where the three countries have agreed to remove trade and other barriers to international trade among themselves. NAFTA was an extension of the Canada–U.S. Free Trade Agreement, which was signed in 1988 and entered into force in 1989. NAFTA was negotiated among the United States, Canada, and Mexico in 1992, ratified in 1993, and entered into force on January 1, 1994. It is an area that accounts for over one-third of the world's GNI and 20 percent of world trade.

NAFTA is quite controversial in the United States. It passed in Congress by a fairly small margin after weeks of acrimonious debate. It was an issue in the presidential campaign of 1992 when Ross Perot gained much political capital by saying that the gigantic sucking sound you hear is the loss of American jobs to Mexico. It was also felt that America had little to gain by admitting Mexico into NAFTA. It was argued that Mexico had a standard of living much lower than the U.S. or Canada. Supporters of Mexico's admission to NAFTA argued that it would create jobs that were higher paying than those that were lost to Mexico. Tariffs would be lower and more manufactured goods would be sold to Mexico. Supporters also argued that American consumers would benefit from the import of lower-cost fruits and vegetables from Mexico.[11]

Tables 13.3, 13.4, and 13.5 present comparisons of NAFTA to the EU. Table 13.3 presents the population, real per capita GNI, and real GNI for the NAFTA countries compared to the EU. Table 13.4 presents U.S. direct investment in Canada and Mexico, and Canadian and Mexican direct investment in the United States for 2003. U.S. direct investment in the EU countries is much larger than it is in Canada and Mexico, and EU direct investment in the United States is much larger than Canadian and Mexican direct investment in the United States. Table 13.5 presents the foreign trade of the NAFTA countries for 2003. Canada is the most important U.S. trading partner, and U.S.–Canadian trade exceeds the entire amount of U.S.–EU trade. Mexico is the

Table 13.3   Population, Per Capita GNI, and GNI for NAFTA, 2004

Country	Population (millions)	Per Capita Gross National Income (GNI) (dollars)	GNI (millions of dollars)
United States	291.0	37,610	10,945.8
Canada	31.6	23,930	756.8
Mexico	102.3	6,230	637.2
Totals	424.9	22,590	12,339.8
World	**6,271.7**	**5,500**	**34,391.5**

Source: The World Bank, *2004 World Bank Atlas*. Washington, D.C.: The World Bank, 2004, pp. 54–55.

Table 13.4 U.S. Direct Investment in Canada and Mexico, and Canadian and Mexican Direct Investment in the United States, 2003 (Millions of Dollars)

U.S. Direct Investment		Direct Investment of Canada and Mexico in U.S.	
Canada	15,024	Canada	12,198
Mexico	4,666	Mexico	2,045
	19,690		**14,243**
European Union	64,023	European Union	22,108

Source: U.S. Department of Commerce, Bureau of Economic Analysis, "U.S. Direct Investment Abroad and Foreign Direct Investment in the U.S.," (2003) www.bea.doc.gov/bea/di/home/directinv.htm

Table 13.5 U.S. Trade with Canada and Mexico, 2003 (Millions of Dollars)

	Exports	Imports	Total
Canada	169,480	224,166	393,646
Mexico	97,457	138,073	235,530
World	723,743	1,259,395	629,176

Source: Industry, Trade, and the Economy: Data and Analysis. (2005) International Trade Administration. www.ita.doc.gov/td/industry/otea/ustrade.html

third most important U.S. trading partner. Furthermore, trade among the NAFTA countries is increasing at a more rapid rate than U.S. trade with the EU.

Provisions of NAFTA

There are several provisions to NAFTA, ranging from the elimination of tariffs and other barriers to the free flow of goods and services among the three countries, to cooperation on environmental problems. These provisions are presented as follows:

Market Access

1. Within fifteen years after its implementation in 1994, all tariffs will be eliminated on North American products traded among Canada, Mexico, and the United States.
2. Within five years after its implementation, 65 percent of all U.S. exports of industrial goods to Mexico would enter tariff-free.
3. Mexico, once the treaty was implemented, would immediately eliminate tariffs on nearly 50 percent of all industrial goods imported from the United States.
4. Government procurement was to be opened up over ten years, with firms of the three countries able to bid on government contracts.[12]

5. Tariffs were to be removed on car imports over a period of ten years. Mexico's import quota on cars were also to be lifted during the same period.

6. Most tariffs between the United States and Mexico on agricultural products were eliminated immediately after implementation of the agreement in 1994.

Investment

1. NAFTA gives U.S. companies the right to establish firms in Mexico and Canada or acquire existing firms.

2. Investors have the right to repatriate profits and capital; the right to fair compensation in the event of expropriation;[13] and the right to international arbitration in disputes between investors and government that involve monetary damage.

3. NAFTA broadens investments to cover such areas as banking, real estate, legal services, consulting, publishing, and tourism.

4. Certain types of investments are restricted. Mexico prohibits foreign investment in petroleum and railroads;[14] Canada prohibits investment in its cultural media; and the United States excludes investments in aviation transport, maritime, and telecommunication.

Intellectual Property Rights

1. NAFTA requires each country to provide for the enforcement of the rights of authors, artists, and inventors against infringement and piracy.

2. It ensures protection for North American producers of computer programs, sound recordings, motion pictures, encrypted satellite signals, and other creations.

3. It locks in the availability of patent protection for most technologies in Mexico, allowing U.S. firms to patent a broad range of inventions in Mexico.

Protection for U.S. Workers

1. NAFTA provides a transition period of up to fifteen years for the elimination of U.S. tariffs on the most labor-sensitive U.S. products, such as household glassware, footwear, and some fruits and vegetables.

2. It provides safeguards that permit a temporary hike in U.S. tariff rates to pre-NAFTA levels to protect U.S. workers and farmers from being injured or threatened with injury by increased imports from Mexico.

3. It provides tough rules of origin to guarantee that the benefits of NAFTA tariff reductions go only to products made in North America.

4. It holds the three countries liable for penalties for nonenforcement of child labor, minimum wage, and health and safety laws.

Other Treaty Provisions

1. Any country can leave the treaty with six months' notice.
2. It allows for the inclusion of any additional country. Chile was to be invited to join in 1996, but there was little support for its membership.[15]

Environment

Environmentalist groups in the United States were opposed to NAFTA on the grounds that the Mexican government had done very little about controlling environmental problems. Major cities such as Mexico City, Guadalajara, and Monterrey had serious air pollution problems.[16] However, the main cause of environmental concern was the U.S.–Mexico border where maquiladora plants were operating from Matamoros to Tijuana.[17] These plants import unfinished goods or component parts from the United States, further process these goods or parts, and re-export them to the United States. The goods produced by maquiladoras enjoy preferential customs and tax treatments by both countries' governments. The plants by themselves create pollution, but they attract thousands of workers to such border cities as Matamoros, Juarez, and Tijuana, creating air and water pollution. To address this concern, the U.S. and Mexican governments created the Border Environmental Plan that covers air, water, hazardous materials, and ground pollution. Its objectives are as follows:

1. To strengthen existing environmental laws
2. To build waste water treatment systems
3. To create joint air pollution monitoring programs
4. To increase cooperative planning, training, and education

Results of NAFTA

The early years of NAFTA were affected by the Mexican currency crisis of December 1994. Mexico's trade deficit increased in 1993 and 1994 to the point that it was losing its foreign financial reserves. In December 1994, at a time when foreign exchange reserves held by the government had dropped from $26 billion to $7 billion, the peso, which had been tied to the dollar at an exchange rate of approximately 3.4 pesos to the dollar, was devalued by about 35 percent against the dollar. To shore up confidence in the Mexican financial system, the Clinton administration provided a $40 billion assistance package to guarantee the sale of Mexican government dollar-denominated

Treasury bonds to foreign investors. The devaluation of the Mexican peso increased Mexican exports to the United States and Canada because they were cheaper than before. U.S. and Canadian exports to Mexico declined because they became more expensive.[18]

In general, criticisms of NAFTA have become rather subdued in the United States. Over the ten-year period, U.S. exports to Mexico were up by 48 percent in 2003 conversely, Mexican exports to the United States increased by 64 percent over the same period. U.S. exports to Canada were up 32.5 percent and U.S. imports from Canada increased by 42 percent. Some U.S. jobs were lost to Mexico, but jobs were also created as a result of an increase in exports to Mexico and Canada. Typically, the jobs created by increased trade with Mexico are in the higher paying, higher value-added industries, such as communications, and the jobs lost to Mexico have been in the lower-paying, lower value-added industries.

THE SOUTH AMERICAN COMMUNITY
OF NATIONS (CSN)

On December 8, 2004, the Cuzsco Declaration was signed by twelve South American countries: Argentina, Bolivia, Brazil, Chile, Colombia, Ecuador, Guyana, Paraguay, Peru, Suriname, Uruguay, and Venezuela. This market combines two formerly separate trading blocs in South America—MERCOSUR and the Andean Community—and incorporates three formerly independent states, leaving only one South American state, French Guyana, outside of the bloc. Complete integration between the formerly separate trading blocs is expected to be accomplished by the year 2007.

Reasons for CSN

The performance of the Latin American countries, particularly when compared to the East Asian countries, was poor during the 1980s.[19] Inflation was high, economic growth rates were low, and currency instability was common. Argentina had a negative growth rate during the 1980s. Its currency problems were so bad that the peso was replaced by a new currency called the astral. Brazil had borrowed heavily in the world capital markets, pledging future revenue from coffee as debt repayment, but the world price of coffee fell during the 1980s. Uruguay had its internal problems with urban terrorists, called the Tupumaros, who made a practice of kidnapping American businessmen. Paraguay was ruled by a military dictatorship and had one of the lowest living standards in South America.

Purpose of CSN

The objectives of CSN go beyond the automatic tariff reductions of MERCO-SUR and the Andean Community. The Treaty of Ascuncion, which established MERCOSUR, agreed to give their firms preferential access to each other's markets and to cut internal tariffs over the period 1991–1995 on goods that accounted for 95 percent of intracountry trade. The formal customs union began on January 1, 1995. In that year, a common external tariff was introduced that would be phased in over a six-year period. At the same time, the four countries would have achieved the transition to a common market governed by the Common Market Council (CMC) and the Common Market Group (CMG). The goals of CSN are to model itself after the EU, with a common parliament, currency, and elimination of passport restrictions between member countries.

CAFTA

On June 30, 2005, the United States Senate approved CAFTA, culminating years of negotiations toward the agreement.[20] This market combines Costa Rica, the Dominican Republic, El Salvador, Guatemala, Honduras, and Nicaragua. The purpose of CAFTA is to develop a free trade zone, and it is viewed as progress toward the establishment of the Free Trade Area of the Americas. CAFTA remains to be ratified by the remaining countries. The agreement would phase out tariffs between participating countries over the course of the next decade. Proponents suggest that CAFTA will:

- Expand economic opportunities for U.S. manufacturers, workers, and farmers.
- Level the playing field for U.S. businesses selling in Central America.
- Advance the U.S. trade agenda; and
- Support democracy, economic reform, and regional integration.[21]

While the majority of trade from Central America is already duty-free, CAFTA will likely benefit Central America most in the areas of investment and intraregional trade.

CRITICISM OF REGIONAL TRADING BLOCS

Regional trading blocs have proliferated like dandelions. In addition to the EU, NAFTA, CAFTA, and MERCOSUR, there are others, including the following:

1. The Central European Free Trade Area (CEFTA): CEFTA consists of the countries of the Czech Republic, Hungary, Poland, Slovak Republic, and Slovenia, Romania, and Bulgaria, with a combined population of 187 million. With the exception of Slovenia, the other countries were formerly a part of the Council for Mutual Economic Assistance (CMEA), dominated by the former Soviet Union.[22] Free trade was liberalized as of January 1, 2000, except for the export of cars to Poland, which was liberalized one year later.
2. Southern Africa Development Community (SADC): SADC consists of fourteen southern African countries, including South Africa, with a population of 223.3 million. Its objective is to eliminate tariff barriers in the region.
3. Common Market for Eastern and Southern Africa (COMESA): COMESA consists of twenty countries in Eastern and Southern Africa, with a population of 413.2 million. It began as a preferential trade area in 1981. It created a common market in 2000 and hopes to eventually create an economic union.
4. Australia-New Zealand Closer Economic Relations (ANZCERTA): ANZCERTA includes two countries with a combined population of 24.5 million and a GDP of $601 billion. Its purpose is to eliminate tariff and nontariff barriers, including subsidies and government procurement policies on all trade between the two countries.
5. Asian Pacific Economic Cooperation (APEC), the largest trade area in the world, is composed of the countries of Australia, Brunei, Canada, Chile, China, Hong Kong, Indonesia, Japan, Malaysia, Mexico, New Zealand, Papua New Guinea, Peru, the Philippines, Russia, Singapore, South Korea, Taipei, Thailand, the United States, and Vietnam.

Regional trading blocs are criticized on the basis of their exclusivity. It is probably good for those countries that belong because it combines their interests toward achieving a common goal. However, by liberalizing trade only with their neighbors, countries are, by definition, discriminating against those not lucky enough to be asked to join the bloc. Some goods will be imported from other members of the free-trade area at the expense of producers elsewhere, and members will begin to specialize in areas in which they lack comparative advantage. Slow progress has also bedeviled regional trade integration. Despite much talk about expanding NAFTA to include every country in North America and South America by early in the twenty-first century, the membership in NAFTA remains stuck at three and will stay there for the foreseeable future. NAFTA also has complicated rules of origin requirements by stipulating how much of a car needs to be made in Mexico to qualify as NAFTA admissible.[23]

There are also arguments for regional trading blocs. The first argument is economic. Regions can achieve additional gains from the free flow of trade and investment among the member countries beyond those normally attainable through trade. They can specialize in the production of goods and services that they can produce most efficiently. Foreign direct investment can stimulate economic growth. In the case of NAFTA, investments in the three countries have increased since its inception in 1994. In that year U.S. direct investment in Canada was $6 billion; in 2004 it was $22.4 billion, a gain of 270 percent, while U.S. direct investment in Mexico increased from $4.5 billion in 1994 to $7.4 billion in 2004, a gain of 66 percent.[24] Conversely, Canadian investment in the United States increased from $4.6 billion in 1994 to $31.8 billion in 2004, a gain of close to 600 percent. Mexican direct investment in the United States has varied widely over the period, beginning at $1.1 billion in 1994 to $5.0 billion in 2000; however, the figure has also been negative for many years during that time.[25]

The second argument for regional trading blocs is political. A main argument for the creation of the European Union is that old enemies would be brought together as trading partners. Within a period of seventy years, France and Germany fought three major wars on French soil, with Germany as the invader. Italy and Austria have also been enemies and have gone to war over territorial claims. Political relationships between the United States and Mexico have been anything but smooth, and CSN brings together two old enemies, Argentina and Paraguay. Thus, by linking neighboring economies and making them more dependent on each other, incentives are created for political cooperation between the countries. In turn, the potential for violence between the countries is reduced.

SUMMARY

The world is rapidly merging into regional trading blocs. The most important one is the European Union, which is more than a trading bloc. Its goal is to achieve the complete economic and political integration of Western Europe. There is a common monetary currency called the euro. Along with the dollar and the yen, it has become a major world currency. The European Union rivals the United States and Japan as a world economic and political superpower. It has achieved the free movement of goods, services, and factors of production among the member countries. There is one central bank, based in Frankfurt, Germany, which coordinates monetary policy. However, the EU Constitution is in limbo, with the recent "no" votes in Belgium and France.

The other regional trading blocs are not nearly as ambitious in their scope. NAFTA involves the regional integration of Canada, Mexico, and the United States into a free trade area. There is no common currency, no common political system, and no common central bank. NAFTA aims at the elimination of tariffs among its members, and the removal of most of the barriers on the cross-border flow of services. CSN is a customs union created from MERCO-SUR and the Andean community. CAFTA is the most recent creation. There are also a number of other regional trading blocs throughout the world.

QUESTIONS FOR DISCUSSION

1. Discuss the differences between NAFTA and the European Union.
2. Discuss the economic and political organization of the European Union.
3. What is the European Monetary Union? What is the euro and why was it created?
4. In what ways is the European Union of importance to the United States?
5. In terms of foreign trade, is the European Union or NAFTA more important to the United States?
6. In terms of foreign direct investment (FDI), is the European Union more important to the United States?
7. Has NAFTA been a success or a failure? Discuss.
8. What are the major provisions of NAFTA?
9. How does CSN differ from NAFTA?
10. Are regional trading blocs good or bad? Discuss.

RECOMMENDED READING

Bureau of Economic Analysis. International Economic Accounts (2005). www.bea.doc
    .gov/bea/di/home/directinv.htm
Europa: Gateway to the European Union On-line. http://europa.eu.int/index_en.htm
Eurostat Yearbook 2004: The Statistical Guide to Europe. Luxembourg: Office for Official
    Publications of the European Communities. 2004.
International Trade Association. Trade Stats Express. http://tse.export.gov/
Nothing's Free in this World: Central America (CAFTA's impact on Central America).
    The Economist. August 4, 2005.

NOTES

1. In May 2004, 10 new Member States joined the original 15 member states of the EU. They included: Cyprus, the Czech Republic, Estonia, Hungary, Latvia, Lithuania, Malta, Poland, Slovakia and Slovenia.

2. Many nonmember nations have preferential tariff agreements with member nations.

3. At that time, Germany became two independent nations: the Federal Republic of Germany (West Germany) and the German Democratic Republic (East Germany). After

the end of World War II, Germany was split into four occupation zones controlled by the British, Americans, French, and Russians. The western part controlled by the British, Americans, and French became West Germany, a capitalist nation, and the Russian part became East Germany, a communist nation.

4. They also form the constitutional foundation of the European Union.

5. This was the first step toward the creation of a common external tariff.

6. In September 1992, the United Kingdom and Italy pulled out of the ERM. In August 1993, the 2.25 fluctuation band widened to 15 percent.

7. The Deutsche Bundesbank was the most powerful bank in Western Europe and the mark was the dominant currency.

8. As new members came in the weighting system was changed, but the mark remained the most important currency.

9. www.europarl.eu.int/members/expert.do?language=en&redirection

10. Luxembourg, the smallest country, has two.

11. This has occurred.

12. Some American firms have won bids in Mexico.

13. This has been an issue in Mexico and the United States since the Mexican government nationalized American and British oil companies in 1938.

14. Prohibition of foreign ownership of petroleum goes back to the Mexican constitution of 1917. The railroads, built by the Americans in the nineteenth century, were nationalized.

15. Chile is a member of APEC and a member of CSN. It has the highest real per capita income of all the Latin American countries.

16. Mexico City is regarded as one of the most polluted cities in the world. The city has expanded its population from 3.2 million in 1950 to around 100 million in 2003. Air pollution is a serious problem.

17. Matamoros is at the entrance of the Rio Grande into the Gulf of Mexico, while Tijuana is across the border from San Diego. The distance between the two cities is about 2,000 miles.

18. American and Canadian firms operating in Mexico lost money because they had to exchange cheaper pesos for more expensive dollars.

19. The growth rates of three of the four countries were negative for the decade. By contrast, the growth rate of South Korea was 8.8 percent for the decade.

20. CAFTA had been cited as a priority goal of President George W. Bush in 2002.

21. www.ita.doc.gov/cafta/why_cafta.asp

22. CMEA consisted of the Soviet Union and the Soviet-bloc countries of East Germany, Poland, Czechoslovakia, Hungary, Romania, and Bulgaria. Most foreign trade was among the members in the form of barter arrangements.

23. NAFTA specifies that, for an automobile to qualify as a North American product, 62.5 percent of its value must be produced in Canada, Mexico, or the United States.

24. www.bea.doc.gov/bea/di/home/directinv.htm. U.S. Direct investment in Canada reached a high of 22.8 billion in 1999; in Mexico it reached a high of 14 billion in 2001. The figures have fluctuated nonlinearly over the 10 year period.

25. www.bea.doc.gov/bea/di/home/directinv.htm

14

Terrorism and Security

For much of the last century, history was made by the two world super powers, the United States and the Soviet Union: the United States which represented the western ideal of democracy with emphasis placed on the free enterprise system, and the Soviet Union which represented communism and which placed emphasis on economic planning to allocate resources. It was not democratic in nature at all although it called itself the Union of Soviet Socialist Republics. It appeared for a while that a clash between the two titans of the world was inevitable because they represented two totally different systems. The Cold War, which began in 1947, continued for 44 years before it ended in 1990. At that time, unnoticed by most western observers, the Soviet Union began to implode, not through war but through its own inefficiency in the resource allocation and also in the satisfaction of requirements of its population in terms of freedom.

By 1991 the former satellites of the Soviet Union had broken away and formed their own countries. The German Democratic Republic (East Germany) was probably the most solid communist regime of them all with a strict regimen of control. The wall between the two Germanys came down, and east and west Germany were unified into one nation. Hungary, which had instituted reforms, became democratic and less controlled by state enterprises. The same happened in Czechoslovakia, with the Czech Republic and the Republic of Slovakia becoming independent entities. Poland, which had not really taken to communism, also became independent in the 1990s, and Romania and Bulgaria followed suit and a number of the former constituent soviet republics went their own way. The Ukraine, Belarus, Moldova, Latvia, Lithuania, and Estonia became separate entities and communism was over.

Once Communism collapsed, many people thought it was the beginning of a new era as the author Francis Fukuyama wrote in his book *The End of His-*

tory and the Last Man.[1] Democracy and the free market would prevail, the democratic ideal would reign supreme and the rest of the world would embrace the free market system, and everybody would be happy and history would be over. There would be no more history to be written, hence the title. There would be a WalMart in such out-of-the-way places as Ulan Bator, Mongolia, Timbuktu, Niger, and La Punta Arenas, Chile. However, a seismographic event occurred that made this thinking rather obsolete.

What Fukuyama could not have predicted was that as Communism fell, another force was arising from a far different source. History had not ended and instead a new force arose to confront the world: Terrorism. The seminal event of the new century, to reinforce this point, was the bombing of the World Trade Center and the Pentagon by terrorists who used airplanes to accomplish their ends. While terror attacks were not unknown to the rest of the world, September 11 shocked the United States and its sense of imperviousness to attack. This new force did not involve big armies as in the past but men who were willing to die for a specific cause and use any method that was feasible to achieve their goals. While terrorism is not new, the responses of the United States as a major superpower are having impacts that are felt throughout the world.

WHAT IS TERRORISM?

There is no universally agreed upon definition of terrorism. Some delineate a difference between terrorism and assassination. Some make a distinction between peacetime and wartime acts. Others would limit terrorism to civilian targets. The United Nations has attempted to come up with a common definition in order to develop a single convention on terrorism, where now there are a dozen conventions to address various aspects of terrorism. However, among the various definitions, some common points emerge:

1) an act of violence which is intended to inspire terror;
2) the focus is on a particular group or population;
3) the actual target is more symbolic than personal;
4) a political or ideological motive underlies the action.

The United States Code, Section 2656f(d), for example, provides the following definition: "The term 'terrorism' means premeditated, politically motivated *violence* perpetrated against *noncombatant targets* by subnational groups or clandestine agents, usually *intended to influence an audience*."[2] These ideas will inform our discussion of terrorism in this chapter.

A HISTORY OF TERRORISM

Some associate the beginnings of terrorism with a group called the Assassins, a religious political group founded in around 1094 AD in the area of Mesopotamia. It was composed of Shiites who were opposed to Sunni groups. It supported rulers who were sympathetic to its ends and deposed rulers through assassination who were not. Followers also used daggers to achieve their ends, hence the term assassin. They were a potent political force in the Middle East for some 300 years and the cult spread in such areas as Syria, Iran, parts of Egypt, all the way over to what is now Pakistan. They were eventually exterminated by the Mongols who were no slouches at terror themselves, except their terror was accomplished through "official" military means.

Another terrorist group was the cult of Kali, which flourished for a time in India around the early part of the nineteenth century. Kali was a deity in the Hindu pantheon of gods. She was the goddess of death and destruction, who wore a necklace of skeleton heads around her neck, a gauntlet of snakes around her waist, and had fangs for teeth. Her anointed instruments of death who worshipped her were called thugs and the method they used to exterminate their victims was called thugee, involving the use of a noose around their necks to choke them to death. For a while this was a rather powerful cult, killing an estimated 100,000 Indians annually. Eventually, the British decided to eradicate the cult and sent in an officer named Sleeman who executed many of them with a vengeance by blowing them out of the muzzles of cannons. Finally, the cult was eliminated and rarely heard of since.

In the early part of the twentieth century, terrorism was frequently associated with anarchists. Anarchism was a political ideology in which followers felt that the state was the root of all problems in any society because it acted at the behest of those who had the power—the landowners, the nobility, wealthy entrepreneurs—whom they contended controlled everything and thwarted any attempt of the majority to improve their position. Anarchists or individuals acting alone have had an enormous impact on the history of the world. For example in March 1891, an anarchist group called the "Narodnaya Volya" or "The People's Will" assassinated Czar Alexander the Second of Russia who had been carrying out a number of economic and social reforms in the country. For one thing he had freed the serfs and was trying to better the life of the average person by giving people more access to the duma. With his death the throne passed to a weaker member of the Romanov dynasty who was eventually responsible for getting Russia into World War I. And when the Bolsheviks overthrew the government, Czar Nicholas was assassinated along with all the members of his family. He simply was too weak to govern. Then another example of an anarchist act with far-reaching consequences was the assassination of the Archduke Ferdinand in Sarajevo in 1914 by Gavril Princep. This act precipitated World War I which changed the map of Europe and also which eventually led to the Second World War.[3] In the United States, President William McKinley was assassinated on September 5, 1901, by a self-professed anarchist. The purpose of these anarchists was to eliminate representatives of states in order to destroy the state.

DOMESTIC TERRORISM

The United States has its own history of terrorism. A particular type of terrorism became associated with the radical organized labor group, the Industrial Workers of the World. The IWW was a radical union that was formed in the northwestern part of the United States in the logging industries of Washington and Oregon and Idaho. It spread to the coal miners, loggers, and farm workers of the west. It did not touch craft workers who thought they were better than the mostly immigrant workers who worked with their hands in coal mines and logging. The IWW did a lot of damage. It was held responsible for the bombing of the Los Angeles Times newspaper building, and for blowing up bridges and other targets that were regarded as the tools of the capitalists. When World War I broke out, then public sentiment was turned against the IWW. When the Bolsheviks destroyed the monarchy in Russia and declared the Communist state, this greatly alarmed many people in the United States and Woodrow Wilson had his attorney general Abraham Lincoln Palmer root out the IWW, who were held to be Communists. Thousands of them were thrown in jail without due process, without bail, without trial. This campaign proved effective in eliminating the IWW.

Another form of terrorism was that of the Ku Klux Klan and other white racist groups. The KKK was first formed in Indiana and eventually spread throughout the south. It was responsible for the lynchings of many thousands of blacks in the United States, particularly in the south and also in areas of the Midwest.[4] Another case of terrorism against blacks occurred in the little town of Rosewood, Florida, south of Gainesville. In 1923 Rosewood was a town primarily inhabited by blacks with several hundred people; it had shops and its people were rather prosperous. A disgruntled white citizen claimed that a shopkeeper had raped a white girl and also other whites claimed that they had been defrauded. The whites resented the prosperity of the blacks, so a mob invaded Rosewood. There was an armed battle followed by killings and lynchings, and eventually the town was destroyed by fire. An investigation was held, but nothing came of it. Sixty years after the fact, the state of Florida apologized and there is a marker today on the highway, showing where Rosewood once was.[5] Lynchings and organized attacks against blacks continued up until the Civil Rights era—in 1963 the 16th Street Baptist Church in Birmingham was bombed, killing four young girls. Well into the late twentieth century, racially motivated church burnings occurred; such events are now classified as hate crimes.

Other random acts of terrorism have occurred in the United States in the late twentieth century. The Simbionese Liberation Army was comprised of educated young people who wanted to liberate the masses from capitalism. They are remembered for the kidnapping of the heiress Patty Hearst, who later joined that particular group. In 1996, bombs exploded during the Atlanta Olympics; white supremacist Eric Robert Rudolph pleaded guilty to the bombings in 2005, along with that of a Birmingham abortion clinic and an Atlanta nightclub. But perhaps the most deadly act of domestic terrorism was the bombing of the Alfred P. Murrah Building in Oklahoma City in April 1995. Timothy McVeigh, a member of a white separatist militia, was convicted and sentenced to death. Terry Nichols has been convicted and imprisoned. The attack killed 168 people, including nineteen children from a daycare center located in the building.

INTERNATIONAL TERRORISM

The late twentieth century witnessed a number of international terrorist attacks which resulted in very high casualties. For example, in 1983 a terrorist attack in Lebanon on the U.S. marine barracks killed 241 marines. In 1998, an attack on the U.S. embassies in Nairobi, Kenya and in Dar es Salaam, Tanzania killed 224 people. In 2002, public trains were bombed in Madrid, Spain, killing 191 people. In that case the terrorists accomplished their goal; the Spanish presidential elections were decidedly swayed, bringing in a new leader who withdrew Spanish troops from the forces in Iraq. Major terrorist attacks of the last twenty years are presented in table 14.1.

The troubling fact about many of these attacks is, of course, civilian casualties. Few attacks were as heart wrenching as the 2004 seizure of a school in Beslan, Russia by Chechen rebels, armed with explosives. The attack was initially a hostage taking, with rebels holding children and teachers. However, after a period of negotiations, the situation turned violent, resulting in the killing of 331 people, at least half of whom were school children.[6] In this case, civilian targets were symbolic, seen as retribution for an earlier hostage taking in Moscow in 2002, in which all of the Chechen rebels were killed.

A great deal of public attention in the United States has been focused on Islamist terrorism; however, terrorist organizations around the world are many and diverse. Table 14.2 presents a sampling of terrorist organizations identified by the U.S. State Department. Organizations are located in Japan, Spain, Ireland, Columbia, Venezuela, Peru, Uganda, Rwanda, and Somalia, to name but a few areas. The Al Q'aida network is distinct in being more geographically disseminated. The State Department report, *Patterns of*

Table 14.1 Major Terrorist Attacks: 1980–2005

Date	Location	Number Killed	Responsible Party
October 23, 1983	Beirut Lebanon—U.S. and French military barracks	231 U.S. Marines and 58 French paratroopers	Shiite suicide bombers
December 21, 1988	Lockerbie, Scotland— Explosion of Pan-Am Boeing 747	259 passengers and 11 on the ground	Libyan suicide bombers
April 19, 1995	Oklahoma City, OK— Explosion of the Afred P. Murrah Federal Building	168 people	U.S. militia members
August 7, 1998	Nairobi, Kenya and Dar es Salaam, Tanzania— Bombings of U.S. Embassies	224 people	Al Q'aida
September 11, 2001	U.S. World Trade Center, U.S. Pentagon, and Shanksville, PA bombings	2,992 people	Al Q'aida
October 12, 2002	Bali, Indonesia	202 people	Jemaah Islamiah
March 11, 2004	Madrid, Spain train bombings	191 people	Al Q'aida
July 7, 2005	London subway bombings	56 people	Al Q'aida affiliated domestic cell
July 23, 2005	Sharm al Sheikh, Egypt resort bombings	88 people	Al Q'aida
October 29, 2005	New Delhi, India marketplace bombings	61 people	Kashmir separatists

Global Terrorism, produced annually, provides information on "Designated Foreign Terrorist Organizations" and "Other Terrorist Groups."

GLOBAL TERRORISM: INCIDENTS AND TRENDS

Many have suggested that since September 11, we have entered a new era of global terrorism, and that the world order has changed. However, this is a broad generalization. Terrorism, as discussed, has taken many forms over the years. The U.S. State Department, in compliance with *Title 22 of the United States Code, Section 2656f(a)*, has been tracking and producing an annual report on international terrorism for almost thirty years. This report, *Patterns*

Table 14.2   Selected Foreign Terrorist Organizations

Organization	Strength	Location
Aum Supreme Truth (Aum)	1,500–2,000	Japan
Basque Fatherland and Liberty (ETA)	200	Spain
Communist Party of Philippines/New People's Army (CPP/NPA)	10,000	Philippines
Al-Gama'a al-Islamiyya (Islamic Group, IG)	1000	Egypt
HAMAS	Tens of thousands	Israel
Hizballah (Party of God)	2000	Lebanon
Jemaah Islamiya (JI)	5000	Indonesia, Malaysia, Singapore, the Philippines, Thailand
Liberation Tigers of Tamil Eelam (LTTE)	8,000–10,000	Sri Lanka
National Liberation Description Army (ELN)—Colombia	3000–5000	Columbia, Venezuela
Al-Qaida	Several thousand*	international
Real IRA (RIRA)	100–200	Northern Ireland
Revolutionary Armed Forces of Colombia (FARC)	9,000–12,000	Colombia, Venezuela, Panama, and Ecuador.
Sendero Luminoso (Shining Path, or SL)	400–500	Peru
United Self-Defense Forces/Group of Colombia (AUC–Autodefensas Unidas de Colombia)	6,000–8,150	Columbia
Lord's Resistance Army (LRA)	1000	Uganda and Sudan
Tupac Amaru Revolutionary Movement (MRTA)	100	Peru

*Al-Qaida probably has several thousand members and associates. (It) also serves as a focal point or umbrella organization for a worldwide network that includes many Sunni Islamic extremist groups, some members of al-Gama'a al-Islamiyya, the Islamic Movement of Uzbekistan, and the Harakat ul-Mujahidin.
    Source: Patterns of Global Terrorism 2002. U.S. Department of State. April 2003. http//www.state.gov/s/ct/rls/

of Global Terrorism, indicates that the overall incidence of international terrorism has been in general decline since a peak of 665 terrorist events in 1987, with the year 2002 witnessing the lowest number of attacks since 1982. The number of deaths and injuries has varied widely from 317 in 1991 to 6,510 in 1998 to 833 in 2003. The main difference, however, is that the United States, which in contrast to other regions of the world, had virtually no terrorist incidents for most of this period, experienced the second highest number of fatalities of any region in 2001 (the highest number of fatalities in a single year was in the African region in 1998).[7]

The State Department follows several types of terrorist activities. These include: hostage taking, kidnapping, skyjacking, armed attacks, bombings, fire bombings, suicide bombings, and arson. Bombings (not specified as suicide or fire bombing) have represented the largest category of terrorist attacks during the twenty-first century: in the year 2001 they represented 207 out of 219 attacks; in 2002, 66 out of 77; and in 2003, 119 out of 208. The category of suicide bombing has received particular attention for its large number of casualties. Robert Pape, in his book *Dying to Win: The Strategic Logic of Suicide Bombers* documents 315 suicide bombing attacks since 1980.[8] Pape argues that suicide bombing is strategic, used against modern democracies occupying territory that terrorists regard as their homeland. It is strategic in that the occupying forces are typically much more powerful, and suicide bombing allows terrorists to kill the maximum number of people given limited resources.

But given the high visibility of suicide bombing, the statistics on the incidences of terrorism are surprising. A comparison of terrorist attacks by region for the period 1997–2002 reveals that Asia has a consistently high number of fatalities from attacks. The only regions to exceed their totals are Africa, in which over 5,000 people were killed in 1998, and in the United States, in which over 4,000 people died in a single day in 2001. The Middle East, while still exhibiting high numbers of deaths due to terrorism, lags behind Asia, and in some years, has fewer than 100 deaths. Figure 14.1 presents the number of terrorist casualties for this period.[9]

In terms of the total *number* of attacks, Latin America has consistently high levels of terrorism, followed by Asia, and then Western Europe. In terms of the total number of attacks for the period 1998–2002, the Middle East had fewer attacks than Latin America, Asia, Western Europe, and Africa. Latin America had the highest number of attacks. Figure 14.2 presents the number of terrorist attacks for this period by region. The highest incidence of terrorist attacks in a single country has been in India.

U.S. LEGISLATIVE RESPONSE

The September 11 attacks prompted a number of new laws and the retooling of old laws designed to protect Americans against terrorism. President Bush enacted seven Executive Orders in the wake of the attacks relating to homeland security and transactions with terrorists. The Airport and Transportation Security Act of 2001 was signed into law in November 2001. The Homeland Security Act was passed on November 26, 2002, and became effective on January 1, 2003. The USA Patriot Act was passed into law on October 26, 2001, and was set to expire on December 31, 2005; however, most of its provisions have been re-authorized. States have also passed antiterrorism legislation. The Terrorism Risk Insurance Act (TRIA) was passed on November 26, 2002. New Jersey passed the Domestic Security Preparedness Act and New York passed the Anti-Terrorism Act of 2001. Several pieces of legislation

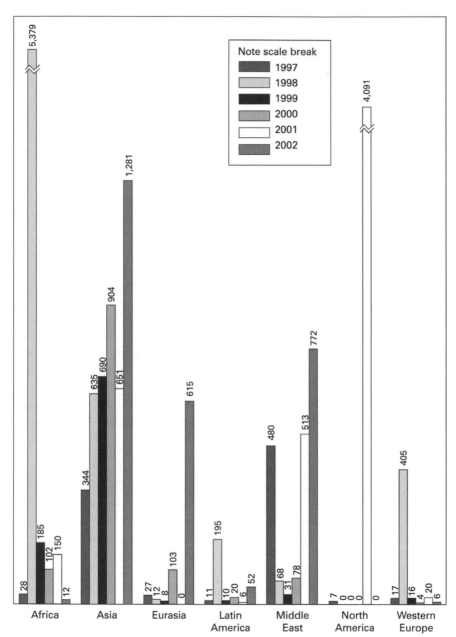

Figure 14.1. Total International Terrorist Casualties by Region, 1997–2002

Source: Patterns of Global Terrorism 2002. U.S. Department of State. p. 163.

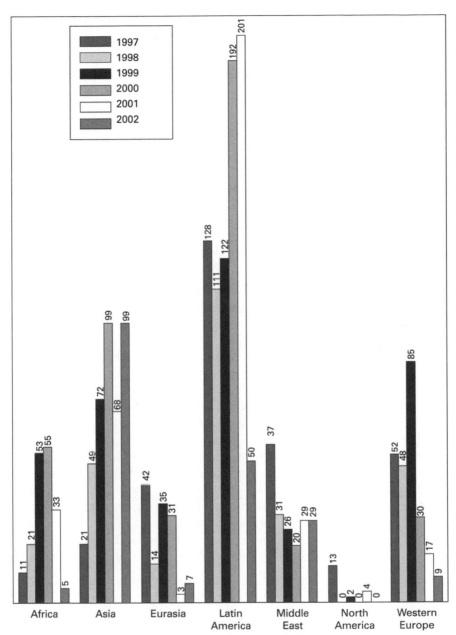

Figure 14.2. Total International Terrorist Attacks by Region, 1997–2002

Source: Patterns of Global Terrorism 2002. U.S. Department of State. p. 162.

have proved controversial in terms of their scope and unintended consequences.

Department of Homeland Security

The Homeland Security Act of 2002 created the Department of Homeland
Security, one of the most massive reorganizations of the federal government
in the last half-century. This was intended to bring the various executive
branch agencies charged with national security into closer communication
with each other. In particular, in the aftermath of September 11, it was found
that the FBI and CIA were not sharing information effectively, to the detri-
ment of national security. The September 11 Commission, among its many
conclusions, found that:

> The missed opportunities to thwart the 9/11 plot were also symptoms of a broader
> inability to adapt the way government manages problems to the new challenges of
> the twenty-first century. Action officers should have been able to draw on all avail-
> able knowledge about al Qaeda in the government. Management should have
> ensured that information was shared and duties were clearly assigned across agen-
> cies, and across the foreign-domestic divide.[10]

Among the various agencies brought together under Homeland Security
were: the Immigration and Naturalization Service; the Transportation Security Administration; the U.S. Customs Service; the Federal Emergency Management Agency; the U.S. Coast Guard; and the U.S. Secret Service.

The creation of an extremely large cabinet level agency out of several
smaller ones has not been without its flaws. In what was viewed as the first
major test of the homeland security reorganization, in September, 2005 the
Federal Emergency Management Agency came under fire for its handling of
the Hurricane Katrina disaster. Citizens waited for some four days without
relief inside the New Orleans Superdome. Reportedly, the first relief troops
to arrive were Canadian. The sluggish FEMA response was seen as evidence
that the agency was not up to handling potential terrorist attacks. The Department of Homeland Security has already announced plans to reorganize
FEMA.

The USA Patriot Act

The USA Patriot Act was designed as an effort to strengthen the counter-
terrorism measures available to the government. It includes a number of provisions, some of which have raised concerns among Americans. The act provides increased funding for antiterrorist measures. It strengthens measures
against money laundering (discussed further below). Enhanced border protection is a key provision. It allows for the creation of funds for victims' fami-

lies. It strengthens criminal provisions against terrorism, and creates definitions that clarify issues relating to terrorism. But the provisions that have caused the most controversy are those that allow for increased domestic surveillance. This includes access to private documents such as medical records, library records, Internet service records, and other records held by third parties. It has also loosened restrictions on the use of the wiretap as a means of surveillance. These provisions have been viewed by some as eroding the civil liberties of citizens. The Titles of the USA Patriot Act are as follows:

I.   Enhancing Domestic Security against Terrorism
II.   Enhanced Surveillance Procedures
III.   International Money Laundering Abatement and Anti-Terrorist Financing Act of 2001
IV.   Protecting the Border
V.   Removing Obstacles to Investigating Terrorism
VI.   Providing for Victims of Terrorism, Public Safety Officers, and their Families.
VII.   Increased Information Sharing for Critical Infrastructure Protection
VIII. Strengthening Criminal Laws Against Terrorism
IX.   Improved Intelligence
X.   Miscellaneous

Impact on the Banking Industry

The Bank Secrecy Act, initially passed in 1970, is now part of the USA Patriot Act, Title III. The Patriot Act recognized the role of the BSA in helping to monitor terrorist activity, therefore it "expanded the Treasury Department's authority initially established under the BSA to regulate the activities of U.S. financial institutions, particularly their relations with individuals and entities with foreign ties."[11] The BSA requires that banks monitor suspicious transactions, and report them to the Financial Crimes Enforcement Network. Bank employees are now trained to complete "Suspicious Activity Reports" on transactions greater than $2,000, if they have reason to suspect illegal activity and on any transaction over $5,000. Table 14.3 provides the federal guidelines for when to complete a Suspicious Activity Report.

In the wake of the September 11 attacks, the FDIC took measures to ensure that banks and bank examiners were familiar with the provisions of the Bank Secrecy Act and the USA Patriot Act. In testimony before the Senate Commission on Banking, Housing, and Urban Affairs, the Inspector General of the FDIC indicated that sanctions had been issued, and that there were difficulties in timely processing of institutional violations. The increased attention to Suspicious Activity Reports has placed increasing pressures for compli-

Table 14.3   Suspicious Activity Report Instructions

When to File a Report:

1. Money transmitters and issuers, sellers and redeemers of money orders and/or travel-er's checks that are subject to the requirements of the Bank Secrecy Act and its imple-menting regulations (31 CFR Part 103) are required to file a suspicious activity report (SAR-MSB) with respect to:

    a. Any transaction conducted or attempted by, at, or through a money services busi-ness involving or aggregating funds or other assets of at least $2,000 (except as described in section "b" below) when the money services business knows, sus-pects, or has reason to suspect that:

        i.   The transaction involves funds derived from illegal activity or is intended or conducted in order to hide or disguise funds or assets derived from illegal activity (including, without limitation, the nature, source, location, ownership or control of such funds or assets) as part of a plan to violate or evade any Federal law or regulation or to avoid any transaction reporting requirement under Federal law or regulation;

        ii. The transaction is designed, whether through structuring or other means, to evade any regulations promulgated under the Bank Secrecy Act; or

        iii. The transaction has no business or apparent lawful purpose and the money services business knows of no reasonable explanation for the transaction after examining the available facts, including the background and possible purpose of the transaction.

    b. To the extent that the identification of transactions required to be reported is derived from a review of clearance records or other similar records of money orders or traveler's checks that have been sold or processed, an issuer of money orders or traveler's checks shall only be required to report a transaction or a pattern of transactions that involves or aggregates funds or other assets of at least $5,000.

2. File a SAR-MSB no later than 30 calendar days after the date of initial detection of facts that constitute a basis for filing the report.

3. The Bank Secrecy Act requires that each financial institution (including a money ser-vices business) file currency transaction reports (CTRs) in accordance with the Depart-ment of the Treasury implementing regulations (31 CFR Part 103). These regulations require a financial institution to file a CTR (IRS Form 4789) whenever a currency trans-action exceeds $10,000. If a currency transaction exceeds $10,000 and is suspicious, a money transmitter, or issuer, seller, or redeemer of money orders and/or traveler's checks must file two forms, a CTR to report the currency transaction and a SAR-MSB to report the suspicious aspects of the transaction. If the suspicious activity involves a currency transaction that is $10,000 or less, the institution is only required to file a SAR-MSB. Appropriate records must be maintained in each case.

Source: Financial Crimes Enforcement Network. United States Department of the Treasury. A Website for Money Services Businesses. www.msb.gov/forms/forms.html

ance on banking institutions. The number of SRAs filed between 2001 and 2004 tripled to over 685,000 reports filed.[12] The American Banking Association now reports that compliance with the Banking Secrecy Act is now ranked as the highest cost of compliance among banking institutions, based on its survey of 1,008 banks nationwide.[13] And the costs of compliance effect banks internationally who do business with American institutions. In the United Kingdom, the costs of antilaundering activities have increased 61 percent over the past 3 years.[14] Lawyers, accountants, insurance companies, casinos, as well as charitable foundations have also been impacted by the increased scrutiny on terrorist financing. Critics suggest, however, that the costs of compliance have not yielded the benefits, and that the fragmentary nature of terrorist cells along with the relatively low costs of carrying out terrorist attacks has made financing difficult to detect. Furthermore, the laws are powerless against informal money transfers and remittances, which are common among foreign nationals living abroad. The international Financial Action Task Force (FATF) has developed a list of recommendations for governments; however, there is no mechanism for enforcement.

Terrorism Risk Insurance Act

The Terrorism Risk Insurance Act (TRIA) was passed in the immediate aftermath of the September 11 attacks because of pressures faced by the insurance industry. Costs to the industry were approximately $40 billion as a direct result of the attacks.[15] Faced with costs that had heretofore been negligible, terrorism reinsurance was reduced or limited on new contracts with insurers. This, in turn, led insurers to reduce the coverage they provided, particularly on property insurance. Price increases were the logical result. Due to the reduced availability and increasing price of terrorism insurance, Congress passed TRIA as a support for U.S. insurers. The legislation was designed to make terrorism insurance affordable and available in the near term, and to give insurers time to respond and to "find ways to price terrorism insurance and develop market-driven resources."[16] The Treasury Department will reimburse insurers for part of their costs due to terrorist attacks; thereby filling the gap left by reinsurers. However, TRIA was intended as a temporary measure, and will expire at the end of 2006. The challenges faced by TRIA have been helped by the fact that there has been no significant terrorist event in the United States since September 11. However, the Treasury Department has been slow to develop the infrastructure to support the insurance industry. In addition, the hoped-for goal of private alternatives had not come to fruition by the December deadline. Thus, the country is still faced with the problem of how victims, private insurers, and the government will bear the costs of another terrorist event.

SUMMARY

While the United States and the international community have had a long history of terrorist activities, the events of September 11, along with the increasing incidence of suicide bombing, have resulted in large-scale changes in how the world does business. Terrorism has impacted tourism, local and international transportation, and civilian recreational and entertainment activities. The threat of terrorism is present in nations all over the world, and attacks on business targets have outstripped military, governmental, and diplomatic targets. A number of laws were passed in the aftermath of September 11 to improve the U.S. government capacity to address terrorism and to increase security in the transportation industry, the banking industry, and the insurance industry. The impact of these laws in the short time frame since their passage remains to be seen, but the vulnerabilities faced by these industries will certainly continue.

QUESTIONS FOR DISCUSSION

1. Has terrorism proved to be an effective political tool for groups?
2. The history of terrorism in the United States can be divided into many types. Discuss.
3. What is anarchism? Was it effective in achieving its aims during its history?
4. What regions evince the greatest incidence of terrorism? What are the differences between the regions?
5. Discuss the changes that have taken place in the United States since September 11, 2001.

RECOMMENDED READINGS

The 9/11 Commission Report: Final Report of the National Commission on Terrorist Attacks Upon the United States. Washington, D.C.: Government Printing Office. July 22, 2004.

BBC News Team. *The Day that Shook the World.* London: BBC Books, 2001.

Pape, R. *Dying to Win: The Strategic Logic of Suicide Terrorism.* New York: Random House, 2005.

Patterns of Global Terrorism 2003. Washington, D.C.: United States Department of State. April, 2004. www.state.gov/s/ct/rls/pgtrpt/2003/

NOTES

1. Francis Fukuyama. *The End of History and the Last Man.* Ithaca NY: Cornell University Press, 1992.

2. United States Code, Section 2656f(d).

3. For a comprehensive history of terrorism, see Roberts, A. "The Changing Faces of Terrorism." BBC News On-line. August 27, 2002.

4. A particularly chilling documentation of lynching is "Without Sanctuary," an internet exhibit containing photographs and postcards featuring grinning whites next to murdered blacks found at www.withoutsanctuary.org/main.html

5. For further information, see "A Documented History of the Incident which Occurred at Rosewood, Florida, in January 1923." Submitted to the Florida Board of Regents. December 22, 1993. www.tfn.net/doc/rosewood.txt

6. Lukov, Y. Beslan Siege Still a Mystery. BBC News On-line. September 2, 2005.

7. Patterns of Global Terrorism 2002. U.S. Department of State. Department of State Publication. April 2003. www.state.gov/s/ct/rls/

8. Pape, R. *Dying to Win: The Strategic Logic of Suicide Terrorism*. New York: Random House, 2005.

9. Patterns of Global Terrorism 2002.

10. Executive Summary. The 9/11 Commission Report. Final Report of the National Commission on Terrorist Attacks Upon the United States. The Department of Homeland Security was created prior to the release of this report.

11. Testimony Before the Committee on Banking, Housing, and Urban Affairs. United States Senate Hearing on Bank Secrecy Act Compliance and Enforcement. *FDIC Office of the Inspector General*. June 3, 2004. p. 4.

12. Financing Terrorism: Looking in the Wrong Places. *The Economist*. October 20, 2005. p. 74.

13. Compliance Watch 2003: Nationwide Bank Compliance Officer Survey. *American Banking Journal*. June 2003. p. 35.

14. Financing Terrorism. p. 74.

15. Terrorism Insurance: Implementation of the Terrorism Risk Insurance Act of 2002. GAO-04-307. *United States General Accounting Office*, 2004. p. 1.

16. Terrorism Insurance. p. 2.

15

Problems of the Less Developed Countries

The countries of the world can be generally classified as more developed and less developed, or as haves and have-nots, and a few are somewhere in between. Unfortunately, many countries can be classified as less developed—and they have around a third of the world's population. Mass poverty exists in the less developed countries and basic consumption needs remain unfulfilled. The magnitude of poverty is all too apparent. We read about it in newspapers and see it on television. A drought in Ethiopia and other parts of Africa was responsible for the death by starvation of thousands of people. The squalor and the number of beggars in the large cities strike anyone who has been to a less developed country. The enormous gap between more and less developed nations increases the potential for social conflict in the world.

This chapter is divided into several parts, the first of which examines the subject of economic development. The second part discusses the characteristics of less developed countries. It looks at population—the causes and consequences of population growth and its link to economic development and performance. The problems of the African continent represent a particular focus of this chapter. Lastly, the Millennium Development Goals are discussed.

ECONOMIC DEVELOPMENT

Although the terms "economic growth" and "economic development" are often used interchangeably, they have different meanings. "Economic growth" can be defined most simply as the ability of a nation to expand its capacity to produce the goods and services its people want. It represents an increase in the real output of goods and services. "Economic development" means not only more real output but different kinds of output from those produced in the past.[1] It includes changes in the technological and institutional arrangements by which output is produced and distributed. There can be economic growth without economic development. For example, a country that relies on the production of oil for export can have its growth rate increase as greater inputs lead to greater output of oil, while its economic development may be minimal. However, the process of economic development almost necessarily depends on some degree of simultaneous economic growth.

A number of factors must exist before economic development can take place in any country. Most of the developed countries in the world have at least several of them:

1. The quantity and quality of a country's labor force has an impact on its economic development. However, the existence of a large labor force does not guarantee economic development. India is an excellent case in point. A labor force has to have education and job skills, both of which are lacking in India because of disparities in the class structure.

2. The quantity and quality of real capital are important for economic development. Real capital is capital goods or inventories in the form of raw materials, machines, and equipment used for the ultimate purpose of producing consumer goods. The supply of real capital depends on the level of savings in a country, which is the difference between its income and its consumption. In countries at a subsistence level, there is little difference between income and consumption.

3. The level of technological attainment in a country must be considered. Technology as a concept deals more with the productive process than with the introduction of new goods. It involves the relationship among inputs of economic resources of land, labor, and capital. The combination of these inputs will determine both the level and type of technology.

4. The quantity and quality of a country's natural resources are also important. Great natural resources contributed to the economic development of the United States. However, it is possible for a country to develop without adequate natural resources. Japan has attained a high level of economic development by importing what it needs.

5. Sociocultural forces also affect economic development. Religion is an example. The role of religion as an economic force can vary considerably among countries. The theocratic society of Iran offers a case in point, where opportunities for women are limited. Other sociocultural forces are the underlying competitive nature of an economy, the distribution of income and wealth, the pattern of consumer tastes, the dominant forms of business organization, and the organization of society.

CHARACTERISTICS OF
LESS DEVELOPED COUNTRIES

A majority of the world's poor live in the less developed countries. Most of the nations of Latin America, Africa, and Asia fall into this category.² However, less developed countries are by no means all alike; some countries are in different stages of economic development from others. There is a vast degree of difference between the lives of, say, the typical slum dweller of Mexico City and an average peasant in Bangladesh or Ethiopia. Although Mexico's per capital income ($6,230) is one-sixth that of the United States ($37,610), it is many times that of Bangladesh ($400) or Ethiopia ($90). Nevertheless, less developed countries possess some common characteristics, and a discussion of each is in order.

Per Capita Income

Whether a country can be classified as developed or less developed, rich or poor, or in between can be determined by the size of its per capita gross national income (GNI). A rough measure of the value of goods and services is produced and available on the average for each country. Among the poorest countries of the world are India, Pakistan, Bangladesh, and Nigeria. These have one-fourth of the world's population and less than 2 percent of the world's GNI. The per capita incomes of each of these countries is less than 5 percent of the annual U.S. figure, which was $37,610 in 2004, and the average of $16,960 for the rich developed countries.³ Nigeria has a per capita income of $320 in 2004, which was less than 1 percent of the per capita income for the United States. The poverty this figure represents shows up in nutritionally inadequate diets, primitive and crowded housing, an absence of medical facilities, and a high rate of illiteracy.

In 2004 there were sixty countries with a per capita income of $765 or less. The countries classified as low income accounted for 41 percent of the world's population but only 3.5 percent of the world's GDP.⁴ Their average per capital GNI was $480. At the opposite end of the spectrum were the wealthy countries of the world, those countries with a per capita GNI of $9,386 or more. These countries had only 15 percent of the world's population, but 80 percent of the world's GDP. The countries in between rich countries and poor countries are classified as lower-middle income countries if they have achieved some stage of economic development and upper-middle income countries. China would be an example of a lower-middle income country, and Poland would be an example of an upper-middle income country.

Sub-Saharan Africa

Africa is a continent with approximately 750 million people. It can be divided into two separate land areas with a totally distinct culture and population—Northern Africa, which is sparsely populated, and Sub-Saharan Africa, which has most of Africa's population. Northern Africa includes such counties as Algeria, Morocco, Tunisia, Libya, and Egypt, which are predominantly Moslem countries. Sub-Saharan Africa includes the great majority of African countries. The Northern African countries, which would be classified as lower-middle income countries, are located on the Mediterranean Sea, a factor that has aided their economic development. The Sub-Saharan countries have not been favored either by climate or geographical location, which has had an adverse effect on their economic development.[5] Heat and humidity have had a deleterious consequence: they have encouraged the proliferation of life forms hostile to humans.

Europeans drew the map of most of the colonial world. It covered all of North America, South America, Africa, Australia, and much of Asia. Thus, Africa and Latin America have much in common with the other colonial possessions of the European countries. All countries that were formerly a part of the British Empire had English as their common language and their legal system is based on English common law, regardless whether the country is Nigeria, India, Belize, or the United States.[6] All countries that were formally a part of the Belgian, Dutch, French, German, Spanish, and Portuguese empires adopted the legal system of these countries, which is code law, usually the Napoleonic code.[7] They have also adopted the language of the country that ruled them.[8] All colonies, regardless of the country to which they belonged, existed for the same reason—to supply their colonizers with raw materials and to serve as a market for manufactured goods.

Colonialism

Africa was the last continent to be colonized by the Europeans even though the British, Dutch, and Portuguese had trading posts at the Cape of Good Hope as early as the 1500s. Because very little was known about it and it possessed nothing of interest to Europeans, Africa was labeled "the Dark Continent."[9] The colonization of Africa took place during two separate periods. The first period occurred around the first part of the nineteenth century, when the British and the French took possession of Northern Africa. The British added Egypt as a colony, and the French acquired Algeria, Morocco, and Tunisia. These colonies were located on the Mediterranean Sea and were of strategic importance to England and France. The opening of the Suez Canal in 1869 made Egypt the crossroads of the British empire. Owning

Egypt enabled England to acquire the Sudan. Algeria and Morocco provided the troops necessary to govern France's empire.

The second wave of colonization of African began in the 1880s. Prior to 1878, the colonies owned by the European countries were mostly located along the seacoasts of Africa. The British and the Dutch had settled South Africa, where the British established the states of Natal and the Crown Colonies, and the Dutch (Boers) established the Orange Free State and the Transvaal. But imperialist rivalries among the European nations began when it appeared that Africa had something to offer of value to the world. The Belgians discovered copper in the Congo, which became the largest copper-producing area in the world, and the British discovered diamonds and gold in southern Africa. Cecil Rhodes, who controlled the diamond interests, began to expand into other parts of South Africa and claimed them for England.[10]

The success of the Belgians and the British provoked the interests of other European countries, and the race began to grab up the rest of Africa. By this time, the British had taken most of the valuable lands in South Africa. To avoid possible wars over territory, the European countries agreed at the Berlin Conference of 1885 to divide up Africa. Five countries shared in this division. England kept what it already had, plus Nigeria, other parts of southern Africa, and the Sudan. France was given the rights to West Africa and recognition to its rights in Tunisia. Germany, which had only been a country for fifteen years, was given parts of East Africa, including the area, which is now the country of Tanzania, and parts of southwest Africa. Belgium got what it already had, and Portugal got what was left, including the areas that are now Angola and Mozambique.

Consequences of European Rule in Africa

There is a distinct similarity today between the problems of the former Yugoslavia and the problems in Africa. The Treaty of Versailles, which ended World War I, created Yugoslavia out of disparate parts of the Austro-Hungarian Empire. Assuming that all Slavs are alike, Yugoslavia became an amalgam of Catholic Slavs, Greek Orthodox Slavs, and Moslem Slavs, all of whom harbored resentment against each other, going back for 600 years.[11] In Africa, the European powers paid no attention to territories or societies. Tribes that had lived separately for centuries found themselves lumped together in the same colonies. When these colonies became countries, historical rivalries were still there, frequently exacerbated by the colonial power structure. The ethnic genocide between the Hutus and Tutsis in Burundi and Rwanda are a tragic example.

The undoubted benefits brought by western medicine and sanitation had the effect of increasing the population, and increasing pressures on the limited supply of land, which in some cases had already been taken up by Europeans. Landless Africans went to work for wages on European farms or in cities, thus further breaking down the traditional society. In the cities they were treated as racial inferiors by the Europeans, prohibited from using the same facilities and given little in the way of housing. The economies of the colonies were run exclusively for the benefit of Europeans. The entire export and import business was in the hands of Europeans and Asians, as were the facilities for credit. Everything produced by African labor was sold at a low price; everything bought by the Africans was expensive.

European penetration quickly undermined the basis on which African society had been organized. The land in most African territories had been held in common by the whole people, and although the tribal leader was responsible for its allocation, he did not himself own it. It was therefore improper for him to have granted any rights to the Europeans, which had the effect of separating the lands from his people. However, the Europeans made use of some tribal leaders for their own purposes, by using them to maintain law and order among the Africans and by using them to collect taxes. The tribal leaders were paid salaries or allowed to keep a share of the taxes. Thus, a feudal society was created by the Europeans instead of the communal society that had once existed.

Each colonial country imposed its educational system upon the Africans. For a long time, primary education was the responsibility of the missionaries, and public education was neglected. Education as a rule involved the conversion of Africans to Christianity, which made the process of Westernization easier. Secondary education was made available for a select few, and graduates were allowed to attend universities in England, France, and the other European countries. Colleges were created in Africa, but their curriculum was based on European conditions and had little relevance to Africa. Graduates were allowed to hold minor colonial offices or work as professionals. The French did a much better job of assimilating Africans into their culture than did the British or Belgians. As in India, the Africans were shut off from social contact with their British masters.

Post Colonial Africa

The postcolonial Africans had no experience with self-government, and leadership often involved being connected with the right tribe. As in the days of the tribal chiefs, strongman rule developed. What this led to was corruption on a grand scale. Bureaucracies expanded to provide jobs for the supporters of the leader, who usually was a military officer. Most foreign aid has ended up in the hands of the rulers. An example was Mobuto Sese Seko, who ruled Zaire for thirty years before he was thrown out.[12] His fortune, which was deposited in Swiss Banks, was said to total billions of dollars.[13] When Zaire achieved its independence from Belgium in 1960, it had 88,000 miles of usable roads; by 1985 this was down to 12,000 miles.[14] The story of what has happened to Zaire can be replicated time and time again in Africa.[15]

Human Development in Poor Countries

In 1990 the United Nations Development Program (UNDP) introduced its human development index (HDI) as a broad measure of economic and social progress. The HDI contains a number of economic and social indicators of well being, including life expectancy, income, adult literacy, infant mortality rate, enrollment in primary, secondary, and tertiary education, health and sanitation facilities, and the status of women.[16] The 177 countries that are included in the index are placed in three categories; (1) countries with a high level of human development; (2) countries with a medium level of human development; and (3) countries with a low level of human development. Table 15.1 presents the HDI for selected countries in each of the three categories. In the high level of human development, Norway ranks first and the United States eighth. The Russian Federation and China are ranked in the medium human development category, at 57 and 94 respectively.[17] The low level of human development category consists of 36 countries, 33 of which are in Africa.[18] Libya is the only African country represented in the United Nations

Table 15.1   Human Development Index for Selected Countries

HDI	Country	Life Expectancy at Birth (Years) 2002	GDP Per Capita (PPP US$) 2002
High Human Development			
1	Norway	78.9	36,600
3	Australia	79.1	29,480
4	Canada	79.3	29,480
8	United States	77	35,750
19	Germany	78.2	27,100
Medium Human Development			
57	Russian Federation	66.7	8,230
68	Venezuela	73.6	5,380
94	China	70.9	4,580
112	Viet Nam	69	2,300
127	India	63.7	2,670
Low Human Development			
142	Pakistan	60.8	1,940
148	Kenya	45.2	1,020
151	Nigeria	51.6	860
153	Haiti	49.4	1,610
170	Ethiopia	45.5	780

Source: Human Development Report 2004, United Nations Development Program (UNDP) pp. 139–42.

category of high human development. Ten African countries have a medium level of human development.

A low rate of economic growth has not helped alleviate the problem of poverty. In some countries, the growth rate has been negative. During the period from 1965 to 1996, the average annual per capita growth rate for Nigeria was 0.1 percent and for Niger it was −2.8 percent. Some of the countries, particularly Botswana, have done well; most have not. Nigeria has been one of the worst performers of all of the African countries. Its per capita income was $780 in 1980; in 2004 it was $320. The countries of North Africa showed a gain during the period 1980–2004; the Sub-Saharan countries did not.

Overpopulation

Although the overall rate of population growth in the world has been declining since the late 1970s, annual world population figures have increased at an average of around 100 million a year. Almost all of this increase is occurring in the poor countries of the world, where birthrates remain high and mortality rates are declining. Conversely, in the rich countries of the world birthrates are declining to the point where the population is not replacing itself. An aging population is a major problem in the poor countries of the world. In either situation, there is a drain on monetary resources.

Poverty

More than one billion people out of the world's population of 6.5 billion people live on less than $1 a day and around two billion people live on less than $2 a day. Poverty is greatest among the African and Asian countries; India and China alone account for close to 50 percent of the world's poor. Table 15.2 presents the poverty rates for selected countries, using the standard of poverty as $2 or less a day. Poverty and population increases are linked. The poorest countries typically have the highest birth rates. India is a case in point. Its population is increasing at a faster rate than growth in real income. It has a population of over one billion people, 79.9 percent of whom live on $2 or less a day.

Africa is by far the poorest continent in the world. It has 14 percent of the world's population and less than 3 percent of its GDP. Sub-Saharan Africa, with a population of 702.6 million, had a combined GDP of $347 billion in 2003, which is less than the GDP of Canada, a country of 31.6 million, and a little larger than the GDP of Belgium, a country of 10 million. Ethiopia, the poorest country in the world, had a per capita income of $90 in 2004, followed by Congo with a per capita income of $100. Nigeria, the largest country in Africa with a population of 135.6 million, had a total GDP of $43 billion in 2003, which is less than half of that of Venezuela with a population

Table 15.2 Poverty Rates for Selected Countries, $2 or Less a Day

Region/Country	Percent of Population Living Below $2 Per Day
World	53
Sub-Saharan Africa	75
North Africa	29
Latin America/Caribbean	26
Eastern Europe	14
South Central Asia	75
Bangladesh	83
China	47
Egypt	44
India	81
Indonesia	52
Nigeria	91
Pakistan	66
Viet Nam	33

Source: Human Development Report 2004, United Nations Development Program (UNDP) p.148.

of 25.5 million. No country in Africa would qualify as a developed country. Libya, which has the highest per capita income of all African countries, produces oil but has a population of only 5 million.

Illiteracy

Some 275 million children throughout the world are illiterate because they live in countries that cannot afford to build enough schools to educate them. Close to one-third of the world's population is illiterate, and two-thirds of those who are illiterate in many countries are women, as far fewer women receive an education than men. Table 15.3 presents the adult illiteracy rate for countries with an illiteracy rate of 40 percent or more of the population. In India close to 40 percent of the adult population is illiterate; in Bangladesh 59 percent of the adult population is illiterate. In India 41 percent of children have not reached a fifth-grade level of education.

Gender Disparity

In the less developed countries of the world most of the activities of women take place in the nonwage sector of the economy for household consumption. According to the United Nations Development Program (1995), informalized labor, if monetized, would constitute "$16 trillion, of which $11 trillion is the non-monetized, invisible contribution of women."[19] This invisible contribution reflects social reproduction, as well as the nonwage work of women,

Table 15.3   The Adult Illiteracy Rate in Selected Countries, 2002

	% Illiterate	
	Female	Male
India	54	31
Bangladesh	69	50
Pakistan	71	47
Nepal	73	38
Indonesia	17	8
Cambodia	41	19
Ethiopia	66	51
Egypt	56	33
Nigeria	41	26
Kenya	22	10
Niger	91	75
China	14	5
Mozambique	69	38

Source: Human Development Report 2004, United Nations Development Program (UNDP) pp. 217–20.

all too frequently in the less developed countries. Piecework, home-based work, domestic work, as well as trafficking in women, are all part of this informalized labor.

Women in less developed countries are less likely to be educated than their male counterparts. In Ethiopia, the gross school enrollment ratio for women is 28 percent, for men 41 percent. In Niger, the literacy rate for women in 9.3 percent, for men 25.1 percent. Women usually have fewer legal rights regarding marital relations, the division of property, or land tenure. In some countries, men can divorce their wives, but not the other way around; also, it is often difficult for the woman to get any form of alimony. Inheritance of property in many countries is limited to male relatives. A disparity in education and resources institutionalizes poverty for women. Control over property conveys power, but it is usually males who control it. There is also a carry-over into such areas as health and life expectancy.

Table 15.4 presents the gender-related development index for developed and less developed countries. As the table indicates, the poorer the country, the lower the life expectancy for both sexes and the lower the rate of literacy, particularly for women. In Pakistan only 28.5 percent of the women are literate; and in India only 46.4 percent of the women are literate. Literacy rates in the least developed countries average 43 percent; literacy rates in the poorest countries are invariably lower for women than for men.[20] The main factor in causing the high rate of illiteracy and poverty among women is the lack of equal educational opportunities. The smaller the percentage of females attending school, the greater the female-male gap; the closer the female percent is to the male percent, the smaller the gender gap.

Table 15.4 Gender-Related Development Index for Selected Countries

GDI	Country	Life Expectancy at Birth (Years) 2002		GDP Per Capita (PPP US$) 2002	
		Female	Male	Female	Male
High Human Development					
1	Norway	81.8	75.9	31,356	53,340
3	Australia	82	76.4	23,643	33,259
4	Canada	81.9	76.6	22,964	36,299
8	United States	79.8	74.2	27,338	43,797
19	Germany	81.1	75.1	18,763	35,885
Medium Human Development					
49	Russian Federation	73	60.7	6,508	10,189
58	Venezuela	76.6	70.8	3,125	7,550
71	China	73.2	68.8	3,571	5,435
187	Viet Nam	71.4	66.7	1,888	2,723
103	India	64.4	63.1	1,442	3,820
Low Human Development					
120	Pakistan	60.7	61	915	2,789
114	Kenya	46.4	44	962	1,067
122	Nigeria	52	51.2	562	1,322
123	Haiti	49.9	48.8	1,170	2,089
137	Ethiopia	46.4	44.6	516	1,008

Source: Human Development Report 2004, United Nations Development Program (UNDP) pp. 217–20.

Population Growth and an Ever-Increasing Labor Force

In 1965 there were 1.3 billion workers in the world. Twenty-one percent of this labor force lived in high-income countries, 27 percent in middle-income countries, and 52 percent in low-income countries (see footnote 9). Twenty-five percent of the world's labor force lived in sub-Saharan Africa and South Asia, the two poorest regions in the world. By 2004, the world labor force had almost doubled, but the percentage of the labor force living in the high-income countries had decreased from 21 percent in 1965 to 15 percent in 2004. Conversely, the percentage of the labor force living in the low-income countries had increased from 52 percent in 1965 to 58 percent in 2004. By 2025, the world labor force is projected to be 3.7 billion, of which 61 percent will be in the low-income countries and 11 percent in the high-income countries. The greatest gains will be in sub-Saharan Africa and South Asia.

Africa's population is growing faster than the population of other continents. This will continue to be a burden for most African countries in terms of resource allocation. Most resources have to be used for consumption. Incomes are low, so human and physical capital is less developed. The population growth affects both the demand for and the supply of savings. Household savings are reduced by the high dependency burdens associated with rapid population growth. At any level of per capita income, greater numbers of dependents cause consumption to rise, so savings per capita will fall. Governments can, within limits, use fiscal and monetary policies to change a country's rate of savings, irrespective of demographic conditions. However, the effectiveness of fiscal and monetary policies is predicated on the existence of a well-developed system of public finance and banking which most African countries do not have.

Even though birthrates have fallen in these countries, they are well above the two-child replacement level, thus increasing the size of future generations. The mortality rate will also decrease. This will increase more entrants into the labor force, compounding problems of education. Increases in the number of school-age children will require increased spending on education. In an age of increased technology, these countries will have to improve their schools both quantitatively and qualitatively, and that is difficult to do because these countries have limited resources. To improve education, they will either have to generate more national savings or reduce spending in other areas.

Population growth has put pressure on the infrastructure of the African countries. There is mass migration from the rural areas to the cities. The end result is that Cairo, Lagos, and other African cities are becoming among the largest in the world. Population pressure leads to poverty and disease. In Nigeria, 36 percent of children under 5 are underweight. In Madagascar, 72 percent of the children do not reach the fifth grade. In Burundi, 78 percent of the population lacks access to an improved water source and health expenditures are $19 per capita, contrasted with $4,887 in the United States. In Ethiopia, there is an average of three physicians per 100,000 people, and only 12 percent of the population has access to improved sanitation.[21]

Income Inequality

Some of the African countries have among the most unequal income distributions in the world. In this respect, they are similar to the Latin American countries. In Kenya, the richest 20 percent of the population received 51.2 percent of total income compared to 5.6 percent for the bottom 20 percent of the population—a ratio nearly 10 to 1. In South Africa, the richest 20 percent of the population received 66.5 percent of income compared to 2.0 percent for the bottom 20 percent—a ratio of 33 to 1. In other countries, the distribution of income is more equal. This is particularly true of the North African countries. In Algeria, the richest 20 percent of the population received 42.6 percent of income, while the poorest 20 percent received 7.0 percent of income—a ratio of less than 6 to 1.

Political and Social Instability

Political and social instability are common problems in the majority of African countries and inhibit their economic development. In 1994 Rwanda was wracked by a civil war that resulted in tribal genocide. A civil war occurred in Zaire that resulted in the ouster of the long-time dictator General Mobutu. Military leaders who have postponed free elections, jailed political opponents, and hanged critics of the government have run Nigeria. Civil war and ethnic genocide continues without end in the Sudan, and in Algeria the internecine struggle between Islamic fundamentalists and the government is a serious threat to the stability of Northern Africa. Terrorism has also occurred in Egypt where Islamic fundamentalists hope to topple the rule of Egyptian President Hosni Mubarak;[22] a 2005 incident in the Gulf of Aden killed eighty-eight people. Genuine political democracy exists in only a handful of African countries.

AIDS

AIDS is the number one economic and social problem in Africa. It is already responsible for over half of the deaths by infectious disease not only in Africa, but also elsewhere in the world. More people suffer from AIDS in Africa than in the rest of the world combined. It has resulted in the lowering of life expectancy in such countries as Nigeria, South Africa, and Zimbabwe. In these and other countries in Africa and Asia, until prevention programs become more effective, life expectancy will fall, the number of orphans will increase, poverty will worsen, and health care resources will come under increased financial strain. The circumstances under which AIDS occurs are different from the developed countries, which will make its eradication more difficult. As table 15.5 indicates, in some of the African countries one-fourth of the adult population is infected by AIDS.

THE FUTURE OF AFRICA

Africa is the world's poorest continent. While the rest of the world has grown more prosperous, Africa has not. Income differences among countries have widened since 1950. For example, real per capita GDP in Kenya in 1950 was $609 and in South Africa $2,251. For South Korea and Taiwan, the respective values were $876 and $922.[23] In 2004 the real per capita GDP for Kenya was $1,055 and for South Africa $3,451, while the real per capita GDP for South Korea was $10,010 and for Taiwan $11,590.[24] It has been argued that climate and cultural factors have worked in favor of South Korea and Taiwan to pro-

Table 15.5 AIDS in Selected African Countries, 2004

Country	Percent of Population aged 15 to 49
Burkina Faso	4.2
Cameroon	6.9
Congo, Democratic Republic	4.2
Ethiopia	6.2
Kenya	6.7
Lesotho	28.9
Malawi	14.2
Mozambique	12.2
Nigeria	5.4
Rwanda	5.1
South Africa	19.8
Tanzania	8.8
Zimbabwe	24.6

Source: Human Development Report 2004, United Nations Development Program (UNDP) pp. 166–67.

mote their economic development, while other climate and cultural factors have worked against the development of the African countries.[25]

At the beginning of the twentieth century, the presence of natural resources was a factor promoting economic development. Countries that had natural resources had something of value to export. The multinational corporations of that time period were resource based. They went to wherever the resources were located. The mass production manufacturing companies that developed during the early part of the twentieth century also depended on resources. The Goodyear Tire Company established rubber plantations in Brazil and Malaysia. Manufacturing firms also needed cheap labor so they built assembly plants abroad. Education was no particular requisite for success during that time period. Unskilled workers could be used for work on banana plantations, while semi-skilled workers could work on the Ford assembly line and make $5 a day.

Today, knowledge is everything, and knowledge depends on education. Poor countries, but particularly those in Africa, differ from rich countries not only because they have less capital but less knowledge. Knowledge is costly to create and that is why most of it is created in the rich countries. Poor countries differ from rich countries in that they have far fewer institutions to impart knowledge and far fewer people attend these institutions. The knowledge gap between the rich and poor countries widened during the 1990s and will continue to widen in the future. International institutions such as the World Bank and the International Monetary Fund can only do so much. Debt forgiveness will only go so far. One way in which to attract technology is through foreign trade and investment, but Africa has received little foreign investment because of corruption, political instability, a weak infrastructure, a poor legal system, low growth rates, and high fiscal deficits.

MILLENNIUM DEVELOPMENT GOALS

At the 2000 United Nations Millennium Summit, world leaders declared a determination to put an end to world poverty. The Millennium Declaration, adopted at the summit, committed the 189 countries represented to a set of goals for the twenty-first century. These eight goals constitute the Millennium Development Goals:

Goal 1: Eradicate extreme poverty and hunger
Goal 2: Achieve universal primary education
Goal 3: Promote gender equality and empower women
Goal 4: Reduce child mortality
Goal 5: Improve maternal health
Goal 6: Combat HIV/AIDS, malaria, and other diseases
Goal 7: Ensure environmental sustainability
Goal 8: Develop a global partnership for development

Progress toward the goals, as of 2004, revealed key regional differences. The regions of East Asia and the Pacific are making progress, but this is largely driven by China and India. Sub-Saharan Africa, by contrast, is falling behind, particularly in the areas of hunger, income poverty, and access to sanitation.[26] Of twenty-seven priority countries—in which the problem is particularly urgent—twenty-one are located in Sub-Saharan Africa.

SUMMARY

Africa appears to continue its state of crisis that has existed during the decade of the 1990s. Although there are some noteworthy exceptions—Botswana, Mauritinis, Tunisia, and a few other countries—the majority of African countries are in a state of chaos. The countries of Sub-Saharan Africa are among the poorest countries in the world. Poverty, gender disparity, illiteracy, and HIV infection all affect the future prosperity of these countries. The Millennium Development Goals have been developed to address these problems; building capacity in these countries is critical in combating the many issues that they face.

QUESTIONS FOR DISCUSSION

1. What is the difference between economic growth and economic development?

2. Even though the population rate is declining in less developed countries, it still remains a problem. Discuss.
3. What impact does corruption have on economic development?
4. What are some of the sociocultural factors that block economic development?
5. The twenty-first century will pose a new set of challenges to the less developed countries. Discuss.

RECOMMENDED READINGS

Lancaster, Carol. *Aid to Africa: So Much to Do, So Little Done*, Chicago: University of Chicago Press, 1998.
Landes, David S. *The Wealth and Poverty of Nations*. New York: W. W. Norton, 1998.
United Nations Development Program. *Human Development Report 2004*. New York: Oxford University Press, 2004.
The World Bank. *World Development Report 2004. Washington, D.C.: Oxford University Press, 2004.*
The World Bank. 2004 World Bank Atlas. Washington, D.C.: The World Bank, 2004.

NOTES

1. Bruce Harrick and Charles F. Kindleberger, *Economic Development*, 4th ed. New York: McGraw-Hill, 1983, 21–23.
2. The United Nations classifies countries on the basis of developed and less developed. The United States, the European Union, Japan, Canada, and Australia, would be developed.
3. The World Bank, *2004 World Bank Atlas*. Washington, DC: The World Bank, 2004, 54–55.
4. Human Development Report 2004. *United Nations Development Program.* pp. 155, 187.
5. David S. Landes, *The Wealth and Poverty of Nations.* New York: W. W. Norton, 1998, p. 130.
6. Common law dates back to 1151 A.D. It is based on legal precedent.
7. Code law dates back before Roman law. It is statutory law. The Napoleonic code was introduced by Napoleon in 1804, and is the law in France, Spain, Portugal, Italy, and Latin America. The Germanic code was introduced in Germany in 1896, and is the law in Germany, Austria, Poland, the Czech Republic, Turkey, and Japan.
8. Senegal and other former French possessions still speak French.
9. The slave trade and ivory were two exceptions.
10. Cecil Rhodes was to England in the nineteenth century what John D. Rockefeller was to the United States. Rhodes became the richest man in England, while Rockefeller was the richest man in America. Both men were unscrupulous. Rhodes made his money in diamonds; Rockefeller made his in oil. Queen Victoria knighted Rhodes; Rockefeller ran afoul of the U.S. antitrust laws. In order to expiate for their sins in this world, Rhodes created the Rhodes Scholarship and Rockefeller created the Rockefeller Foundation.

11. The battle of Kosovo, which was fought between the Serbs and Turks in 1389, is a national shrine even though the Serbs lost. For that matter, so is the Alamo, which the Texans lost. As a Polish friend told the author, if we build a monument to every battle we lost, we would run out of territory.

12. Zaire was formerly the Belgian Congo. Now, it is the Democratic Republic of the Congo.

13. Much of this money came from the United States, which regarded him as a friend.

14. David S. Landes, *The Wealth and Poverty of Nations.* New York: W. W. Norton, 1998, p. 510.

15. Idi Amin, dictator of Uganda, is one of many examples.

16. Many women die in childbirth or of malnutrition.

17. The World Bank, *World Development Report, 2004*, p. 9.

18. The World Bank, *World Development Report, 2004*, pp. 84–88.

19. United Nations Development Program, *Human Development Report*, 1995, page 6.

20. Lesotho is a notable exception, with 90.3 percent literacy rate for women and 73.7 percent for men.

21. Human Development Report 2004.

22. Mubarak received more than 80 percent of the vote in the 2005 elections.

23. Angus Maddison, *Monitoring the World Economy, 1820–1992.* Paris: OECD, 1997, p. 206.

24. Maddison, 1997, pp. 204–205.

25. David S. Landes, *The Wealth and Poverty of Nations.* New York: W. W. Norton, 1998, Africa, pp. 499–507; South Korea, pp. 377, 436–38, 475–77; Taiwan, pp. 377, 437, 438, 475; climate, temperate v. tropical, pp. 5–16.

26. Human Development Report 2004, pp. 129–33.

16

Wealth and Income Inequality in America

Money may not buy you happiness, but it will enable you to buy a yacht so you can pull up alongside it.

Author unknown

In the movie *Wall Street,* a young junior executive asked the chief executive Gordon Gecko (Michael Douglas), "How much money is enough?" Gecko is taken aback, because he never thought about it one way or another. So he tells the young man "Greed is good. Greed is right. Greed works. Greed clarifies, cuts through and captures the essence of the evolutionary spirit. Greed, in all of its forms—greed for life, for money, knowledge—has marked the upward surge of mankind and greed—you mark my words—will not only save Teldar Paper but that other malfunctioning corporation called the USA."[1] As he says this he looks out his Manhattan skyscraper window at the scene below and he thinks of himself as a titan of industry looking over all that he surveys and controls. He also thinks about his house up in Westchester County and what he has bought. So his point to the boy is that you can never have enough money.

That seems to be the American spirit as epitomized by what has happened in the last ten or twelve years. But it is simply one of a number of cycles in the history of the United States. The Roaring Twenties was a period of "get rich" which led to the collapse of the stock market and the ruination of the American economy, which was revitalized only by our entrance into World War II. But the last ten years are probably worse than what we had in the 1920s and the outcome remains to be seen.

The Robber Barons

Some form of wealth and income inequality has existed in the United States since the beginning of the nineteenth century. The first tycoons in America were the merchant traders such as Cornelius Vanderbilt and others who made fortunes trading with the settlers and with the Indians in the West. They had ships that enabled them to reach large parts of America by boat. When the

343

railroads were built and began to open up America, that increased their opportunity for fortunes and they were able to expand their markets. Vanderbilt himself eventually began to control railroads as well as shipping.

Then during the latter part of the century the so-called robber barons came to the front as the leading entrepreneurs of America. They all had one thing in common; they didn't have much in the way of formal education. John D. Rockefeller[2] had a fourth grade education and went to work as a clerk in a hardware store in Cleveland, Ohio at the sum of $4 a week. By the end of the nineteenth century he was the richest man in the United States. He made his money during and after the time of the Civil War through oil. When oil was discovered he was able to put together entities that eventually grew so large that they were called the Standard Oil Trust (the trust form of development of entrepreneurship)

Then there was Andrew Carnegie who came to this country from Scotland at the age of 13 with little formal education. He started at the bottom in a mill as a sweeper and eventually rose to the top and put together the Carnegie Steel Company, the entity that came to be known as United States Steel.

Another person who made a fast fortune was James B. Duke for whom Duke University is named. He too had little formal education; he was an itinerant salesman and opened up markets for tobacco both domestic and foreign. He was a born salesman. He introduced the Chinese to cigarette smoking by successfully marketing the product in a package that displayed nude women to titillate the Chinese smoker. He also made it acceptable for women to smoke and he put together the American Tobacco Trust, a conglomerate of a number of tobacco companies that dominated as did Standard Oil their specific industry. So those were three men who became very prominent in the latter part of the nineteenth century.

During that time period among the more popular novels for boys were the Horatio Alger stories written by an Episcopal priest. The theme of the stories was always the same. Young man starts at the bottom as a shoe shine boy, is very diligent and hard working, catches the attention of a banker who has his shoes shined and observes how conscientious and hard working the boy is, and offers him a position in his Bank. The boy starts at the bottom and through diligence and hard work he eventually works his way up the corporate ladder, marries the banker's daughter, and he too becomes President of the bank. That really was part of the Protestant work ethic, that good hard work and thrift builds success and character, and certainly Rockefeller, Carnegie, and Duke are examples.

And there were other tycoons as well who made their money one way or the other. Leland Stanford made his money in railroad construction, Jay Gould in financing railroads. For the most part with few exceptions they had little formal education. Eventually what happened roughly from 1870 to 1900 was the formation of the trust as a business enterprise. A trust simply gathered under it a conglomerate of industries of the same type like Standard Oil

Trust and the American Tobacco Trust. They dominated their industries and the men such as Rockefeller, Duke, and Carnegie were very wealthy indeed! Eventually the Sherman and Clayton acts discussed earlier broke the power of the trusts.

The Roaring Twenties

The 1920s ushered in a second cycle of business entrepreneurship in which some people became very wealthy. It was known as the Roaring Twenties, a period of unlimited prosperity. The stock market went up and up and people invested in it. The 1920s were stimulated by a building boom in which speculation in real estate was common and Florida became the "in" place to buy and build. Also two major industries developed which stimulated the "Roaring Twenties." The first was the development of the automobile industry and the second was the development of electrical products such as washing machines, dryers, refrigerators, and radios.

The two men associated with those two industries—Henry Ford and Thomas A. Edison—were somewhat similar to Duke, Carnegie, and Rockefeller. Neither had much in the way of formal education. Ford was an itinerant mechanic who developed an automobile, eventually put together the Ford Motor Company and produced one of the most successful cars of all time, the Model T. Through mass production he was able to produce the Model T to sell at a price of around $300 which was affordable by the masses and the Ford Motor Company sold some 3,000,000 Model Ts during the time it was produced.

Thomas Edison started life as a telegraph operator in the office of a railroad company but through tinkering with electricity he formed the G. E. Company, which mass produced refrigerators, ovens, and consumer durables.

Then there was speculation in real estate with Florida being the prime example. This development was stimulated by the building of a railroad by Henry Flagler from the top of Florida all the way to Key West. This made land very popular, particularly when Miami was opened up for development. So thousands of investors poured their money into unseen real estate that usually did not exist. Fancy hotels were constructed and a building boom occurred. But the Stock Market Crash of 1929 ended all this. It wasn't really until World War II began that America eventually got itself out of the Depression.

Corporate Scandals of the Early Twenty-first Century

After World War II there was a period of rapid expansion in the American economy. Pent up demand for consumer goods, which were scarce during the war, stimulated economic activity and provided jobs for returning veterans.

The Cold War, which began in 1947, also lent impetus to demand, as defense expenditures increased. This continued until the collapse of Communism in 1991. The Korean Conflict beginning in 1951 also stimulated demand. When the Russians sent a man into space, this contributed to expenditures on space exploration under President Kennedy, followed by President Johnson. The Vietnam War also stimulated the American economy.

Another factor continually adding to the increased expenditures in the American economy were the tax cuts by Ronald Reagan during the 1980s. The 1990s were highlighted by the collapse of Communism and expenditures on technology. All of these factors led to increased consumer spending and investment.

Many Americans took the "Greed is Good" philosophy to heart during the latter part of the 1990s when the rage was to invest in the dot com stocks, no matter that these companies weren't earning anything. It was what people expected that they would do in the future that counted. After all, during the 1920s, General Motors and General Electric and other companies did very well and continued eventually to become corporate giants.

But that didn't happen to the technology stocks because the majority of them did not earn a cent and went bankrupt. As a result many Americans who optimistically and confidently invested in these companies lost their money. But the corporate executives who became the quintessential paladins of greed more than outdid themselves.

Enron

In the late 1990s, Enron was a fast growing energy company recognized as one of America's coming corporations. It was heralded for its innovative financial practices, but those practices proved to be its downfall in November 2001. In the process, Kenneth Lay, the President of Enron, Andrew Fastow, the Chief Financial Officer, and Jeffrey Skilling, the Chief Executive Officer, along with several other Enron executives, were indicted, and the whole Enron apparatus fell apart and became one of the largest bankruptcies in American history. The "innovative" accounting processes began with a means for reporting future energy purchases on the current balance sheet, then evolved to a series of "structured deals" which turned out to be nothing more than a means for hiding debt on an off-balance sheet.[3] Enron, under Fastow, under-reported losses. All told, the thicket of accounting practices baffled insiders and analysts alike; but Skilling and Fastow derided them for not being progressive enough in their thinking.[4]

Late in 2001, with their share price falling, Enron experienced a series of business failures and market shocks which ultimately led to the realization of massive debt that had been accumulating for years. Ultimately, thousands of employees lost their jobs and retirement savings. But perhaps the most astonishing thing about the collapse of Enron was the retinue of players that ended up being involved. The long respected accounting firm of Arthur Anderson was found complicit, and ended by being broken up. Several banks, the Canadian Imperial Bank of Commerce, Citigroup, and JP MorganChase were also sued for their roles in Enron's "structured deals."[5] While Fastow and his wife were found guilty, Lay and Skilling have yet to be tried. However, Skilling has been criticized for the cutthroat business culture that he fostered, which may have created fertile ground for accounting fraud. And Lay, known as "Kenny Boy," came off looking, if not culpable, simply clueless, raising questions about executive accountability.

WorldCom

While the Enron case caught national attention, the WorldCom case a year later resulted in the nation's largest accounting scandal totaling around $11 billion. As a result thousands of people lost their jobs and life savings while WorldCom President Bernard Ebbers and CFO Scott Sullivan, particularly the latter, lived opulent lives with mansions and all the accoutrements of what is considered American success. And while Enron's accounting measures were too complex for most to understand, by comparison "WorldCom cooked its books with a scheme that even an Accounting 101 student could have devised."[6] Ebbers took pride in characterizing himself as a simple Mississippi country boy who rode around in a pickup truck. His erstwhile Chief Financial Officer Scott Sullivan, who is said to have masterminded the fraud, testified against Ebbers, who now is serving twenty-five years in prison. In exchange for his testimony, Sullivan was sentenced to five years in prison and was forced to sell his mansion to satisfy part of the debt incurred by the company.

Sarbanes-Oxley Act of 2002

In the wake of the corporate scandals of the early 2000s, Congress passed the Sarbanes-Oxley Act. The act has several major requirements. They include regulations on timely filing of financial reports and corrections. The act also provides for financial auditor independence, which was sadly lacking in the Enron case. Finally, it provides for greater criminal and civil penalties for executives who knowingly produce inaccurate financial statements.

Individualistic Capitalism v. Communitarian Capitalism

Since capitalism has become the sine qua non of the world's present and future existence, what is left to compare? The answer is to compare various types of capitalism. One way in which capitalism can be compared is by distinguishing between individualistic Anglo-Saxon capitalism and communitarian European and Japanese capitalism. This two-pronged comparison, which is based on a distinction made by George C. Lodge, forms part of the foundation of Lester Thurow's *Head to Head: The Coming Economic Battle Among Japan, Europe, and America.*[7] The Anglo-Saxon variant of capitalism dominated the last two centuries, with the United Kingdom dominant in the nineteenth century and the United States in the twentieth century. Who, then, will dominate the twenty-first century? According to Thurow, it will be the communitarian capitalism of Europe.

Individualistic Capitalism

Individualistic capitalism is associated with the writings of John Locke and Adam Smith. It was Locke who developed the argument that the right to govern rests in the hands of the governed, not the governor. Prior to Locke, it had been assumed that the king, not the people had the right to rule. According to Locke, the individual is a fulcrum of society and has certain inalienable rights, including the right to own property.[8] According to Adam Smith, the individual, if permitted to pursue his or her self-interest, will promote the well being of all. This will not result from charitable motives, but from the inexorable logic of the free market—the "invisible hand."[9] Stated simply, if all people are motivated to work at full capacity, whether as laborers, artisans, or executives, the net supply of goods and services available for consumption by all will be increased.

According to Thurow, individualism in the United States and other Anglo-Saxon countries takes a number of forms: large income differentials, brilliant entrepreneurs such as Bill Gates, the founder of Microsoft and the richest man in America, and short-term profit maximization. In the tradition of individualism each person is responsible for his or her own personal success. Life is a competitive struggle where the fit survive and those who are unfit do not. Individuals owe no particular loyalty to a company; they are free to leave for higher-paying jobs. Conversely, companies feel no loyalty to their employees; they can be laid off when times are bad or for that matter when times are relatively good, as witnessed by the downsizing of many American corporations. Neither employers nor employees owe each other anything.[10]

Communitarian Capitalism

The term *communitarian* has a number of connotations, but basically it means deriving satisfaction from being part of a group process as opposed to functioning as an individual. The role of the state is greatly expanded under communitarian ideology. It plays roles in stimulating economic growth and providing social welfare programs, and it also is involved in public investment expenditures for such things as job training. There is less job changing and more loyalty to the employer in communitarian capitalistic countries. Employers think more in terms of job retraining and teamwork. Companies think in terms of long-term strategies and often function as part of a group. Close cooperation between companies and the government can also exist. Communitarian capitalism is the result of different cultural and historical developments in Europe and Japan, where government often as a matter of necessity played an important role in economic development.[11]

Germany and Japan are examples of communitarian capitalist countries. In Germany the state has played an important role since the time of Bismarck. There is codetermination between labor and management, with labor representatives sitting on the boards of directors of German companies. German banks are major shareholders in German companies. Job training is also the responsibility of companies and the government. In Japan the overwhelming emphasis is on the group and one's responsibility to it. Companies (including banks) are often part of a group of companies. Employees are loyal to a company, and there is very little job switching. There is cooperation between business and government and between business and labor. Business thinks in terms of long-term objectives as opposed to short-term profit maximization.

A Comparison

Income inequality is far greater in the individualistic countries than it is in those countries that are communitarian, and that country that has the greatest income inequality among the high-income nations is the United States. And although England has a lower level of income inequality it is still greater than the European countries and Japan. The same is true for Canada. The income inequality is greater in Canada than it is in the communitarian societies. That does not necessarily mean that communitarian societies are superior to individualistic societies, because they have their own problems.

One problem they face is the aging of the population, which bodes ill for these countries because the costs of the welfare state are increasing. If you look at the benefits offered by countries such as Sweden, France, and Germany, they are considerable and expensive. The individuals and the companies basically pay them. But the point is as these societies age and they are not reproducing themselves, then the costs of these benefits are going to increase and the wherewithal to pay for them is not going to be there. They will have to take rather drastic measures to perhaps curtail the benefits that people receive in the European countries or raise taxes on a dwindling labor force and that is something that has to be considered. In some cases, notably Germany, the population is not reproducing itself, thus creating a serious

Table 16.1   A Comparison of Income Inequality for Individualistic and Communitarian Countries

Countries	Gini	Percent Share of Income or Consumption	
		lowest 20%	highest 20%
Individualistic			
United States	40.8	5.4	45.8
United Kingdom	36	6.1	44
Canada	33.1	7	40.4
Australia	35.2	5.9	41.3
New Zealand	36.2	6.4	43.8
Communitarian			
Belgium	25	8.3	37.3
Denmark	24.7	8.3	35.8
Finland	26.9	9.6	36.7
France	32.7	7.2	40.2
Germany	28.3	8.5	36.9
Netherlands	32.6	7.3	40.1
Norway	25.8	9.6	37.2
Sweden	25	9.1	36.6

Source: World Development Report 2005, The World Bank, Washington, DC, 2005, 258–59

problem that has to be contended with in the future. Also, in these countries, the unemployment rate, for example in Germany is quite high and has been high for a number of years.

Also it can be said that in communitarian countries there is no particular burning desire to embrace what is called Western style individualistic capitalism, and as the governments of various European countries have had to work with declining revenues and rising welfare costs, friction occurs. For example France has attempted to raise taxes and encourage business development and has met opposition from the people.[12] A poll from the French magazine *Le Monde* showed 80 percent of the French people opposed to what they call American capitalism so you have a totally different value system that is not receptive to the individualistic type of capitalism as practiced by the United States. The same holds true in Germany where the German companies are very much regulated by the government in terms of hiring practices, firing practices, opening time in the morning, and closing time at night. The German government strictly regulates starting a new company, and of course this affects employers' decisions to invest and to hire. The employer in Germany and in the other European states basically bears the cost of the welfare state. So there are good points and bad points of communitarianism.

The Rich and the Hyper-Rich

At the turn of the twentieth century, Thorstein Veblen, an economist at the University of Chicago wrote a book called *The Theory of the Leisure Class.*[13] Its theme was thus: the rich set the trends in America. His book developed the concept of conspicuous consumption. For example, when the first cars appeared, very few could afford them. They were beyond the reach of 99 percent of Americans. The rich could pay $30,000 to $40,000 for a Stanley Steamer or other cars that were produced at that time. The average worker made $1,000 a year at best, so a $40,000 car was beyond his means. Naturally, there were those who liked to have cars and they wanted them because they provided a degree of status, emulating the rich. Eventually, Henry Ford developed the mass production of the Model T Ford car, and the introduction of the 40-hour workweek got the income of many workers up to the point where they could buy cars rolling off the assembly line. The Model T was utilitarian; it was manufactured in one color and that was black. Then General Motors introduced style changes that made the Model T obsolete. Because car purchasers wanted more from their cars than just getting to and from work, it became "keeping up with the Joneses." If the neighbor had a car with style and color, he would be envied, so planned obsolescence developed, introducing style changes every year and a choice of various models, like moving from Chevrolet, Buick, Pontiac, to Oldsmobile up to Cadillac with different types of styles. Then, as people got wealthier, they could afford really fancy and expensive cars like the Duisenberg, the really expensive cars that movie stars drove around. Looking at fashions, the rich set the fashion tones, the consumption tones, and the rest of the population followed suit, in a watered-down version. The rich could go to Neiman Marcus; the middle class could buy the same model in a department store in New Orleans, or Indianapolis, for example. It wouldn't be elite, but it would be the same type of dress or suit. So the idea of conspicuous consumption, the tone of which was set by the wealthy, emanated with the patterns of the leisure class and permeated on down to the lower income individuals.

In 2005, *The New York Times* published a series of articles entitled "Class in America." The series illustrates that, although the U.S. views itself as a classless nation, the forces of class still play a large role in such areas as health care, education, and other matters. Income mobility, or the American Dream that anyone can "make it here," is actually far less in the United States than once believed. And while Americans have more luxuries than their parents ever expected, the gap between the rich and poor has widened dramatically.

Figure 16.1 indicates the dramatic changes in income distribution from the period 1980–1992. This period is traditionally associated with the "Reagan Revolution" in which trickle down economics and Laffer curves supported

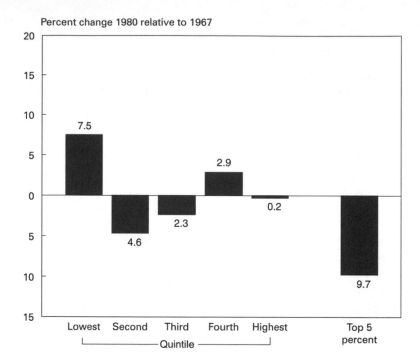

Percent change 1980 relative to 1967

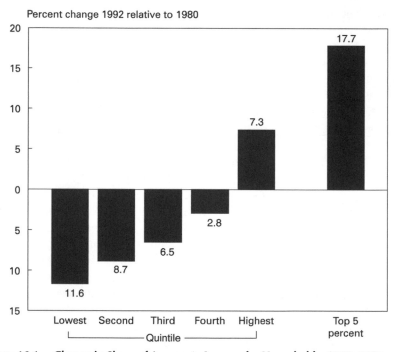

Percent change 1992 relative to 1980

Figure 16.1.   Change in Share of Aggregate Income for Households, 1967–1992

Source: U.S. Census Bureau. Current Population Survey. March 1968, 1981, and 1993.

the conventional wisdom that, if you increased spending at the top income levels, the economy would grow, raising all ships. Not all economists agreed with this line of thought, however. But the growing gap cannot be solely attributed to this trend. The increase in two-income households, the growth in high skilled, technology based employment all contributed to this trend.

Of particular significance to the *Times* authors, however, was the growth in the class they refer to as the "hyper-rich." While many data sources report on the income levels of the top fifth, or top 5 percent, the hyper-rich constitute the top 0.1 percent of income earners, some 145,000 taxpayers. The bottom income for this group is $1.6 million. And the wealth of this group is on the rise, doubling from 1980 to some 7.4 percent of national income. This group will benefit from more than 15 percent of the Bush administration's proposed tax cuts, while the "merely rich" shoulder the burdens.[14]

The gap between the rich and the hyper-rich is particularly apparent in traditional moneyed strongholds such as Nantucket Island, where real estate can sell for upwards of $15 million, extra houses are needed for staff and storage, and it is a bone of contention at cocktail parties what kind of plane or boat one has. The elite clubs are dropped in favor of more elite clubs. Old money, unaccustomed to flaunting itself, sniffs at the ostentation of the *nouveau riche*. Says one resident: "What has happened in America is that achievement is so important that everyone wants everyone else to know what they have done . . . and in case you don't know, they want to tell you with a lethal combination of houses, cars, and diamonds."[15]

Witness the laundry list of excess: A G-IV transcontinental jet, a 200 foot Fed Ship, a personal baseball field (but if you build it, they are not allowed to come); one's very own lighthouse. Among the recently indicted heads of industry, L. Dennis Kozlowski, former CEO of Tyco International, boasted a $6,000 shower curtain, a $2,000 elephant's foot for guest umbrellas, and a "vodka-spewing ice sculpture fashioned after Michelangelo's David."[16]

But is such excess a problem, or just a signal that America is the land of opportunity, for some? In other words, is income inequality, or excessive consumption, truly a *weakness* for the United States? As we shall see in chapter 17, it is a factor that sets us apart from other nations.

SUMMARY

The United States is a nation with unprecedented income inequality. The ethic that creates such inequality appears to be on the rise. In the early 2000s, a number of corporate scandals highlighted indifference on the part of corporate CEOs to their employees, stakeholders, and pensioners. The level of inequality has been on the increase for the past three decades. While the United States has been called "the land of opportunity," it turns out that income mobility between classes is relatively stagnant. The level of consumption in the United States, unbalanced by the level of savings, may put us at a disadvantage compared with other countries.

RECOMMENDED READING

Class in America (series). *New York Times*. May–June, 2005.

Eichenwald, Kurt. *Conspiracy of Fools*. New York: Broadway Books, 2005.

Jones, Arthur F., Jr. and Weinberg, Daniel H. The Changing Shape of the Nation's Income Distribution. *Current Population Reports*. Washington, D.C.: U.S. Census Bureau. June 2000.

Philips, Kevin. *Wealth and Democracy*. New York: Broadway Books, 2002.

Thurow, Lester C. *The Future of Capitalism*. New York: William Morrow and Company, 1996.

NOTES

1. Movie: *Wall Street.* 1987.

2. Rockefeller was the wealthiest man in America. His fortune was valued at close to $1 billion dollars. Accounting for inflation, he would still be the wealthiest man in America today. Nobody would be even close. He himself was a very frugal man who read his Bible every night, and attributed his success to the fact that God had chosen him to succeed.

3. Eichenwald, K. *Conspiracy of Fools.* New York: Broadway Books, 2005.

4. McLean, B. and Elkind, P. *The Smartest Guys in the Room.* New York: Portfolio, 2004.

5. Farrell, G. "CIBC Agrees to Pay $2.4 billion in Enron Settlement." *USA Today*. August 3, 2005.

6. Kadlec, D. "WorldCon." *Time*. July 8, 2002.

7. George C. Lodge, *The New American Ideology.* New York: Knopf, 1975.

Lester Thurow, *Head to Head: The Coming Battle among Japan, Europe, and America* New York: Morrow, 1992. The battle never occurred.

8. John Locke, *Second Treatise on Civil Government*, 1681. Government comes into existence, said Locke, because of property. If there is no property, there is no need for government.

9. Adam Smith. *An Inquiry into the Nature and Causes of the Wealth of Nations.* Indianapolis: Liberty Classics, 1981. p. 660.

10. This is a part of English Common Law.

11. An example is Germany. Massive government intervention occurred prior to World War I when Germany was trying to catch up with England as a major economic power.

12. It also imposed a 35-hour workweek on employers for the purpose of making them employ more workers. All it did was to increase the French unemployment rate, which is now over 10 percent.

13. Veblen, T. *The Theory of the Leisure Class.* Penguin, 1994. Originally published in 1899.

14. Scott, J. and Leonhardt, D. "Shadowy Lines that Still Divide." *New York Times.* May 15, 2005.

15. Fabrikant, G. "Old Nantucket Warily Meets the New." *New York Times.* June 5, 2005.

16. Fabrikant, 2005.

17

Who Will Dominate the Twenty-first Century?

> My name is Ozymandias, king of kings.
> Look on my works ye Mighty and despair.
>
> —Percy Bysshe Shelley, 1817

The poem "Ozymandias" is an appropriate introduction for this chapter. Empires come and empires go, and that is the point of this poem. Certainly Ramases was a great pharaoh of Egypt, and Egypt was at its aegis when he was ruler. He built a great pyramid to himself to immortalize his accomplishments. The same was true of the pharaohs who followed him; there is nothing left of them except the pyramids that they erected to their glory. Then there was the Assyrian empire, the Babylonian empire, followed by Athens and Sparta, and the Roman Empire that endured for 300 years.

It is not given to any country to be dominant forever. Spain became the dominant European power during the fifteenth and sixteenth century. Its discovery of gold in a new world enabled it to finance its armies, and through its conquests dominate Europe. Then after Spain came France which then became the leading power of Europe. Then it was Holland with its naval power and its wealth and its army which dominated Europe. It was replaced by England, which after the Battle of Waterloo in 1815 put together its empire and became the dominant world power of the nineteenth century. But England is just another country today and its empire has long since disappeared.

The last century was the American century in which America was dominant through its economic strength including its wealth. Then, it had the good fortune of being isolated from the destruction of World War I and World War II. Its whole economic might was undamaged. Then the Soviet Union collapsed in 1991, and America became by default the leading economic power of the world. It is expected to continue to be the leading world economic power for this century as well. So for 200 years presumably the United States will dominate and for this century a pax americana like a pax romana will dominate.

So then who will dominate the twenty-first century? No one would have thought that the mighty British Empire would become a thing of the past during the last century. Britannia ruled the waves and the British Empire extended from New Zealand all the way to Canada and included almost one half of the world's population. What destroyed the British Empire was World War I and then World War II but World War I created the seeds of destruction of the empire because Britain did not have the wherewithal to finance the wars. It had the men from all over the empire to fight in France but it had to borrow from the United States and the Rothchild banking system to finance the war.

The United States became the leading creditor nation of the world and emerged as the economic power of the century after World War I. Now it is the leading debtor nation. The British were also in debt to the Rothchild's and promised them through the Balfour Agreement of 1916 to create a new homeland for the Jews. It wasn't decided where this new homeland would be, but eventually it turned out to be where it is today, in the Middle East in the former Palestine. Germany, which had been shriven by two major wars and perhaps could have been dominant at least in Europe for the entire century and could have posed a challenge to the United States, simply lost too much in the last century to figure in the process. To conjecture perhaps is pointless, but we will start by comparing the United States with China and the European Union, comparing their strong points and weak points. However, we can only speculate and portend what the future holds.

THE UNITED STATES

At the beginning of the last century the population of the United States was 76 million. By the end of the century the population had increased to 291 million. Successive waves of immigration from Europe and Latin America were responsible for most of the increase. The United States also endured two major wars and the Depression of the 1930s. However, it was a prosperous century, particularly the last fifty years.

The United States is by far the wealthiest country in the world with a total GNI of $13 trillion, which is larger than the combined GNIs for Japan, China, Germany, and France. It has a land area larger than that of the European Union.[1] It leads the world in such areas as banking, computer technology, drugs, heavy equipment, and machine tools. For better or worse, its music and fast food are popular throughout most of the countries of the world, from such exotic places as Ulan Bator, Mongolia and Nairobi, Kenya. Our university system is considered to be the best in the world and thousands of students from other parts of the world attend here. Many foreign tourists travel to the United States each year, which benefits the U.S. economy.

However, it was not always such. In the late 1980s many experts were confident that Japan would dominate the twenty-first century. Ezra Vogel wrote a book called *Japan as Number One* in which he predicted that Japan would overtake the United States. Clyde Prestowitz wrote a book called *Trading Places* in which he also predicted that Japan would replace the United States as number one. There were a number of others who were confident that Japan would supplant the United States as the world's leading economic power of the twenty-first century. The Japanese were smarter, their primary education was better; and their culture was superior, because they stressed family values over the individual and their management style was superior to ours. But these predictions did not materialize, because a number of serious flaws developed in the Japanese economy, particularly in the area of banking which was overladen with debt, and many bankruptcies occurred. On the other hand, the American economy, led by the technology boom and the rise in stock prices, achieved unprecedented prosperity during the latter part of the 1990s.

Problems in the American Economy

There are problems in the American economy. The technology boom ran its course, leaving many bankruptcies and led to a fall in stock prices. The September 11 terror attack on the World Trade Center in New York City changed its economic landscape. Then came the unpopular war with Iraq, which has widened the gap between broad-based segments of the society that have nothing in common. In an economy that was already beginning to sag, Hurricane Katrina, which caused widespread damage in the South, necessitated increases in government expenditures. This was exacerbated by damage to oil platforms in the Gulf, which hastened a spike in automobile fuel and home heating oil prices.

The United States is far from being an egalitarian society. As mentioned in chapter 16, the gap between the haves and have-nots has widened in recent years. The wealthy have access to power, and they influence the political decision-making process.

The United States is the largest exporter and importer of goods and services in the world, and this goes a long way toward explaining why we are the world's leading debtor nation. To put it simply, we buy more goods and

Table 17.1   U.S. Federal Budget Totals, 2002–2008 (Projected)

In billions of dollars:	2002	2003	2004	2005	2006	2007	2008
Receipts	1,853	1,836	1,922	2,135	2,263	2,398	2,521
Outlays	2,011	2,140	2,229	2,343	2,464	2,576	2,711
Deficit	−158	−304	−307	−208	−201	−178	−190

Source: Budget of the U.S. Government Fiscal Year 2004. (U.S. GPO: 2003) p. 311.

services from other countries than we sell to them. We buy more cars from the Japanese than we sell to them, meaning more money for them and better cars for American consumers.

We have a deficit in our trade account with the Japanese and with the Chinese. But China has cheap labor and has incurred the wrath of American politicians who hold it responsible for the loss of American jobs, for example in the textile industry. China has a huge labor supply of mostly unskilled and semi-skilled workers. On the other hand, China imports capital goods and consumer durable goods from the United States. Soft drinks, beer, and McDonalds hamburgers are also very popular in China. Table 17.2 presents the current account balances of the United States, the European Union, and China over a ten-year period. As indicated in chapter 12, the current account consists of merchandise trade, services (including travel, financial, royalties, etc.) income from U.S. assets abroad, foreign assets in the United States, and remittances.

Table 17.2 Summary of Payments Balances on Current Account (Billions of U.S. Dollars)

	1997	1998	1999	2000	2001	2002	2003	2004	2005	2006
United States	−136.0	−209.6	−296.8	−413.5	−385.7	−473.9	−530.7	−665.9	−724.5	−749.8
Euro area	99.7	64.3	30.5	−28.5	13.1	53.5	25.8	35.6	50.1	52.2
China	34.4	31.6	15.9	20.5	17.4	35.4	45.9	70.0	76.5	81.6

Source: World Economic Outlook April 2005. (International Monetary Fund) pp. 237, 241.

Table 17.3 Comparative Growth Performance of Select Countries, 1978–1995

	GDP Per Capita
South Korea	6.6
China	6
Taiwan	6
India	2.8
Japan	2.7
United Kingdom	1.7
United States	1.5
France	1.3
Germany	1 *
USSR/Russia	−2.3*

*Figures affected by boundary changes
Source: Angus Maddison (1998) Chinese Economic Performance in the Long Run. Table 3.4. Comparative Growth Performance, 24 Countries, 1913–1995 (selected data from 1978–1995), Chinese Economic Performance in the Long Run, (c) OECD 1998. p. 59.

CHINA

To understand contemporary China, it is necessary to look at its history. China is an old country. It was a world power for several hundred years. Its economy and standard of living was the highest in the world. But China was eclipsed and fell into disarray for some 400 years while Europe became the leading entity of the world. There are those who argue that a new rebirth in China could propel it into the dominant position, but that is unlikely. For one thing the GDP of the United States is almost ten times that of the GDP of China. But on the other hand, when you apply deflators to each, you find that the real gross national product of China is not far below that of the United States. Certainly China has an educated population, one that is growing in terms of skills, industry, and education. But there is nothing really that would indicate that the United States would fall to number two, for the simple reason that there is no competition outside of perhaps China.

In the tenth century, China was the world's leading economy in terms of per capita income. Europe was still in the Dark Ages when China developed a civil service system based on competitive examinations. It developed gunpowder, yet never learned to make modern guns. It had a road system and its merchants traded through East Asia. It developed an efficient system of public finance. It outperformed Europe in level of technology, the intensity with which it used its natural resources, and its capacity for administering a large empire. Between 1500 and 1800 Europe gradually overtook China in real income technology and scientific capacity. China had been adversely affected by the Mongol conquest and by internal dynastic rivalries.

In 1820 China had the highest level of real GDP in the world. Its GDP was $199 billion compared to $22 billion for Japan, $35 billion for England, and $12 billion for the United States.[2] Its population was 381 million. But the twentieth century proved to be the undoing of China. Its political system had become fragile and twice British and French armies, with the resultant loss of territory, invaded China. For all practical purposes, China became an economic enclave of England and France. It served as a market for British and French goods and provided raw material for England and France. China was ruled by a succession of weak leaders. The culminating blow to China came in 1900 with the Boxer Rebellion, which prompted military intervention by an international army consisting of troops from the United States, England, Germany, France, and Japan. The result was a Chinese defeat and the division of a part of its territories into economic enclaves controlled by the aforementioned countries.

Chaos dominated China during the first half of the twentieth century. In 1911 the Manchu dynasty was overthrown by a revolution. This was followed by a prolonged civil war that destroyed much of China and encouraged the Japanese to invade China in 1937. Japan already had territorial designs on

China, seizing Formosa (now Taiwan) from the Chinese in 1895. After the defeat of the Japanese in 1945, two rival factions fought for dominance of the country. One faction, who had American support, was the Kuomintang, which was created by Chiang Kai-shek in 1928. He established a republican form of government and his armies controlled much of the western part of China when the Japanese invaded China in 1937. The second faction was the Chinese Communist Party, which was created in 1921 and dominated much of the rural areas of China. A civil war between the two factions broke out in 1946, and the Communists eventually won in 1949.

Over a little more than one hundred years, China had lost two wars with Japan and was invaded three times by England and France and once by Russia and the United States. Its rulers were corrupt and incompetent and were eventually replaced. Its warlords were no better. China went backward, while the rest of the world went forward. Its real per capita GDP declined and its share of world GDP fell from one-third to one-twentieth. Its real per capita income fell from parity to a quarter of the world average. When the Communists took over in 1949, the economy had nowhere to go but up. The first thing they did was to expel foreign companies, including Coca-Cola, and expunge foreign influence.

In December 1978 the Central Committee of the Communist Party convened in Beijing. The session declared that if China were to develop successfully, it must turn from class struggle to modernization and completely restructure its economy. The Four Modernizations Program, originally started by Premier Chou-en-Lai in 1975, was incorporated into a Ten-Year Plan that called for increases in grain output, steel production, and capital construction through the purchase of foreign plants and technology. The program emphasized the development of four major economic sectors—agriculture, industry, science, and technology—and national defense. The centerpiece of the program was to be the creation of the massive Baoshan steel complex, which would turn out 6.7 million tons of steel a year with the most advanced technology imported from Japan, West Germany, and the United States. Baoshan was an expensive failure, however, caused in part by China's inability to assimilate foreign technology and in part by an unrealistic emphasis on the role of heavy industry in developing the Chinese economy. A period of retrenchment and reappraisal of Chinese economic goals set in.

The early 1980s marked a liberalization of the Chinese economy as the ambitious goals of the Four Modernization Program were scaled down and the government turned its attention to more immediate objectives, such as improving productivity and increasing output. It introduced more competition into the economy, not only by permitting private business to exist, but also by turning over small, unprofitable state-owned enterprises to private collectives. In 1984 a number of reforms were introduced to improve the structure of the Chinese economy. There was a separation of government from state enterprise functions. The purpose was to give state enterprises more autonomy over their operations. Prices were restructured away from uniform prices set by the state and toward a floating price system for some products and free prices for others. In enterprises, differences in wages among various trades and jobs were widened to apply fully the principle of awarding the diligent and punishing the indolent. These and other measures promoted rapid economic growth during the 1980s.

CHINA VS. THE UNITED STATES

A 2005 article in *The Economist* posits "How China Runs the World Economy." It suggests that Chinese practices, as well as its status as "the fastest growing emerging economy" place China in the position of having an enormous impact on the American trade deficit, labor, and interest rates. The sheer size of China represents a very real "butterfly effect" for the rest of the world. Its large labor force and growing economy represent not only increased exports, but also increased imports. The result is that China "has increased the world's potential growth rate, helped to hold down inflation, and triggered changes in the relative prices of labor, capital, goods, and assets."[3]

Its vast workforce has reduced overall wages in the developed nations. Cheaper production has lowered the price of goods, and thus worldwide inflation. This, in turn, has lowered worldwide interest rates. And this trend has not yet peaked; China still has a surplus of underemployed workers to meet the demands of a growing economy. Chinese frugality also plays a role. Whereas Americans are fond of spending beyond their means, China has an ethic of saving. As a result, Chinese banks have purchased American debt. All of these factors combined suggest that China, while not the economic superpower of the United States, holds increasing influence in the future of the global economy.

Table 17.4   Shares of World GDP, 1700–1995

	Shares of World GDP, 1700–1995 (percent)					
	1700	*1820*	*1890*	*1952*	*1978*	*1995*
China	23.1	32.4	13.2	5.2	5	10.9
India	22.6	15.7	11	3.8	3.4	4.6
Japan	4.5	3	2.5	3.4	7.7	8.4
Europe	23.3	26.6	40.3	29.7	27.9	23.8
United States	0	1.8	13.8	28.4	21.8	20.9
USSR/Russia	3.2	4.8	6.3	8.7	9.2	2.2

Source: Angus Maddison, Chinese Economic Performance in the Long Run, Table 2.2a Shares of World GDP, 1700–1995, (c) OECD 1998. p. 40, 41

EUROPEAN UNION

As described in chapter 15, the EU is a congerie of twenty-five different nations with different languages and different cultures joined together as a United States of Europe. Collectively they have a population that is larger than that of the United States and a gross domestic product that comes close to that of the United States. But the key to the future success of the European Union is Germany, because it is the largest country within the European Union with a population of 82 million people, far larger than the population of France, Italy, or the United Kingdom. Germany has been the dominant force in Europe going back to the beginning of the last century. It began with the unification of the various German principalities in 1871. Then came the Franco-Prussian War and the development of Germany under the leadership of the Iron Chancellor, Otto von Bismarck. By the time of the First World War, Germany was the leading power in Europe. Its industrial capacity matched that of England and its empire. It had a dynamism about it that drove it ahead and when World War I began, it was a force to be reckoned with. Its military power made it the most powerful country in Europe. It took on most of the world—Russia, the United Kingdom, France, Italy, and later the United States. It more than held its own for four years until the weight of the Allied armies and the total industrial production that was added to by the United States when it entered the war did ultimately defeat the Germans. Reparations were very stiff against the Germans and its war losses were very high. Germany was saddled with its war debts and by the Treaty of Versailles it lost most of its territory, which was formed into new countries.

Within a relatively short time, again it became the major power in Europe and under Hitler preparations were made for a second war that occurred in 1939 and lasted until 1945. Again the Germans took on the forces of Russia, the United Kingdom and its empire, and the United States. It held its own for several years, conquering the major part of Russia. But eventually it lost the war and had to rebuild its economy that was almost totally destroyed. It did so through the aid of the U.S. Marshall Plan, which was not so much charity but was really done because the United States feared the threat of a Communist takeover of the weakened Europe. Germany rebounded again with the so-called economic miracle, Soziale Markwirtschaft, and regained its status as the leading economic force of Europe even after the split into West Germany and East Germany and the construction of the Berlin Wall in 1960. West Germany became the leading economy of Western Europe and by the same token the East German economy was superior to that of most countries in the Soviet bloc. It had a higher standard of living than any country in the bloc including that of the Soviet Union.

With the collapse of Communism in 1989, the Berlin Wall came down, and East Germany and West Germany were reunited into one country. At that time Germany regained much of the land area that it had and the two Germanies in terms of population amounted to around 78 million people. The rebuilding of East Germany and the various forms of aid given to the East Germans cost in the billions of dollars. Even now the East Germans lag behind the West Germans in terms of living standards. It was a very expensive endeavor, and starting the decade the German growth rate fell to almost zero and has continued to be virtually nil during the first part of the twenty-first century. As of October 15, 2005, 5 million Germans are unemployed. The unemployment rate in Germany is the highest of any major country in Europe. The population is aging and the labor force is declining so there are fewer workers to support the very elaborate social welfare system that has existed in Germany since the rule of Bismarck. As Germany goes, so goes the rest of Europe. Some other countries, Spain, for example have an unemployment rate about that of Germany, and the Spanish economy is not nearly as strong as that of Germany.

The recent German election in the latter part of September does not auger well for the future of Germany in that it was a virtual tie between the Christian Democrats as represented by Angela Merkel and the Social Democrats as represented by Chancellor Gerhardt Schroeder. The Christian Democrats won by a very small majority of about one percent over the Social Democrats and there are other parties affiliated with the two major parties. Angela Merkel was declared the winner, so she will govern with a coalition of parties and whether or not she can accomplish anything remains to be seen.

Thus, while many have suggested that a combined European Union represents a new economic superpower to be reckoned with, the fate of the largest EU countries rests on an unstable foundation of the welfare state, an aging labor force, high unemployment, and low birth rates. These factors compromise the promise of the EU, both politically and socially. The successful reform efforts of Prime Minister Tony Blair, and the pressures for reform in France and Germany, make the future of the EU difficult to predict. Thus, while the EU represents perhaps the most successful and ambitious examples of regional trading blocs, its potential as a global player has yet to be realized.

OTHER FORCES IN THE NEW MILLENNIUM

Others suggest that the predominating forces facing the new century will not be states. The forces of international globalization cross and transcend state boundaries. Certain global corporations, for example Wal-Mart, represent "economies" larger than those of most states. The mobility of global capitalism, the availability of cheap labor, and the technologies that make possible decentralization of production and labor all create new and significant pressures on the world of the twenty-first century. It is these sorts of pressures that will have the largest impact, for better or worse, on both the wealthy and the poor nations, as well as the formation of regional trading blocs.

But they have another, more troubling consequence. In the previous century, terrorism was a known entity; however, the events of the year 2001 were completely unpredictable, at least to Americans. Some would contend that the threat of terrorism is a direct result of global capitalism; at the very least, the same forces which promote globalization also facilitate terrorism. Terrorism is increasingly *not* confined to, or associated with, particular states. Terrorist cells are part of a diffuse, decentralized network that is not readily traceable. Global flows of funds support terrorist activities; yet are difficult to follow. Instability in newly emerging and developing states provides a seedbed for terrorist recruits. And, the ready transmission of information via television and the Internet provides a means of communication, learning, and mimesis among possibly unconnected terrorist groups. All of these factors are poorly understood, reflecting a world in flux, in which it is difficult to predict future outcomes.

Perhaps more significant is not terrorism itself, but the response of world powers to it. While other countries had experienced terrorism for decades, the United States had been relatively free from it. The United States has long been in a unique position of imperviousness to foreign invaders; the September 11 attacks resulted in a system shock not seen since Pearl Harbor in 1941. The *response* of the United States also has profound effects for the global future. Security, torture, travel, relationships with global allies, privacy, surveillance, racial and cultural relations, immigration, even ability to respond to natural disasters—all of these factors once taken for granted or regarded as terrains on which we were progressing, all of these have changed. These factors affect not only the United States, but also its relationships with other nations.

Last, but not least, environmental issues are likely to play a significant role in the twenty-first century. The oil shocks of 2005, following the passage of a new Energy Bill, suggest pressures for the exploration of alternative fuels. Brazil is now not only producing but also exporting biofuels made from corn. The growth of China, and its reliance on fossil fuels, has significant effects on the supply and price of oil and coal. As China grows, its ecological footprint, already large, is likely to become larger. China's relative lack of natural resources will also impact world supplies of other goods.

SUMMARY

The question of who will dominate the twenty-first century seems, on the one hand, relatively simple. The U.S. position is unchallenged at this point. However, forces are occurring which are changing the entire playing field.

The formation of the EU coupled with the long slow decline of powerful developed European nations; the rise and rapid economic growth of China, coupled with its high population—both of these factors will shift the traditional Western power balance. Globalization, with its accompanying influences on poor nations, suggests changing economic flows. Terrorism, increasingly detached from states, appears to be increasing in influence as a tactic of extremist groups, as well as impacting the actions and interactions of large nations. Environmental forces, such as international supply and demand for natural resources, are shifting. All of these forces suggest tectonic shifts that have the potential to determine "who will dominate the twenty-first century." However, predictions at this point are anyone's guess; and there will be no lack of attempts to answer this question.

RECOMMENDED READINGS

Fishman, T. *China, Inc.: How the Rise of the Next Superpower Challenges America and the World.* New York: Scribner Publishing, 2005.
How China Runs the World Economy. *The Economist.* July 28, 2005.
Harvey, D. *A Brief History of Neoliberalism.* New York: Oxford University Press, 2005.

NOTES

1. Statistical Abstract of the United States, 2004–2005. *U.S. Bureau of the Census.* U.S. Government Printing Office: 2005, p. 7.
2. Angus Maddison, "Chinese Economic Performance in the Long Run," Development Centre Studies, OECD, 1998. pp. 40, 41.
3. Special Report: China and the World Economy. *The Economist.* July 30, 2005. pp. 61–63.

Index

AARP. *See* American Association of Retired Persons

ACLU. *See* American Civil Liberties Union

ADA. *See* Americans with Disabilities Act of 1990

ADEA. *See* Age Discrimination Employment Act of 1967

administrative agencies: types of, 24–26, 39n2; rule-making by, 110–11

advertising: criticisms of, 115; deceptive, 112, 113–14, 132, 133n9, 133nn21–22; Internet, 233–34; prescription drugs, 130–31; purpose of, 106, 112–13, 133n24

affirmative action, 148–54 , 157. *See also* discrimination cases

AFL-CIO, 43, 52, 62

Africa: AIDS crisis, 338, *339*, 340; economic growth, 338–40; European colonialism and, 329–32, 341–42nn6–10, 342n15; gender disparities, 334–35, 342n20; human development index (HDI), *332*–33; income distribution, 337; Northern, 329, 333, 337, 338; political instability in, 288n20, 338; population growth, 336–37; poverty in, 333–*34*, 340; Sub-Saharan, 329, 333, *334*, 340; United States and, 268, 342n13. *See also* Ethiopia; Nigeria; South Africa; Zaire

Age Discrimination Employment Act of 1967 (ADEA), 31, 140, 141

airlines: deregulation, effects of, 202–3, 207–8; deregulation measures, *35*, 38, 197–98; federal laws regulating, 197, 206; hubbing, 202–3; mergers among, 205–6, 207; safety issues, 204–5; service issues, 203–4; Southwest, 203, 206; US Airways, 204, 205. *See also* Civil Aeronautics Board; Federal Aviation Administration; transportation regulation cases

American Association of Retired Persons (AARP), 39n13, 40–41, 45–46, 130

American Civil Liberties Union (ACLU), 238

American Family Publishers, 114, 115

American Federation of Labor-Congress of Industrial Organizations. *See* AFL-CIO

Americans with Disabilities Act of 1990 (ADA), 31, 32, 140–41, 149

American Telephone and Telegraph Company. *See* AT&T

America Online. *See* AOL

antitrust cases: *Addyston Pipe and Steel Company v. United States*, 61; *Albrecht v. Herald Company*, 71, 72; *American Tobacco Company v. United States (1946)*, 67, 68; *Appalachian Coals, Inc. v. United States*, 64, 66; *Arizona v. Maricopa County Medical Society*, 72;

Pape, Robert: *Dying to Win: The Strategic Logic of Suicide Bombers*, 317
Peckham, Rufus Wheeler, 61
Philadelphia, 219–20
Poland, 15, 272, 328
political action committees (PACs), 49–51, 52, 55. *See also* Bipartisan Campaign Reform Act of 2002
political campaign contributions, 49–53, 56nn17–18
pollution: abatement, costs of, 13, 160, 178–80; air, 44, 45, 160, 164–65, 169, 303, 309n16; effects of, 160, 165, 169; as global problem, 29, 161–64, 169; government and, 13, 170, 191–92; greenhouse gases, 161–62, 163–64, 191; water, 44, 45, 160, 168, 169. *See also* environmental problems; Environmental Protection Agency (EPA
population: aging of, 10, 14, 35–36, 45–46, 349–50; growth of, 333, 336–37
Porter, Michael: *The Competitive Advantage of Nations*, 262–63, 287
Powell, Lewis F., Jr., 154, 220
presidential elections (United States), 46, 49–54 , 56nn9–10
product liability, 122; *BMW of North America v. Ira Gore Jr.*, 128–29, 134nn38–40; costs of, 126, 127; *MacPherson v. Buick Motor Company*, 126, 127, 132; tort law and, 125–28, 132
Publishers Clearing House, 114, 115
Pure Food and Drug Act of 1906, 107–8

railroads: Amtrak, 201, 208; Conrail, 200–201; CSX, 200, 201; deregulation, effects of, 199–200, 202; federal laws regulating, 79, 195–96; mergers among, 199–200, 201, 208; Norfolk Southern, 200, 201; safety issues, 201–2; Union Pacific, 200, 202
Reagan, Ronald, 33, 245, 346, 351
regional trading blocs. *See* international trade
regulation: characteristics of, 198–99; cost-benefit analysis of, 32–*33*; criticisms of, 199; direct costs, 31–32, 39n7; economic, 12, 17, 25, 38; indirect costs, 32; reasons for, 12; regulatory impact anal-

ysis (RIA), 33–34; social, 12, 17, 25, 38. *See also* government; deregulation
Rehnquist, William, 54, 181, 239
Republican Party, 42, *51*, *52*, 79
Resource Conservation and Recovery Act, 171, 174, 180, 190
Ricardo, David, 260, 287n5
Robinson-Patman Act, 26, 84, 88–97, 119. *See also* Clayton Antitrust Act
Rockefeller, John D., 44, 63, 341–42n10, 344, 354n2
Roman Empire, 3, 18n2, 259, 356
Roosevelt, Franklin Delano, 197, 211
Roosevelt, Theodore, 45, 62, 63, 108
Russia: economy of, 39n10, *359*, *362*; human development index (HDI), *332*; political instability, 277; terrorism in, 312, 314; women, status of, *336*. *See also* Soviet Union

savings and loan industry, 215–16
SBC Communications, 226, 227, 228, 230, 244
Scalia, Antonin, 180–81, 182, 221, 226, 227–28, 232
SEC. *See* Securities and Exchange Commission
Securities and Exchange Commission (SEC), 26–27, 31
Senate, United States, 26, 40, 49, 122, 130, 211, 305
September 11, 2001, terrorist attacks, 159n43, 206–7, 311, 317, 320–24, 358, 365
Sherman Antitrust Act: amendments to, 74–75; damages under, 59, 62, 80, 88; enforcement of, 78–79, 90, 97–98; labor unions and, 62–63, 64–66, 67, 70; penalties under, 59–60, 75; provisions of, 30, 59, 68–69, 70, 98; violations of, 39n4, 59, 61, 63–74 , 87, 88, 93, 95, 96. *See also* antitrust cases
Sinclair, Upton: *The Jungle*, 107–8, 133n8
Smith, Adam, 18n5, 105, 260, 287n5, 348
Social Security, 8–9, 48, 267; expenditures on, *6*, 7; problems, 35–36, 45; reform of, 8, 36, 39n11, 56
Souter, David, 97, 221, 227
South Africa, 337, 338, *339*

United States: balance of payments (BOP) account, 265–69, 286, 287, 288n13; demographic disparities in income, 136–*37*; direct investment abroad, *268, 298–99, 301*, 308; dollar, 273, 286, 287, 296; economic predominance of, 356, 357, 358–*59*, 365–66; European Union and, *264*, 298–*99*; exports and imports, 263–*64*, 265, 284, *299*, 358–59; foreign direct investment in, *269, 269, 301*, 307, 308; gross domestic product (GDP), 7, *362*; gross national income (GNI), *300*, 357; human development index (HDI), *332*; income inequality, 135–36, 158n4, 349, *350*, 351–54, 358; individualistic capitalism and, 348, 350; international trade deficit, 7, 264, 265, 286, 358–*59*; NAFTA and, 300–304, 307–8; women, status of, 137–38, *336*.
USA Patriot Act, 317, 320–21

VAWA. *See* Violence Against Women Act
Veblen, Thorstein: *The Theory of the Leisure Class*, 351
Venice, 3, 18n3, 259
Verizon Communications, 226, 227, 228, 230, 244. *See also* communications industry cases
Violence Against Women Act (VAWA) of 1994, 148
Virginia, 41, 47, 56nn12–13, 107, 245–46

Wall Street (motion picture), 343, 346
Water Pollution Control Act of 1972, 170, 171, 179, 181–84, 187
welfare state, 4, 16, 364
Wexler, Ann, 48
Wheeler-Lea Amendment of 1938, 87, 99, 113–14, 120. *See also* Clayton Antitrust Act
White, Byron Raymond, 244–45
White, Edward Douglass, 196
Wilson, Woodrow, 83, 210
women. *See* Africa; discrimination; Violence Against Women Act; world; *and individual countries*
world: developed countries, 327, 341n2; financial system, 222; gender disparities, 137, 334–35, 342n16; illiteracy problem, 334, *335*; labor force, 336; low income countries, 328; Millennium Development Goals, 340; population growth, 333; poverty, 333; United States trade with, *301. See also* globalization; United Nations
World Bank Group, 275, 288n16, 339
WorldCom, 228–29; scandal involving, 347
World Trade Organization (WTO), 29, 285–86
World War I, 4, 18n6, 42, 270, 312, 357, 363
World War II, 263, 313, 345, 357, 363, 365
WTO. *See* World Trade Organization

Zaire, 331–32, 338, 342nn12–13

About the Authors

Robert Langran is professor of political science at Villanova University. His area of expertise is American constitutional law, and he also teaches a course on Government and Business. He has won the Lindback Award for Distinguished Teaching and the Faculty Service Award. He has published a casebook on the Supreme Court, which is in its fifth edition, a book on the history of the Supreme Court, plus numerous articles.

Martin Schnitzer is Professor Emeritus of international management at Virginia Tech. He has taught economics at the University of Arkansas, the University of Florida, and Virginia Tech. He has published many books, including *Comparative Economic Systems*, which is in its eighth edition, and has served as a consultant to the Joint Economic Committee of the U.S. Congress and the House Ways and Means Committee. He is former editor of the *Virginia Social Science Journal*.